88938

D0074813

THE
PRINCIPLES OF
HISTORY

AND OTHER WRITINGS
IN PHILOSOPHY OF HISTORY

R. G. COLLINGWOOD

Edited with an Introduction by

W. H. DRAY

and

W. J. VAN DER DUSSEN

OXFORD
UNIVERSITY PRESS

OXFORD

UNIVERSITY PRESS

Great Clarendon Street, Oxford OX2 6DP

Oxford University Press is a department of the University of Oxford
It furthers the University's objective of excellence in research, scholarship,
and education by publishing worldwide in

Oxford New York

Athens Auckland Bangkok Bogotá Buenos Aires Calcutta
Cape Town Chennai Dar es Salaam Delhi Florence Hong Kong Istanbul
Karachi Kuala Lumpur Madrid Melbourne Mexico City Mumbai
Nairobi Paris São Paulo Singapore Shanghai Taipei Tokyo Toronto Warsaw

with associated companies in Berlin Ibadan

Oxford is a registered trade mark of Oxford University Press
in the UK and in certain other countries

Published in the United States
by Oxford University Press Inc., New York

British Library Cataloguing in Publication Data

Data available

Library of Congress Cataloging in Publication Data

Collingwood, R. G. (Robin George), 1889–1943.
The principles of history: and other writings in philosophy of
history / R.G. Collingwood; edited with an introduction by
W.H. Dray and W.J. van der Dussen.
Includes bibliographical references and index.
1. History—Philosophy.   I. Dray, William H.
II. Dussen, W. J. van der.   III. Title.
D16.8.C592   1999   901—dc21   98–49637

ISBN 0-19-823703-0 (hbk)
ISBN 0-19-924315-8 (pbk)

1 3 5 7 9 10 8 6 4 2

Typeset by Hope Services (Abingdon) Ltd.
Printed in Great Britain
on acid-free paper by
Biddles Ltd.,
Guildford and King's Lynn

ACKNOWLEDGEMENTS

The editors' special thanks are due to Mr Peter Momtchiloff, Philosophy Editor of Oxford University Press, whose proposal it was that they undertake the present project, to Mrs Teresa Smith, Collingwood's daughter, not only for the permission she gave us to publish the chosen manuscripts, but also for the freedom she allowed with regard to their selection, and to Mr Colin Harris, Principal Library Assistant, Dept. of Special Collections and Western Manuscripts at the Bodleian Library, whose interest and assistance greatly facilitated our study of the Collingwood collection over a considerable period. Others who gave much appreciated help on specific points include Dr Rik Peters, Dr Grace Simpson, Professor Rex Martin, Professor David Gallop, and Dr Leofranc Holford-Strevens, who assisted with the verification and translation of passages in Greek. The editors would like also to acknowledge with gratitude the continuing support they received from the Collingwood Committee of Oxford University Press, and especially from Mr William Rieckmann and Professor David Boucher.

The editors would also like to express warm thanks to Ms Charlotte Jenkins, Assistant Philosophy Editor, for facilitating the correction in the present edition of a number of errors and omissions in the original version.

CONTENTS

ABBREVIATIONS

References to the following works of Collingwood in the footnotes and within brackets in the text will be abbreviated thus:

Books

A	*An Autobiography* (1939)
EM	*An Essay on Metaphysics* (1940; rev. edn. 1998)
EPH	*Essays in the Philosophy of History* (1965)
EPM	*An Essay on Philosophical Method* (1933)
IH	*The Idea of History* (1946; rev. edn. 1993)
IN	*The Idea of Nature* (1945)
NL	*The New Leviathan* (1942; rev. edn. 1992)
PA	*The Principles of Art* (1938)
RB	*Roman Britain* (rev. edn. 1932)
RBES	*Roman Britain and the English Settlements* (1936)
RP	*Religion and Philosophy* (1916)

Manuscripts published in the revised edition of The Idea of History

For ease of identification, the abbreviations L26, L27, and L28
will be used for these sources, but page numbers will be from
The Idea of History, rev. edn.

L26	'Lectures on the Philosophy of History' (1926)
L27	'The Idea of a Philosophy of Something and, in Particular, a Philosophy of History' (1927)
L28	'Outlines of a Philosophy of History' (1928)

Unpublished manuscripts

CHBI	'Can Historians be Impartial?' (1936)
CNM	'Conclusions to Lectures on Nature and Mind' (1934, 1935)
HUP	'History as the Understanding of the Present' (1934)

IRN   'Inaugural: Rough Notes' (1935)
NHH   'Notes on the History of Historiography and
        Philosophy of History' (1936)
NHV   'Notes on Historiography' (1938–9)
NTM   'Notes towards a Metaphysic' (1933–4)
PH   'The Principles of History' (1939)
RAH   'Reality as History' (1935)

EDITORS' NOTE

Our policy has been to make as few changes as possible from the original texts of the manuscripts, and to acknowledge all but the most minimal of them in footnotes. Collingwood's handwriting is generally quite legible, but in the few cases where we had to guess, we explain the problem. We have corrected occasional inconsistencies or errors of punctuation, spelling, or hyphenation without notice, but where a missing word has been supplied, or the case or tense of a word has been altered, our correction is enclosed in square brackets. We have followed Collingwood in hyphenating 're-live' and 're-enact' because these are quasi-technical terms of his and because they are generally hyphenated in the critical literature. Where Collingwood himself supplied a footnote, we mark this with a dagger to distinguish it from our own footnotes, and any additions we make to his footnotes are enclosed in square brackets. In the few cases where we have inserted a paragraph break, or changed a tense, or filled in a reference that Collingwood left blank, or slightly reordered material, or italicized a heading, or removed numbers from a manuscript heading, or even supplied a heading where one seemed to be missing, we call attention to this in a footnote. We have rendered ordinal numbers in words, e.g. writing nineteenth for 19th. From time to time, we have printed, with an explanation, and usually in a footnote, a passage which Collingwood himself struck out, or on which another text was pasted. In general, where we have intruded editorially, we have tried to make it easy to challenge or to verify the practice we have adopted.

EDITORS' INTRODUCTION

1. *Collingwood's philosophy of history*

R. G. Collingwood made signal contributions to several branches of philosophy, but he is best known for his work in philosophy of history.[1] Many would regard him, indeed, not only as a theorist of the first rank in this field, but as the only English-speaking philosopher of whom that could be said: the thinker whose ideas have effectively set the agenda for those working in it ever since his untimely death in 1943. It is remarkable that he gained this commanding position principally through a posthumous work, *The Idea of History*, which was put together by his literary executor, Sir Malcolm Knox, largely out of lecture notes and manuscripts, although this was supplemented by his own account of the development of his view of history in his *Autobiography*, published in 1939. Besides the latter work, and excluding *Speculum Mentis*, a monograph of 1924 which antedated his interest in history as a form of inquiry, there were, during his lifetime, just a few scattered essays on philosophy of history which appeared in the 1920s but were little noticed at the time,[2] an 'interim report' on the progress of his thought on history in 1930 entitled *The Philosophy of History* which was published as a leaflet by the English Historical Association, and two public lectures: 'The Historical Imagination', an inaugural lecture which Collingwood delivered to the University of Oxford in 1935 on the occasion of his election to the Waynflete Chair of Metaphysics, and 'Human Nature and Human History', an address which he gave to the British Academy in 1936. Knox included both of these in the Epilegomena to *The Idea of History* (*IH*, 205–49).

Central to Collingwood's thought on history was the idea that historical inquiry is or ought to be 'autonomous', and, more

---

[1] *The Times Literary Supplement* listed *IH* among the one hundred most influential books since the Second World War (6 Oct. 1995, 39). For Collingwood's contributions to philosophy of mind, art, nature, religion, politics, and philosophy itself, see e.g. *PA*, *IN*, *RP*, *NL*, *EPM*, *EM*.

[2] These were collected by William Debbins and republished in 1965 as *EPH*.

particularly, that its investigative methods and conceptual framework differ significantly, despite certain similarities, from those of the natural sciences. Among the well-known Collingwoodian doctrines associated with this stance are the need for historians to base conclusions on evidence, not testimony; to appreciate the crucial role of systematic questioning in their inquiries; to exercise a disciplined imagination when endeavouring to reconstruct the past; to place expressions of thought at the centre of their interest; to seek understanding of actions by re-enacting in their own minds the thoughts which they expressed. Still others are a stress upon the individuality of the historian's subject-matter; upon its unpredictability; upon its processive character; and upon its necessary relativity to the historian's own present. Important, too, was Collingwood's insistence that philosophers of history should work from a close knowledge of the way historical inquiry actually proceeds, elaborating philosophical criticism of it only 'from the inside'. Because of this emphasis, reinforced as it was by his claim to have derived his own theory of history from first-hand experience of historical research, Collingwood has often been seen as the historian's philosopher of history *par excellence*. He is certainly unusual among philosophers writing about history in having attained the status of a practising historian and archaeologist in his own right, as is evidenced by the simultaneous appointments he held at Oxford in Roman history and philosophy,[3] by the two books and numerous articles he wrote on the history of Roman Britain, and by his many publications in archaeology—among them two standard works—a genre of inquiry which he always regarded as continuous with history.[4] In fact, during his lifetime, his work in these 'secondary' fields gained him more

---

[3] Besides holding a philosophy fellowship at Pembroke from 1912 to 1935, Collingwood was from 1927 to 1935 University Lecturer in philosophy and Roman history.

[4] *RB* (1923, rev. edn. 1932), and most of *RBES* (1936), co-authored with J. N. L. Myres. His books on archaeology are: *The Archaeology of Roman Britain* (London, 1930; repub. London, 1996), and the posthumously published *The Roman Inscriptions of Britain*, i: *Inscriptions on Stone*, with R. P. Wright (Oxford, 1965). For information about his articles on history and archaeology, see D. S. Taylor, *R. G. Collingwood: A Bibliography* (New York, 1988), 157–64, or Christopher Dreisbach, *R. G. Collingwood: A Bibliographic Checklist* (Bowling Green, Oh., 1993), 5–14.

recognition than the philosophical work which, he always insisted, was his ultimate purpose in undertaking it.

One of the difficulties encountered by an interpreter of Collingwood's writings is the fact that, partly because he worked quickly and partly because he did not mind 'thinking on paper',[5] his ideas sometimes appear to change significantly over time, and in some cases over a very short time. The first attempt to periodize the development of his thought was made by Knox, who, in his preface to *The Idea of History*, distinguished an early, formative period up to the publication of *Speculum Mentis* in 1924, a long second period during which he saw Collingwood as being at the height of his powers, the period in which *An Essay on Philosophical Method* and most of the lectures which became *The Idea of History* were written, then a period of decline into scepticism and irascibility, of which he considered *An Autobiography*, *An Essay on Metaphysics*, and *The New Leviathan* to be characteristic expressions. But Knox was more concerned with Collingwood's view of philosophy than with his view of history. A way of periodizing which is more directly relevant to his theory of history as a form of inquiry—philosophy of history in what Collingwood himself sometimes called a narrow sense[6]—is suggested by the account he gave in the *Autobiography* of a philosophical 'illumination' he had in 1928, when he first came to formulate the idea that historical understanding requires a re-enactment of past thought (*A*, 107, 111–12). By contrast with this major turning-point, later changes in his view of history could be seen as relatively minor, although he did himself regard the work he did in his last years as distinctive enough to make it somewhat hazardous to lump together, as Knox did, the writings of 1935–6, the period when most of *The Idea of History* was written, and those of 1938–9, the period of the *Autobiography* and 'The Principles of History'.[7] Still another way of looking at Collingwood's

[5] NTM, prefatory note; see also *A*, 116.

[6] As will appear in § 2, what Collingwood planned for PH would have been philosophy of history in the narrow sense in Books I and II, and in the wide sense in Book III. On the distinction between a narrow and wide sense of a philosophy of history, see *IH*, 6–7.

[7] Another way of periodizing Collingwood's work on history is to distinguish three main periods of creative activity: 1925–30, 1935–6, 1938–9. See *IH* rev., pp. xxxii–xxxvii.

development might be as a journey from the realistic philosophy in which he was raised to a form of idealism about history, although Collingwood himself rejected the epithet 'idealist' (*A*, 56). In fact, in his writings dealing specifically with history, one can often find traces of both positions.

In his editor's preface to *The Idea of History*, Knox reported that, in the period immediately before his death, Collingwood had been working on an account of the nature and significance of history which he envisaged as a culmination of his more than two decades of work on the subject. This he planned to publish as a companion volume to a book which, based on university lectures he had been giving since 1936, would offer a historical survey of the development of European thought about history from the Greeks to the present day—essentially what later appeared as parts I–IV of *The Idea of History*. The companion volume would bear the title 'The Principles of History'.[8] At the time of his death, Collingwood had completed a mere third of what he had planned for the latter, this while on a voyage through the Dutch East Indies in 1939. But Knox, after deciding to put together a single volume under the title *The Idea of History* out of Collingwood's papers on history, rather than the two that were originally planned, chose to include only three selections from the manuscript of 'The Principles of History', less than half of what was available. The rest he judged to be of insufficient interest or of insufficiently high quality to justify publication.

As interest in Collingwood's philosophy of history burgeoned throughout the 1950s and 1960s, nurtured by the appearance of several major works of interpretation and, as well, a growing article literature on various aspects of his thought,[9] this decision

---

[8] Collingwood had arranged with Oxford University Press that these volumes would fit into an even larger publication scheme. Three categories of works were envisaged: the first, 'Philosophical Essays' (*EPM* and *EM*); the second, 'Philosophical Principles' (*PA* and PH); the third, 'Studies in the History of Ideas' (*IN* and *IH*).

[9] See e.g. Alan Donagan, *The Later Philosophy of R. G. Collingwood* (Oxford, 1962; repr. Chicago, 1985); Lionel Rubinoff, *Collingwood and the Reform of Metaphysics* (Toronto, 1970); L. O. Mink, *Mind, History, and Dialectic* (Bloomington, Ind., 1969; repr. Middletown, Conn., 1987). For references to other writings on Collingwood's ideas, see Taylor, *Bibliography*, 177–268; Dreisbach, *Checklist*, 35–75.

of Knox's was often regretted. The regret was made the more poignant by the high value that Collingwood himself had placed upon what he intended to say; he referred more than once to the projected volume as the work for which he believed his whole philosophical experience had especially prepared him, and for which he most hoped to be remembered.[10] Thus, when it was announced, early in 1978, that several thousand pages of Collingwood's unpublished manuscripts had been deposited by his widow Kate in the New Bodleian Library at Oxford, it was generally hoped that among them would be found the original manuscript of 'The Principles of History'. The deposit did include a wealth of materials on a large number of philosophical, historical, and archaeological subjects, many of them relating to philosophy of history; and a further deposit in 1980, mainly of lecture notes on moral philosophy from 1921 to 1940, also bore at various points upon problems in philosophy of history.[11] Many of these sources have since become objects of close study by scholars interested in the development of Collingwood's ideas, and some have now been published, in whole or in part.[12] But the manuscript of 'The Principles of History' was not among them. Inquiries made at Oxford University Press suggested that this manuscript was probably destroyed when Knox finished working with it, as would apparently have been normal practice at the time, and that its contents were therefore irretrievably lost.[13] One could only speculate about what it probably contained, guided by a terse and rather tantalizing outline of what was intended which Collingwood recorded in a manuscript entitled 'Notes on Historiography' just before he began to write.[14]

---

[10] For further details, see § 10 below.

[11] For details of both deposits, see Taylor, *Bibliography*, 51–84; Dreisbach, *Checklist*, 25–33.

[12] Some were included in the revised editions of *IH*, *NL*, and *EM*. Sizeable extracts from a number of manuscripts appear in Taylor, *Bibliography*, and in W. J. van der Dussen, *History as a Science: The Philosophy of R. G. Collingwood* (The Hague, 1981).

[13] See e.g. W. J. van der Dussen, 'Collingwood's Unpublished Manuscripts', *History and Theory*, 18 (1979), 309.

[14] Included in the present volume.

2. *The lost manuscripts*

It was therefore quite electrifying when, early in 1995, Oxford University Press announced that the original manuscript of 'The Principles of History' had been found in its archives.[15] With it were discovered two earlier Conclusions which Collingwood had written for his Lectures on Nature and Mind, which Knox had discarded in favour of a third when editing *The Idea of Nature*, the posthumous volume for which those lectures were the source. The manuscript of 'The Principles of History' contained some surprises. It sets forth some new doctrines about historical inquiry, and develops some old ones in ways which can be expected to generate controversy. But the major surprise was the extent to which the recovered text was found to deviate from the outline, the 'Scheme for a Book', that Collingwood had sketched for it in his 'Notes on Historiography'.[16]

The plan for the work, as set forth in the Scheme, was as follows. It was to consist of three books, the first two divided into four chapters, the content of the third being indicated only in a more general way. After an introduction tracing changes of meaning undergone by the word 'history' with a view to calling attention especially to what Collingwood calls its 'specialized' or 'scientific' sense, the first book would set forth the chief characteristics of the science of history as it now exists.[17] A first section would explicate the idea of evidence, contrasting this with mere testimony and what Collingwood calls the scissors-and-paste history which dependence on testimony yields. A second would expound the idea of human action, or *res gestae*, contrasting this with mere process or change, which was categorized as pseudo-history. A third would expound the idea of historical under-

[15] By the archivists, Peter Foden and Jenny McMorris, to whom the thanks of all students of Collingwood's thought on history are due. For further details of the find, see Jan van der Dussen, 'Collingwood's "Lost" Manuscript of *The Principles of History*', *History and Theory*, 36 (1997), 33–4; and David Boucher, 'The Significance of R. G. Collingwood's *Principles of History*', *Journal of the History of Ideas*, 58 (1997), 313–14.

[16] Included in NHV in this volume; see also remarks by Knox in the preface to the original edition of *IH*, p. v.

[17] Collingwood always insisted that history has become a science, although different from natural science. See e.g. L28, 490; *IH*, 18–19, 209.

standing as involving a re-enactment of past thought, the idea of
the past as still living in the present rather than as dead and
finished. A fourth would expound Collingwood's view of historical study as self-knowledge of mind, and explain why other
ways of studying mind must fall short of this.

In a second book, it was proposed to trace the relation of history, so conceived, to other kinds of inquiry. A first chapter
would explore its relation to natural science, representing the
two as irreducibly different, and stressing the dependence of
science upon historical thinking rather than, as more commonly
believed, that of history upon science.[18] A second would compare history with the other human sciences, including the so-
called social sciences, arguing that the latter, even when they try
to distance themselves from history and historical methods, still
amount to a kind of crypto-history.[19] A third chapter would
examine the relations between history and philosophy. In a
third book, the relations between history, as characterized, and
practical life would be considered. It would be argued that upon
historical thinking about human relations can be based a characteristic approach to morality, and, indeed, a whole mode of
civilization, which could replace the science-oriented one we
have now, which Collingwood believed to have proved disastrous. Essential to such a change would be a breaking down of
the traditional distinction between subject and object, and
between theory and practice, and an approach to human relations centred upon re-enactive understanding rather than upon
attempts to master or to manœuvre.[20]

In what he completed of 'The Principles of History',
Collingwood got no further than Book I, and of this he completed only the first three chapters, making no more than a brief

[18] The assertion that history cannot be reduced to science echoes the warning in *IH*, 223, that a scientific approach to human affairs 'dementalizes' it, and
prefigures the attack on psychology mounted in PH, Ch. 3, and more fully
worked out in *EM*, 101–42.
[19] See the note on 'Crypto-history' in NHV.
[20] Collingwood's plan to make a case for a morality, indeed a whole civilization, saturated with the idea of history shows how deeply entrenched was his
idea, noted in passing in *IH*, 7, and alluded to in *A*, 147 ff. and at the end of
IRN, of eventually elaborating a complete philosophy from a historical point
of view. This idea is considered further in the editor's introduction to *IH* rev.,
p. xxxix.

beginning on Chapter 4.[21] Appended to the latter is a single page on 'History and Philosophy', which would presumably have been incorporated eventually into Book II, Chapter 3. The promised preliminary discussion of various senses of the word 'history' does not appear. Chapter 1, which contains Collingwood's now well-known critique of scissors-and-paste history and his account of similarities and differences between historical inquiry and crime detection, follows his outline strictly. Chapter 2 departs somewhat from the plan. Although it argues that the proper subject-matter of history is human action, it also reverts to the question of how historians argue from evidence, expanding considerably the theory of evidence set forth in the preceding chapter, and making connections between 'The Principles of History' and *The Principles of Art*. It does not discuss process, change, and pseudo-history, as was promised in the Scheme. Chapter 3, which was to have been about re-enactment, never mentions this idea.[22] It does, however, explore implications of the related notion that, as a study of action, all history is history of thought, this leading to a clearer contrast being drawn between human and natural history than is found in most of Collingwood's other writings. The latter, however, is a topic which was to have been treated in Book II, Chapter 1. Chapter 4, rather than addressing the question of how mind achieves self-knowledge by thinking historically, embarks upon a discussion of what is entailed by the idea that historical inquiry is about the past. There is thus a progressive departure from the original plan: some deviation from it in Chapter 2; only a slight connection with it in Chapter 3; and none at all in what was completed of Chapter 4, although the latter has some slight relevance to what was to have been treated in Chapter 3.

Thus what we have is really not even a first third of what was promised by Collingwood's Scheme. The manuscript does contain some challenging new ideas, however, such as the likeness it asserts between interpreting historical evidence and understanding language, and the assurance it gives that irrational actions fall well within the purview of the historian. It also

---

[21] Since there are summaries appended to the first three chapters, we can assume that they are at any rate complete drafts.

[22] On this see § 11 below.

develops further some ideas already familiar to readers of Collingwood, such as the way the actual practice of history must function as a touchstone for philosophical pronouncements on the nature and possibilities of historical thinking, or the wide gap alleged to exist between history and biography, despite some appearance of their being similar genres of inquiry, or the dangers of historical naturalism. Important connections are made, too, with Collingwood's writings in cognate fields, notably with *The Principles of Art*, from which is now drawn an analysis of the relation between thought and emotion which leads to a startling revision of what was previously said about the place of the latter in the historian's subject-matter.[23] There are also useful recastings of familiar doctrines, and new exemplifications, which can be expected to throw light on a number of issues which have been matters of controversy.

But given what is now known of 'The Principles of History', together with whatever might have been added if Collingwood had been able to complete the work more or less as planned, is there any reason to share his own expectation, as expressed, for example, in a letter to his son of 14 February 1939, that it would become recognized as his 'masterpiece'?[24] We are inclined to think this unlikely; but there is some danger of an illusion of perspective here. It is hard for us, who are familiar with *The Idea of History* and the *Autobiography*, to imagine ourselves in a situation where the first of these was known only in the form of oral presentations to students who attended Collingwood's lectures,[25] and the second had only been written on the eve of his

[23] This may be seen as vindication of the stress placed by commentators like Louis Mink, e.g. in *Mind, History, and Dialectic*, 163 ff., on the relevance of *PA* for Collingwood's theory of history. For commentators criticizing Collingwood for paying too little attention to emotions in his theory, see van der Dussen, *History as a Science*, 82–3.

[24] See van der Dussen, *History as a Science*, 61.

[25] Although various individuals have expressed deep appreciation of Collingwood's lectures, the latter never gained the status of treasured texts circulating among devoted followers in the way Wittgenstein's lectures did (for the appreciation of Collingwood as a lecturer, see David Boucher, *The Social and Political Thought of R. G. Collingwood* (Cambridge, 1989), 6). It is indicative of how little Collingwood's ideas on history were valued or even known in his lifetime that his name does not appear among the contributors to Raymond Klibansky and H. J. Paton (eds.), *Philosophy and History: Essays Presented to Ernst Cassirer* (Oxford, 1936), one of the few significant publications on the subject in English during the 1930s.

departure for the Dutch East Indies as a hurried anticipation of
some things he hoped to say, but feared he might not have the
opportunity to say, in a final work on history. It is especially
important to remember that, in 1939, the original Metaphysical
Epilegomena to the lectures which Collingwood delivered in
1936 had not been published; nor is there any indication that he
intended their publication.[26] It needs to be kept in mind, too,
that, brilliant as they undoubtedly are, the two previously published essays which Knox included in the Epilegomena to *The
Idea of History* were offered by Collingwood in the mid-1930s
simply as interim reports on the direction in which his thought
was tending, not as definitive statements of his theory of history.[27]

Considerations such as these make Collingwood's own view
of the nature and prospective importance of his 'Principles of
History' somewhat more plausible. Yet, important as this work
certainly is as the last thing he wrote on the subject he had so
much made his own, and valuable and novel as many parts of it
certainly are, it does not seem to us that it can be regarded as
more than a welcome and often illuminating further addition to
the corpus of his writings on history. Although it contains fresh
developments of ideas promulgated earlier, it is hard to see it,
taken as a whole, as a culminating work; it does not articulate a
position towards which all Collingwood's previous work can be
seen as a progressive movement. For example, what he wrote
about evidence in the unusually well worked through lectures of
1926 and 1928, which have recently been made available in a
revised edition of *The Idea of History*, is in some ways superior
to what he wrote on this subject in the 1930s, and should be read
along with it (L26, 368–90; L28, 482–96). Much of what he had
to say in some of the published essays of the 1920s about the relativity and perspectivity of historical thought, too, is neither

[26] The original Metaphysical Epilegomena to the lectures of 1936 consisted
of three parts: 'Re-enactment of Past Experience the Essence of History', 'The
Subject-matter of History', and 'Progress'. Knox incorporated these into *IH* as
§§ 4, 5, and 7 of that volume's Epilegomena, slightly changing the titles of the
first and third. To avoid confusion, we will hereafter use 'Epilegomena' to refer
to the whole of part V of *IH*, and 'Metaphysical Epilegomena' to refer only to
the three sections derived from the lectures of 1936.

[27] Collingwood's essay of 1930 for the English Historical Association, *The
Philosophy of History* (*EPH*, 121–39), is an earlier interim report.

repeated in, nor superseded by, what came later.[28] Nor does anything he wrote after 1935 quite match his discussion of the systematic 'picture-building' which he attributed to scientific historians in his inaugural lecture (*IH*, 241 ff.). In his case, at any rate, it seems fair to say that last is not necessarily best.[29] In seeking to come to grips with his thought on history, it is wise therefore to range over all of it.

In his preface to *The Idea of History*, Knox expressed some distaste for what he found in Collingwood's manuscripts after 1936: they were written, he said, in his 'later manner', this not being intended as a compliment. Yet it is difficult to see how, as pieces of philosophical writing, the previously unpublished parts of 'The Principles of History' are any better or any worse than most of what Collingwood wrote on the theory of history. They do sometimes tend to meander, this being especially true of Chapter 2, and they are sometimes carelessly expressed. But these are not blemishes from which his philosophical writings are characteristically free. As has often been noted, Collingwood was an intuitive writer, and frequently an impatient and testy one. He saw a great deal at once, and did not always make allowances for the lesser intellects among those who might be his readers. Nor can it be said that his work, here or elsewhere, is always free from opacity, or even contradiction. When he wrote 'The Principles of History', furthermore, he was in a hurry. Rapidly declining health and the near-certainty of an early death seemed only to drive him on; and what he accomplished in the last three or four years of his life beggars belief. Even earlier, however, no matter how important he thought the subject-matter, he had been more likely to produce stimulating and highly readable pieces of writing than finely crafted ones. He confessed himself that his *Essay on Philosophical Method*, a work of great elegance and power published in 1933, was the

[28] Much the same might be said of Collingwood's notion of the 'ideality' of history, which almost drops out of sight after the lectures of 1928.

[29] In this connection, it should not be forgotten that PH, far from being a finished work, was in effect a first draft; also that while writing it, Collingwood was not in a position to consult his previous writings and notes on the subject. That he sometimes did consult his previous writings when working further on a subject is made clear by an observation he made in 1935 on his lectures of 1928 (L28, 470, n. 16); also by a later addition to the table of contents of those lectures (L28, 437).

only book which he had been able to finish as well as he knew
how (*A*, 118). Yet even his least finished texts are, in our view,
uniquely valuable as stimuli to fruitful reflection upon the
nature of history. The unfinished 'Principles of History' is no
exception.

3. *The aims of this book*

The chief aim of the present book is to make the newly discovered manuscript of 'The Principles of History' available to
students of Collingwood, and along with it some further unpublished writings of his of the 1930s on philosophy of history,
selected in all but one case from those now on deposit at the
New Bodleian Library. The additional manuscripts have been
chosen for their general interest, their relevance to what
Collingwood has to say in 'The Principles of History', and their
bearing upon his other writings in the field. Also included are
the newly found Conclusions to the Lectures on Nature and
Mind because, although much of what is discussed in them is
somewhat remote from the concerns of Collingwood's philosophy of history, at any rate in what he called the narrow sense,
they contain some arguments that bear directly on it, and passages, too, which it is interesting to compare with other things
he wrote at about the same time. The result is a volume which,
together with *The Idea of History* and the *Autobiography*, may
be regarded as rounding out our knowledge of Collingwood's
thought on history in the middle and late 1930s, somewhat as
the recent publication of his lectures of 1926 and 1928, together
with the published articles collected by Debbins in *Essays in the
Philosophy of History*, has done for his thought of the 1920s.

Among the manuscripts now at the New Bodleian Library
there are some other short pieces from the 1930s which contain
material relevant to Collingwood's philosophy of history.[30]

---

[30] These manuscripts include a draft of Collingwood's British Academy
Lecture of 1936, which, however, does not differ from the final version as much
as the draft of the inaugural lecture (IRN), included in this volume, differs
from the version now found in *IH*. Other items of interest are fragments from
Collingwood's lecture notes on philosophy of history for 1931 and 1932, and a
group of individual pages from his lectures of 1936. A manuscript of great
interest for philosophy of history, 'Goodness, Rightness, Utility', which
formed part of Collingwood's lectures on moral philosophy in 1940, now

None of these seem to us to have as strong a claim to be included as the ones we have selected. There remains one long manuscript, however, which does have great potential significance for Collingwood's view of history. This reports studies he made of European folklore in the late 1930s, which led him to outline, in effect, a philosophy of anthropology with marked affinities to his philosophy of history.[31] Some excerpts from this work have already appeared in print, and since there is some prospect that the whole manuscript will eventually be published intact, we have refrained from drawing upon it here.

We have not thought it necessary to offer in this Introduction a summary of the quite complicated arguments of 'The Principles of History', and still less to review all the doctrinal claims made in the shorter manuscripts. We will, however, call attention at section length to four issues treated in that manuscript which seem to us of special interest: the nature of argument from historical evidence; the scope of the historian's proper subject-matter; the difference between human history and natural history; and the dangers of historical naturalism—in each case relating what Collingwood says here to what he had to say elsewhere on the same or connected issues. With a view to helping to launch the discussion of each which Collingwood's often provocative pronouncements may be expected to evoke, our comments will be critical as well as expository. We shall then, also at section length, try to answer three large questions which we think most readers will want to ask about the manuscript of 'The Principles of History': why Knox incorporated only part of it into *The Idea of History*; why Collingwood left it in an unfinished state; and why the idea of re-enactment, so closely associated with his theory of history elsewhere, makes no appearance in it. Finally, we shall comment seriatim, but necessarily more briefly, on the general character of each of the

appears as an appendix to *NL* rev. (see esp. 469–79). This stresses the close relationship which he sees between the individualizing thought of history, regarded as the highest form of theoretical reason, and the individualizing morality of duty, regarded as the highest form of practical reason.

[31] For more information about this manuscript and some extracts from it, see van der Dussen, 'Unpublished Manuscripts', 303 ff.; or Taylor, *Bibliography*, 73–7. The text is of special interest for Collingwood's theory of evidence, re-enactment, emotion, social groups, and, more generally, the relation between history and the social sciences.

xxvi EDITORS' INTRODUCTION

shorter manuscripts we have included, and on a few of the particular issues they raise. We have printed the latter roughly in the order of their composition, except for the Conclusions to Nature and Mind, which are placed at the end where their status as essentially an appendix to the volume will be most evident. The shorter manuscripts, it might be remarked, are rather a heterogeneous lot. One (HUP) is a mere fragment; two (NHH, NHV) amount to no more than notes which Collingwood recorded to guide him in later writing; one (RAH) he described himself as an experimental essay aimed only at seeing what could be made of a certain hypothesis; another (IRN) is a draft of a public lecture which, in the end, distanced itself considerably from the draft; still another (CHBI) is a paper read to a student philosophical society, an occasion on which Collingwood may perhaps be excused for trailing his coat; another again (NTM) consists of short extracts from a larger 'workpiece', which inevitably suffer somewhat from the loss of their original context.

A word of explanation should be offered of some of the editorial policies we have followed.[32] We thought it best to publish the whole text of 'The Principles of History', including the parts which Knox incorporated into *The Idea of History*, i.e. those entitled 'Evidence', 'Freedom', and 'Heads or Tails', as well as the ones which he left out. One reason for this is that it will facilitate the reading of the previously published parts in their proper context, the context of a continuous argument—for example, Chapter 2 as an emendation and expansion of Chapter 1.[33] Another is that the newly recovered text of two of the sections which Knox used differs in some details from what appears in *The Idea of History*. Discrepancies of this sort raise a problem to which we shall return in § 9: that of the nature and extent of Knox's editorial intrusions into the text of the latter as we have become familiar with it. It might be added that, since the manuscript, as it was found, begins at Chapter 2—or, more precisely, half-way through Collingwood's summary of Chapter

---

[32] For our policy on orthography etc., see the initial Editors' Note.

[33] A corresponding benefit is that readers of *IH* may thereby be encouraged to read that work along with its original Metaphysical Epilegomena (that is, §§ 4, 5, and 7 of the present Epilegomena to *IH*), i.e. imaginatively excising the pieces Knox added from PH, and the two public lectures he reprinted.

1, which Knox unfortunately ignored—it has been necessary to reprint as Chapter 1 exactly what now appears as 'Historical Evidence' in the Epilegomena of *The Idea of History*, despite the very real possibility that it, too, may not be identical with its original, which remains lost. This makes it the more unfortunate that the first half of the summary of Chapter 1 was not found with the recovered manuscript.

Something should also be said in support of our decision to publish materials in this volume which are hardly ever in what might be regarded as final form. This is true even of the manuscript of 'The Principles of History', which was at least written with eventual publication in mind; but it is even more true of the shorter manuscripts, where the case for posthumous publication of incomplete and possibly defective work may appear even harder to make. It seems unlikely that Collingwood himself would have recommended publication of all the pieces collected in this volume. However, he left no unambiguous directions as to what might or might not be published after his death. Indeed, he was quite ambivalent about it, telling some that he wanted all his papers destroyed, and others that he had no objection to the publication of any which were judged to be of more than ephemeral interest.[34] He left a specific authorization for the publication of what he had finished of 'The Principles of History' on the manuscript itself, should his wife judge this to be appropriate. Two generations later, Collingwood's writings, published and unpublished, finished or exploratory, constitute the richest single resource possessed by English-speaking philosophy of history; and we think that by now it ought to be permissible to decide what in them, within the bounds of practicality, and despite some roughnesses and internal tensions, would best serve to promote research in the subject generally, and to clarify further the meaning and development of Collingwood's own ideas. That is one of the principles on which we have selected items for this volume, and it is one, happily, on which the Collingwood family and Oxford University Press concur.

---

[34] For further details, see D. Boucher, 'The Principles of History and the Cosmology Conclusion to The Idea of Nature', *Collingwood Studies*, 2 (Swansea, 1995), 141–6.

In a sense, of course, the question whether selected unpublished writings of Collingwood's should be made available posthumously was settled in principle when it was decided, soon after his death, to go ahead with *The Idea of Nature* and *The Idea of History*, both of which were based on lectures left in manuscript. It seems likely, furthermore, that there would have been still further publication of Collingwood's papers at that time had Knox not opposed the idea.[35] Since 1978, the manuscripts which remain unpublished, but can be examined in the Bodleian Library, have come increasingly into public view, as studies of them have appeared, and extensive quotations from them have been included in articles dealing with various aspects of Collingwood's thought.[36] Our including in this collection, along with the manuscript of 'The Principles of History', some of Collingwood's more casual writings thus simply opens to a wider readership resources which have been available to a select group of researchers for some time.

4. *Evidence and interpretation*

The first of the four issues to be discussed is Collingwood's conception of history's relation to evidence. What he says on this matter in the first chapter of 'The Principles of History' has become part of the common knowledge of all those who have any acquaintance with his philosophy of history.[37] He draws a sharp distinction there between evidence and mere testimony: between historical accounts which merely repeat, arrange, and to some extent extrapolate from what has been found in previous accounts, all the way back to reports of eyewitnesses, and ones which draw conclusions from present relics of the human past which sometimes go beyond what even those who lived at the time may have known. The language in which he puts this doctrine has been incorporated into the normal vocabulary of philosophers of history. Pre-scientific history, Collingwood maintains—meaning almost all historical writing until well into

[35] Boucher, 'The Significance', 311–12.
[36] See e.g. van der Dussen, *History as a Science*, 127–99; and commentaries in Taylor, *Bibliography*, 51–84.
[37] As noted earlier, the text of Ch. 1 is the same as *IH*, 249–82. Only what remains of the chapter's summary is new.

the nineteenth century—tries to base itself upon 'ready-made' knowledge, and its method is 'scissors and paste'.[38] Putting the point in another way, he declares that scientific history is autonomous: the point of departure for a historian is not what his sources report, but what he himself is prepared to say about the fact that they report it.[39]

Associated with this now famous analysis is a stress upon the role of systematic questioning in historical thinking. In this respect, Collingwood avers, history is not unlike natural science. He sometimes puts his point by declaring that nothing can be considered as evidence by a historian until it is seen as answering a question he wants to ask. A second associated doctrine is Collingwood's categorizing as relatively unimportant for theory of history the distinction traditionally drawn between written and unwritten sources. Since what interests a scientific historian is not what a piece of evidence says but what can be inferred from it, both are simply evidence. Still a third associated doctrine, and one that is obscured if one thinks of history as dependent on ready-made statements preserved in documents, is a claim that anything which is here and now perceptible may conceivably function as evidence for a historian. As Collingwood observes elsewhere (L28, 491; IH, 247; A, 86), some of the most significant advances in historiography have been made by historians who discovered how to use as evidence relics of a kind which had not hitherto been regarded in that way.

But if one asks precisely how Collingwood thought reasoning from evidence proceeds in history, it is easier to say what he denied than what he asserted. He denied that such reasoning is either deductive or inductive, the kinds characteristic of mathematics and natural science respectively. He nevertheless insisted that, like mathematical reasoning, historical reasoning can be compulsive, leaving no room for alternative conclusions. It would have been of interest to have been given at this point an example of historians actually reasoning to certain conclusions.[40]

[38] For previous uses of this expression, see e.g. L28, 488; IH, 33, 143; EM, 94, 235; A, 79, 99, 114, 131, 133, 145.
[39] This point is also put in Ch. 1, and more explicitly in Ch. 2, by declaring that the historian's interest is in what a source means, not what it says.
[40] Collingwood's own pronouncements as a historian and archaeologist sometimes suggest, however, that he regards particular conclusions as

What we are offered instead is a fictional account of crime detection, which, although instructive in some ways, neither elaborates in detail a chain of reasoning from the standpoint of an investigator, nor makes clear how any of the inferences involved could properly be considered certain. In fact, Collingwood himself admits that the analogy between historical and forensic reasoning is imperfect, not least because the latter is generally 'pegged down' in the end by a confession. If anything like this were encountered in a historical inquiry, he points out, it would only raise the further problem of its own authenticity.[41]

Collingwood returns to the questions of evidence and historical inference in the newly discovered Chapter 2.[42] Rather surprisingly, in attempting to clarify the nature of historical evidence further, he does not focus on cases in which the relics considered are artefacts, this despite the emphasis he had placed in his detective story on how much can be learned from dabs of paint, footprints, and the like, and his assertions elsewhere of how much historical inquiry resembles archaeological prac-

---

'compulsive'. For example, he maintains that excavations of 1911 by the archaeologists J. P. Gibson and F. G. Simpson definitively proved that what we now call Hadrian's Wall was built by Hadrianus and not by Severus as was previously believed, and made it 'absolutely certain' that it 'dates from the first half of the second century' ('Hadrian's Wall: A History of the Problem', *Journal of Roman Studies*, 11 (1921), 62). He elsewhere says that 'it is more certain than ever that the forts [on Hadrian's Wall] were built before the stone Wall', and that '[i]t is certain . . . that the Antonine Wall was finally evacuated, as such, in or about 181' ('The Roman Frontier in Britain', *Antiquity*, 1 (1927), 23, 28). With regard to the latter statement, Dr Grace Simpson observed to the editors that Collingwood was in error in thinking that forts came before Hadrian's Wall. We should like to thank Dr Simpson for this information and for the reference to the excavation made by her father.

[41] The analogy with crime detection is also considered in IRN under the heading 'History and the Detective', and in the section of NHH headed 'A Note on Evidence and Certitude'.

[42] His ostensible reason for doing this is that, in order to consider its designated topic, the object of historical inquiry, he must first probe more deeply into the nature of historical method, this on the principle that what determines the subject-matter of a type of inquiry is the method it brings to bear, not the other way around. In Ch. 3, § 5, the section on 'Freedom', he comes back to the relation between history *a parte subjecti* and *a parte objecti* (on this see also L28, 429, 434). Somewhat the same line is taken, but more gingerly, in *IH*, 212–13, where Collingwood is at least prepared to consider the question whether the method actually employed by historians covers the whole field proper to their subject.

tice.[43] Instead, he considers a more conventional type of historical problem: how a certain document, alleged to be a charter
issued by Henry I, is to be interpreted.[44] The analysis he offers
of this example is significantly different from anything found
elsewhere in his writings. A striking feature of it is the link he
now claims to see between an adequate theory of historical
thinking and the theories of language and imagination which he
had worked out two years earlier in *The Principles of Art*.

According to Collingwood, a historian endeavouring to interpret Henry's charter can expect to be involved in four kinds of
problems, these identifying four levels of thought at which a
historian may have to operate when trying to make use of a
potential piece of evidence. First, if the document is a copy of an
original, he must consider whether it is a true copy; second, he
must satisfy himself that the original was what it purported to be
and not, say, a forgery; third, he must be able to read it, to find
out what it says; and fourth, he must determine, in the light of
what he believes it to be saying, what it means—what its author,
in issuing it, was trying to accomplish. At the first of these levels, what is required, he observes, is a species of practical judgement. At the second, it is an exercise of textual scholarship. At
neither of these levels, however, does anything strictly describ-
able as historical thinking yet take place: what occurs is no more
than propaedeutic to it. Even at level three, there is no truly historical judgement; what is required there of the historian is an
aesthetic skill, an ability to read an expression of thought as
such. Only at level four, where the implications of what has been
read are probed, can full-blown historical thinking be said to
occur. Thus, in the case of the charter, the historian determines
at level three that the relic before him granted certain privileges
to certain subjects: that is what it says. At level four, he discovers how the king sought to serve his own ends by this means.[45]

---

[43] In L28, 427, 490–2, 496 Collingwood even calls archaeology, apparently
taken in a broad sense, the 'empirical methodology' of history, and in *A*, 24–6
he characterizes it as his 'laboratory' of historical thought and knowledge in
general. On the relevance of archaeology, see further *A*, 82, 108.

[44] He implicitly extends his analysis later to citations of material evidence.

[45] The distinction between interpretation at the third and fourth levels is
anticipated sketchily in L26, 377, 382. Collingwood does not go into the question whether the document's implicit claim to grant the privileges is valid,

Collingwood insists that historical judgements made at level three are not inferential. This applies the theory worked out in *The Principles of Art* about the way language is understood, where it is held that grasping what someone says involves 'attributing to him the idea which his words arouse in yourself; and this implies treating them as words of your own' (*PA*, 250). The grasping is immediate, not a matter of ratiocination. Such an account of linguistic understanding, however, is not intended to imply that the interpretation of evidence in history is not inferential at all—a position which would have blatantly contradicted both what Collingwood affirmed so strongly in Chapter 1 and what he would go on to affirm in the rest of Chapter 2[46]— since judgements made at level four, an integral aspect of historical thinking as a whole, would still be inferential. But if the contention is that inference occurs only at level four, this raises some problems.

One is how the present, more complicated analysis of the way historians appeal to evidence is to be related to Collingwood's claim that their conclusions can be as certain as those of mathematics. Clearly, in the four-level scheme, the truth of what is asserted at the fourth level is dependent upon the truth of what is asserted at the third; for what third-level interpretations provide, in effect, is premisses for inferences to be drawn at level four. In *The Principles of Art*, however, it is denied that interpreting expressions of another person's thought can ever attain certainty (*PA*, 251, 309), and if third-level pronouncements must thus remain uncertain, the uncertainty will surely infect any inferences which historians draw from them at level four.[47] It is conceivable that what Collingwood meant to claim for inferences at level four was only certainty relative to their third-level premisses. But if that is his position, there is little hint of it in what he actually says.

This problem leads to others. In Chapter 1, as was noted,

consideration of which might have forced him to complicate further his account of the relation between levels three and four.

[46] It would also have contradicted what he said about historical inference in relation to the interpretation of evidence at many other points: see e.g. L26, 382, 407; L28, 435, 483; CNM 1934, par. 38; *IH*, 234, 282. The idea that inferences are to be drawn from evidence is pivotal, too, in the idea of archaeology as the empirical methodology of history.

[47] See p. 17 for Collingwood's picturesque way of putting this point.

Collingwood said little of a positive nature about what a reputable historical inference would look like. Stress was placed upon the need for questioning and for evidence, but there was no suggestion that historians have available to them some third kind of logical route from premises to conclusion, a route quite different from that offered by the deductive or inductive sorts of inference which Collingwood denied them. What is said in Chapter 2 about there being a role here also for the historian's imagination is a further complication. In *The Principles of Art*, the interpretation of thought-expressions, i.e. the understanding of language, is described as a work of imagination (*PA*, 225, 251). It therefore seems reasonable to conclude that what is conceived to function at level three in lieu of inference is a species of historical imagination. But in Chapter 2, historical thinking at level four is also characterized as a work of the imagination; and since inference is also said to be involved at this level, this can hardly mean imagination in the same sense. One could wish that Collingwood had gone on to link what he says in 'The Principles of History' about the role of the historical imagination with what he said about it briefly, yet powerfully, in his inaugural lecture (*IH*, 241 ff.), and, under the rubric 'The interpolative imagination', in the draft for it included in this volume. There a constructive historical imagination is said to elaborate an increasingly detailed 'picture' of a portion of the past through an interplay of what can be inferred, although not 'proved', from sources, critically analysed, and what is required by certain a priori principles. But even in Collingwood's Scheme for 'The Principles of History', and certainly in the approach he takes in Chapter 2, there appears to be little place for such a view of the way historical reconstruction proceeds.[48]

[48] Although Collingwood left his conception of the relation between imagination and inference insufficiently worked out, there is early evidence of his intention to bring together something like the analyses he presented in 'The Historical Imagination' and 'Historical Evidence' in a note he added at a later date to the table of contents of L28 listing 'topics to be worked in'. One of these was 'Historical imagination (i.e. closer study of nature of historical *inference*)' (L28, 437). 'The Historical Imagination' might thus be read as implicitly a discussion of historical inference. Such a combined view of imaginative and inferential reasoning, it might be observed, is typical of the notion of 'abduction' as conceived by Charles Peirce: what he also calls 'hypothetical inference' (on this see van der Dussen, 'Collingwood's "Lost" Manuscript', 48 n. 33).

It needs also to be asked whether Collingwood's four-level analysis can be given general application as easily as he appeared to think. As noted already, the example he used in introducing it was the most plausible kind: the interpretation of a document. He goes on to make it clear, however, that he regards the same theory as applying to cases where material evidence is used—to the reconstruction of the past of an imaginary ancient site he calls Highbury, for example, where no documentary evidence is available at all, and historians are obliged to use only archaeological methods. In his analysis of this example, little is said about the first two levels of interpretation, and it is difficult to see how they could have applied to it. It is difficult enough to see how even the idea of level-three interpretation applies without stretching it considerably. The connecting link, as Collingwood sees it, is that all human artefacts are expressions of past thought, and, as such, are 'in the nature of' language. But what does he think the triangular objects which he imagines being identified as loom weights actually 'say'? Identified as such, their discovery certainly supports Collingwood's conclusion that the people who made or used them must have been weavers. But do they say anything in the sense that Henry's charter does? Is there anything more than implicit tautology or intriguing analogy here?[49]

5. *Broadening the subject-matter*

Collingwood's declared goal in Chapter 2, although he digresses from it somewhat as he develops his theory of evidence further, is to show that the subject-matter of history is human actions, *res gestae*,[50] and that since an action, in the intended sense, is an expression of an agent's thought, all history is history of thought (see also *IH*, 216; *A*, 110).[51] To the likely charge that this is to

[49] If certain objects are seen as loom weights one may indeed conclusively conclude that they were used by people who wove. But this statement is simply tautological, and the compulsive nature of substantive historical inference therefore remains obscure.

[50] This claim is also made in *IH*, 9, in a part of the 1936 lectures probably revised by Collingwood in 1940.

[51] If by thought here is meant what Collingwood called 'reflective' thought in *IH*, 308, the subject-matter will seem even more unacceptably narrow. But there are conflicting interpretations of what he meant there by 'reflective': see

conceive history's proper subject-matter far too narrowly, he implicitly responds in three ways.[52]

He argues, first, that, although conceiving history as a study of actions understood as expressions of thought implies that it will be concerned with exhibitions of human reason, its subject-matter can include instances of human irrationality. Reiterating a view of human nature which he had expressed in *The Idea of History* and elsewhere, he concedes that human reason is a relatively weak instrument, and that human beings seldom act in perfectly rational ways (*IH*, 41, 116, 227). As a comment on facts of human nature this is hardly controversial. More problematic, however, is Collingwood's uncompromising assertion that, while history is not properly concerned with mere 'psyche'— that 'apanage' of mind consisting of perceptions, feelings, animal appetites, and the like—irrational human actions belong to mind proper, and are thus fully within the range of the historian's interests and techniques. There is a difference, he observes, between an absence of reasons and the presence of bad ones.[53]

Those who have regarded Collingwood's view of history's subject-matter as too narrow because it seems to exclude all but the fully rational in human life will welcome such a forthright statement to the contrary. However, the brief remarks he makes on the matter here leave an important problem unaddressed. Had he been discussing, as his Scheme had suggested he would in this chapter, the idea that only past thoughts which can be re-enacted are properly the subject-matter of history, he might have been expected to go on to explain how irrational as well as rational thoughts can be re-enacted. And it is difficult to see how he could have done this, at any rate as the idea of understanding by re-enactment has commonly been interpreted, namely, as involving the attribution to the agent of a valid practical argument which enjoins the performance of the action.[54] Of course,

e.g. Boucher, *NL* rev., pp. xxvii ff.; W. H. Dray, *History as Re-enactment* (Oxford, 1995), 110 ff.

[52] The main points made in this section are considered in greater detail in W. H. Dray, 'Broadening the Subject-Matter in *The Principles of History*', *Collingwood Studies*, 4 (1997), 2–33.

[53] There is a close approach to this position in *IH*, 116.

[54] See e.g. Rex Martin, *Historical Explanation* (Ithaca, NY, 1977), 95 ff.; or Dray, *History as Re-enactment*, 55 ff.; or Heikki Saari, *Re-enactment: A Study in R. G. Collingwood's Philosophy of History* (Åbo, 1984), 108 ff.

there are different kinds of less-than-rational actions. Collingwood discussed one kind in his *Autobiography*, controversially, when he pointed to the difficulty of reconstructing the thoughts of agents whose actions were unsuccessful because they misconceived the situations they were in.[55] There would appear to be no reason deriving from the idea of re-enactment itself why actions which are irrational in this sense could not be re-enactively understood, provided sufficient evidence of the way the agents did conceive their situations can be obtained. But it would be another matter entirely to claim re-enactive understanding of actions which were irrational in the sense not just of being badly informed, but of being confused or illogical; for such actions would express no valid argument to be re-enacted.[56] Thus, if the extension of the historian's subject-matter which Collingwood proposes here were accepted without qualification, a major revision of the very idea of re-enactment might be required; and it is far from clear what this could be like.

A second extension of the historian's subject-matter as Collingwood is generally thought to have conceived it is suggested by what he says about the relevance of certain kinds of emotion to human action. It has long been a source of dissatisfaction with his view of history that, besides excluding mere feelings and purely animal activities from its field of interest, it also excludes emotions. Not that the position Collingwood seemed to take on this matter is entirely without ambiguity. At several points, for example, he observed that what historical inquiry is about is thought 'in the widest sense', which, in one instance, he declared to include 'all the conscious activities of the human spirit' (L28, 444–5)—these presumably encompassing human emotions. In his lectures on moral philosophy and his writings on folklore, he represents at least what he there calls 'rational' emotions as fully understandable in the properly historical way.[57] Even in *The Idea of History*, he takes some steps

[55] *A*, 70. On the controversy occasioned by this example, see Herman Simissen, 'On Understanding Disaster', *Philosophy of the Social Sciences*, 23 (1993), 352–67.

[56] The idea of re-enactment will be discussed further in § 11.

[57] 'Lectures on Moral Philosophy' 1933, Collingwood MSS, Bodleian Library, dep. 8, 125; 'Folklore', ibid., dep. 21, part IV. The first is discussed in *NL* rev., p. xxxv.

towards his present doctrine, as when he commends Hegel for holding that, although history is a story of passion, it is a story of passion in the service of reason, this at least suggesting that there can be reasons (not just determining causes) for people having the passions, i.e. emotions, that they have (*IH*, 116).

It is therefore of some interest that, in Chapter 2 of 'The Principles of History', Collingwood explicitly includes in history's subject-matter what he calls 'essential' emotions, by which he means ones which necessarily accompanied the thoughts ascribed by historians to the human agents whose actions they study. He offers the following example. When a military officer, in the course of a campaign, builds a fort with a view to providing protection against a perceived danger, we can infer, he says, that in acting for such a motive, the officer felt a certain emotion. He may, of course, have felt many emotions; but in the case of most of them, we either lack evidence that they were experienced, or we can disregard them as having no relevance to the building of the fort. Unfortunately, although Collingwood gives examples of what he means by inessential emotions, he offers no concrete example of what he would consider an essential one. And it may well be doubted that there are any emotions which, in any strict sense, are essentially connected with acting in certain ways. It is not as if we have been shown, by means of an analysis of the concepts concerned, that certain emotions are necessarily connected with certain types of action, as Collingwood might plausibly claim to have done with regard to the connection between action and thought.[58] Nor

---

[58] Rex Martin has suggested to the editors that, in the context sketched, Collingwood is more likely to have had a causal relationship than a logical one in mind. But this, for Collingwood, he maintains, could hardly have meant conceiving an essential emotion as a condition which is nomologically necessary for action of the kind exemplified; it must mean one which was necessary to the particular action performed in the sense of providing the agent with his motive for acting, thus becoming a cause of the action in the special non-nomological sense in which Collingwood held that actions could alone be caused. On this interpretation, an essential emotion would be a necessary part of the true non-nomological explanation of an action (Martin would call it a 'contributory cause'), and proper subject-matter for a given history to the extent that the action itself was considered such. Such a resolution of the problem, it might be noted, would admit essential emotions into history's subject-matter on the same basis as any other reason for acting, including an agent's perceptions of

does *The Principles of Art*, to which we are sometimes referred in Chapter 2, offer any further illumination on the point.

Yet even if Collingwood had been able to establish that certain emotions are essential to certain kinds of actions, and that historians have the means to discern them, that would have opened the door only slightly to viewing human emotions as a proper part of history's subject-matter. For it would fall far short of recognizing that human emotions may sometimes, like human actions, afford historians a legitimate topic of investigation in their own right. It would make no room, for example, for something like a study of 'The Great Fear' that swept through French society in the summer of 1789, and which historians have often found an intriguing as well as a puzzling phenomenon.[59] Nor is it clear that Collingwood assigns to emotions—even to essential ones—any possibly explanatory role. We are told that such emotions can be inferred from associated actions; but there is no suggestion that they might constitute even part of their explanation: for example, the officer's fear of enemy raids as a reason why he built the fort just where, when, and how he did. Still less does Collingwood even hint that essential emotions, any more than any other kind, might themselves be rationally, i.e. re-enactively, explained. Thus, although there is some widening of the subject-matter of history here, it appears to be minimal, and even rather arbitrary.[60]

Still a third way in which Chapter 2 may be seen as endeavouring to expand the view of the historian's proper subject-

his situation, which could then with equal propriety be called essential perceptions.

[59] See e.g. Crane Brinton, *A Decade of Revolution* (New York, 1934), 35.

[60] The question of not only the relation between emotion and (rational) action or thought, but also between emotion and feeling is not altogether clear in Collingwood's philosophy of mind and history. In *RP*, 10, for instance, emotions and feelings are put on a par, and it is stated that emotion should be seen in close relation to the other faculties of mind. In *PA*, however, Collingwood explicitly distinguishes feelings from emotions: whereas the first belongs to the psychical level studied by psychology (164), thought and emotion are seen as related to each other (266–7). In *NL* feeling is called an 'apanage' of mind (18), and it is said of the object of 'any form of consciousness, however highly developed', that its immediate object 'always carries an emotional charge' (25). For a discussion of this subject, see also Mink, *Mind, History, and Dialectic*, 92–106, van der Dussen, *History as a Science*, 262–6, and Dray, 'Broadening the Subject-Matter', 8–15.

matter generally ascribed to Collingwood is implied by the
attack which he mounts in its final section on biography conceived as a specialized genre of history—an attack quite as slash-
ing as the one which he is notorious for having levelled against
psychology conceived as a science of mind (on this, see § 7
below). In the Epilegomenon to *The Idea of History* entitled
'The Subject-matter of History', he had already contrasted
biography, sometimes conceived as tracing the history of a
human individual, with history proper on the ground that its
structure is determined by biological considerations. What a
biography is about, Collingwood observes, is the birth, life, and
death of some human organism; and the human experiences it
tends to stress are those, especially emotions, which are bound
up with the bodily life that sets its limits. As he puts it, in a striking phrase: historical currents pass through biography 'like sea-
water through a stranded wreck' (*IH*, 304).[61] In 'The Principles
of History', we are offered a more extended account of how
Collingwood believes biographies deviate from history proper.
Much of what they typically include, he maintains, is in no sense
expressive of thought; and even what does express thought is
not typically included for that reason. The principle of selection
into a biography is 'gossip-value'. Or, more specifically, it is
what best serves the chief purpose of biographers, namely, to
arouse the emotions of readers, especially those of sympathy or
malice, these being ones which Collingwood sees as closely
bound up with a subject's bodily life.[62]

One can hardly complain that Collingwood here characterizes
incorrectly either the content of many biographies, or the
motives of many biographers. But his apparent claim that his
account of biography has general application raises questions
about the philosophical status of what he is saying. In earlier
works, he had insisted that the business of philosophy is not
merely to report empirical facts, but to make clear what is

---

[61] For an earlier look at biography, see L26, 398.

[62] The penchant of biographers for exhortation and moral-pointing, he
observes, invites a comparison with what in *PA* he calls amusement art and
magical art, depending on whether the purpose is to stir emotion with a view to
discharging it in the aesthetic experience itself, or to hoarding it for the fuelling
of practical life (*PA*, 57–104). An analogous distinction by reference to their
purposes is drawn here between amusement biographies and magical biographies.

universal and necessary in a subject-matter.[63] When he points out that the overarching structure of a biography, since it is determined by biology, is not that of a work of history, he clearly remains within that conception of the philosophical task. But when, without offering a reason similarly derived from the very idea of biography, he maintains that biographies *must* be determined by gossip-value, he clearly goes beyond it.[64]

What is of more interest for our immediate purpose, however, is the curious sting in the tail of the section on biography. Collingwood argues that disposing of biography's claim to be a branch of history will help to dissolve the common illusion that, since history is, in effect, a sum of innumerable biographies, it is tied to knowledge of what particular individuals did in the past. To this he replies that, although it is concerned with thought, history has 'nothing to do with the names of the people who think it'. As a reminder that history can be about what anonymous individuals thought—the members of a trade union, for example, or the courtiers of Queen Elizabeth—this may be salutary. But there are surely times when historians need to be able to assign thoughts to identifiable individuals, as Collingwood's own histories of Roman Britain so splendidly show.[65] To imply that, as an account of past thought, an ideal history would not mention human individuals at all, is, at best, an overstatement of a valid and important point: that history can be about thought even when no individual thinker is identified. Yet, unlike what Collingwood said about finding a place for unreason and emotion in history, finding even such a place for the anonymous does entail a considerable widening, at any rate of the view of the historian's subject-matter which has often been ascribed to him. It makes clear at least, if by an argument

[63] e.g. in L27, 352–7, where empirical is contrasted with transcendental analysis.

[64] One wonders how Collingwood would have applied the present analysis to his own *Autobiography*, which contains many evocative pronouncements, and clearly has the intention of leaving the world better than it found it. The historicity of an adequately researched autobiography seems to be assumed in *IH*, 219.

[65] In an essay of the 1920s, Collingwood himself rejected a prediction by Spengler that a new Caesar would arise at a later stage of our civilization as falling short of historical knowledge not because it predicted the future, but because Spengler could not say who the new Caesar would be. 'Oswald Spengler and the Theory of Historical Cycles', *EPH*, 69.

more arresting than carefully formulated, that he was far from being the extreme methodological individualist that some of his critics have made him out to be.[66]

6. *Human history and natural history*

In Chapter 2, § 4, Collingwood goes on to point out that the subject-matter of history is not just human actions, but human actions performed in the past. In other words, it is about events, events of a certain kind, each with a definite position on a time scale.[67] The same thing, however, could be said of natural science; and, according to Collingwood, this similarity between modern history and modern science has prompted cosmologists and philosophers of science like Whitehead and Alexander to look for still further likenesses. In a paper entitled 'The Historicity of Things', a paper which so impressed (and worried) Collingwood that he returned to it several times in his writings,[68] Alexander maintained that modern physics, with its emphasis on 'process', on the 'timefulness' of its subject-matter, was becoming increasingly like history, and opined that, because of the common 'historicity' of their subject-matters, and the long experience historians have had in studying change, scientists may have much to learn from them. The true 'mistress' of the sciences, in Alexander's view, is not physics, but history—a remarkable reversal of the position, dominant since the seventeenth century, that all modes of inquiry should model themselves on natural science. But flattering as this may be to historians, and while not wanting to reject the idea out of hand, Collingwood felt obliged to resist it, indeed to mount a case against it.[69] For he saw it as a way of thinking that might place in jeopardy much of what had been achieved by the very recent

---

[66] Donagan calls him a methodological individualist 'in the strongest sense of that disputable term' (*Later Philosophy*, 206).

[67] As noted in *IH*, 214, Collingwood contrasts actions not with events, but with 'mere' events; in PH that contrast is clarified.

[68] See e.g. *IH*, 210; RAH, § 1, § 5; CNM 1935, beginning. As a reader for Oxford University Press, Collingwood had seen this paper in advance of its publication in Klibansky and Paton (eds.), *Philosophy and History*, 11–25.

[69] As is suggested by his image of the Tiger and the Lady, he considered this new, ostensibly benign attempt to 'swallow' history even more dangerous than older, more malign ones.

rise of history to the status of a mature and autonomous discipline.

Collingwood's initial response to Alexander's thesis is an
uncompromising declaration that, even though nature may
exhibit process, it has no history. He concedes that natural science, in its current phase of development, may manifest many of
the marks of a historical inquiry: for example, it may trace
developments, produce narratives, identify epochs, discover
origins. But all this he characterizes as mere chronology. There
is nothing in natural science, he points out, even when its prac-
titioners treat its subject-matter as process, that corresponds to
the historian's ascertaining the thoughts expressed in past
events by 'reading' present relics for their meaning. Natural science simply does not work with a concept of 'readable' evidence
in the historian's sense. Collingwood reinforces this position by
contrasting the approaches that would be taken by geologists
and archaeologists to the task of reconstructing what took place
over a period of time at a now-ruined site. Both, he observes,
would use stratigraphical methods to reach their conclusions,
but only the archaeologist (who, for Collingwood, is really a
special sort of historian) would treat the materials found as
language.[70]

This may be acceptable as far as it goes; but some of
Collingwood's pronouncements appear to push his thesis too
far. He has drawn attention to an important difference between
human history and any account of a natural process that someone like Alexander might call history. But that only shows that
anything which is plausibly called natural history will differ in
at least one significant way from a history of human affairs; it
does not show that there is nothing appropriately called natural
history.[71] This point is obscured when Collingwood dismisses
as 'mere chronology', a mere 'framework' for genuine history,
any tracing of changes or developments in a subject-matter
which does not find in them the kind of intelligibility that can be

[70] For slightly different ways of drawing the contrast between the two
approaches, see *IH*, 212; *A*, 107–8.
[71] What is in view here is not, of course, natural history in the sense of a
merely classificatory and observation-based generalizing science (for example,
elementary botany), but something more like a history of the changing surface
of the earth, or of evolving biological species.

found in history of thought. For a scientific account of a development in nature would normally be a great deal more than that, as Collingwood himself allows at other points in his writings on history (e.g. L28, 474; *IH*, 115; CNM 1934, par. 39 ff.).[72]

In fact, far from having no idea of natural history, no theory of what would constitute an intelligible series of natural events by contrast with a mere series of them, he seems to have at least two such theories, not obviously compatible with each other. In 'Reality as History', he begins by sketching a view of history, whether dealing with a human or a natural subject-matter, which finds intelligibility, indeed necessity, in the actual course of events studied, this to be discerned by a radically individualizing sort of judgement.[73] It is only towards the end of his analysis that he goes on to observe that, while all history exhibits sequences which are in some sense necessary, only human history has the further property of being expressive of thought, this making it uniquely capable of exhibiting rational necessity. In still other writings, he seems content enough, where an inquiry deals with a natural subject-matter, with something like a positivist account of how individual sequences are made intelligible, namely, by being seen, successively, as falling under laws (*IH*, 205, 214; *EPH*, 27, 32; RAH, § 3). The first of these two views of intelligibility in natural history is clearly controversial; but its acceptability is not the point at issue here. What is important is that Collingwood had no need to offer, and in some other contexts did not offer, a choice only between successions rendered intelligible by the thoughts expressed and successions composed of just one unintelligible thing after another.

In 'The Principles of History', Collingwood does not apply the derogatory epithet 'pseudo-history' to alleged cases of natural history; but he does so in his Scheme, and elsewhere in the

[72] In his philosophical writings on history, Collingwood frequently appears to use the history of nature as a kind of a dummy to be put up against his own view of human history, which is in consequence not very well considered in itself (see e.g. L28, 445). However, at other times (e.g. in NTM, CNM, *IN*), he examines the characteristics of history of nature more deeply.

[73] The generic sense of history expounded in RAH, § 3, is the idea of any individualized but understandable directional change through time: history in a broad sense, rather than the narrow one exemplified by Collingwoodian history of human affairs. In many contexts (e.g. *IH*, 216), however, he restricts the meaning of the term history to the latter.

'Notes on Historiography' which he wrote in preparation for it.[74] It may therefore be worth pointing out that, occasional lapses apart, what he generally meant by pseudo-history was not just accounts of sequences in which no expressions of thought were discerned, but ones in which, given the nature of the subject-matter, such expressions *should* have been discerned—as would be the case, for example, where social and cultural changes are recounted as if the process were a natural one.[75] Such accounts are properly called 'pseudo' because they pretend to make a processive subject-matter intelligible in a way which is appropriate to it, yet fail to do so. In the latter sort of case, the sort which most concerned Collingwood, it might have been less misleading to speak of pseudo-human-history. This suggests that part of the problem here is his tendency to use the term 'history' in two different senses, generally without notice: a narrow one applying only to human history as he conceived it, and a wider one applying to any attempt to render individual changes through time intelligible.

It is a curiosity of Collingwood's discussion of the feasibility of natural history that he maintains at one point that anything offered as such would necessarily fail to be genuine history because, like human history before its Copernican Revolution, it would have to use the method of scissors and paste.[76] For he gives the lie to such a strange view himself in his 1934 Conclusion to Nature and Mind, where he speaks of the natural world before the emergence of life as 'a real past stage in the

[74] See also *A*, 107, with explicit reference to geology, palaeontology, and astronomy so far as they assume narrative form. In *IH*, 212, geology is more ambiguously referred to as 'quasi-historical'.

[75] See e.g. the discussion of Collingwood's attack on naturalistic historiography in § 7. In *IH*, 223, Spengler is accused of treating 'cultures' as if they were 'natural products', i.e. of writing human history as if it were natural history.

[76] If he has in mind the original account he gave of 'scissors-and-paste history', this would mean, implausibly, that natural history would necessarily be based on testimony rather than evidence—as was assumed in Collingwood's no more acceptable criticism of biography as an affair of scissors and paste in PH, Ch. 2, § 8. The valid point underlying what he says here is just that natural history does not (and cannot) interpret past events as expressions of thought. However, in the way the latter idea is associated with the former, two different issues are confused: what sort of thing is being claimed (that a certain event expressed a thought) and the likelihood of its being true (this depending on whether mere testimony or solid evidence is cited).

evolution of nature', and of the physicist as reconstructing this stage from present physical remains 'as the surgeon reconstructs a past attack of appendicitis from the present condition of a body'. Here a genuine likeness between human and natural history is stressed: their both being reconstructions of the past from what is at present perceived.[77] The difference, of course, lies in the nature of the reconstruction and the kind of intelligibility each seeks. In passages like this, where Collingwood is not driven by his determination to protect human history from contamination by patterns of thought appropriate only to natural science, he is able to take natural history seriously, to see it as something of interest and value in itself. In most of his writing on history, however, the way researchers in the natural sciences discover past processes in nature is not at the centre of his interests. And this is to be regretted, since a careful elaboration of a Collingwoodian theory of natural history might, through comparison and contrast, have shed further light on Collingwood's account of the nature of human history too.

7. Historical naturalism

In Chapter 3 of 'The Principles of History', Collingwood analyses and discusses historical naturalism, a recurring concern of his, in a more extensive and systematic way than he does elsewhere.[78] He begins by distinguishing, and then discussing separately, two ways in which he thinks naturalistic assumptions can deform the work of historians. As he mentions also in his Scheme, they can do this by substituting natural facts for the historical facts which ought to be the objects of the investigation, or they can do it by recognizing the historical facts, but referring them to natural facts as their causes. The first alternative shows itself in the demand, ever since the eighteenth

[77] CNM 1934, par. 39. There are other important likenesses: the idea of evidence (whether or not the word was used) would have a legitimate place in a well-conceived theory of natural history, as would some of the structural concepts, like period, stage, or episode, which figure in Collingwood's embryonic account of historical narrative.

[78] At the same time, he considers certain relations between history and natural science, thus anticipating what was to have been the central topic of the first chapter of Book II, where history and natural science were to be shown irreducible to each other.

century, that history either be transformed into, or replaced by, a true science of human nature, which would not just record, but would explain what happened, perhaps in the light of what is found to be typical of human beings of various kinds. The second is represented by environmental approaches to historical explanation, which trace what historians discover to external conditions studied by existing natural sciences like geography, meteorology, or botany. Both approaches, Collingwood argues, misconceive the nature of the 'facts' which concern historians: they treat them as if they were natural facts, things simply to be reported, organized, and theorized about.

In an amusing vignette extending the story of *Gulliver's Travels*, Collingwood offers an imaginary example of the way he thinks a naturalistically conceived science of human nature is bound to miss its target. The target in this case is music as enjoyed by a subsection of a certain population, and the scientific approach to it confines itself to what investigators can discover by weighing and measuring bodily changes undergone by those who listen. Clearly, such an inquiry will uncover nothing resembling what historians, seeking always to discern what certain occurrences express, would call musical facts.[79] To find a real rather than imagined example of the same sort of inconsequence, Collingwood thinks we need look no further than to psychology, conceived as a natural science of mind.[80] His central claim here is that a true science of human nature, if it is really to deal with human mentality, must take seriously the self-critical nature of thought, which, he insists, a natural science of mind does not and cannot do. A true science of mind must be 'criteriological': sensitive to the fact that human action expresses values in ways long studied in traditional sciences of mind like logic, ethics, aesthetics, or economics, which psychology conceives itself as replacing.[81]

---

[79] Collingwood's main point might have been clearer here if his investigators had been able to hear sounds but not to grasp their musical significance, thus being unable even to frame questions, nomological or otherwise, about genuinely musical facts (e.g. resolutions of discords, modulations of key, recurrences of theme, etc.).

[80] Psychology is similarly treated in *IH*, 173, 231; *PA*, 35–6, 171 n.; *EM*, 101 ff.; *A*, 92–4, 112, 116, 143. See also Collingwood's remarks on sociology and anthropology in RAH, § 3.

[81] On the idea of a criteriological science see PH, Ch. 3, § 2; *PA*, 171 n.; *EM*, 109–11.

Collingwood points in this connection to what he sees as a lurking contradiction in the whole programme of a naturalistic science of mind. For although psychology, pursued as a natural science, abjures the study of human actions considered as applications of criteria, it necessarily indulges, in its own investigations, in the same criteria-applying kinds of activities which it excludes, on principle, from its own subject-matter. At least part of what is being said here, it would seem, is that historical facts are partly value-constituted. If so, then—although he does not explicitly say so here—Collingwood appears to be committing himself also to the idea that history is a value-discerning, i.e. value-judging, kind of study.[82]

Collingwood takes a somewhat softer line in considering the second, the environmental, form of naturalism, this because he thinks that, in looking for causes of human action beyond human nature itself, it proposes at least to offer explanations which are not circular. The notion that explaining human actions in terms of a naturalistically conceived human nature would be circular is a rather puzzling one. Presumably Collingwood would not want to rule out, as similarly reasoning in a circle, explanations of physical events by reference to physical conditions and laws. However, he has another and more serious reservation about explanations of actions in terms of environmental causes: that they are likely to represent the latter, falsely, as having the same sort of 'direct' effects on action that they have on bodily conditions like skin colour or sexual maturation. What causes human beings to act, he insists, is not nature itself, but what they make of nature, given their enterprise, knowledge, and level of technological achievement.[83] It is not the natural fact of the ocean's proximity that explains the way those living on its shores respond to it, but whether they regard it as an obstacle or an opportunity. Collingwood nevertheless concedes a role for natural conditions in the explanation of action in history provided the explanation is seen as going 'through the mind'. His position here calls to mind the distinction he drew in his *Essay on Metaphysics* between merely

[82] This idea is pursued further in CHBI, when he discusses impartiality in a second sense. For a contrary view, see L26, 402–4, *EPH*, 76.

[83] On this see further L28, 474; *IH*, 200; the section of NHH entitled 'The Idea of Historical Efficacy'; and *EM* 98.

xlviii   EDITORS' INTRODUCTION

necessary conditions and fully causal ones (*EM*, 285–312). For one way of putting his point would be to say that, although a full explanation of a human action would require reference to the natural environment as well as to agents' thoughts, it is always the thoughts, and never the environment, that should be accorded the status of cause.

This doctrine is bound to be controversial. It may be felt, for example, that insufficient reason has been provided for regarding it as a universal principle that, while agents' thoughts and what they are about may both be relevant to the explanation of an action performed, it is never the latter that should be considered the cause. But such criticism pales by comparison with the resistance a further apparent development of Collingwood's position here is likely to evoke. As he says himself, the view of environmental explanation so far propounded gives nature itself at least a secondary or background role in the causation of actions. But even this, he goes on to maintain, is to assign more to nature and less to thought than can be allowed in the case of a historical subject-matter. For merely believing, even if falsely, that natural conditions are a certain way is quite as efficacious as a cause of action as knowing the way they really are. And whereas citing an agent's knowledge of conditions as a cause of his acting a certain way retains an explanatory role for the conditions themselves, citing his mere beliefs about them does not. Collingwood dramatizes his position by saying that the 'hard facts' composing the situation in which an agent has to act consist entirely of his thoughts. The situation itself, in other words, is explanatorily irrelevant.[84] He drives the point home by asking what would really be meant by saying of a certain population,

---

[84] It is interesting to note that the German logician Gottlob Frege in his famous article 'Ueber Sinn und Bedeutung' of 1892 (translated as 'On Sense and Reference') works out a position similar to Collingwood's. Frege develops in his article the thesis that in a main sentence that refers to a subordinate one containing a thought as its referent, it is not the latter's truth value that is at issue, but the sense of the thought concerned. 'If, toward the end of the battle of Waterloo, Wellington was glad that the Prussians were coming', Frege argues, 'the basis for his joy was a conviction. Had he been deceived, he would have been no less pleased so long as his illusion lasted; and before he became so convinced he could not have been pleased that the Prussians were coming— even though in fact they might have been already approaching' ('On Sense and Reference', in *Translations from the Philosophical Writings of Gottlob Frege*, ed. Peter Geach and Max Black (Oxford, 1970), 67).

overrun by an enemy, that it 'had' to give in to 'brute force'. What is called brute force in such cases, he insists, is simply the victims' conviction, whether true or not, that they were no longer in a position to resist.

There is clearly a good deal that is true and important in this doctrine; but there is also much to which exception could be taken. An obvious problem is that it will surely matter a good deal to the agents envisaged whether the threat they faced was real or only perceived, if, after deciding to resist, many of them are then maimed or killed. In other words, although their (incorrect, as it turns out) thought about the situation they faced may explain their decision to resist, it will not explain their failure to resist successfully. And Collingwood is adamant at a number of points, both in 'The Principles of History' and in other writings (e.g. *A*, 70, 72), that the historian's proper concerns include whether and why intended actions were successfully carried out.[85] It may seem that he makes some allowance for this consideration when, after insisting that an agent's situation consists entirely of thoughts, he adds: 'his own and other people's'. But this hardly meets the problem for two reasons. First, it is not the enemy's thoughts but his sabres and muskets that will maim and kill. Second, the expressed thoughts of other people (i.e. their actions) impinge upon an agent's own possibilities of action in much the same way that natural conditions do: they permit and prevent expressions of his own will. As Collingwood himself says, in discussing the implications of his analysis for human freedom, an agent must so position himself that expressions of his own thoughts fit into the 'interstices' between those of his neighbours. Taken strictly, therefore, it is hard to see how his apparent attempt not just to diminish, but to eliminate, the causal role of the physical can be sustained.

All this begins to encroach upon what Collingwood wrote in the section entitled 'Freedom' towards the end of Chapter 3, a version of which was included in the Epilegomena to *The Idea of History*. The argument here is more tortuous than in most other parts of 'The Principles of History'. Perhaps its most problematic contention is the connection it asserts to hold between the rise of scientific history and a secure realization that

[85] See also n. 55.

human action is free. In the practice of scientific history, Collingwood maintains, the historian discovers simultaneously his own freedom as inquirer and the freedom of man as historical agent. He also puts his position by saying that, just as the scientific historian is free from the domination of natural science, so human history is free from the domination of nature, this allegedly instantiating the principle, first stated in his lectures of the 1920s and reiterated in a slightly different form in 'The Principles of History', that history *a parte subjecti* and *a parte objecti* must correspond (see e.g. L27, 429–30; L28, 434; PH, Ch. 2, § 1). But this rather startling declaration surely exploits an ambiguity in the term 'free' as Collingwood employs it. For the sense in which historical inquiry is declared to be free from natural science seems to be conceptual or logical (i.e. it can make its subject-matter appropriately intelligible without offering scientific explanations of it), while the sense in which human history is declared to be free from nature seems to be empirical or causal[86] (i.e. human beings can act in ways not nomologically determined by natural causes). Collingwood himself seems more concerned to answer in advance another likely objection to his position here, namely, that it was surely known that man was free long before the rise of scientific history, this, according to his own account, not antedating the eighteenth century. Many of his readers will surely feel that his response that it was indeed known, but only to a few exceptional individuals, or only dimly, requires more evidential support than he is able to provide for it here.

8. *Two fragments*

The manuscript of 'The Principles of History' peters out after the summary appended to Chapter 3. Only two further short fragments were found. One, entitled 'The Past', consisting of a little more than a page, makes a start on Chapter 4. A second, running just under a page, is headed 'History and Philosophy'. However, although short, both fragments are of some interest.

What the piece destined for Chapter 4 considers is not the way scientific history achieves self-knowledge of mind, as

---

[86] Causal, of course, in the nomological or positivist sense, not in Collingwood's special sense of cause as motive or reason (*EM*, 286, 290).

Collingwood's Scheme had stipulated for this chapter, but the sense in which history is a study of the past.[87] In his previous writings, Collingwood had raised many issues that one might have expected him to pursue further under a heading like 'The Past'. For example, he might have expanded on his doctrine, first expounded in the lectures of 1926 and never entirely withdrawn, that the past is not real, but only ideal (L26, 364); or explicated further the sense in which historians, as he maintained in 'The Historical Imagination', must bring an a priori idea of the past to their work (*IH*, 248); or considered again a distinction drawn earlier between the past as historians conceive it and their own specious present, which is conceded to possess some duration (RAH, last section); or argued again for the idea that the past is 'necessary' in the sense of being conclusively retrodictable (L26, 412). Instead he sets off in a direction not found in earlier works, although it is prefigured in his 'Notes on Historiography' in the section on 'Pseudo-history'. Historical inquiry, he holds, is not about the past in the sense in which things are sometimes said to be of 'purely historical interest'— as if to be historical is to be remote, cut off from the exigencies of ordinary life. More particularly, the past, as historians conceive it, bears no relationship to a past regarded as an escape from the present: what might be called an 'emotional past'. Using language reminiscent of Michael Oakeshott, Collingwood insists that the historical past is the past 'as such', a claim which he underscores by observing that a letter received from one's solicitor is quite as much a historical document as an ancient charter is.[88] It is of interest to compare the rather austere objectivism about the historical past which this suggests with what Collingwood has to say in 'Can Historians be Impartial?' about proper and improper motives for studying history. Clearly, he sees no special connection between being emotionally attached to the past and writing emotional history, for which, in the latter paper, he confesses to a certain fondness.

[87] Collingwood introduces the topic with the observation that a continued examination of historical method shows that the subject-matter of history must be, not just actions (as at first maintained) but actions done in the *past*, since what historians interpret is traces (see also PH, Ch. 2, § 4). For a different route to the same conclusion, see L28, 439.

[88] See M. Oakeshott, *Experience and its Modes* (Cambridge, 1933), 102 ff. Collingwood's position here is anticipated in *IH*, 219.

The title of the second fragment, 'History and Philosophy',
also suggests a number of questions that one might have
expected Collingwood to consider in a piece so named. For
example, he might have explained further some of the implications of his doctrine, first stated in the lectures of 1920s, that
philosophy of history is the a priori methodology of history
(L27, 347; L28, 492), or expanded on his not obviously compatible claim, in his 'Notes on Historiography', that the branches
of philosophy are one and all 'historical sciences';[89] or shown
more precisely how his warning against 'consulting philosophers' in 'The Principles of History', Chapter 2,[90] relates to
the essentially critical role which he assigned to philosophers of
history elsewhere (L27, 346; *IH*, 203, 213); or offered further
justification for an earlier contention that while philosophical
writing ought to be confessional, historical writing is properly
didactic (*EPM*, 210–11). Such themes would doubtless have
been among the ones treated at length in Book II, Chapter 3,
had Collingwood gone on to compose it in accordance with the
plan he laid down in his Scheme. What he in fact considers—
this perhaps also among the topics to be treated more fully in
Book II, Chapter 3—is the common belief that, while philosophical conclusions may be asserted with demonstrative certainty, historical ones never attain more than a degree of
probability. Against this he argues, as he did also in the first two
chapters of 'The Principles of History', that historical inference
can also achieve certainty, declaring, indeed, that history has no

[89] See the sections entitled 'That History is the Only Kind of Knowledge',
'Logic an Historical Science', and 'Ethics as an Historical Science'.

[90] The attack on 'consulting philosophers' is an extreme example of
Collingwood's tendency to assert the autonomy of history at times not only in
the sense of being independent of testimony (e.g. *IH*, 236), but also in the sense
of being independent of 'external' criticism. Earlier in PH, and in some other
works (e.g. L28, 494–6; *IH*, 8), this takes the form of maintaining that only a
practitioner of a discipline, in this case the historian himself, can understand
and thus criticize its procedures—although that did not prevent Collingwood
himself from making philosophical pronouncements on the nature of the natural sciences without having practised any of them (see e.g. RAH, CNM, *IN*,
EM). A less truculent form of the doctrine is the declaration that philosophers
should only ask how, not whether, history is possible (*A*, 77). A still more reasonable one is the demand that philosophers take actual historical practice as
their point of departure rather than simply theorizing about historical knowledge a priori (L26, 381).

more to do with probability than any other science does.[91] He goes on to give a brief explication of what he understands by probability, elucidating the idea in terms of expectation. The essentially subjectivist theory of the concept which he adumbrates may well be felt to offer rather a thin theoretical underpinning for the probability judgements that historians routinely make, and that he frequently made himself when functioning as a historian (see e.g. *A*, 131; *RBES*, 215).

9. *The selective publication*

We turn now to the first of the three questions which it was said in § 3 would be raised about the newly found manuscript of 'The Principles of History'. As was remarked earlier, Collingwood had intended to publish *The Idea of History* and 'The Principles of History' as two separate volumes, one on the origin and development of scientific history, the other on its present nature and significance. Since he managed to complete only about one third of what had been planned for the second volume, it is understandable that Knox should have decided to publish what was available as a single volume. What is less understandable is his using only parts of the incomplete manuscript, especially in view of a note which Collingwood had written to his first wife on its title page authorizing its publication.

The decision to fragment the manuscript in this way was entirely Knox's. In a letter to Oxford University Press of 31 March 1945, he explained it as follows: 'In spite of the authority given for publication, I think it would be a mistake to publish "The Principles of History" as it stands. It is divided into three chapters. A good deal of the second and third chapters is contained already in the *Autobiography* and the *Essay on Metaphysics*, and I am not satisfied that we ought to press the wording of a note written in all probability when R.G.C. was unusually ill.'[92] In his editor's preface to *The Idea of History*, Knox made a great deal of Collingwood's declining health in the

---

[91] On this see also the section entitled 'A Note on Evidence and Certitude' in NHH; and *EM*, 60. For a treatment of the concept of probability, see the same section of NHH.

[92] *IH* rev., p. xii. In fact, Chs. 2 and 3 contain much that is not found in the books mentioned, and the manuscript of PH had more than three chapters.

last years of his life, calling it the 'decisive factor which cast a dark shadow over all his later work' (*IH*, p. xxi). What he found problematic about the 1939 manuscript was, in part, what he saw as its consequent irascibility and impatience. Even the parts which he decided, albeit reluctantly, to include in *The Idea of History*, he complained, sometimes exhibit a 'style and temper' which is 'rather out of key with the rest of the book' (*IH*, p. vi). Even if true, however, this seems an odd justification to offer for excluding some parts of a manuscript while including others. It seems odder still when one remembers that the *Autobiography* and the *Essay on Metaphysics* were written at roughly the same time, and thus also, one must suppose, in Collingwood's 'later manner', not to mention the parts of *The Idea of History* which Collingwood himself revised. It must be allowed that there are traces of asperity, and even of what Knox called 'hectoring', in what Collingwood completed of 'The Principles of History'. But these are not characteristics of his writing only in his final years.

What bothered Knox most about the manuscript was clearly less its style than certain aspects of its content. There is evidence of this in some of the editorial changes he made in the text (of which more below), and in the misgivings he confessed about having allowed anything from this source to go to publication at all.[93] It is only partly true, however, that, in Chapters 2 and 3 of 'The Principles of History', Collingwood simply repeated what he also wrote elsewhere. There are no parallels in his other writings, for example, to his stress in this manuscript on the idea of evidence as language; on the alleged analogy between the historical and the aesthetic imagination; on the different relations to human action of essential and inessential emotions; or on the radical unlikeness of history and biography. As we have seen, the new manuscript also contains valuable clarifications and extensions of his case against historical naturalism; his conception of the autonomy of history; his view of the specifically historical past; his idea of rationality; and his understanding of the

---

[93] Knox also opined that Collingwood's other unpublished manuscripts on history contained little that would have been worth publishing. However, records at Oxford University Press suggest that, of the manuscripts included in the present volume, Knox saw only CHBI, although there is internal evidence that he must also have seen NHV.

concept of probability in its application to history as well as to other fields. Of course, given the unfavourable climate of philosophical opinion in which Collingwood worked for most of his professional life, Knox could hardly have been expected to anticipate the remarkable surge of interest in his ideas after his death, and the widespread desire to have available for study virtually everything he wrote. Nor can it be denied that what Collingwood completed of 'The Principles of History', although displaying flashes of brilliance and insight, is uneven in quality, and sometimes suffers from careless overstatement. It tends, as well, to deteriorate as it progresses, the first chapter, which Knox included in *The Idea of History*, being by far the best written.

In deciding to publish only parts of 'The Principles of History', Knox made an editorial judgement which, with the full manuscript available, we are now in a better position to appraise. One unfortunate result of his publishing only Chapter 1 is that the incompleteness of that chapter's argument, which is developed further in Chapter 2, is thereby obscured. Another is that the close connection which Collingwood came to see between his theory of history and positions he took in *The Principles of Art* is thereby left unstated and unexamined. But in putting together what we now know as *The Idea of History*, Knox made other, more detailed, editorial judgements which look even more questionable. It can now be seen, for example, how much he manipulated the text of 'The Principles of History', and, in consequence, also that of *The Idea of History*, by reordering materials, introducing omissions, and rephrasing what Collingwood originally wrote, sometimes in ways that alter the sense.[94] The changes thus introduced are in many cases relatively innocuous; but not all of them are. And the fact that most remained unacknowledged cannot but raise questions about the way *The Idea of History* as a whole was edited.

The section of 'The Principles of History' which Knox included in *The Idea of History* under the title 'History and Freedom' offers a striking example of reordering (*IH*, 315–20). This section is taken out of its original context, where it represents the penultimate stage of Collingwood's chapter-long argument against naturalism, and is given the appearance of a friendless intruder into the Epilegomena, where it follows hard upon a discussion of the kinds of subject-matter which can be considered properly historical on the ground of being re-enactable (*IH*, 302–15). There are also changes of the original wording in the introductory sentences, and in a few other places, which, to say the least, appear gratuitous. For example, the passage beginning with 'because I wish', and ending with 'that claim is groundless' (*IH*, 319), is mainly Knox's own invention. In the manuscript Collingwood refers back to the end of § 1 of Chapter 2, where he makes a link between history *a parte subjecti* and *a parte objecti*, maintaining that the first has a priority. The passage found in *The Idea of History* is quite different from the corresponding one in the manuscript, which runs as follows: 'But I do not leave the matter exactly there; because what I have already said in the first section of the second chapter carries it a stage further. It was said in that section that only by using historical methods could we find out anything about the objects of historical study' (PH, Ch. 3, § 5). At the very least, a connection of importance to Collingwood is lost by the changes.

Even more meddlesome editing is evident in the section entitled 'Heads or Tails' which follows. As Knox himself acknowledged, much of this was inserted into *The Idea of History* at the point (part III, § 8) where Collingwood's historical survey of theories of history reaches the theories of Hegel and Marx. This involves a somewhat dubious incorporation of 1939 material into a 1936 document. What is worse, Knox derives the beginning of that section, i.e. the text on page 122 and the first paragraph of page 123 up to 'in which bankers think about banking', from Collingwood's lectures on philosophy of history of 1936, this sentence appearing on page 116 of those lectures, one of the few pages which has survived. The rest of the section comes from 'The Principles of History', although the phrasing of the original is not left intact. And there appears to be a philosophical bias in some of the changes made. A case in point is the way some of Collingwood's assertions about Hegel have been reworded, and thereby partly denatured, with cumulative effect. For example, where the manuscript reads 'natural science from which Hegel had in principle proclaimed it free,' Knox deletes the words 'in principle' (*IH*, 125). On the same page, where the text reads 'had not been fully achieved', the word 'fully' is Knox's own addition. Where it reads 'in which he [Hegel] mainly contented himself with scissors-and-paste methods', the word 'mainly' has been added. A further change of sense which seems to be doctrinally inspired appears in Knox's substituting for 'history ordinarily so-called' the hardly equivalent phrase 'what he [Hegel] ordinarily called history' (*IH*, 125).

But the most surprising change that Knox made in this material, and one that appears clearly to be aimed at mitigating the criticism that Collingwood levelled against Hegel, is the omission of a whole paragraph on Hegel's view of the relation of history to logic. This can now be found towards the end of Chapter 3 of 'The Principles of History'. There Collingwood argues that Hegel only *seemed* to recognize an autonomous status for history, since he subordinated it to a structure of logical 'ideas', this, in his view, amounting to a misconception of the same nature as Marx's submission of history to natural science. Because Knox omitted most of the passage in which this view was developed, he also found it necessary to make changes in the first two sentences of the paragraph which follows, where the text of the manuscript is quite different from that of *The Idea of History*.[95] Such editorial treatment of the parts of Chapter 3 which were incorporated into *The Idea of History* cannot but make one wonder how much of Chapter 1, the original version of which unfortunately has not been found, may also have been emended. One wonders similarly about the integrity of the text of parts I–IV of *The Idea of History*, which a few surviving pages show not to have gone completely unscathed.[96]

10. *The unfinished manuscript*

Even more puzzling than Knox's decision to publish only part of what was available of 'The Principles of History' is

[95] Other examples of overly free editing are the way Knox incorporated Collingwood's review of Bury's *Selected Essays*, ed. H. Temperley (Cambridge, 1930), into *IH*, 147–51—the original text in the *English Historical Review*, 46 (1931), 461–5, is significantly different—and the way some of the quotations included in his preface, pp. xii–xiii, diverge from the text of NHV from which they are apparently drawn.

[96] See remarks by van der Dussen in *IH* rev., pp. xvii–xix.

Collingwood's having left the work unfinished. He began it with a clear and coherent plan, and he worked on it with purposeful speed for a period of several weeks. He apparently placed great value upon the project, and there is evidence of late date that he fully intended to complete it. On 14 February 1939, while working on Chapter 1, he wrote to his son: 'I have begun writing *The Principles of History*, which will go down to posterity as my masterpiece. I suddenly began it, quite unexpectedly, as my boat was approaching Soerabaja, and spent my whole time in that damnably hot town writing it as hard as I could.'[97] After his return to England late in the spring, he wrote to his friend, the archaeologist Gerald Simpson: 'in the last 6 months I have written two books and begun a third. . . . The third, of which I wrote some 40,000 words in Java, is called *The Principles of History* and is the book which my whole life has been spent in preparing to write. If I can finish that, I shall have nothing to grumble at.'[98] That Collingwood intended as late as the autumn of that year to finish the work is further evidenced by a letter he wrote to Oxford University Press on 19 October 1939, in which he explicitly refers to 'The Principles of History' as volume ii of his projected works on 'Philosophical Principles'.

In his preface to *The Idea of History*, Knox offers the following explanation of Collingwood's failure to finish what he began: 'Diminished physical strength, and preoccupation with *The New Leviathan* are two obvious answers. But the true answer is that his project had become either impossible or unnecessary' (*IH*, p. xvii). It was now impossible, according to Knox, because Collingwood had come to believe that 'philosophy had been absorbed by history', and that 'theory and practice had been identified', doctrines supposedly found in *An Essay on Metaphysics* and *An Autobiography* respectively. A philosophical analysis and critique of historical thinking in the style of *The Idea of History* and earlier works was therefore ruled out. All that was left for a would-be philosopher of history to do was to articulate his own experience of historical thinking; and

---

[97] Quoted in van der Dussen, *History as a Science*, 61. The reference is to the town of Surabaya (here given the Dutch spelling) on the north coast of the island of Java.

[98] One of several letters donated by Dr Grace Simpson to the Bodleian Library. The first two books referred to were *A* and *EM*.

this in Collingwood's case was no longer necessary, since he had done it already in his *Autobiography*. But what Knox here calls the 'true answer' is not very convincing. For what is envisaged in the *Autobiography*, on which Collingwood was working concurrently with 'The Principles of History', is not an identity but a *rapprochement* between philosophy and history, and a similarly mutual relationship between theory and practice. Philosophy is urged to become more historically aware, and history to become more philosophically sophisticated.[99] It must not be forgotten, too, that, as we have seen, as late as October 1939, Collingwood himself gave no sign of seeing any theoretical reason why he should not finish 'The Principles of History'. Nor do the parts which he did complete give much support to Knox's diagnosis. The way they treat various topics in the philosophy of history is, for the most part, quite consistent with the way they are dealt with in relevant earlier works, including *The Idea of History*.

David Boucher has suggested a different reason why 'The Principles of History' was never finished. He notes that the relation between history and practice, which was to have been the subject of Book III, was later dealt with in *The New Leviathan*, and had been considered to some extent also in the *Autobiography*.[100] Thus, despite the value that Collingwood originally placed upon completing 'The Principles of History', this work may have become less important to him, not because he saw any flaw in its arguments, but simply because, at this crucial point in his life, he had little time for saying the same thing twice. But there are difficulties with this idea, too. For the practical implications of historical thinking are not discussed in any explicit way in *The New Leviathan*, and Boucher's suggestion leaves unexplained why not just Book I, but also Book II of 'The Principles of History', which was to have examined the relation

[99] *A*, ch. 12. See also Boucher, 'The Principles', 168–9; van der Dussen, 'Collingwood's "Lost" Manuscript', 35.

[100] Boucher, 'The Principles', 168–9. Boucher argues that *EM*, and to some extent *IN*, also contain material that would have found a place in PH had Collingwood gone on to complete it. Indeed, he suggests that Collingwood did, in effect, complete his PH project through these other writings. In considering this idea, it should be remembered, however, that *EM* was finished in first draft when Collingwood began work on PH, and that *IN* is based on lectures given in preceding years.

between history and other sciences, was not finished either. It is true that, as Knox also observed, Collingwood's completing 'The Principles of History' was made less likely by his preoccupation with *The New Leviathan*. But that seems to have been due largely to the outbreak of war in September 1939. Collingwood himself writes, in a letter to the archaeologist O. G. S. Crawford: 'When the war broke out I saw that the whole business was due to the fact that everybody concerned was in a completely muddled condition about the first principles of politics and, examining my own mind, I saw that I had plenty of ideas which it would be a public service to state.'[101] It seems plausible to say, therefore, that Collingwood postponed his work on 'The Principles of History' in response to a moral imperative: a perceived duty to act immediately, and not at some future and more convenient time, on a matter which he considered of great public importance.

More mundane factors, like worsening health and far from ideal working conditions on his voyage through the Indies, also played a part. The Scheme for the book was written on 9 February, on a ship approaching Surabaya. According to Collingwood's diary, he worked on 'The Principles of History' from the 10th to the 13th of that month. On 14 February, he put up at a hotel in the town of Yogyakarta. The next day he worked again on the manuscript, 'finishing and tidying up chapter 1'. He continued to write during the following days, with the exception of 18 February, when his diary records: 'tired and slack this day after a bad night: kept off the book.' On 20 February, it reads: 'Writing most of the day. Much annoyed by uproarious fellow-guests, the hotel wireless and other incessant discomforts.' The next day he took the early morning train to Batavia (the present-day Jakarta), arriving on 22 February. Of this trip he remarks: 'Comfortable journey, revising ms., lunching, writing a poem.' In Batavia, where again he stayed at a hotel, he remarks in his diary: 'Some points in favour of being back in civilization. Have been long enough in the Dutch East Indies.' So strong indeed were his feelings of discomfort that, on the same day, he arranged his passage home on the ship *Rhesus*, scheduled to sail on 4 March. Then we read in the diary:

[101] Bodleian Library, Oxford, MS Crawford, 4, 118.

'late in the afternoon received and read proofs of my autobiography.'

The last entry calls attention to another important part of the explanation: Collingwood's involvement with two other books during his trip through the Dutch East Indies. When he left England on 21 October 1938 he had finished his *Autobiography*. On the outbound voyage, from 24 October to 13 November, he worked on *An Essay on Metaphysics*. On the latter day, his diary records: 'Revising all day; wrote new chapter XXVII (last).' After receiving the proofs of his *Autobiography* on 22 February 1939, he worked the following two days not only on that book, but also again on *An Essay on Metaphysics*. From then on, he worked almost daily on the latter, both in Batavia and on the return voyage, apparently revising substantial parts of it (when published, it bore the notation: 'off Cape St. Vincent, 2 April 1939'). The diary makes it clear, too, that, through this period, Collingwood was also making his *Autobiography* ready for the press, and on 19 March he rewrote its last chapter. 'The Principles of History' is mentioned only twice. On 26 March we read: 'Playing with *Principles of History*'; and on the following day: 'Tried to begin ch. IV of *Principles of History* in the morning—stuff wouldn't flow. Stomach worse, in fact worse than it has been yet. Very idle and uncomfortable all afternoon.' The next day's entry reads: 'Spent day in bed nursing my stomach and starving.' And that was the last time he worked on 'The Principles of History'.

Collingwood's failure to finish this long-projected volume thus owes a good deal not only to fortuitous circumstances like poor accommodation, chronic insomnia, and noisy neighbours, but also to his involvement with other projects towards the end of his trip to the East. After his return, he was engaged in lecturing and in making his *Essay on Metaphysics* ready for the press, thus again having little opportunity to complete 'The Principles of History'. At the end of June, perhaps with a view to restoring his health, he departed unexpectedly on an almost two-month trip to the Greek islands with a group of foreign students, returning only a few days before the outbreak of the war. In the autumn of 1939, he had no less than five projects under way. In his letter of 19 October, he informed Oxford University Press that 'The Principles of History' and *The Idea of History* were 'in preparation', and that *The Idea of Nature* was 'now in its lecture stage, i.e. being tried on the dog'. He also prepared *The First Mate's Log* for the press, this giving some impressions of his trip through the Greek islands, and began work on *The New Leviathan*.[102] Early in 1940, he lectured on 'Goodness, Rightness, Utility', writing the lectures out in full, as was his habit, from December to February.[103] If one takes into account also his continuing struggle with worsening health, which forced him to resign his chair in 1941, it is hardly surprising that he failed to finish any of the projects which he mentioned in his letter to Oxford University Press. Indeed, it was an accomplishment of the first order that he went on to complete *The New Leviathan*.[104]

Puzzles do remain; but there appears to be no great need to look to content or to subject-matter for reasons why Collingwood failed to complete 'The Principles of History'. The serious health problems he increasingly faced, the difficult conditions in which he had to work on his voyage to the Indies, the interference of other projects, the unexpected trip to Greece, and the priority he felt duty-bound to give to *The New Leviathan* offer reasons enough.[105] Given the remarkable speed with which he could work, it is hardly to be doubted that he could have finished 'The Principles of History' in a few weeks of uninterrupted work. But even that amount of leisure was no longer available to him, as it was not either for completing *The Idea of History* and *The Idea of Nature*.

11. *The idea of re-enactment*

The most surprising aspect of what Collingwood completed of 'The Principles of History' is its failure to develop further the

[102] He also wrote 'Fascism and Nazism' and 'The Three Laws of Politics', now included in *Essays in Political Philosophy: R. G. Collingwood*, ed. David Boucher (Oxford, 1989), 187–96, 207–23.

[103] Now an appendix to *NL* rev., 391–479.

[104] It would be difficult for anyone who has even skimmed *NL* to take seriously the idea that failing intellectual powers provide any part of the explanation why Collingwood never finished PH.

[105] One other possible reason relating to content, the difficulty of adapting the idea of re-enactment to the broader historical subject-matter envisaged in PH (also mentioned by Boucher), will be considered in § 11.

idea that historical inquiry requires a re-enactment of past thought on the part of the historian. According to his Scheme, this idea was to have been the main topic of Book I, Chapter 3, and it had been mentioned with favour several times in the preparatory 'Notes on Historiography'. It had a prominent place in much of Collingwood's philosophical writing on history since he worked it out for the first time at Die in France in 1928 (L28, 441 ff.). It is present in both the historical and systematic parts of *The Idea of History*, which, as we saw, he began revising for publication during the same period as he worked on 'The Principles of History'. Indeed, the title borne by the first section of the Metaphysical Epilegomena to the lectures on philosophy of history of 1936 from which *The Idea of History* was derived referred to re-enactment as the 'essence' of history—an indication of the importance ascribed to the idea by Collingwood which, in producing the book, Knox edited out by substituting the title 'History as Re-enactment of Past Experience' (*IH* rev., pp. xiii–xiv). The notion that historical thinking involves re-enactment was also explicitly propounded in the *Autobiography*, and it survived with no apparent difficulty Collingwood's revision of that book during his stay in Java and on his return trip. Yet in 'The Principles of History' there is only silence on this supposedly central Collingwoodian doctrine. Even the word 're-enactment' never appears.

The puzzlement which this is bound to engender will be deepened by another curious fact. As already noted, Collingwood's own Scheme, known since 1978, raised what now turns out to be the false expectation that 'The Principles of History' would enlarge upon the re-enactment doctrine. This expectation was further encouraged in 1981, when Margit Hurup Nielsen, author of one of the best-known studies of Collingwood's idea of re-enactment, reported that Knox had told her, in a conversation of 1975, that the reason he 'disregarded' Collingwood's note on the manuscript of 'The Principles of History' authorizing the publication of all he had completed of it was that, in his judgement, it would have been 'disastrous' to offer the public at any rate its first seven sections, all of which, he said, dealt with re-enactment.[106] One can only speculate as to

---

[106] To this opinion Nielsen plausibly attached the suspicion that Knox did not, in any case, hold Collingwood's view of history as re-enactment in very

how Knox could have made such an astonishing mistake. Did he perhaps, some years after the event, confuse what Collingwood promised in his Scheme with what, in the end, he actually did? We are at any rate faced with the fact that, in his final pronouncements on history, Collingwood said nothing at all about re-enactment. And this calls for explanation.[107]

An explanation which suggests itself, but which it is hard to take seriously, is that the idea of re-enactment may have been a good deal less important to Collingwood than has generally been assumed. And the notion that he may simply have jettisoned it as unnecessary baggage in the end, perhaps thinking its work better done by less problematic ideas, may seem to derive some credibility from the fact that it is missing also from another late work, *An Essay on Metaphysics*, which is, in some of its aspects, a theory of intellectual history;[108] and is mentioned only once in passing, and not clearly with the usual theoretical intent, in his last work, *The New Leviathan*, also a work closely related to philosophy of history (*NL*, 69).[109] Not too much weight can be placed upon this, however, since in some other late works—for example, the *Autobiography*—the idea is very much present. Nor should it be forgotten that at least one major piece of writing of the mid-1930s, the inaugural lecture, makes no mention of re-enactment either, although one might have expected it to do so, since it contains Collingwood's most extensive discussion of the historical imagination, often regarded as a

high regard. See her 'Re-enactment and Reconstruction in Collingwood's Philosophy of History', *History and Theory*, 20 (1981), 2–3.

[107] It also calls for retractions of supposedly informed guesses offered by various authors, including both the present editors, about the likely content of the missing parts of the manuscript.

[108] It is also a work which presents a problem for re-enactment theory as outlined in *IH* and *A*, since absolute presuppositions, not being held for reasons, do not appear to be the kind of thoughts that could be re-enacted. Boucher has argued that they are nevertheless re-enactable (*NL* rev., pp. xxix ff.) and Rex Martin that, although not re-enactable, there can still be a Collingwoodian history of them ('Collingwood's Doctrine of Absolute Presuppositions and the Possibility of Historical Knowledge', in Leon Pompa and W. H. Dray (eds.), *Substance and Form in History* (Edinburgh, 1981), 100 ff.).

[109] Boucher has argued that *NL* is a philosophical history of mind as it has developed in Western civilization, and that *EM* is, in its own way, a work in philosophy of history (*NL* rev., p. xviii).

closely related idea, prior to what he said about it in 'The Principles of History'.[110] The idea of re-enactment is also missing from a famous article of early 1938, 'On the So-Called Idea of Causation',[111] which, again, is surprising, since it has a good deal to say about causation in history conceived as a relationship between what agents think and what they do, and missing also from the discussion of the relation of history to duty in 'Goodness, Rightness, Utility', Collingwood's lectures on moral philosophy of 1940.

Boucher has suggested that Collingwood's surprising silence about re-enactment in 'The Principles of History' may have been due to the difficulty of applying the idea to the broadened subject-matter which he there assigned to history.[112] And it is notable that the major divergence from his original plan begins in Chapter 3, this following his claim in Chapter 2 that certain kinds of emotion belong properly to the historian's subject-matter. In Boucher's judgement, Collingwood needed at this point either to drop the requirement that history deals only with the re-enactable, or to expand the idea of re-enacting thought in such a way that it has clear relevance to the added subject-matter.[113] He does neither of these things, however; he simply passes on to other matters. But he could scarcely have ignored the problem for long, since an important role had also been assigned to re-enactment in the arguments to be offered in Books II and III. Boucher thinks it unfortunate that Collingwood did not persevere with the problem because he sees his frequent references in Chapter 2 to the theory of language and imagination developed in *The Principles of Art* as pointing to a solution. For there, he holds, emotions are in effect shown to be re-enactable after all.

[110] Conceivably relevant to Collingwood's apparent inconsistency here is his declared antipathy to the use of technical terms in philosophy (*EPM*, 202–8). There are other cases, too, in which he used a term quasi-technically for a time and later dropped it, e.g. 'ideality', which was prominent in the lectures of the 1920s, and then disappeared, although vestiges of the idea lingered on.

[111] *Proceedings of the Aristotelian Society* (1937–8), 86–9 (the substance of this article was later incorporated into *EM*, part IIIc); *NL* rev., 467 ff.

[112] Boucher, 'The Significance', 326–30.

[113] Collingwood's claim (considered in § 5 above) that the historian's subject-matter includes action done for bad reasons as well as for good raises a similar problem, which would seem to call for a similar solution.

In considering this proposed way out of Collingwood's apparent difficulty, it is important, first, not to overstate the problem to which it is hoped *The Principles of Art* may provide a solution. For although the idea of re-enactment makes no explicit appearance in 'The Principles of History', it might plausibly be regarded as implicit in the way Collingwood presents and discusses some of his historical examples. A case in point is his description of the way the granting of a charter by Henry I would have to be understood; what the historian must do, we are told, is to discover 'how the king envisaged the situation he was dealing with, and how he intended that it should be altered' (Ch. 2, § 3). The same sort of thing is said about the way a historian would have to understand the issuing of an Edict of Prices by Diocletian or the revoking of the Edict of Nantes by Louis XIV. In fact, it is quite remarkable how closely these examples, and what Collingwood says about them, resemble what is presented in other works as exemplifying re-enactive understanding: for example, the well-known case of the promulgation of the Theodosian Code (*IH*, 283). Collingwood goes on to observe that it is 'the special business of the historian' to interpret his evidence as implying that the agent 'envisaged the situation in which he found himself in a certain manner, was discontented with it for certain reasons, and proposed to amend it in a certain way'. It may well be that, in view of what he wrote elsewhere, he simply took it for granted that, in using language of this sort, he would be understood to be talking about re-enactment. Much the same might be said of his references at several points to historical understanding as achieved by 'reconstructing' an agent's thoughts. Some interpreters of Collingwood have claimed that the notions of re-enacting and of reconstructing thoughts are equivalent in his writings.[114] Whether or not that is generally true, the two do seem to have much the same sense in some of these cases.

[114] See e.g. L. B. Cebik, 'Collingwood: Action, Re-enactment and Evidence', *Philosophical Forum*, 2 (1970), 79; Nielsen, 'Re-enactment and Reconstruction', 24; P. Skagestad, *Making Sense of History* (Oslo, 1975), 91. The term 'reconstruction' is sometimes used for deriving historical conclusions from evidence (*IH*, 209); but in other cases it is a near-equivalent of 're-enactment' (*IH*, 310). It is also sometimes used by Collingwood to designate the recovery of the physical past (CNM 1934, par. 39), in which case it clearly excludes re-enactment.

EDITORS' INTRODUCTION lxvii

It might also be argued that the idea of re-enactment is present, at least as an implied background, in much of what Collingwood had to say about natural history in Chapter 3. The topic announced in the Scheme for this chapter was a contrast between a past conceived as dead and one conceived as re-enactively understandable. In 'The Principles of History' Collingwood does not actually describe the natural past as dead; but his contention that only a past viewed as expressing thought is truly historical seems related to that original theme, especially when taken in conjunction with the contrast he draws elsewhere between a dead past and a re-enactable one. He draws this contrast explicitly, for example, in his 'Notes on Historiography' when discussing pseudo-history. It is drawn also in his critique of Toynbee in *The Idea of History*, where the naturalism alleged to taint that author's view of history is attributed to the fact that 'he never reaches the conception of historical knowledge as the re-enactment of the past in the historian's mind', this having the consequence that 'history is converted into nature, and the past, instead of living in the present, as it does in history, is conceived as a dead past, as it is in nature' (*IH*, 163–4).[115]

All this, however, concerns the re-enactive understanding of actions, not of emotions. Boucher concedes that any satisfactory account of how emotions might be re-enactively grasped by historians would have to be considerably different from the one Collingwood offered in *The Idea of History* with the understanding of actions in view. We would simply stress how very different such an account would indeed have to be. As the example of Henry I's charter well illustrates, where the problem is understanding an action, it is essential to the re-enactment of its expressed thought that the agent's intention in performing the action be discerned. In the case of emotions, the element of intention or will is missing. The historian seeking re-enactive understanding of an action must ask: What was this agent trying to achieve? There is no comparable question with regard to understanding his emotions. It makes no sense to ask: What was this agent trying to feel?[116] And that leads on to a further

[115] Collingwood's referring to a past as 'dead' because not expressive of thought is rather inappropriate in the case of the natural past, which cannot be said ever to have been 'alive'.

[116] On the question of emotions and feelings, see n. 60.

difficulty. For, as Collingwood said repeatedly, the re-enactive understanding of an action must be critical—in fact, doubly critical: the historian must interpret critically whatever evidence he has for attributing a particular thought, and he must re-think the thought itself critically in the sense of appraising its validity—or, as Collingwood himself sometimes says, he must ask whether it was right or wrong (*IH*, 215–16).[117] It is difficult to see how a supposed re-enactment of a past emotion could be regarded as critical in the second of these ways. Yet it is tempting to talk about discerning emotions in at least a quasi-re-enactive way, as is done in *The Principles of Art*. For it is no more plausible to treat emotions as mere psychic phenomena, to be dealt with like other natural occurrences, than it is to see them as expressions of an agent's will. Clearly there is much here to ponder for anyone interested in developing Collingwood's theory of history further.

12. *The shorter manuscripts*

As we have already noted, most of what Collingwood wrote on philosophy of history was not completed in a form he considered ready for publication. Even the lectures of 1936, which became the basis of the posthumous *Idea of History*, he only began transforming into a book; and those of 1926 and 1928, although completely written out, were never intended for publication at all. Of the shorter pieces he wrote on history during the 1920s, most were published as articles at the time; but almost all of the ones he wrote during the 1930s were left in manuscript form. For the present volume, we have selected eight pieces from the latter group. All but the 'Notes on Historiography' of 1939 were written in the middle 1930s just after Collingwood completed *An Essay on Philosophical Method* and his part of *Roman Britain and the English Settlements*. None of them, of course, has the authority of a book or an article prepared for publication by its author; but all contain material which, for one reason or another, we think too valuable not to be made generally available. In earlier discussion of 'The

---

[117] The question is whether the study of emotions can be what Collingwood called 'criteriological'. For references to the idea of a criteriological science, see n. 81.

Principles of History', we have already made occasional references to some of these pieces. In this section we offer more systematic but necessarily still brief comments on them seriatim.

The several selections brought together under the heading
'Notes towards a Metaphysic' are culled from a very long manuscript of that title which Collingwood wrote in 1933–4. This
explores ideas he was then developing on cosmology, in preparation for the lectures which eventually became *The Idea of Nature*.
The sections of the manuscript entitled 'Nature has no History'
and 'History' are of special interest for his philosophy of history.
The first culminates in one of the strongest assertions of the viability of natural history found anywhere in his writings, although
he still insists that this is history only in a secondary sense. He
nevertheless makes it clear that, even in this sense, history is not
just a story of change, even of directional change: there must be
not only change within certain forms, but also change of the
forms themselves.[118] Thus a seacoast may have a history since its
eroding tides, over time, change their own pattern of ebb and
flow. In the same manuscript, a contention worth remarking is
that history in the full sense goes back at least to the first flint
chipper, this despite our being told that human history is to be
conceived as a work of freedom, self-consciously exercised. The
claim is especially surprising when read in conjunction with what
is said in 'The Principles of History' about the necessary connection allegedly holding between historical consciousness and
knowledge of freedom. In the section on 'History', Collingwood
advances a view of the historian's proper object that may also
seem surprising, given ways in which human history is represented in some of his other writings. The historian's object of
thought, we are told, is abstract, not concrete, quite as abstract as
the object of thought in natural science. The difference is that
while natural scientists study abstract generalities, historians
study abstract individualities. It follows that neither history nor
science can give complete accounts of their objects.[119]

The short section on Gentile, whose view of history
Collingwood characterizes as an 'arthritic' version of Croce's,
dismisses as 'subjective idealism' any view of the past as a mere

[118] For an application of this idea to human history, see CNM, par. 34.
[119] Cf. CNM 1934, par. 36 on concrete eternal objects; NHV, in the section
entitled 'No Completeness in History'.

'abstraction' from the present, and cautions against stressing the role of perspective in history while ignoring the question of the relation of perspectives. It is of some interest to read this along with Collingwood's own treatment of the latter problem in 'The Nature and Aims of a Philosophy of History' (*EPH*, 53 ff.). Other ideas worth remarking in this manuscript include Collingwood's claim that the relation between human and natural history exemplifies a scale of forms as explicated in the *Essay on Philosophical Method*; that the human world contains its own past within itself in a way that the natural world does not; that historical objectivity consists, in one sense at least, in the use by historians of a shared system of concepts; that the course of historical events not only exhibits necessity, but also exemplifies phases of self-developing concepts. There is an intriguing if inconclusive consideration of the idea that the velocity of time may differ in nature and in history, and a rather puzzling insistence that, despite important differences, causality in nature and in history both require an active response on the part of the 'patient'.[120] There is also an anticipation, although in a very different context,[121] of the attempt in 'The Principles of History' to soften the contrast between thought and emotion in the declaration that 'persistent' emotions, at least, can be assimilated to thought.

The manuscript 'History as the Understanding of the Present', which is thought to have been written in 1934 or 1935, is no more than a very brief fragment, but it touches on a number of recurring Collingwoodian themes. It contains an early version of the claim, also found in 'The Principles of History', that, to speak strictly, historians do not infer the past from present evidence; for to discover what the evidence really is (e.g. a piece of Flavian pottery) is already to interpret it—to see it as a relic of a certain past state of affairs. Collingwood also stresses the limited extent to which he thinks historians can explain the present by reference to the past.[122] At the same time, he links

---

[120] On this see also CNM 1934, par. 34.

[121] The context is a discussion of the emotional dimension of religion, a topic considered extensively later in the folklore MSS when treating the phenomenon of magic.

[122] This claim is based on the position, worked out in RAH as well, that the present is not completely determined by the past, since there is always a 'free' element involved in it.

historical explanation, uncharacteristically, with discovering origins, an approach not easily reconciled, on the face of it, with his insistence, in the 'Notes on Historiography', that there are no beginnings in history. There is also an anticipation of the contention in the British Academy lecture, which later became a focus of considerable critical discussion, that, in history, knowing what happened is indistinguishable from knowing why it happened (*IH*, 214). Collingwood's historical indeterminism, which appears in different guises in different writings, is in this manuscript given the unusual form of declaring that the past only determines possibilities in the present, a position which meshes well with what he says at greater length in 'Reality as History' about the way and the extent to which an agent's character may determine his actions. The main thrust of the piece, however, is a rather extreme version of the 'presentism' which is a recurring feature of Collingwood's writings on history: the assertion that the ultimate aim of historical inquiry is not to discover the past, but to understand the present. This doctrine is weakened, but still not withdrawn, by the concession that knowing what the present really is entails knowing how it came about.

As the name suggests, the manuscript entitled 'Inaugural: Rough Notes' is a draft for the public lecture 'The Historical Imagination', which Collingwood gave when he was elected to the Chair of Metaphysics at Oxford in 1935. The draft covers the same ground as the lecture, but there are differences that make it worth independent study. Besides giving further insight into the way Collingwood worked at a topic, it offers useful clarifications or expansions of some of his ideas in passages that were substantially rewritten for the lecture itself, or were omitted from it altogether. The draft treats the common-sense view of history more gently than the lecture does, and it makes more of the methodological necessity of recognizing provisional authorities. It discusses the use of unwritten sources more concretely, and makes more explicit the role envisaged for the auxiliary sciences of history. The important contrast drawn in the lecture between critical and constructive history is given a rather different look, the continuing part necessarily played by critical history within scientific history being stressed. And the way criticism and construction supplement each other when historians construct imaginative webs or 'pictures' of the past is more clearly expounded in the draft—in a manner, furthermore, that better explains why Collingwood refused to characterize historical inference as either deductive or inductive, as well as suggesting a role for re-enactment in it. There is a strong passage asserting the ineradicable presence of 'brute fact' in historical narrative, which needs to be considered along with apparent denials of this in some other writings;[123] and the idea that historical inquiry has as its goal the construction of a narrative is broadened, an interesting comparison being offered between history and literature. Collingwood's problematic notion of a necessity which resides entirely in individuals, and which appears also in 'Reality as History', is stated forthrightly, with examples. And even where draft and lecture display no apparent divergences of doctrine, the use of different illustrations in the draft is sometimes illuminating.

'Reality as History', the next manuscript, is described by Collingwood himself as aimed simply at determining how far one can press the thesis of Alexander and some other cosmologists that the idea of history applies, not just to human life, but to all that exists. This is a problem to which he returns in later works (e.g. *IH*, 210 ff.; PH, Ch. 2, § 4). But it gets its most extended consideration in this essay, where Collingwood's discussion of it leads him to take some quite controversial positions on a number of interrelated issues in philosophy of history.[124]

The discussion has three stages: first, an examination of what, in general, a historical sequence is like and how it should be understood; second, an account of some features of historicity as exemplified in human action and human affairs; and third, an analysis of how, despite important similarities, the historicity of a natural process must differ fundamentally from that of a human one. At the first stage, Collingwood contrasts his own view of what would constitute a truly historical approach to human experience with approaches which he regards as typical

[123] See e.g. PH, Ch. 3, § 1 and § 5, although it is a moot point whether the idea of 'fact' is used there in quite the same sense.

[124] Among those not touched on above are the possibility of nomological knowledge of mind; the explanatory role of continuity; the limits of all explanation; the explanatory use of rules; the ultimate uselessness of natural science; the equivalence of the ideas how and why in history; the logical relation of historical to scientific thinking.

EDITORS' INTRODUCTION lxxiii

of the ancient and early modern worlds. Both of the latter saw
the flow of experience as understandable only by reference to
generalities of some kind: for the ancients, transcendent ones;
for the early moderns, immanent—the general laws and concepts according to which things occur. A truly historical
approach, Collingwood maintains, would find intelligibility in
the flow of experience itself, and, more specifically, in the continuities it exhibits; and he welcomes the assurance of Alexander
and others that this is just what modern physical science
increasingly does. In defending what he calls this fundamental
'principle of history', Collingwood anticipates in a remarkable
way later debates about the nature of historical explanation,
and, more particularly, about the viability of a 'covering law'
conception of it.[125] However, his resistance to this idea employs
arguments quite different from those he generally used against
it later (see e.g. *IH*, 214), and they are rather loosely formulated.
Collingwood seizes the opportunity, in passing, to continue his
quarrel with naturalistic psychology, charging it with falsely
presupposing that its subject-matter is unintelligent; and he
warns of destructive social consequences that he thinks are
likely to flow from adopting ways of thinking derived from early
modern science in this and other fields. In both cases, concerns
are anticipated which are expressed even more forcibly in his
writings of 1938–9.

In the second stage of his discussion, Collingwood argues that
human nature is resolvable without residue into historical
process, thus rejecting any view of it as a changeless entity, or as
determined by natural causes.[126] Of special interest here is the
way he believes we should regard the relation of human character to human action. With a view to clarifying his own position,
and at the same time clearing it of any appearance of extreme
libertarianism, he offers an extensive analysis of what is
involved in acting in or out of character, and of the sense
in which character can explain action, which seeks to give due

---

[125] On this controversy, see R. H. Weingartner, 'Historical Explanation', in
Paul Edwards (ed.), *The Encyclopedia of Philosophy* (New York, 1962), iv 7–12.
For further references, see Harry Ritter (ed.), *Dictionary of Concepts in History*
(New York, 1986), 75–9.
[126] This in a section entitled 'Human Nature and Human History', the same
title he was to give his British Academy Lecture a few months later.

consideration both to the weight of a formed character in human decision, and to the freedom possessed by human beings to form their own characters. A person's character, he maintains, is just a residue of his past alive in his present, this making certain actions more or less difficult to perform, but never completely determining decision. Collingwood sums up his position by affirming that, while what nature brings to the present is compulsion, what history brings is simply fact. He goes on to consider certain practical implications of such an analysis for public policy: for example, how and whether war, conceived as a consequence of accumulating human choices rather than natural instincts, can be avoided. All this amounts to a resounding metaphysical defence of the idea that human beings are responsible for the world they make—useful background for what was eventually to be said along these lines in the *Autobiography* and *The New Leviathan*.

At the third stage of his discussion, Collingwood argues that, although nature, on the modern view of it, is clearly historical, it is less historical than human nature and human affairs.[127] Much of his effort is nevertheless devoted to showing just how historical the natural world must be conceived to be. Thus it is argued that, since life arose out of nature at a certain point, the natural world must exhibit not just a directional development but a unique one, in which important things may happen just once. This leads Collingwood to observe that, unless nature had already had a history (in what turns out to be a broader sense), human nature could not have experienced one (in the special, narrower sense appertaining only to it). The difference between the historicity of natural things and of human beings is formulated in several ways, but a striking one is the following. Although, on the modern view, what natural things are, just as what human beings are, consists in their characteristic patterns of activity, each of these requiring an appropriate period of time to become established, human being is not temporal in quite the same sense that natural being is. Whereas natural things are what they do, human beings are what they have done (here

---

[127] In other writings (e.g. IRN), Collingwood contrasted the two by insisting that nature has no history, or that natural history, unlike human history, consists only of particular facts. Here (as in NTM) the contrast drawn is based on the idea that historicity can be a matter of degree.

Collingwood implicitly calls upon his earlier analysis of human character). Upon this difference he bases the claim that, while in nature different causes may produce the same effect, in human life, since a unique past experience is conserved in its present, there is only one possible past, and thus only one possible explanation, of any given present. If correct, this is clearly a matter of great importance for the viability of retrodictive argument from present evidence in human history.

The piece entitled 'Can Historians be Impartial?' is a paper which Collingwood delivered to a historical society at Oxford in 1935. It is the only considerable record we have of his views on what might surely be regarded as a major issue facing his theory of historiography: the place of value judgement in historical thinking, although there are passing remarks on this issue in some other writings (e.g. *EPH*, 15, 76; L26, 397 ff., 402–4). The discussion is structured by two distinctions: first, between historians showing partiality in the sense of being prejudiced and showing it in the sense of making value judgements at all; and second, between their having a duty to avoid partiality and their being able, in fact, to avoid it. Collingwood argued that prejudice is difficult or impossible to avoid when the subject-matter is closely related to a historian's practical concerns. This, however, and somewhat surprisingly, is said to be no bad thing, mainly on the ground that, without the 'head of steam' afforded by prejudice, many great historical works would never have been written.[128] The historian as eunuch, he observes, is not really what we want. With regard to making value judgements at all—and such judgements, we are reminded, include far more than narrowly moral ones[129]—Collingwood maintains, as some later philosophers of history were to do, that it may be impossible to grasp the full nature of a historical fact if value judgements are ruled out. Even such an apparently simple fact as who a certain Gildas was, he argues, is partly value-constituted; and value judgements are said to enter a historian's conclusions through his conception of what matters most in the subject-matter.

[128] In another mood (e.g. *IH*, 203–4), Collingwood denigrates accounts which deliberately express partisan feelings as mere pseudo-history.
[129] To the kinds of value judgements Collingwood lists here, readers of PH, Ch. 2, § 8, can now add the 'gossip-value' which is there ascribed to some biographies.

Collingwood does not seem to notice, or at any rate does not say, that the arguments he offers with regard to prejudice and with regard to value judgement are fundamentally different in character: what he says about the first relates to what is practically or psychologically possible, while what he says about the second concerns what is involved in the very concept of a historical fact. It may be felt, too, that he somewhat exaggerates the methodological benefits of prejudice—although this is perhaps excusable in a piece written for an occasion on which he was doubtless expected to be provocative. In fact, despite some overstatement and internal strains, it is difficult to think of a piece of comparable length better calculated to generate fruitful reflection on the problems it addresses.

Collingwood's 'Notes on the History of Historiography and Philosophy of History' were preparatory to writing a new set of lectures on philosophy of history in 1936.[130] Since these lectures eventually formed the basis of *The Idea of History*, the 'Notes' are of special value for better understanding some of the positions taken in that book. They are divided into sections, one or several paragraphs long, on a variety of topics. Of the ones which have been included here, the note entitled 'The Idea of Historical Efficacy' is of unusual interest because it discusses a problem, the meaning of importance in history, which is almost ignored in Collingwood's other writings, published or unpublished. The part of the 'Note' which is printed here follows an extensive critique of some views of Eduard Meyer, and is implicitly a commentary on them.[131] A puzzling aspect of what Collingwood has to say is his complete extrusion of the idea of intrinsic importance from historical thinking, an idea to which he seems himself committed at other points (e.g. *IH*, 179; *RB*, 69). However, he also rejects the idea that would generally be contrasted with it: the idea that historical importance is determined by consequences; and he explicates clearly some of the difficulties that acceptance of the latter notion would entail. The

---

[130] He had lectured on the subject from 1926 to 1931 (and prepared notes for 1932, a year in which he was for most of the time too ill to lecture). Besides the full text of the lectures given in 1926, 1927, and 1928, now printed as an appendix to *IH* rev., there remain fragments of what was delivered in 1929 and 1931, and of what would have been delivered in 1932.

[131] The gist of the commentary can be found in *IH*, 176–81.

problems raised by his own alternative—the claim that 'historically important' means either 'important to the agent' or
'important to the historian'—are more sketchily treated.[132] As
part of his analysis, Collingwood rejects, as he does in some
other writings (e.g. L26, 356), the commonly accepted idea that
selection is a fundamental problem for theory of historiography.
However, his position on this, too, is not easy to reconcile with
theoretical claims he makes elsewhere—for example, his coup-
ling of 'selection' with 'construction' and 'criticism' in 'The
Historical Imagination' (*IH*, 236)—or with his own practice as
a historian—for example, his declaration that Britain's 'partial
conquest and occupation by Rome' was what its history in
Roman times was 'primarily' about (*RBES*, 5).

The first of two Notes entitled 'Human Nature and Human
History' shows Collingwood still thinking through, with
refreshing candour, the problem of how far 'down the scale' one
can hope to find rationality in human affairs, this prefiguring
what he had to say on the subject later (e.g. in *IH*, 227; PH, Ch.
2, § 3). A second offers a terse but useful summary of metaphysical and epistemological doctrines against which his philosophy
of history should be read. In a Note on 'Eternal Objects', the
normal objects of historical interest are represented as 'struc-
ture-patterns', an idea which appears also in the 1934
Conclusion to Nature and Mind, and which helps to undermine
the common view of Collingwood as an extreme methodological
individualist. The same Note contains a strong, if somewhat
intricate, discussion of his theory of understanding as re-
enactment in which Collingwood draws a distinction, as he does
nowhere else, between four senses of 'thought' which, he says,
need to be kept in mind if this doctrine is to be fully grasped. At
the same time, it is made clear, although with an element of
overstatement which appears again in what he says in 'The
Principles of History' (Ch. 3, § 5) about historical situations
always being conceived situations, that re-enactment, on his
view, has a constitutive as well as explanatory role to play in historical reconstruction, the political situation faced by Duke
William at Hastings, for example, being said to have itself consisted of thoughts: his own and other people's. A final Note on

---

[132] For the notion of historical importance, see also the section under that
heading in NHV.

'Evidence and Certitude' offers a subjective explication of the idea of probability in history which, although he concedes it to be 'paradoxical', Collingwood still maintains in the extant fragment of Chapter 4 of 'The Principles of History'. The context here is a contrast drawn between the way evidence is treated in history and in the law courts, a recurring interest of his.

The piecemeal notes which follow, Collingwood's 'Notes on Historiography' of 1939, were composed on the same voyage on which he wrote 'The Principles of History'. Almost all of its eighteen items consist of very short paragraphs, heterogeneous in subject-matter, and some quite terse in expression. Among the ones selected for this volume is the 'Scheme for a Book' which Collingwood composed in February 1939 with 'The Principles of History' in mind, although, as was pointed out earlier, he did not subsequently follow its outline strictly. The passage entitled 'That History is the Only Kind of Knowledge' contains the notorious statement, 'Thus philosophy as a separate discipline is liquidated by being converted into history', which Knox, in his preface to *The Idea of History*, took to be indicative of an extreme historicism on Collingwood's part (*IH*, p. x).[133] The note 'Historical Naturalism' calls to mind Collingwood's treatment of this subject in 'The Principles of History', Chapter 3, §§ 1, 2, and the one on 'Nature and History' sketches the argument he developed in § 4. The notes on 'Pseudo-history' and 'Crypto-history'[134] explain better than is done elsewhere (e.g. *A*, 107, 109; *IH*, 300) what he mainly intended by those terms of abuse, and the one entitled 'Historical Importance' echoes some of the conclusions reached on this matter in the 'Notes' of 1936. The brief discussions of

[133] Since Knox took this to imply that philosophy had been 'absorbed' by history, he saw it as offering the 'true answer' to the question why Collingwood did not finish PH (*IH*, p. xvii). But this, as was argued in § 10, is hardly plausible, since in *A*, written at about the same time, Collingwood called only for history and philosophy to become more closely related, not to fuse with each other. It remains true, however, that in e.g. *EPM* and *EM* he developed apparently conflicting views on the nature of philosophy. One needs to keep in mind, too, the important difference between Collingwood's frequent reminders that philosophy *has* a history—which, as in the case of all human enterprises, is part of, or 'incapsulated in', its present nature—and his apparent contention here that philosophy simply *is* history.

[134] Collingwood's later MSS on folklore were to show in considerable detail what he means here by calling anthropology 'crypto-history'.

'Accident 'and 'Contingency' appropriate these terms exclusively for the human studies (see also *EM*, 289; *NL*, 110, 117), and supplement views expressed by Collingwood elsewhere on the nature of historical causation. The even briefer note on 'The Comparative Method' makes it clear why he questions the validity of this approach to history, although in some other contexts (e.g. *IH*, 67; *RBES*, 302–4) he seems to grant it some heuristic value.[135] In the fifth, sixth, eleventh, and twelfth notes the indispensability of the idea of re-enactment for the theory of historiography is taken for granted, despite its later absence from 'The Principles of History'; and in the one entitled 'No Endings in History', re-enactment is appropriately linked with the idea of a past still living in the present, a theme to which Collingwood frequently returns.[136]

Most problematic are the fourth, eighth, and ninth notes arguing Collingwood's position that all the human studies, including philosophy, even ethics and logic, are, or should be, historical in nature. A puzzle worth pursuing in this connection is how the alleged historicity of such inquiries is to be related to the declaration in 'The Principles of History' that the same studies, and certainly 'scientific' history as Collingwood understands it, are all criteriological enterprises, as such requiring investigators to engage in critical appraisal of the human activities which form their subject-matter.[137] Perhaps helpful, in this connection, would be an examination of the relation between the historical and systematic parts of Collingwood's *Idea of History*, or between *The Idea of Nature* and its various conclusions, or between the historical and theoretical elements of *The New Leviathan*. It seems clear, at any rate, that despite apparent difficulties raised by the present claim, Collingwood still, in his

[135] This interprets Collingwood's exposition of Vico's view of history at this point as an approving one, which may, of course, be contested. There seems little room, however, for denying that Collingwood himself sometimes thought it appropriate to use a comparative approach in his own historical work.
[136] What Collingwood says two paragraphs earlier against the idea of beginnings in history might need some reformulation to make it clearly consistent with his description of history in HUP and elsewhere as a search for origins, given the tendency in ordinary speech not to distinguish sharply between these ideas. For examples of history conceived by Collingwood as a search for origins, see *IN*, 10; CNM 1935.
[137] See n. 81.

final writings, assigned a critical role not only to the historian, but also to the philosopher of history—even if the vehemence of his attack, in the second chapter of 'The Principles of History', on the pretensions of 'consulting philosophers' might lead a reader to think otherwise. Collingwood's claim that metaphysics, at least, is a historical science, specifically mentioned in his note 'That History is the Only Kind of Knowledge' and developed later at length in the *Essay on Metaphysics*, has already become a focus of critical discussion.[138] What is said here about logic and ethics may broaden the battleground.

13. *The Conclusions to Nature and Mind*

Something needs finally to be said about the second recently discovered manuscript, the Conclusions to Collingwood's Lectures on Nature and Mind, which he delivered in 1934, 1935, 1937, 1939, and again, after substantial revision and under the title 'The Idea of Nature in Modern Science', in 1940. We print the entire manuscript, although much of it has only marginal relevance to philosophy of history as exemplified by most of the other pieces in this volume, i.e. as an account of the nature and significance of history as a form of inquiry. Its contents are related most closely to the studies which Collingwood recorded in his 'Notes towards a Metaphysic', written at about the same time.[139] Since the manuscript consists of Collingwood's conclusions to lectures which were later to form the basis of his posthumous book *The Idea of Nature*, its contents are also, of course, closely related to the latter. As found, it contains a shorter and a longer Conclusion, which we present here more discretely than they appear in the original text.[140] When Collingwood gave the lectures for the last time in 1940, he wrote a third Conclusion, and at the same time changed their title to 'The Idea of

[138] See e.g. Rex Martin, 'Collingwood's Claim that Metaphysics is a Historical Discipline', *Monist*, 72 (1989), 489–525.

[139] In 1933–4, immediately after the completion of *EPM*.

[140] It was apparently H. H. Price who first distinguished the first from the second Conclusion by inserting a 'B' between them on the manuscript (not reproduced here). For a consideration of the relation of the two Conclusions and on Knox's policy with regard to them, see Boucher, 'The Principles', 147 ff. Boucher also gives reasons for believing that Knox's editing of *IN* (as of *IH*) was more heavy-handed than he admitted.

Nature'.[141] It was this Conclusion which Knox chose to print in the volume he edited under that name, a decision questioned at the time by H. H. Price.[142]

From the standpoint of philosophy of history, the Conclusion of 1935 is the more interesting of the two earlier ones. In it Collingwood concedes, as he did also in 'Reality as History' and 'Notes towards a Metaphysic', that nature, as is shown by the way his review of changing views of it culminates, is now conceived as a temporal process which not only suffers change, but, in changing, brings new forms of itself into being. To that extent, as Alexander had insisted in 'The Historicity of Things', and contrary to the view of it that prevailed in the nineteenth century, it is historical in nature. In the history of human affairs, Collingwood observes, it is a familiar idea that, in tracing the history of something like England, what is found to change is not just certain details, but the very essence of the thing. England (like human nature generally) is itself a product of a historical process, the whole of it changing while at the same time remaining itself by virtue of continuity with its past.[143]

[141] In the Conclusion of 1935, Collingwood says we need to proceed from the idea of nature to the idea of history in order to find out what difference there is, if any, between human and natural historical processes—i.e. how far historicity can be generalized. In the Conclusion Knox printed in *IN*, the reason given for proceeding from nature to history is that scientific thinking depends for its validity on historical thinking. In both cases, however, attention is directed towards what will be said in subsequent lectures. The third Conclusion does not do this any more effectively than the second: it simply does it differently. Rex Martin discusses the nature and relation of Collingwood's Conclusions in 'Collingwood's *Essay on Metaphysics* and the Three Conclusions to the *Idea of Nature*', *British Journal for the History of Philosophy*, 7 (1999), 333–51.

[142] The reason Knox gave in his prefatory note to *IN* for printing only the Conclusion of 1940 as a 'Transition from Nature to History' is that he believed Collingwood to have become 'dissatisfied' with 'the sketch of his own cosmology' which closed the original lectures. The latter phrase, however, only makes sense as a reference to the long Conclusion of 1934, not to the short Conclusion of 1935, which, in this note, Knox curiously ignores.

[143] This might be compared with what Collingwood says in RAH about the historical nature of human 'character'. It is unfortunate that the idea of continuity, on which Collingwood depends heavily at this point, is explicated neither here nor anywhere else in his writings. Presumably he would want to say, e.g., that although Roman Britain was in one sense continuous with Anglo-Saxon Britain, in another sense it was not; and the way such senses are related needs discussion. One wonders, too, how Collingwood thought his notion of

Collingwood holds that matter is now seen, on analogy with a changing human nature, as something brought into existence by its own process and is to be taken as identical with it. This seems to imply a full acceptance of the idea of natural history on his part, and the beginnings of a theory of its nature. But there is a fundamental difference, he insists, between human and natural process which makes the idea of historicity applicable to nature in no more than an analogical sense.[144] Since Collingwood announces here that in the following term's lectures on the idea of history he will spell out what this is, we can extrapolate. The distinguishing mark of human history, or of history as 'strictly and properly' conceived, will be found to be the re-enactability of what takes place in it.[145] In other words, what he envisages here is a criterion of genuine historicity not obviously identical to the one he was to offer later in 'The Principles of History' (being derived from evidence which can be 'read'), or which he envisaged in the 1934 Conclusion to Nature and Mind (a development which cumulates).

The longer Conclusion sets the idea of history in a broader framework of evolutionary metaphysics. In effect, Collingwood sketches a natural history of the world at the most general cosmological level, tracing, with a sharp eye for interesting details of the hierarchy of discernible forms, a development from matter to life to mind. The 'essence' or 'general principle' of the process, he maintains, is a movement from outwardness to inwardness. The first is illustrated, at the most elementary level, by the fact that material particles are completely outside each other in space and time, each having its being, as it were, in

continuity in history applied to the cosmological shift from matter to life, and from life to mind discussed in the Conclusion of 1934, where the crucial feature seems to be not continuity but discontinuity. He does say that continuity means an absence of 'breaks', but that idea is enmeshed in the same problems as 'continuity'.

[144] The idea that historical process is different from natural process, which is introduced in the Conclusion of 1935, is more fully developed in Collingwood's subsequent writings, e.g. RAH, NHH, the British Academy Lecture 'Human Nature and Human History', his lectures on philosophy of history of 1936, and is elaborated still further in Ch. 3 of PH.

[145] It is notable that Collingwood here and elsewhere, with a considerable appearance of arbitrariness, takes human history as paradigmatic, asking how far natural history approximates to it, not how far human history approximates to history of nature.

itself, and merely interacting with others. The second is illustrated by the capacity of mind to transcend spatial location by sharing the experience, i.e. activities, of other minds (mind simply *being* activity of a certain kind), and temporal location by living not only in a perceived present, but also in a remembered past and an envisaged future. Collingwood pushes his cosmological reflections to the point where they intersect with theological concerns. The processive course of nature, he avers, can be seen as the 'life of God', a process in which he develops himself from the status of mere Creator to that of Spirit. The related question of whether the human spirits which develop themselves in the same process can attain the final inwardness of immortality he toys with, but, in the end, pronounces unanswerable.[146]

Of special interest for the elucidation of the idea of history more narrowly conceived is the use Collingwood makes in the 1934 Conclusion of the theoretical notions outwardness opposed to inwardness, nisus, and eternal object. The history of the world at the highest level he characterizes as a movement from outwardness to inwardness. The latter may appear at first to be a merely synthesizing or ordering idea, similar in use to ideas like the Industrial Revolution or the westward march of the American frontier in human historiography; and so conceived, the detailed argument in support of its application is illuminating enough, if not very problematic. At more than one point, however, Collingwood appears to treat the idea as an explanatory one—maintaining, for example, that, at a certain stage of the physical world's development, merely material forms of activity are succeeded by at least embryonic forms of life 'because' outwardness can no longer develop significantly in the direction it has been moving up to that point. What appears, on the face of it, as a 'jump' in the evolutionary process taken as a whole is thus declared to be a perfectly understandable, and, indeed, necessitated, development of it, although not a normal

[146] Given the controversy over whether Collingwood reduced philosophy, in the end, to history of ideas (e.g. in *EM*, or in NHV), it is worth remarking (as Knox observes with regard to *EPM* in *IH*, pp. ix–x) that, at this point at least, he appears to distinguish philosophy quite clearly from history, offering his own cosmological conclusions, however tentatively, as based in part on what he accepts as contemporary findings of natural science.

one in the sense of being like developments occurring within the material, living, and mental domains.[147]

And this leads to a consideration of the second rather puzzling theoretical notion that Collingwood employs. What is required to maintain the direction of the world-process, we are told, both at the levels of ordinary self-development and that of the larger movements just noted, is a pre-existing 'nisus' towards the end result. Those already familiar with Collingwood's writings in philosophy of history, and his historical writings as well, will surely be surprised at his easy adoption of such a holistic and highly speculative form of teleological explanation, a way of thinking about a subject-matter that he would certainly pro-scribe for human historiography. Nor is his use of the idea of 'nisus' here a unique aberration. He calls upon it also in his 'Notes towards a Metaphysic',[148] and in some of his still unpub-lished manuscripts on folklore. It might, perhaps, be observed that, if the idea of nisus were in fact considered applicable to ordinary human history, the result would be about as far as it is possible to go from the methodological individualism of which, as has been noted, Collingwood is sometimes accused. But a denial that he was an extreme individualist no more needs such drastic support than it does the extreme views Collingwood expressed in 'The Principles of History' about the non-historicity of biography. Should we take it, then, that he thinks that different methodological standards are appropriately applied in human history and in natural history at the cosmo-logical level? In fact, he appears to hedge a bit, at times, about the nature and role of nisus even in cosmological history. Thus, although he speaks of mind as 'wanting' to perceive the world, and of the world, in its turn, as 'wanting' to be perceived, with respect to the latter at least, he has the grace to add 'figuratively speaking'.[149]

---

[147] Collingwood draws an even more puzzling a priori conclusion from his analysis here: that the development of any other world, no matter how differ-ent in content from ours, would necessarily exemplify the same formal princi-ple of movement. Is he here, one wonders, simply stating a conclusion which he believes to be analytically derivable from the very idea of 'development'?

[148] See e.g. van der Dussen, *History as a Science*, 197–9.

[149] Collingwood employs the idea of nisus at various points in *IN* itself, e.g. 15, 83–4, 92, 110, 124, 161, 164, 169, pointing out on p. 83 that, for Greek philosophy at least, nisus was not just change, but effort or tendency 'to change

The third problematic theoretical notion, that of there being 'eternal objects' in history, appears about two-thirds of the way through the 1934 Conclusion in what looks like a short digression on Whitehead's view of the matter. Whitehead had insisted that the reduction of nature to process, the insistence upon its historicity, upon the fact that everything passes away, does not rule out the idea that there are eternal objects in the world. In his view, a certain shade of blueness (indeed, any quality) would be an eternal object, since it is something which can be instantiated and re-instantiated in the world-process at various times. Collingwood accepts this, but holds that the thesis regarding eternal objects can be maintained in a stronger, or at any rate different, sense, which is of greater interest for the theory of history. According to him, all historical events are eternal objects in the sense that, once having occurred, they remain in being, if not in existence, as unchangeable stages of the historical process, which can become objects of present-day historical thought if sufficient evidence of them survives. Where Whitehead's eternal objects are abstract (universals), Collingwood's are concrete (particulars).[150] Collingwood describes the former as no more than aspects of the latter, illustrating this

in certain definite ways'. Rik Peters has drawn the attention of the editors to the fact that Collingwood used the term 'nisus' only after completing *EPM*, and that, in a part of NTM not reproduced in this volume (bk. A, fos. 6, 16), he characterized nisus as a force which drives a development from a lower to a next higher form on a scale of forms—a 'strain' towards a later 'actuality' in an earlier 'virtuality'. He also likened it to Spinoza's notion of immanent causality, but conceded that it was a frankly teleological idea. Peters plausibly suggests that Collingwood's cosmological use of the idea has the appearance of an early attempt at elaborating a fully historicized philosophy, and that in this use it is, in effect, 'a naturalized version of reason'. In considering such an idea, however, it should be remembered that what would here be 'naturalized' would be a reason supposedly at work in human history at the holistic level, an idea which, given what Collingwood has to say at various points about 'corporate minds' in history, he appears never to have completely embraced (see e.g. *IH*, 34, 95, 116, 122, 219). Peters notes that the term 'nisus' was used by Leibniz and by earlier writers, but not clearly in Collingwood's sense (see Joachim Ritter et al. (eds.), *Historisches Wörterbuch der Philosophie* (Basel, 1971–)); and we have found no evidence of his having adopted (or adapted) it from any previous author.

[150] Cf. Collingwood's discussion of Whitehead and the remarks on the Norman Conquest in the section on 'Historical Events as Eternal Objects' in NHH.

with the claim that although, on Whitehead's theory, when King James II threw the Great Seal into the Thames, the exact configuration of the splash may be regarded as an eternal object, it is still not an eternal *historical* object. Only the whole event, the throwing of the Seal into the river, can properly be so regarded.

All this may cast some light on a passage in *The Idea of History* which has sometimes given commentators pause: one in which the Roman Constitution and the Augustan modification of it are called eternal objects on the ground that they 'can be apprehended by historical thought at any time' (*IH*, 218).[151] But the point is further developed there by Collingwood in a way that diverges from the position he takes in the present manuscript; he maintains that what makes an event historical is not its having happened in time but its having become known to us by our re-thinking the thought which created it. In the present manuscript, by contrast, he appears to accept the idea that natural as well as human history 'generates' eternal objects in the same concrete rather than abstract sense, the 'eternality' of the natural ones in this sense being what makes them 'reconstructible', if not 're-enactable', by natural historians.[152] Again we come up against Collingwood's recurring ambivalence about similarities and differences between natural and human history.

Collingwood did not further elaborate his studies on cosmology after the mid-1930s, but they had fruitful consequences for his developing view of history in the contrasts he ever more sharply drew, on the one hand, between natural and historical processes and, on the other, between the study of nature and of history. This is evidenced by many passages in the 'Notes towards a Metaphysic', 'Reality as History', 'Notes on History of Historiography and Philosophy of History', 'Notes on Historiography', and 'The Principles of History'; and the same contrasts pervade *The Idea of History*. Deriving from these contrasts are not only Collingwood's well-known insistence that all

---

[151] The idea also appears in *A*, 67–8, where Collingwood declares that 'any historical fact could be called eternal because it had happened once for all'.

[152] Collingwood here seems quite prepared to commit himself to the anti-constructionist notion that nature had a 'real' past which can be discovered—he offers the example of the physical world at a cosmological stage before life appeared. For a constructionist interpretation of his theory of history, see Leon Goldstein, *The What and the Why of History* (Leiden, 1996), 273–336.

history is history of thought, but also his somewhat visionary call for a civilization based on history rather than on natural science, signalled in the plan for Book III of 'The Principles of History' and adumbrated in the *Autobiography*. More generally, Collingwood's Conclusions are of interest because they make clearer the cosmological context within which his later philosophy of history developed. It is of interest, too, that, towards the end of his career, Collingwood should have given his cosmological studies a distinctly historical turn by focusing on the history of the idea of nature as expressed in the history of natural science, an approach that has gained increasing acceptance since the Second World War, although Collingwood's contribution to it has scarcely yet been recognized.

PART I

THE PRINCIPLES OF HISTORY

INTRODUCTION TO BOOK I[1]

'History,' said Bury, 'is a science; no less, and no more.'

Perhaps it is no less: that depends on what you mean by a science. There is a slang usage, like that for which 'hall' means a music-hall or 'pictures' moving pictures, according to which 'science' means natural science. Whether history is a science in that sense of the word, however, need not be asked; for in the tradition of European speech, going back to the time when Latin speakers translated the Greek ἐπιστήμη by their own word *scientia*, and continuing unbroken down to the present day, the word 'science' means any organized body of knowledge. If that is what the word means Bury is so far incontestably right, that history is a science, nothing less.

But if it is no less, it is certainly more. For anything that is a science at all must be more than merely a science, it must be a science of some special kind. A body of knowledge is never merely organized, it is always organized in some particular way. Some bodies of knowledge, like meteorology, are organized by collecting observations concerned with events of a certain kind which the scientist can watch as they happen, though he cannot produce them at will. Others, like chemistry, are organized not only by observing events as they happen, but by making them

The title page has a note saying: 'To E.W.C. [Collingwoods first wife Ethel] If this ms. comes into your hands and I am prevented from finishing it, I authorize you to publish it with the above title, with a preface by yourself explaining that it is a fragment of what I had, for 25 years at least, looked forward to writing as my chief work.'

[1] The Introduction was placed by Knox at the beginning of 'Historical Evidence', § 3 of the Epilegomena of *The Idea of History* (249–52). Since Collingwood meant it as an introduction to the whole of Book I of 'The Principles of History', it has been separated from the first chapter here. The text was missing from the manuscript of 'The Principles of History', along with the text of Chapter 1, and has therefore been copied from *The Idea of History*. The 'Notes on Historiography', written during his trip through the Dutch East Indies, contain a first draft of the beginning of the Introduction which differs slightly from this one (see pp. 248–9).

happen under strictly controlled conditions. Others again are organized not by observing events at all, but by making certain assumptions and proceeding with the utmost exactitude to argue out their consequences.

History is organized in none of these ways. Wars and revolutions, and the other events with which it deals, are not deliberately produced by historians under laboratory conditions in order to be studied with scientific precision. Nor are they even observed by historians, in the sense in which events are observed by natural scientists. Meteorologists and astronomers will make arduous and expensive journeys in order to observe for themselves events of the kinds in which they are interested, because their standard of observation is such that they cannot be satisfied with descriptions by inexpert witnesses; but historians do not fit out expeditions to countries where wars and revolutions are going on. And this is not because historians are less energetic or courageous than natural scientists, or less able to obtain the money such expeditions would cost. It is because the facts which might be learned through such expeditions, like the facts which might be learned through the deliberate fomenting of a war or a revolution at home, would not teach historians anything they want to know.

The sciences of observation and experiment are alike in this, that their aim is to detect the constant or recurring features in all events of a certain kind. A meteorologist studies one cyclone in order to compare it with others; and by studying a number of them he hopes to find out what features in them are constant, that is, to find out what cyclones as such are like. But the historian has no such aim. If you find him on a certain occasion studying the Hundred Years War or the Revolution of 1688, you cannot infer that he is in the preliminary stages of an inquiry whose ultimate aim is to reach conclusions about wars or revolutions as such. If he is in the preliminary stages of any inquiry, it is more likely to be a general study of the Middle Ages or the seventeenth century. This is because the sciences of observation and experiment are organized in one way and history is organized in another. In the organization of meteorology, the ulterior value of what has been observed about one cyclone is conditioned by its relation to what has been observed about other cyclones. In the organization of history, the ulterior value of what is known about the Hundred Years War is conditioned, not by its relation to what is known about other wars, but by its relation to what is known about other things that people did in the Middle Ages.

Equally obvious is the difference between the organization of history and that of the 'exact' sciences. It is true that in history, as in exact science, the normal process of thought is inferential; that is to say, it begins by asserting this or that, and goes on to ask what it proves. But the starting-points are of very different kinds. In exact science they are assumptions, and the traditional way of expressing them is in sentences beginning with a word of command prescribing that a certain assumption be made: 'Let ABC be a triangle, and let AB = AC.' In history they are not assumptions, they are facts, and facts coming under the historian's observation, such as, that on the page open before him there is printed what purports to be a charter by which a certain king grants certain lands to a certain monastery. The conclusions, too, are of different kinds. In exact science, they are conclusions about things which have no special habitation in space or time: if they are anywhere, they are everywhere, and if they are at any time they are at all times. In history, they are conclusions about events, each having a place and date of its own. The exactitude with which place and date are known to the historian is variable; but he always knows that there were both a place and a date, and within limits he always knows what they were; this knowledge being part of the conclusion to which he is led by arguing from the facts before him.

These differences in starting-point and conclusion imply a difference in the entire organization of the respective sciences. When a mathematician has made up his mind what the problem is which he desires to solve, the next step before him is to make assumptions which will enable him to solve it; and this involves an appeal to his powers of invention. When an historian has similarly made up his mind, his next business is to place himself in a position where he can say: 'The facts which I am now observing are the facts from which I can infer the solution of my problem.' His business is not to invent anything, it is to discover something. And the finished products, too, are differently organized. The scheme upon which exact sciences have been traditionally arranged depends on relations of logical priority and posteriority: one proposition is placed before a second, if under-standing of the first is needed in order that the second should be understood; the traditional scheme of arrangement in history is a chronological scheme, in which one event is placed before a second if it happened at an earlier time.

History, then, is a science, but a science of a special kind. It is a science whose business is to study events not accessible to our observation, and to study these events inferentially, arguing to them from something else which is accessible to our observation, and which the historian calls 'evidence' for the events in which he is interested.

EVIDENCE[2]

1. *History as Inferential*

History has this in common with every other science: that the historian is not allowed to claim any single piece of knowledge, except where he can justify his claim by exhibiting to himself in the first place, and secondly to anyone else who is both able and willing to follow his demonstration, the grounds upon which it is based. This is what was meant, above, by describing history as inferential. The knowledge in virtue of which a man is an historian is a knowledge of what the evidence at his disposal proves about certain events. If he or somebody else could have the very same knowledge of the very same events by way of memory, or second sight, or some Wellsian machine for looking backwards through time, this would not be historical knowledge; and the proof would be that he could not produce, either to himself or to any other critic of his claims, the evidence from which he had derived it. Critic, not sceptic; for a critic is a person able and willing to go over somebody else's thoughts for himself to see if they have been well done; whereas a sceptic is a person who will not do this; and because you cannot make a man think, any more than you can make a horse drink, there is no way of proving to a sceptic that a certain piece of thinking is sound, and no reason for taking his denials to heart. It is only by his peers that any claimant to knowledge is judged.

This necessity of justifying any claim to knowledge by exhibiting the grounds upon which it is based is a universal characteristic of science because it arises from the fact that a science is an organized body of knowledge. To say that knowledge is inferential is only another way of saying that it is organized.

---

[2] This chapter is missing in the recovered manuscript. Since it has been edited in *The Idea of History*, 252–82 (under the title 'Historical Evidence'), it is copied from that book.

What memory is, and whether it is a kind of knowledge or not, are questions that need not be considered in a book about history: for this at least is clear, in spite of what Bacon and others have said, that memory is not history, because history is a certain kind of organized or inferential knowledge, and memory is not organized, not inferential, at all. If I say 'I remember writing a letter to So-and-so last week', that is a statement of memory, but it is not an historical statement. But if I can add 'and my memory is not deceiving me; because here is his reply', then I am basing a statement about the past on evidence; I am talking history. For the same reason, there is no need in an essay like this to consider the claims of people who say that when they are in a place where a certain event has occurred[3] they can in some way see the event going on before their eyes. What actually happens on occasions like this, and whether the people to whom it happens thereby obtain knowledge of the past, are certainly interesting questions, but this is not the right place to discuss them; for even if these people do obtain knowledge of the past, it is not organized or inferential knowledge; not scientific knowledge; not history.

2. *Different Kinds of Inference*[4]

Different kinds of science are organized in different ways; and it should follow (indeed, this would seem to be only the same thing in other words) that different kinds of science are characterized by different kinds of inference. The way in which knowledge is related to the grounds upon which it is based is in fact not one and the same for all kinds of knowledge. That this is so, and that therefore a person who has studied the nature of inference as such—let us call him a logician—can correctly judge the validity of an inference purely by attending to its form, although he has no special knowledge of its subject-matter, is a doctrine of Aristotle; but it is a delusion, although it is still believed by many very able persons who have been trained too exclusively in

---

[3] The text of *IH* says 'recurred' (253) but this is apparently a mistake.

[4] In a table of contents found in the manuscript the subtitle reads 'Kinds of Inference'.

the Aristotelian logic and the logics that depend upon it for their chief doctrines.[5]

The main scientific achievement of the ancient Greeks lay in mathematics; their main work on the logic of inference was naturally, therefore, devoted to that form of inference which occurs in exact science. When at the end of the Middle Ages the modern natural sciences of observation and experiment began to take shape, a revolt against Aristotelian logic was inevitable; in particular, a revolt against the Aristotelian theory of demonstration, which could by no manner of means be made to cover the technique actually used in the new sciences. Thus, by degrees, there came into existence a new logic of inference, based on analysis of the procedure used in the new natural sciences. The textbooks of logic in use today still bear the marks of this revolt in the distinction they draw between two kinds of inference, 'deductive' and 'inductive'. It was not until late in the nineteenth century that historical thought reached a stage of development comparable with that reached by natural science about the beginning of the seventeenth; but this event has not yet begun to interest those philosophers who write textbooks of logic.

The chief characteristic of inference in the exact sciences, the characteristic of which Greek logicians tried to give a theoretical account when they formulated the rules of the syllogism, is a kind of logical compulsion whereby a person who makes certain assumptions is forced, simply by so doing, to make others. He has freedom of choice in two ways: he is not compelled to make the initial assumption (a fact technically expressed by saying that 'the starting-points of demonstrative reasoning are not themselves demonstrable'), and when once he has done so he is still at liberty, whenever he likes, to stop thinking. What he cannot do is to make the initial assumption, to go on thinking, and

---

[5] † The reader will perhaps forgive me a personal reminiscence here. I was still a young man when a very distinguished visitor addressed an academic society on an archaeological subject that came within my special field of studies. The point he made was new and revolutionary, and it was easy for me to see that he had proved it up to the hilt. I imagined, foolishly enough, that so lucid and cogent a piece of reasoning must convince any hearer, even one who previously knew nothing about its subject-matter. I was at first much disconcerted, but in the long run greatly instructed, by finding that the demonstration had quite failed to convince the (very learned and acute) logicians in the audience.

to arrive at a conclusion different from that which is scientifically correct.

In what is called 'inductive' thinking there is no such compulsion. The essence of the process, here, is that having put certain observations together, and having found that they make a pattern, we extrapolate this pattern indefinitely, just as a man who has plotted a few points on squared paper and says to himself 'the points I have plotted suggest a parabola', proceeds to draw as much of the parabola as he likes in either direction. This is technically described as 'proceeding from the known to the unknown', or 'from the particular to the universal'. It is essential to 'inductive' thinking, though the logicians who have tried to construct a theory of such thinking have not always realized this, that the step so described is never taken under any kind of logical compulsion. The thinker who takes it is logically free to take it or not to take it, just as he pleases. There is nothing in the pattern formed by the observations he or someone else has actually made which can oblige him to extrapolate in that particular way, or indeed to extrapolate at all. The reason why this very obvious truth has been so often overlooked is that people have been hypnotized by the prestige of Aristotelian logic into thinking that they see a closer resemblance than actually exists between 'deductive' and 'inductive' thinking, that is, between exact science and the sciences of observation and experiment. In both cases there are, for any given piece of thinking, certain starting-points, traditionally called premisses, and a certain terminal point, traditionally called a conclusion; and in both cases the premisses 'prove' the conclusion. But whereas in exact science this means that they enforce the conclusion, or make it logically obligatory, in the sciences of observation and experiment it means only that they justify it, that is, authorize anybody to think it who wishes to do so. What they provide, when they are said to 'prove' a certain conclusion, is not compulsion to embrace it, but only permission; a perfectly legitimate sense of the word 'prove' (*approuver*, *probare*), as there should be no need to show.

If in practice this permission, like so many permissions, amounts to virtual compulsion, that is only because the thinker who avails himself of it does not regard himself as free to extrapolate or not, just as he pleases. He regards himself as under an obligation to do so, and to do it in certain ways: obligations which, when we inquire into their history, we find to have their roots in certain religious beliefs about nature and its creator God. It would be out of place to develop this statement more fully here; but not, perhaps, to add that if today it seems to some readers paradoxical, that is only because the facts have been obscured by a smoke-screen of propagandist literature, beginning with the 'illuminist' movement of the eighteenth century and prolonged by the 'conflict between religion and science' in the nineteenth, whose purpose was to attack Christian theology in the supposed interests of a 'scientific view of the world' which in fact is based upon it and could not for a moment survive its destruction. Take away Christian theology, and the scientist has no longer any motive for doing what inductive thought gives him permission to do. If he goes on doing it at all, that is only because he is blindly following the conventions of the professional society to which he belongs.

3. *Testimony*

Before trying to describe the special characteristics of historical inference positively, we shall find it useful to describe them negatively: to describe something that is very often, but mistakenly, identified with it. Like every science, history is autonomous. The historian has the right, and is under an obligation, to make up his own mind by the methods proper to his own science as to the correct solution of every problem that arises for him in the pursuit of that science. He can never be under any obligation, or have any right, to let someone else make up his mind for him. If anyone else, no matter who, even a very learned historian, or an eyewitness, or a person in the confidence of the man who did the thing he is inquiring into, or even the man who did it himself, hands him on a plate a ready-made answer to his question, all he can do is to reject it: not because he thinks his informant is trying to deceive him, or is himself deceived, but because if he accepts it he is giving up his autonomy as an historian and allowing someone else to do for him what, if he is a scientific thinker, he can only do for himself. There is no need for me to offer the reader any proof of this statement. If he knows anything of historical work, he already knows of his own experience that it is true. If he does not already know that it is true, he does not know enough about history to read this essay with any profit, and the best thing he can do is to stop here and now.

When the historian accepts a ready-made answer to some question he has asked, given him by another person, this other person is called his 'authority', and the statement made by such an authority and accepted by the historian is called 'testimony'. In so far as an historian accepts the testimony of an authority and treats it as historical truth, he obviously forfeits the name of historian; but we have no other name by which to call him.

Now, I am not for a moment suggesting that testimony ought never to be accepted. In the practical life of every day, we constantly and rightly accept the information that other people offer us, believing them to be both well informed and truthful, and having, sometimes, grounds for this belief. I do not even deny, though I do not assert it, that there may be cases in which, as perhaps in some cases of memory, our acceptance of such testimony may go beyond mere belief and deserve the name of knowledge. What I assert is that it can never be historical knowledge, because it can never be scientific knowledge. It is not scientific knowledge because it cannot be vindicated by appeal to the grounds on which it is based. As soon as there are such grounds, the case is no longer one of testimony. When testimony is reinforced by evidence, our acceptance of it is no longer the acceptance of testimony as such; it is the affirmation of something based upon evidence, that is, historical knowledge.

4. *Scissors and Paste*

There is a kind of history which depends altogether upon the testimony of authorities. As I have already said, it is not really history at all, but we have no other name for it. The method by which it proceeds is first to decide what we want to know about, and then to go in search of statements about it, oral or written, purporting to be made by actors in the events concerned, or by eyewitnesses of them, or by persons repeating what actors or eyewitnesses have told them, or have told their informants, or those who informed their informants, and so on. Having found in such a statement something relevant to his purpose, the historian excerpts it and incorporates it, translated if necessary and recast into what he considers a suitable style, in his own history. As a rule, where he has many statements to draw upon, he will find that one of them tells him what another does not; so both or all of them will be incorporated. Sometimes he will find that one of them contradicts another; then, unless he can find a way of reconciling them, he must decide to leave one out; and this, if he is conscientious, will involve him in a critical consideration of the contradictory authorities' relative degree of trustworthiness. And sometimes one of them, or possibly even all of them, will tell him a story which he simply cannot believe, a story characteristic, perhaps, of the superstitions or prejudices of the author's time or the circle in which he lived, but not credible to a more enlightened age, and therefore to be omitted.

History constructed by excerpting and combining the testimonies of different authorities I call scissors-and-paste history. I repeat that it is not really history at all, because it does not satisfy the necessary conditions of science; but until lately it was the only kind of history in existence, and a great deal of the history people are still reading today, and even a good deal of what people are still writing, belongs to this type. Consequently people who know little about history (some of whom, in spite of my recent farewell, may still be reading these pages) will say with some impatience: 'Why, this thing that you say is not history, is just history itself; scissors and paste, that is what history is; and that is why history is not a science, which is a fact that everybody knows, in spite of groundless claims by professional historians magnifying their office.' I shall therefore say a little more about the vicissitudes of scissors-and-paste history.

Scissors and paste was the only historical method known to the later Greco-Roman world or the Middle Ages. It existed in its simplest form. An historian collected testimony, spoken or written, using his own judgment as to its trustworthiness, and put it together for publication: the work which he did on it being partly literary—the presentation of his material as a connected, homogeneous, and convincing narrative—and partly rhetorical, if I may use that word to indicate the fact that most ancient and medieval historians aimed at proving a thesis, in particular some philosophical or political or theological thesis.

It was only in the seventeenth century, when the post-medieval reform of natural science had attained completion, that historians began to think their house also needed to be set in order. Two new movements in historical method now began. One was a systematic examination of authorities, in order to determine their relative credibility, and in particular to establish principles according to which this determination should be carried out. The other was a movement to broaden the basis of history by making use of non-literary sources, such as coins and inscriptions and suchlike relics of antiquity which hitherto had been of interest not to historians but only to collectors of curiosities.

The first of these movements did not overstep the limits of scissors-and-paste history, but it permanently altered its character. As soon as it became understood that a given statement, made by a given author, must never be accepted for historical truth until the credibility of the author in general and of this statement in particular had been systematically inquired into, the word 'authority' disappeared from the vocabulary of historical method, except as an archaistic survival; for the man who makes the statement came henceforth to be regarded not as someone whose word must be taken for the truth of what he says, which is what was meant by calling him an authority, but as someone who has voluntarily placed himself in the witness-box for cross-examination. The document hitherto called an authority now acquired a new status, properly described by calling it a 'source', a word indicating simply that it contains the statement, without any implications as to its value. That is *sub judice*; and it is the historian who judges.

This is 'critical history', as it was worked out from the seventeenth century onwards, and officially acclaimed in the nineteenth as the apotheosis of the historical consciousness. There are two things to observe about it: that it was still only a form of scissors and paste; and that it had already, in principle, been superseded by something very different.

(1) The problem of which historical criticism offers a solution is a problem interesting to nobody but the practitioner of scissors-and-paste history. The presupposition of the problem is that in a certain source we have found a certain statement which bears on our subject. The problem is: Shall we incorpo-

rate this statement in our own narrative or not? The methods of historical criticism are intended to solve this problem in one or other of two ways: affirmatively or negatively. In the first case, the excerpt is passed as fit for the scrap-book; in the second, it is consigned to the waste-paper basket.

(2) But many historians in the nineteenth century, and even in the eighteenth, were aware that this dilemma was fallacious. It was by now a commonplace that if in some source you found a statement which for some reason could not be accepted as literally true, you must not on that account reject it as worthless. It might be a way, perhaps a well-established way according to the custom of the time when it was written, of saying something which you, through ignorance of that custom, did not recognize as its meaning.

The first person to make this point was Vico, at the beginning of the eighteenth century. It is true that in Germany, the home of 'critical history' in the late eighteenth and early nineteenth centuries, the importance of Vico's work was not as widely recognized as it ought to have been; but he was not entirely unknown there; indeed, some very famous German scholars, like F. A. Wolf, actually borrowed some of his ideas. Now, any-one who had read Vico, or even a second-hand version of some of his ideas, must have known that the important question about any statement contained in a source is not whether it is true or false, but what it means. And to ask what it means is to step right outside the world of scissors-and-paste history into a world where history is not written by copying out the testimony of the best sources, but by coming to your own conclusions.

Critical history is of interest to the student of historical method today only as the final form taken by scissors-and-paste history on the eve of its dissolution. I will not venture to name any historian, or even any historical work, as one from which the last traces of it have disappeared. But I will venture to say that any historian (if there is any) who practises it consistently, or any historical work written entirely on this method, is at least a century out of date.

So much for one of the two movements which gave new life to history in the seventeenth century. The other, the archaeologi-cal movement, was totally hostile to the principles of scissors-and-paste history, and could have arisen only when those principles were moribund. No very profound knowledge of coins and inscriptions is needed in order to realize that the assertions they make are by no means uniformly trustworthy, and indeed are to be judged more as propaganda than as statements of fact. Yet this gives them an historical value of their own; for propaganda, too, has its history.

If any reader still thinks that history as practised today is a scissors-and-paste affair, and is willing to go to a little trouble in order to settle the question, let him take the history of Greece down to the end of the Peloponnesian War, which I mention as an example peculiarly favourable to himself because Herodotus and Thucydides have there maintained the position of 'authorities' to a quite peculiar degree, and compare in detail the account of it given by Grote with that given in the *Cambridge Ancient History*. Let him mark in each book every sentence of which he can find the original in Herodotus or Thucydides; and by the time he is through with the job he will have learnt something about how historical method has changed in the last hundred years.

5. *Historical Inference*

In § 2 it was pointed out that proof might be either compulsive, as in exact science, where the nature of inference is such that nobody can affirm the premisses without being obliged to affirm the conclusion also, or permissive, as in 'inductive' science, where all a proof can do is to justify the thinker in affirming its conclusion, granted that he wishes to do so. An inductive argument with a negative conclusion is compulsive, that is to say it absolutely forbids the thinker from affirming what he wishes to affirm; with a positive conclusion, it is never more than permissive.

If history means scissors-and-paste history, the only kind of proof known to the historian is of this latter kind. For the scissors-and-paste historian, there is only one kind of problem which is capable of being settled by any sort of argument. This is the problem whether to accept or reject a certain piece of testimony bearing upon the question in which he is interested. The sort of argument by which he settles a problem of this kind is, of course, historical criticism. If criticism leads him to a negative conclusion, viz. that the statement or its author is untrustworthy, this forbids him to accept it, just as a negative result in an 'inductive' argument (for example, a result showing that events of the kind in which he is interested happen in the absence of that kind of event which he hopes to identify as their cause) forbids the inductive scientist to affirm the view he hoped to affirm. If criticism leads him to a positive conclusion, the most it gives him is a *nihil obstat*. For the positive conclusion is in effect that the man who made the statement is not known to be either ignorant or mendacious, and that the statement itself bears upon it no recognizable marks of being untrue. But it may be untrue for all that: and the man who made it, though in general he bears a good name for being well informed and honest, may on this one occasion have fallen a victim to misinformation about his facts, misunderstanding of them, or a desire to suppress or distort what he knew or believed to be the truth.

To avert a possible misunderstanding, it may be added here that one might think there was another kind of problem for the scissors-and-paste historian, beside the kind which consists in whether to accept or reject a given piece of testimony, which therefore has to be settled by methods other than those of historical criticism: the problem, namely, of what implications follow from a piece of testimony that he has accepted, or would follow if he did accept it. But this is not a problem specially belonging to scissors-and-paste history; it is a problem which arises in history or pseudo-history of any kind whatever, and indeed in any kind of science or pseudo-science. It is simply the general problem of implication. When it occurs in scissors-and-paste history, however, it presents one peculiar feature. If a certain statement coming to the historian by way of testimony has a certain implication, and if this implicational relation is a compulsive one, nevertheless if the inference which leads him to accept the testimony is only permissive the same permissive character attaches to his assertion of its implication. If he has only borrowed his neighbour's cow, and she has a calf in his field, he cannot claim the calf as his own property. Any answer to the question whether the scissors-and-paste historian is obliged or only permitted to accept certain testimony carries with it a corresponding answer to the question whether he is

obliged or only permitted to accept the implications of that testimony.

One hears it said that history is 'not an exact science'. The meaning of this I take to be that no historical argument ever proves its conclusion with that compulsive force which is characteristic of exact science. Historical inference, the saying seems to mean, is never compulsive, it is at best permissive; or, as people sometimes rather ambiguously say, it never leads to certainty, only to probability. Many historians of the present writer's generation, brought up at a time when this proverb was accepted by the general opinion of intelligent persons (I say nothing of the few who were a generation ahead of their time), must be able to recollect their excitement on first discovering that it was wholly untrue, and that they were actually holding in their hands an historical argument which left nothing to caprice, and admitted of no alternative conclusion, but proved its point as conclusively as a demonstration in mathematics. Many of these, again, must be able to recollect the shock of discovering on reflection that the proverb was not, strictly speaking, an error about history, history as they were practising it, the science of history, but a truth about something else, namely scissors-and-paste history.

If any reader wishes to rise here on a point of order and protest that a philosophical question, which ought therefore to be settled by reasoning, is being illegitimately disposed of by reference to the authority of historians, and quote against me the good old story about the man who said 'I'm not arguing, I'm telling you', I can only admit that the cap fits. I am not arguing; I am telling him.

Is this wrong of me? The question I want settled is whether an inference of the kind used in scientific history, as distinct from scissors-and-paste history, yields compulsion or only permission to embrace its conclusion. Suppose the question had been not about history but about mathematics. Suppose somebody had wanted to know whether Euclid's proof of what is called Pythagoras' theorem compels or merely permits a man to adopt the view that the square on the hypotenuse is equal to the sum of the squares on the other two sides. I speak with submission; but for myself I can think of only one thing that a sensible man in that situation would do. He would try to find somebody

whose mathematical education had got as far as Euclid I. 47, and ask him. And if he did not like his answer, he would look for other people similarly qualified to give one, and ask them. If all else failed to convince him, he would have to get down to it and study the elements of plane geometry for himself.

The one thing that he will not do, if he is a man of any intelligence, is to say 'This is a philosophical question, and the only answer I will be satisfied with is a philosophical answer.' He can call it anything he pleases; he cannot alter the fact that the only way of knowing whether a given type of argument is cogent or not is to learn how to argue that way, and find out. Meanwhile, the second best thing is to take the word of people who have done so for themselves.

6. *Pigeon-holing*

Scissors-and-paste historians who have become disgusted with the work of copying out other people's statements, and, conscious of having brains, feel a laudable desire to use them, are often found satisfying this desire by inventing a system of pigeon-holes in which to arrange their learning. This is the origin of all those schemes and patterns into which history has again and again, with surprising docility, allowed itself to be forced by such men as Vico, with his pattern of historical cycles based on Greco-Roman speculations; Kant, with his proposal for a 'universal history from a cosmopolitan point of view'; Hegel, who followed Kant in conceiving universal history as the progressive realization of human freedom; Comte and Marx, two very great men who followed Hegel's lead each in his own way; and so on down to Flinders Petrie, Oswald Spengler, and Arnold Toynbee in our own time, whose affinities are less with Hegel than with Vico.

Although we find it as late as the twentieth century and as early as the eighteenth, not to mention isolated occurrences even earlier, this impulse towards arranging the whole of history in a single scheme (not a chronological scheme merely, but a qualitative scheme, in which 'periods' each with its own pervasive character follow one another in time, according to a pattern which may be necessary *a priori* on logical grounds, or may be forced upon our minds by the fact of its frequent repetition, or may be a bit of both) is in the main a nineteenth-century phe-nomenon. It belongs to the period when scissors-and-paste his-tory was on its last legs; when people were becoming dissatisfied with it but had not yet broken away from it. This is why the people who have indulged [in] it have been, in general, men with a high degree of intelligence and a real talent for history, but a talent which has been to some extent thwarted and baffled by the limitations of scissors and paste.

It is typical of this condition that some of them described their pigeon-holing enterprise as 'raising history to the rank of a science'. History as they found it meant scissors-and-paste his-tory; that, obviously, was no science, because there was nothing autonomous, nothing creative, about it; it was merely the trans-shipment of ready-made information from one mind into another. They were conscious that history might be something more than this. It might have, and it ought to have, the charac-teristics of a science. But how was this to be brought about? At this point the analogy of the natural sciences came, they thought, to their aid. It had been a commonplace ever since Bacon that a natural science began by collecting facts, and then went on to construct theories, that is, to extrapolate the patterns discernible in the facts already collected. Very well: let us put together all the facts that are known to historians, look for pat-terns in them, and then extrapolate these patterns into a theory of universal history.

It proved to be not at all a difficult task for anybody with an active mind and a taste for hard work. For there was no need to collect all the facts known to historians. Any large collection of facts, it was found, revealed patterns in plenty; and extrapolat-ing such patterns into the remote past, about which there was very little information, and into the future, about which there was none, gave the 'scientific' historian just that sense of power which scissors-and-paste history denied him. After being taught to believe that he, as an historian, could never know any-thing except what his authorities told him, he found himself dis-covering, as he fancied, that this lesson had been a fraud; that by converting history into a science he could ascertain, entirely for himself, things that his authorities had concealed from him or did not know.

This was a delusion. The value of each and all of these pigeon-holing schemes, if that means their value as means for discovering historical truths not ascertainable by the interpretation of evidence, was exactly nil. And in fact none of them ever had any scientific value at all; for it is not enough that science should be autonomous or creative, it must also be cogent or objective; it must impress itself as inevitable on anyone who is able and willing to consider the grounds upon which it is based, and to think for himself what the conclusions are to which they point. That is what none of these schemes can do. They are the offspring of caprice. If any of them has ever been accepted by any considerable body of persons beside the one who invented it, that is not because it has struck them as scientifically cogent, but because it has become the orthodoxy of what is in fact, though not necessarily in name, a religious community. This was to some extent achieved by Comtism, and to a much greater extent by Marxism. In these cases, or at any rate in the case of Marxism, historical schemes of the kind in question proved to have an important magical value, as providing a focus for emotions and in consequence an incentive to action. In other cases they have had an amusement value, not without its function in the life of a jaded scissors-and-paste man.[6]

And the delusion was not complete. The hope that scissors-and-paste history would one day be replaced by a new kind of history that should be genuinely scientific was a well-grounded hope, which has in fact been realized. The hope that this new kind of history would enable the historian to know things that his authorities could not or would not tell him was also well grounded, and has also been fulfilled. How these things have happened, we shall very soon see.

7. Who Killed John Doe?

When John Doe was found, early one Sunday morning, lying across his desk with a dagger through his back, no one expected that the question who did it would be settled by means of testimony. It was not likely that anyone saw the murder being done.

[6] The subjects of emotions, magic, and amusement, especially in relation to art, are discussed by Collingwood in *The Principles of Art*, 31–2, 65–9, 78–104.

It was even less likely that someone in the murderer's confidence would give him away. It was least likely of all that the murderer would walk into the village police-station and denounce himself. In spite of this, the public demanded that he should be brought to justice, and the police had hopes of doing it; though the only clue was a little fresh green paint on the handle of the dagger, like the fresh green paint on the iron gate between John Doe's garden and the rector's.

This was not because they hoped that, in time, testimony would be forthcoming. On the contrary, when it did come, in the shape of a visit from an elderly neighbouring spinster asserting that she killed John Doe with her own hand because he had made a dastardly attempt upon her virtue, even the village constable (not an exceptionally bright lad, but kindly) advised her to go home and have some aspirin. Later in the day the village poacher came along and said that he had seen the squire's gamekeeper climbing in at John Doe's study window; testimony which was treated with even less deference. Finally the rector's daughter, in a state of great agitation, rushed in and said she had done it herself; the only effect of which was to make the village constable ring up the local Inspector and remind him that the girl's young man, Richard Roe, was a medical student, and presumably knew where to find a man's heart; and that he had spent Saturday night at the rectory, within a stone's throw of the dead man's house.

There had been a thunderstorm that night, with heavy rain, between twelve and one; and the Inspector, when he questioned the rectory parlour-maid (for the living was a good one), was told that Mr. Roe's shoes had been very wet in the morning. Questioned, Richard admitted having gone out in the middle of the night, but refused to say where or why.

John Doe was a blackmailer. For years he had been blackmailing the rector, threatening to publish the facts about a certain youthful escapade of his dead wife. Of this escapade the rector's supposed daughter, born six months after marriage, was the fruit; and John Doe had letters in his possession that proved it. By now he had absorbed the whole of the rector's private fortune, and on the morning of the fatal Saturday he demanded an instalment of his wife's, which she had left to him in trust for her child. The rector made up his mind to end it. He knew that John

Doe sat at his desk late into the night; he knew that behind him, as he sat, there was a french window on the left and a trophy of Eastern weapons on the right; and that on hot nights the window was left open until he went to bed. At midnight, wearing gloves, he slipped out; but Richard, who had noticed his state of mind and was troubled about it, happened to be leaning out of his window and saw the rector cross the garden. He hurried into his clothes and followed; but by the time he reached the garden the rector was gone. At this moment the thunderstorm broke. Meanwhile the rector's plan had succeeded perfectly. John Doe was asleep, his head fallen forward on a pile of old letters. Only after the dagger had reached his heart did the rector look at them, and see his wife's handwriting. The envelopes were addressed 'John Doe, Esq.' Until that moment, he had never known who his wife's seducer had been.

It was Detective-Inspector Jenkins of Scotland Yard, called in by the Chief Constable at the entreaty of his old friend's little girl, who found in the rectory dustbin a lot of ashes, mostly from writing paper, but including some from leather, probably a pair of gloves. The wet paint on John Doe's garden gate—he had painted it himself that day, after tea—explained why the gloves might have been destroyed; and among the ashes were metal buttons bearing the name of a famous glove-maker in Oxford Street whom the rector always patronized. More of John Doe's paint was found on the right cuff of a jacket, ruined as to shape by a recent wetting, which on Monday the rector bestowed on a deserving parishioner. The Detective-Inspector was severely blamed, later on, for allowing the rector to see in what direction his inquiries were tending, and thus giving him an opportunity to take cyanide and cheat the hangman.

The methods of criminal detection are not at every point identical with those of scientific history, because their ultimate purpose is not the same. A criminal court has in its hands the life and liberty of a citizen, and in a country where the citizen is regarded as having rights the court is therefore bound to do something and do it quickly. The time taken to arrive at a decision is a factor in the value (that is, the justice) of the decision itself. If any juror says: 'I feel certain that a year hence, when we have all reflected on the evidence at leisure, we shall be in a better position to see what it means,' the reply will be: 'There is something in what you say; but what you propose is impossible. Your business is not just to give a verdict; it is to give a verdict now; and here you stay until you do it.' This is why a jury has to content itself with something less than scientific (historical) proof, namely with that degree of assurance or belief which would satisfy it in any of the practical affairs of daily life.

The student of historical method will hardly find it worth his while, therefore, to go closely into the rules of evidence, as these are recognized in courts of law. For the historian is under no obligation to make up his mind within any stated time. Nothing matters to him except that his decision, when he reaches it, shall be right: which means, for him, that it shall follow inevitably from the evidence.

So long as this is borne in mind, however, the analogy between legal methods and historical methods is of some value for the understanding of history; of sufficient value, I think, to justify my having put before the reader in outline the above sample of a literary genre which in the absence of any such motive it would, of course, be beneath his dignity to notice.

8. *The Question*

Francis Bacon, lawyer and philosopher, laid it down in one of his memorable phrases that the natural scientist must 'put Nature to the question'. What he was denying, when he wrote this, was that the scientist's attitude towards nature should be one of respectful attentiveness, waiting upon her utterances and building his theories on the basis of what she chose to vouchsafe him. What he was asserting was two things at once: first, that the scientist must take the initiative, deciding for himself what he wants to know and formulating this in his own mind in the shape of a question; and secondly, that he must find means of compelling nature to answer, devising tortures under which she can no longer hold her tongue. Here, in a single brief epigram, Bacon laid down once for all the true theory of experimental science.

It is also, though Bacon did not know this, the true theory of historical method. In scissors-and-paste history the historian takes up a pre-Baconian position. His attitude towards his

authorities, as the very word shows, is one of respectful attentiveness. He waits to hear what they choose to tell him, and lets
them tell it in their own way and at their own time. Even when
he has invented historical criticism, and his authorities have
become mere sources, this attitude is at bottom unchanged.
There is a change, but it is only superficial. It consists merely in
the adoption of a technique for dividing witnesses into sheep
and goats. One class is disqualified from giving testimony; the
other is treated exactly as authorities were treated under the old
dispensation. But in scientific history, or history proper, the
Baconian revolution has been accomplished. The scientific historian no doubt spends a great deal of time reading the same
books that the scissors-and-paste historian used to read—
Herodotus, Thucydides, Livy, Tacitus, and so forth—but he
reads them in an entirely different spirit; in fact, a Baconian
spirit. The scissors-and-paste historian reads them in a simply
receptive spirit, to find out what they said. The scientific historian reads them with a question in his mind, having taken the
initiative by deciding for himself what he wants to find out from
them. Further, the scissors-and-paste historian reads them on
the understanding that what they did not tell him in so many
words he would never find out from them at all; the scientific
historian puts them to the torture, twisting a passage ostensibly
about something quite different into an answer to the question
he has decided to ask. Where the scissors-and-paste historian
said quite confidently 'There is nothing in such-and-such an
author about such-and-such a subject', the scientific or
Baconian historian will reply 'Oh, isn't there? Do you not see
that in this passage about a totally different matter it is implied
that the author took such-and-such a view of the subject about
which you say his text contains nothing?'

To illustrate from my fable. The village constable does not
arrest the rector's daughter and beat her periodically with a rub-
ber truncheon until she tells him that she thinks Richard did the
murder. What he tortures is not her body, but her statement
that she killed John Doe. He begins by using the methods of
critical history. He says to himself: 'The murder was done by
somebody with a good deal of strength and some knowledge of
anatomy. This girl certainly hasn't the first, and probably
hasn't the second; at any rate, I know she has never attended

ambulance classes. Further, if she had done it she wouldn't be in such a hurry to accuse herself. The story is a lie.'

At this point the critical historian would lose interest in the story and throw it in the waste-paper basket: the scientific historian begins to be interested in it, and tests it for chemical reactions. This he is able to do because, being a scientific thinker, he knows what questions to ask. 'Why is she telling a lie? Because she is shielding someone. Whom is she shielding? Either her father or her young man. Is it her father? No; fancy the rector! Therefore it is her young man. Are her suspicions of him well founded? They might be; he was here at the time; he is strong enough; and he knows enough anatomy.' The reader will recollect that in criminal detection probability is required, of a degree sufficient for the conduct of daily life, whereas in history we demand certainty. Apart from that, the parallel is complete. The village constable (not a clever lad, as I explained; but a scientific thinker does not have to be clever, he has to know his job, that is, know what questions to ask) has been trained in the elements of police work, and this training enables him to know what questions to ask and thus to interpret the untrue statement that she did it herself into evidence for the true conclusion that she suspects Richard Roe.

The constable's only mistake was that in the excitement of answering the question 'Whom does this girl suspect?' he lost sight of the question 'Who killed John Doe?' This is where Inspector Jenkins, not so much because he was a cleverer man as because he had learned the job more thoroughly, had the advantage of him. The way I see the Inspector going to work is like this.

'Why does the rector's daughter suspect Richard Roe? Probably because she knows that he was involved in something queer which happened at the rectory that night. We know that one queer thing happened at the rectory: Richard was out in the storm, and that was quite enough to make the girl suspicious. But what we want to know is, did he kill John Doe? If he did, when did he do it? After the thunderstorm broke, or before? Not before, because here are his tracks going both ways in the mud of the rectory garden path: you see them beginning a few yards from the garden door, going away from the house; so that is where he was, and that is the direction he was going in, when the downpour began. Well, did he carry mud into John Doe's

study? No: none there. Did he take off his shoes before going in?
Think a moment. What position was John Doe in when he was
stabbed? Was he leaning back or sitting upright in his chair? No;
because the chair would have protected his back. He must have
been leaning right forward. Possibly, indeed probably, asleep in
the position in which he still lies. How exactly did the murderer
proceed? If Doe was asleep, nothing easier: step quietly inside,
take the dagger and in it goes. If Doe was awake and merely
leaning forward, the same might be done, but not so easily.
Now, did the murderer pause outside to take off his shoes?
Impossible. In either case, speed was the first thing necessary:
the job had to be done before he leaned back, or woke up. So the
absence of mud in the study lets Richard out.

'Then, once more, why did he go into the garden? For a walk?
Not with that thunderstorm growling about. For a smoke? They
smoke all over the house. To meet the girl? No signs that she
was in the garden; and why should he? They had had the draw-
ing-room to themselves ever since dinner, and the rector isn't
one to shoo young people off to bed. Broad-minded sort of chap.
Had trouble, I shouldn't wonder. Now, why did young Richard
go into that garden? Something must have been going on there.
Something queer. A second queer thing that night at the rectory, one we don't know about.

'What could it have been? If the murderer had come from the
rectory, which that paint suggests he did, and if Richard saw
him from his window, it might have been that; because the murderer got to Doe's house before the rain began, and Richard was
caught in it ten yards from the garden door. Just time. Let's see
what would follow, if the murderer did come from the rectory.
Probably he went back there afterwards. No tracks in the mud;
why? Because he knew the garden well enough to keep on the
grass all the way, even in that pitch darkness. If so, he knew the
rectory very well and also spent the night there. Was it the rector himself?

'Now why does Richard refuse to say what made him go into
the garden? It must be to keep somebody out of trouble; almost
certainly, trouble about the murder. Not himself, because I've
told we know he didn't do it. Somebody else. Who? Might
be the rector. Can't think of anybody else it might be. Suppose
it was the rector; how would he have worked it? Very easy. Go

out about midnight, in tennis shoes and gloves. Quite silent on the rectory path—no gravel on them. Reach that little iron gate into John Doe's garden. Does he know it's wet paint? Probably not; it was only painted after tea. So he grabs it. Paint on glove. Probably paint on jacket too. Walk on the grass to Doe's study window. Doe is leaning forward in his chair, or likelier asleep. Now for a bit of quick work, easy for a good tennis-player. Left foot inside, right foot to the right, grab that dagger thing, left foot forward, in it goes.

'But what had John Doe been doing at that desk? Nothing on it, you know. Queer. Does a man spend the evening sitting at an empty desk? There must have been something there. What do we know about the chap at the Yard? Blackmailer, that's it. Had he been blackmailing the rector? and gloating over the letters, or what not, all evening? And did the rector, if it was the rector, find him asleep on top of them? Well, that's not our business. We'll pass it on to the defence, for what it's worth. I'd rather not use a motive like that in prosecution.

'Now then, Jonathan, don't go ahead too fast. You've got him in there, you've got to get him out again. What exactly does he do? About now it begins to rain cats and dogs. Back he goes through it. More paint at the gate. Walk on grass, no mud brought in. Back in the house. All soaked: gloves covered with paint, too. Wipe paint off door-knob. Lock up. Put letters (if it was letters), and anyhow gloves, in the hot-water furnace—the ashes may be in the dustbin now. Put all clothes in the bathroom cupboard; they will be dry by morning. And so they are; but the jacket will be hopelessly out of shape. Now what did he do with that jacket? First, he'd look for paint on it. If he found paint, he'd have to destroy the thing; and I pity the man who tries to destroy a jacket in a house overrun with women. If he didn't find any, he would certainly give it away on the quiet to a poor man.

'Well, well: there's a pretty story for you; but how can we tell whether it's true or not? There are two questions we've got to ask. First: can we find the ashes of those gloves? And the metal buttons, if they are like most of his gloves? If we can, the story is true. And if we can find a lot of writing-paper ash as well, the blackmail bit is true, too. Second: where is that jacket? Because if we can find the tiniest speck of John Doe's paint on it, there's our case.'

I have gone to some length in this analysis because I wish to bring home to the reader the following points about the questioning activity which is the dominant factor in history, as it is in all scientific work.

(1) Every step in the argument depends on asking a question. The question is the charge of gas, exploded in the cylinder-head, which is the motive force of every piston-stroke. But the metaphor is not adequate, because each new piston-stroke is produced not by exploding another charge of the same old mixture but by exploding a charge of a new kind. No one with any grasp of method will go on asking the same question all the time, 'Who killed John Doe?' He asks a new question every time. And it is not enough to cover the ground by having a catalogue of all the questions that have to be asked, and asking every one of them sooner or later: they must be asked in the right order. Descartes, one of the three great masters of the Logic of Questioning (the other two being Socrates and Bacon), insisted upon this as a cardinal point in scientific method, but so far as modern works on logic are concerned, Descartes might never have lived. Modern logicians are in a conspiracy to pretend that a scientist's business is to 'make judgments', or 'assert propositions', or 'apprehend facts', and also to 'assert' or 'apprehend' the relations between them; suggesting that they have no experience whatever of scientific thinking, and wish to palm off, as an account of science, an account of their own haphazard, unsystematic, unscientific consciousness.

(2) These questions are not put by one man to another man, in the hope that the second man will enlighten the first man's ignorance by answering them. They are put, like all scientific questions, to the scientist by himself. This is the Socratic idea which Plato was to express by defining thought as 'the dialogue of the soul with itself', where Plato's own literary practice makes it clear that by dialogue he meant a process of question and answer. When Socrates taught his young pupils by asking them questions, he was teaching them how to ask questions of themselves, and showing them by examples how amazingly the obscurest subjects can be illuminated by asking oneself intelligent questions about them instead of simply gaping at them, according to the prescription of our modern anti-scientific epistemologists, in the hope that when we have made our minds a perfect blank we shall 'apprehend the facts'.

9. *Statement and Evidence*

It is characteristic of scissors-and-paste history, from its least critical to its most critical form, that it has to do with ready-made statements, and that the historian's problem about any one of these statements is whether he shall accept it or not: where accepting it means reasserting it as a part of his own historical knowledge. Essentially, history for the scissors-and-paste historian means repeating statements that other people have made before him. Hence he can get to work only when he is supplied with ready-made statements on the subjects about which he wants to think, write, and so forth. It is the fact that these statements have to be found by him ready made in his sources that makes it impossible for the scissors-and-paste historian to claim the title of a scientific thinker, for this fact makes it impossible to attribute to him that autonomy which is everywhere essential to scientific thought; where by autonomy I mean the condition of being one's own authority, making statements or taking action on one's own initiative and not because those statements or actions are authorized or prescribed by anyone else.

It follows that scientific history contains no ready-made statements at all. The act of incorporating a ready-made statement into the body of his own historical knowledge is an act which, for a scientific historian, is impossible. Confronted with a ready-made statement about the subject he is studying, the scientific historian never asks himself: 'Is this statement true or false?', in other words 'Shall I incorporate it in my history of that subject or not?' The question he asks himself is: 'What does this statement mean?' And this is not equivalent to the question 'What did the person who made it mean by it?', although that is doubtless a question that the historian must ask, and must be able to answer. It is equivalent, rather, to the question 'What light is thrown on the subject in which I am interested by the fact that this person made this statement, meaning by it what he did mean?' This might be expressed by saying that the scientific historian does not treat statements as statements but as evidence: not as true or false accounts of the facts of which they profess to be accounts, but as other facts which, if he knows the right questions to ask about them, may throw light on those facts. Thus in my fable the rector's daughter tells the constable that she killed John Doe. As a scientific historian, he begins attending seriously to this statement at the point where he stops treating it as a statement, that is, as a true or false account of her having done the murder, and begins treating the fact that she makes it as a fact which may be of service to him. It is of service to him because he knows what questions to ask about it, beginning with the question: 'Now why does she tell this story?' The scissors-and-paste historian is interested in the 'content', as it is called, of statements: he is interested in what they state. The scientific historian is interested in the fact that they are made.

A statement to which an historian listens, or one which he reads, is to him a ready-made statement. But the statement that such a statement is being made is not a ready-made statement. If he says to himself 'I am now reading or hearing a statement to such and such effect', he is himself making a statement; but it is not a second-hand statement, it is autonomous. He makes it on his own authority. And it is this autonomous statement that is the scientific historian's starting-point. The evidence from which the constable infers that the rector's daughter suspects Richard Roe is not her statement 'I killed John Doe', but his own statement 'the rector's daughter tells me that she killed John Doe'.

If the scientific historian gets his conclusions not from the statement that he finds ready made, but from his own autonomous statement of the fact that such statements are made, he can get conclusions even when no statements are made to him. The premisses of his argument are his own autonomous statements: there is no need for these autonomous statements to be themselves statements about other statements. To illustrate once more from the story of John Doe. The premisses from which the Detective-Inspector argued to the innocence of Richard Roe were all premisses of the Detective-Inspector's own stating, autonomous statements resting on no authority but his own: and not one of them was a statement about statements made by anybody else. The essential points were that Richard Roe had got his shoes muddy while going away from the rectory, that no mud was to be seen in John Doe's study, and that the circumstances of the murder had been such that he would not have stopped to clean or remove his shoes. Each of these three points,

in its turn, was the conclusion of an inference, and the statements upon which they severally rested were no more statements about other people's statements than were these three
points themselves. Again: the ultimate case against the rector
did not logically depend upon any statements made by the
Detective-Inspector about statements made by other persons. It
depended upon the presence of certain objects in a certain dustbin, and of certain paint-smears on the cuff of a jacket made in
the conventional clerical style and shrunk by wetting; and these
facts were vouched for by his own observation. I do not mean
that the scientific historian can work better when no statements
are made to him about the subjects on which he is working; it
would be a pedantical way of avoiding scissors-and-paste history to avoid occasions of this type which might be a trap for the
weaker brethren; what I mean is that he is not dependent on
such statements being made.

This is important because it settles by appeal to principle a
controversy which, even if it is no longer so urgent as it was, has
not yet ceased to echo in the minds of historians. This was the
controversy between those who maintained that history was
ultimately dependent on 'written sources', and those who maintained that it could also be constructed from 'unwritten
sources'. The terms were unhappily chosen. 'Written sources'
were not conceived as excluding oral sources, or as having any
special connexion with handwriting as distinct from chiselling
in stone or the like. 'Written sources', in fact, meant sources
containing ready-made statements asserting or implying alleged
facts belonging to the subject in which the historian was interested. 'Unwritten sources' meant archaeological material,
potsherds, and so forth, connected with the same subject. Of
course, the word 'source' was in no sense applicable to these, for
a source means something from which water or the like is drawn
ready made; in the case of history, something from which the
historian's statements are drawn ready made, and the point of
describing potsherds as 'unwritten sources' was to indicate that,
not being texts, they contained no ready-made statements and
were therefore not sources. (Inscribed potsherds or 'ostraka'
were, of course, 'written sources'.)

In effect, this was a controversy between people who believed
that scissors-and-paste history was the only possible kind and

people who, without impugning the validity of scissors-and-paste methods, claimed that there could be history without them. According to my own recollection the controversy was alive, though giving one an impression of obsolescence, in academic circles in this country thirty years ago; all statements of the issue, so far as I can recall them, were extremely confused, and the philosophers of the time, though it gave them an excellent opportunity for doing a useful job of work on a subject of high philosophical interest, cared for none of these things. My impression is that the controversy fizzled out in the feeblest of compromises, the partisans of scissors-and-paste history accepting the principle that 'unwritten sources' could give valid results, but insisting that this could happen only on a very small scale and when they were used as an auxiliary arm to 'written sources'; and only about low matters like industry and commerce, into which an historian with the instincts of a gentleman would not inquire. This amounted to saying that historians brought up to regard history as an affair of scissors and paste were beginning, very timidly, to recognize the possibility of something quite different; but that when they tried to convert this possibility into an actuality they were still too incompletely fledged for any but the shortest flights.

10. *Question and Evidence*

If history means scissors-and-paste history, where the historian depends on ready-made statements for all his knowledge about his subject, and where the texts in which he finds these statements are called his sources, it is easy to define a source in a way which has some practical utility. A source is a text containing a statement or statements about the subject; and this definition has some practical utility because it helps the historian to divide the whole of extant literature, once he has determined his subject, into texts which might serve him as sources, and must therefore be looked at, and those which cannot, and may therefore be ignored. What he has to do is to run over his library shelves, or his bibliography of the period, asking himself at every title: 'Could this contain anything about my subject?' And, in case he cannot give the answer out of his head, aids of several kinds have been provided: notably indexes and special-ized or classified bibliographies. Even with all these aids, he may still miss an important piece of testimony, and thus provide sport for his friends; but on any given question the amount of testimony that exists is a finite quantity, and it is theoretically possible to exhaust it.

Theoretically, but not always practically: for the amount may be so large, and some parts of it so difficult of access, that no his-torian can hope to see it all. And one sometimes hears people complaining that nowadays so much raw material for history is being preserved that the task of using it is becoming impossible; and sighing for the good old days when books were few and libraries small, and an historian could hope to master his sub-ject. What these complaints mean is that the scissors-and-paste historian is on the horns of a dilemma. If he possesses only a small amount of testimony about his subject, he wants more; because any new piece of testimony about it would, if really new, throw new light on it, and might make the view he is actu-ally putting forward untenable. So, however much testimony he has, his zeal as an historian makes him want more. But if he has a large amount of testimony, it becomes so difficult to manipu-late and work up into a convincing narrative that, speaking as a mere weak mortal, he wishes he had less.

Consciousness of this dilemma has often driven men into scepticism about the very possibility of historical knowledge. And quite rightly, if knowledge means scientific knowledge and history means scissors-and-paste history. Scissors-and-paste historians who brush the dilemma aside with the blessed word 'hypercriticism' are only confessing that in their own profes-sional practice they do not find that it troubles them, because they work to such a low standard of scientific cogency that their consciences become anaesthetized. Such cases in contemporary life are highly interesting, because in the history of science one often meets with them and wonders how such extraordinary blindness was possible. The answer is that the people who exhibit it have committed themselves to an impossible task, in this case the task of scissors-and-paste history, and since for practical reasons they cannot back out of it they have to blind themselves to its impossibility. The scissors-and-paste historian protects himself from seeing the truth about his own methods by carefully choosing subjects which he is able to 'get away' with, exactly as the nineteenth-century landscape-painter protected himself from seeing that his theory of landscape was all wrong by choosing what he called paintable subjects. The subjects must be those about which a certain amount of testimony is accessible, not too little and not too much; not so uniform as to give the historian nothing to do, not so divergent as to baffle his endeavours to do it. Practised on these principles, history was at worst a parlour game, and at best an elegant accomplishment. I have used the past tense; I leave it to the conscience of historians who are capable of self-criticism to decide how far I might justly have used the present.

If history means scientific history, for 'source' we must read 'evidence'. And when we try to define 'evidence' in the same spirit in which we defined 'sources', we find it very difficult. There is no short and easy test by which we can decide whether a given book is or is not capable of providing evidence about a given subject, and indeed no reason why we should limit our search to books. Indexes and bibliographies of sources are of no use at all to a scientific historian. This is not to say that he cannot use indexes and bibliographies; he can and does; but they are indexes and bibliographies not of sources but of monographs or the like: not of evidence, but of previous discussions which he can take as a starting-point for his own. Consequently, whereas the books mentioned in a bibliography for the use of a scissors-and-paste historian will be, roughly speaking, valuable in direct proportion to their antiquity, those mentioned in a bibliography for the use of a scientific historian will be, roughly speaking, valuable in direct proportion to their newness.

In my fable there is only one obvious characteristic common to all the pieces of evidence used by the Detective-Inspector in his argument: they are all things observed by himself. If we ask what kind of things, it is not easy to give an answer. They include such things as the existence of certain footprints in certain mud, their number, position, and direction, their resemblance to prints produced by a certain pair of shoes, and the absence of any others; the absence of mud on the floor of a certain room; the position of a dead body, the position of a dagger in its back, and the shape of the chair in which it is sitting; and so on, a most variegated collection. This, I think, we can safely say about it: that no one could possibly know what could or could not find a place in it until he had got all his questions not only formulated but answered. In scientific history anything is evidence which is used as evidence, and no one can know what is going to be useful as evidence until he has had occasion to use it.

Let us put this by saying that in scissors-and-paste history, if we allow ourselves to describe testimony—loosely, I admit— by the name of evidence, there is potential evidence and there is actual evidence. The potential evidence about a subject is all the extant statements about it. The actual evidence is that part of these statements which we decide to accept. But in scientific history the idea of potential evidence disappears; or, if we like to put the same fact in these other words, everything in the world is potential evidence for any subject whatever. This will be a distressing idea to anyone whose notions of historical method are fixed in a scissors-and-paste mould; for how, he will ask, are we to discover what facts are actually of service to us, unless we can first of all round up the facts that might be of service to us? To a person who understands the nature of scientific thinking, whether historical or any other, it will present no difficulty. He will realize that, every time the historian asks a question, he asks it because he thinks he can answer it: that is to say, he has already in his mind a preliminary and tentative idea of the evidence he will be able to use. Not a definite idea about potential evidence, but an indefinite idea about actual evidence. To ask questions which you see no prospect of answering is the fundamental sin in science, like giving orders which you do not think will be obeyed in politics, or praying for what you do not think God will give you in religion. Question and evidence, in history, are correlative. Anything is evidence which enables you to answer your question—the question you are asking now. A sensible question (the only kind of question that a scientifically competent man will ask) is a question which you think you have or are going to have evidence for answering. If you think you have it here and now, the question is an actual question, like the question 'What position was John Doe in when he was stabbed?' If you think you are going to have it the question is a deferred question, like the question 'Who killed John Doe?'

It was a correct understanding of this truth that underlay
Lord Acton's great precept, 'Study problems, not periods.'
Scissors-and-paste historians study periods; they collect all the
extant testimony about a certain limited group of events, and
hope in vain that something will come of it. Scientific historians
study problems: they ask questions, and if they are good historians they ask questions which they see their way to answering. It
was a correct understanding of the same truth that led Monsieur
Hercule Poirot to pour scorn on the 'human blood-hound' who
crawls about the floor trying to collect everything, no matter
what, which might conceivably turn out to be a clue; and to
insist that the secret of detection was to use what, with possibly
wearisome iteration, he called 'the little grey cells'. You can't
collect your evidence before you begin thinking, he meant:
because thinking means asking questions (logicians, please
note), and nothing is evidence except in relation to some definite
question. The difference between Poirot and Holmes in this
respect is deeply significant of the change that has taken place in
the understanding of historical method in the last forty years.
Lord Acton was preaching his doctrine in the heyday of
Sherlock Holmes, in his inaugural lecture at Cambridge in
1895; but it was caviare to the general. In Monsieur Poirot's
time, to judge by his sales, the general cannot have too much of
it. The revolution which dethroned the principles of scissors-
and-paste history, and replaced them by those of scientific
history, had become common property.

11. *Summary*[7]

. . . creation of a new kind of history that should be scientific, but
did not see how to achieve this. Schemes of this kind are uniformly unscientific; they are creatures of fantasy; at highest they
serve the purposes of magic, at lowest those of amusement.

§ 7. An outline of a 'detective novel' is given, following
the usual present-day conventions of the *genre*. Similarities and

---

[7] Knox did not use this summary in his edition of Chapter 1 in *The Idea of
History*. Items 1 to 5 and the first part of item 6 of the summary are missing
from the manuscript as found.

differences are noted between the types of inference used in detection and those used in history.

§ 8. There is no science without questioning. A scientist's training consists in learning what questions to ask. This is equally true of a detective. The best detective, like the best scientist, is the one who is best able to ask the right questions in the right order. Ability to do this depends on training in method. To forget this, and pretend that the essential element in discovery is the 'apprehension of facts', 'affirmation of propositions', etc., is to undermine the foundations of science.

§ 9. Scissors-and-paste history is composed of ready-made statements, with trimming and padding of various kinds. Scientific history contains no ready-made statements whatever. Hence the scientific historian is in no way limited to the employment of what are called 'written sources' (i.e. those which contain ready-made statements about his subject); and there is no difference of principle between the way in which he uses these and the way in which he uses 'unwritten sources'. In either case, the evidence from which he argues does certainly consist of statements, but these are his own autonomous statements (i.e. made on his own authority), to the effect that certain facts have come under his notice. Among these facts may or may not be the fact that a certain statement has been made by a certain person.

§ 10. In scissors-and-paste history the quantity of extant testimony relating to any given subject is finite. It can therefore, theoretically, be collected and reviewed, as a preliminary step to criticizing it and dividing it into reliable and unreliable. Practically, this is not always possible. In scientific history there is nothing corresponding to this. Anything is evidence which can be used as evidence, and no one can tell what is going to serve him as evidence for answering a certain question until he has formulated the question. Question and evidence are correlative. A competent scientific thinker asks only such questions as he thinks he has, or will have, evidence for answering.[8]

[8] Dated '15.2.39'.

2

ACTION[9]

1. Eppur si Muove

There are two questions to be asked whenever anyone inquires into the nature of any science: 'what is it like?' and 'what is it about?' If the reader prefers words of more syllables, the first question concerns the subjective characteristics of the science, its peculiarities as a kind of thinking; the second concerns the

[9] The first page of this chapter was pasted over an earlier version, which runs as follows: 'The subject of the foregoing chapter is not yet exhausted. It has been said that evidence is something here and now coming within the historian's observation; that of all the things which at a given time come within his observation, those are evidence which, of whatever kind they are, serve him as evidence in relation to the question he is asking; and that serving him as evidence in relation to that question means enabling him, and not only enabling him but compelling him, to answer it in a certain way. There is more to be said about it; but that will be easier to say when our preliminary review of the more obvious characteristics of history is a little less incomplete than it is at the present time.

Such a review will naturally fall into two parts. The word history, and the same is true of the words which serve in other European languages as equivalents for it, stands both for a certain type of science and also for the kind of things which a person pursuing that type of science is trying to find out about. These two things both called history, a "subjective" thing or a certain way of thinking and an "objective" thing or a certain kind of thing thought about, necessarily stand in a somewhat intimate relation. Their respective peculiarities dovetail into one another. Granted that the way of thinking is a success, and really gives us knowledge of the thing thought about, it follows that the way of thinking is adapted to the peculiarities of its object; so that a person who understood what was meant by saying that "a way of thinking is adapted to the peculiarities of its object" could discover, by investigating the characteristics of that way of thinking, what the peculiarities of its object are.

How is anybody to know whether a given way of thinking is a success or not? How is he to know whether it really gives us knowledge of the thing thought about? It has sometimes been fancied that in order to get a reply to this question we must refer it to a special kind of person, a "consulting scientist" (as we speak of a consulting engineer or a consulting physician) whose business it is to study the methods of ordinary scientists, or systematic thinkers of every kind, watching them at work partly in order to' [from 'of ordinary scientists' to 'in order to' has been crossed out].

characteristics of its object, that which in the course of this thinking people come to know.

What I shall try to show in this section is not only that of these two questions the one I have put first must necessarily be asked before the one I have put second, but that when in due course we come to ask the second we can answer it only by a fresh and closer consideration of the first.

The first question has been answered, in a preliminary and superficial manner, in the preceding chapter. We have seen that history, as a kind of thinking, goes to work like any other science by asking questions, and that it answers them by using something called evidence. We have seen that evidence is something here and now falling under the historian's observation; that of all the things which at any given time fall under his observation, those are evidence, of whatever kind they may be, which enable him, and not only enable him but compel him, to answer the question he is asking, and answer it in a certain way.

The present chapter is intended to give a similar answer to the second question. And in this section I am considering how we are to set about finding the answer. The difficulty is this. By merely studying a certain kind of thought, it is certainly possible to discover what the people who think in that way think that they are thinking about, but hardly (it would seem) to discover whether they are right. There are cases in which people think they are studying one thing and are really studying something else. On the other hand, you cannot hope to answer a question of this kind by going behind the back of the science about which you ask it. The science must be its own witness as to what it is about. This does not mean that we are forbidden to ask whether its testimony about itself is true or not; it only means that the principles on which this question should be answered are a very delicate matter.

In the present case, the question 'what is history about?' resolves itself into two sub-questions: 'what do historians think it is about?' and 'are they right?'

The answer to the first sub-question is easy. Historians think and always have thought that history is about *Res Gestae*, deeds, actions done in the past.

As to the second sub-question, there is one way in which it obviously cannot be answered. If a fortune-teller claims to be able to discover things about my past life, and the things he tells me conflict with what I recollect, I regard him as a fraud. But this cannot be done in the case of history. No one will claim that he knows more than historians do about certain actions done in the past concerning which historians claim to have knowledge, and knows this in such a way that he can satisfy both himself and other people of that claim's groundlessness.

There is a second approach that must be ruled out. It has sometimes been fancied that there are persons, consulting scientists one might call them, whose business it is to study the methods of ordinary scientists, watching them at work partly to see how they do it and partly to see whether they are doing it right. These consulting scientists, who are called philosophers, are supposed to have the right of saying to this or that group of scientists, 'your belief that your way of thinking is giving you knowledge of the things you are thinking about is erroneous. I have studied your methods, and it is my duty to tell you that they are faulty.'

Talking like that gives a man a very pleasant feeling of superiority to other people. And the attractiveness of the philosophical profession undoubtedly depends in part upon the fact that those who adopt it see themselves in the position of inquisitors, entitled by virtue of their holy office to sit in judgment upon all who in their various ways pursue knowledge, and on occasion denouncing them as heretics. The traditional structure of European society for the last three centuries, in Protestant countries at any rate, has been such that these denunciations produce no effect. They are verdicts of a spiritual court, whose only function is to flatter the self-conceit of the court that gives them. No executive does anything about putting them into practice. But the structure of European society is changing rather rapidly. One of the most obvious ways in which it is changing is that the seventeenth-century principles of toleration, free speech, and a free press are being attacked, and new forms of persecution are being instituted. In this state of things it is no longer wise to let philosophers denounce this or that group of scientists merely because their denunciations are futile. It is time to inquire into their credentials.

If a scientist, told by a philosophical inquisitor that his methods are faulty and that the science they yield can never give him genuine knowledge, thought it worth while to give any answer at all, the right answer for him to give would be: '*Eppur si muove*. My science is a going concern. I ask myself questions. I invent ways of answering them. I find the answers convincing. As I go on working, I find my old problems dissolving, and new ones taking their place. I claim no infallibility; as my work goes forward, I find myself constantly correcting my own past mistakes; and if it is allowed to go forward in the future I shall discover and correct others that I am making now. And I am no individualist; I welcome criticism; but only if it is well-informed criticism, that is, criticism by men who understand what I am trying to do and can give me grounds for thinking that they can show me how to do better.'

This position seems to me unassailable. It would be quite legitimate for a philosopher to claim an inquisitorial status in relation to, say, modern relativistic physics, if he could say to the modern physicist: 'I already know by my philosophy the true answers to the questions you are trying to answer by your physics, and in the light of this knowledge, which you of course do not share, I am able to tell you that your answers are wrong: so your methods must be wrong, because they lead to what I know to be wrong answers.' A modern philosopher will hardly say this in so many words; but something very like it is working in his mind. When he was young, he learned enough physics to become thoroughly indoctrinated with the methods and theories then current; because he did not pursue the subject seriously, he did not discover the fatal flaws in these methods and theories, which are matters of common knowledge (and therefore not much talked about) among physicists today; not being conscious of these flaws, he does not understand why anybody should labour at inventing new methods and theories which shall avoid them; and so, when confronted by these new methods and theories, he condemns their inventors as motiveless busybodies, and does his best to put them down, or at least bring them into contempt, by appeal to his inquisitorial powers. He thinks he is using these powers in order to defend against wanton paradox-mongers a knowledge about physical matters which he derives from a source other than physical science: from 'common sense' or what not. This is an hallucination. He is using them to defend the now obsolete physical science of his youth against the further developments which have rendered it obsolete.

This is the formula according to which inquisitorial powers are always used. In the sixteenth century, they were used not to protect religion against science, but to protect medieval science against Renaissance science. In modern Germany, the official condemnation of modern anthropology as a 'Jewish' (that is, an anti-patriotic) science is not a measure to protect patriotism against anthropology, it is a measure to protect the 'Race-theory' of eighteenth-century anthropology against the twentieth-century anthropology that has proved it a delusion.

No science can be criticized except from inside. The only way in which anybody can find out whether a science is a success, and gives knowledge about the things of which it professes to give knowledge, is by engaging in it for himself and finding out by experience, since there is no other way, whether or not it does in the experience of those who practise it answer the questions it asks. The idea of philosophy as a 'consulting science', criticizing the work of the other sciences and judging it as sound or unsound, is merely a disguise for a kind of inquisition whose unavowed purpose is to save inquisitors the trouble of growing up.

We cannot, therefore, find out behind the historian's back what are the special characteristics of the object he is studying, and then proceed to examine his methods in order to find out whether they are well adapted to the study of this peculiar object. It is only by entering into the historian's work for ourselves that we can discover what the object he is thinking about looks like to him; and it is only by asking whether the arguments that he uses are cogent or not—that is to say, whether their actual function, for a mind that thinks in that way, is or is not compulsive—that we can settle whether the look of that object to him is 'mere appearance' or 'objectively valid'.

This is why any systematic consideration of history must begin by discussing history *a parte subjecti*, history as a special form of thinking which goes on in the minds of historians, and go on afterwards to discuss history *a parte objecti*, history as a special kind of thing about which it is the business of historians to acquire knowledge. And this is also why, having shown that the arguments used in history *a parte subjecti* are compulsive and not permissive, we are logically bound to answer all questions as to the nature of history *a parte objecti* by finding out how it is that historians, in using their own methods, are led to conceive the thing they are studying.[10]

2. Res Gestae

As we have seen, historians traditionally say that history is about *Res Gestae*; doings or rather deeds; things that have been done, past actions.[11] And this means actions done by human beings. Actions done by other animals are traditionally recognized as legitimate subjects of historical interest only [in] so far as they impinge upon human affairs: actions done by God, only in so far [as] they either impinge upon human affairs or are done through human agents, *gesta Dei per Francos*.

Traditional sayings about history, we have already seen, sometimes apply not to history proper, but only to scissors-and-paste history. This may be a case in point. Yet, if all the traditional ideas about history, without exception, applied only to scissors-and-paste history, there would be no community of nature at all between scissors-and-paste history and history proper; and if that were so, the relation between the two things would be unintelligible. In particular, there would be no sense in saying that scissors-and-paste history had been superseded by history proper unless the two were attempts, one unsuccessful and the other successful, to do the same thing; and if one is an unsuccessful attempt, and the other a successful attempt, to get knowledge, the second can only have superseded the first if they were attempts to get knowledge about the same kind of object. We start, then, with the probability that when scissors-and-paste historians described their study as concerned with *Res Gestae*, they were stating the purpose not of scissors-and-paste history but of history in general: a purpose, it may be,

---

[10] Dated '16.2.39'.

[11] Before this sentence the following has been crossed out: 'What is history about? And, as the only possible way of answering that question, what do historians think it is about? That question, again, is best approached by asking another: what do they habitually say they think it is about? The answer to that is easy.'

which scissors-and-paste history failed to achieve, but which was nevertheless its purpose.

Closer examination of the formulae actually used by scissors-and-paste historians will reveal details appropriate only to scissors-and-paste methods. Thus, when Herodotus tells us that he writes his book in order that certain deeds shall not be forgotten, he is saying that history is concerned not only with deeds, but with deeds that somebody now remembers, and that their memories are to serve him as authorities for his own work; the purpose of this work being to conserve them, that is, to tell posterity what it is that his informants remember. This implies that he is incorporating in his book the statements which he finds his informants making: in other words, it implies a true scissors-and-paste programme. Not necessarily an uncritical one. The most that can be said in favour of the vulgar doctrine that Herodotus was uncritical is that he criticized his sources not systematically and according to principles, but according to his own judgment, and that his judgment was sometimes at fault; as in the curious case where he condemns a story as false on account of the very feature which incontestably proves it true.[12]

The Herodotean formula thus falls into two parts, one applying to scissors-and-paste history alone, the other perhaps admitting of wider application. And if we study the work of modern scientific historians, we certainly find that human deeds provide their subject-matter. All the same, it might be argued from this that history as now practised is still in some ways immature, not that this limitation of subject is inherent in history as such. We shall not be able to do justice to this contention until we see why it is that historians have traditionally accepted a limitation which at first sight appears so arbitrary.

It is not mere clannishness. It is not that the historian, as a human being, takes an interest in whatever concerns human beings. The proof is that a great many things which deeply concern human beings are not, and never have been, traditionally included in the subject-matter of history. People are born, eat and breathe and sleep, and beget children, and become ill and

---

[12] † The Egyptians who claimed to have circumnavigated Africa clockwise alleged that in the southern part of the voyage the sun was on their right. 'A statement, to me, incredible', says Herodotus with sturdy common sense.

recover again, and die; and these things interest them, most of them at any rate, far more than art and science, industry and politics and war. Yet none of these things have been tradition-ally regarded as possessing historical interest. Most of them have given rise to institutions like dining and marrying and the various rituals that surround birth and death, sickness and recovery; and of these rituals and institutions people write his-tories; but the history of dining is not the history of eating, and the history of death-rituals is not the history of death. What men have done and undergone simply in their capacity as animals, human animals but still animals, done under the stress of animal inclination and suffered under the compulsion of animal des-tiny, is traditionally no part of their history. And it is because other animals are traditionally believed to do and suffer nothing but things of this kind, that other animals do not traditionally interest the historian. Man, says the traditional doctrine of European science, is not only animal, but *animal rationale*; and it is in virtue of his rationality that he not only eats but dines, not only copulates but marries, not only dies but is buried. On a foundation of animal life his rationality builds a structure of free activities, free in the sense that although they are based on his animal nature they do not proceed from it but are invented by his reason on its own initiative, and serve not the purposes of animal life but the purposes of reason itself. *Res Gestae* are not the actions, in the widest sense of that word, which are done by animals of the species called human; they are actions in another sense of the same word, equally familiar but narrower, actions done by reasonable agents in pursuit of ends determined by their reason.[13]

---

[13] After this, the following text is crossed out: 'Characteristic of supersti-tious ages is the fear of words, for words are magic. One of the most fashionable modern superstitions is to be frightened of the word reason. "Monstrous" (it will be said by persons trying to rationalize their superstitious terror) "to pre-tend that the actions studied by history are always, or even often, actions pro-ceeding from reason! Most of them, to say the least, obviously proceed from the extremest unreason." But this is to pick a quarrel about a word. I mean by rea-son, as people have meant for a good many centuries now, thinking. My critic, to dignify him by that name, calls thinking unreason when he personally dis-agrees with it. I do not object. I will admit that Ethelred the Unready behaved unreasonably when he paid blackmail to the Danes. But an unreasonable rea-son is still a reason, though a bad one. A beast that wants discourse of reason does not pay blackmail.'

These include—is it necessary to add?—acts done by an unreasonable agent in pursuit of ends (or in the adoption of means) determined by his unreason; for what is meant by unreason, in a context of this kind, is not the absence of reasons but the presence of bad ones; and a bad reason is still a reason. A brute that wants discourse of reason does not make a fool of itself.

The actions traditionally studied by history are actions in this narrower sense of the word: actions in which reason, in a high or a low degree, reason triumphant or reason frustrated, wise thought or foolish thought, is not only at work but recognizably at work. The old belief that man is the only 'rational animal' may well be mistaken, not so much because it implied too much rationality in man; it never did that, for it never implied that man was more than feebly, intermittently, and precariously rational; as because it implied too little in non-human animals. And yet it may be true enough for the purposes of history, if the rationality of non-human animals is so much feebler, more intermittent, and more precarious than our own, or so concealed from us by defective powers of communication, that we can never lay a finger on any action of a non-human animal and say with confidence 'here reason is at work; here the animal is not obeying its instincts but acting out its thoughts'.

As an example of what I mean, the American writer Ernest Thompson Seton, some years ago, published a series of books in which he professed to reconstruct, from such evidence as that of their tracks, the processes of reason which had determined the actions of various wild animals. If genuine, these were real history of *Res Gestae*. But many readers must have doubted whether they were not sentimentalized portraits falsified by a desire to find in the wild animals he loved a resemblance to human beings closer than actually exists. However that may be, this is clear, that the question whether history of non-human deeds is possible is to be answered not by arguing, but by trying to write it.[14]

---

[14] Dated '16.2.39'.

3. *Evidence and Language*[15]

The principle was laid down at the beginning of this chapter, which professes to deal with the object of historical knowledge, that there is no way of finding out what the object of a science is, except to study that science itself; and (which is really the same thing) that there is no way of finding out whether it studies that object successfully, except to find out whether it solves its own problems to the satisfaction of those who ask the questions and answer them: the only competent judges.

It follows that, so long as any unanswered questions remain about the object of historical knowledge, the only way in which we can answer them is by inquiring more closely into the nature of historical thinking. Obviously, such a question does remain. In the foregoing section it was stated that the object of historical knowledge, according to historians themselves, is *Res Gestae*, understood as the deeds, or past actions, of human beings not in their capacity as animals of a certain species but in their capacity as rational animals. The deeds which historians study are therefore, according to the tradition, deeds embodying or expressing thoughts.

It was pointed out that this is what historians traditionally say. It may be untrue; or it may be true, but true of scissors-and-paste history, not of scientific history. This, then, is our unanswered question: is the traditional statement as to what history is about true?

This question, we know, must be answered by an examination of historical method. And unless it is already what Socrates called 'rolling about in front of our feet', which I do not think it is, our previous examination of historical method has not gone far enough. We must take it further. This I propose to do in the present section. I will give away the result in advance so far as to say that whereas in the preceding chapter things like footprints, paint-smears, ashes, and buttons were described as evidence, we shall here conclude that strictly speaking evidence consists not in these things themselves but in something else which may

---

[15] Collingwood originally wrote 'Evidence as Language' and replaced 'as' by 'and'.

be roughly defined as 'what they say'. The relation between historical evidence and the conclusions drawn from it, historical knowledge, is the relation between what such things 'say' and 'what it means'.

First of all, I shall try to show that this conclusion is implied in the traditional view of history as concerned with *Res Gestae*: then I shall go on to show that it tallies with the way in which evidence is actually used by scientific historians.[16]

If the actions studied by the historian are actions in which thought is recognizably at work, it follows that the evidence for them must be something which reveals to him the presence of thought. In other words, it must be expressions of thought, or language: either language itself, the bodily gestures by which a thinker expresses his thought to himself and to others, or a 'notation' of language, the traces left by these gestures in the perceptible world, or a trustworthy copy of these traces, from which a person able to read them can reconstruct the gestures in his imagination, and so reconstruct as an experience of his own the thought they express.

For a rational animal, in so far as he is rational (and in the case of man, I repeat, that is never very far), every action has the character of language: every action is an expression of thought. Every trace of his action left upon the world he inhabits has the character of writing: every such trace is evidence, to a person who can read it, of what his thought was. A man climbing a snow-covered mountain is putting into practice his plan for getting to the top; and if he sticks to his plan, his movements during the ascent make up a continuous piece of language, from which an understanding watcher can make out, with as much precision as if he were listening to a running commentary given by the climber in words, what the plan is. And because he leaves tracks in the snow, which as long as they remain legible preserve a tolerably complete notation of his movements, it remains possible to read his movement-language after he has ceased to utter it, and reconstruct the history of his ascent from the evidence of his footprints.

'Great men', said Pericles, 'have the whole world for their tomb'. It is only little men who need epitaphs describing what

---

[16] Dated '17.2.39'.

they have done; great men leave footprints behind them, from which all who can read may know of their deeds: good laws in the city, peace and plenty in the country-side.[17]

Res Gestae are not mere action, they are rational action, action which embodies thought. To embody thought is to express it. To express thought is to be language. The historian's task is not merely to know that a certain action was done in certain conditions by a certain person at a certain time; in some ways it may be less than that, for much may be historically known about a person (such as the author of the Junius letters)[18] who remains unidentified; in one way it must always be more, for it must always include knowing what the person who did the action, as we say, 'meant by it', what thought his action embodied. To know that Diocletian issued an Edict of Prices, or that Louis XIV revoked the Edict of Nantes, is not historical knowledge; it is at most the dry bones of historical knowledge; before we can make it into historical knowledge we must 'read' it, that is, find out what Diocletian or Louis meant by it; then (and this is the special business of the historian) we must interpret it as implying that he envisaged the situation in which he found himself in a certain manner, was discontented with it for certain reasons, and proposed to amend it in a certain way. He may have been mistaken as to what the situation was; he may have known what it was, but have been foolish to be discontented with it; he may have envisaged it correctly and been justly discontented with it, but mistaken in thinking that his action would lead to anything better. Whether in these various ways he was right or wrong is also an historical question, or rather three different historical questions; not to be burked on the plea that the historian is only concerned with 'what exactly happened', events as such, and not with 'judgments of value'. The historian's only concern with events as such is to read them as evidence of the thoughts they embody; and a person who merely knows what a thought was, but does not know whether it was right or wrong, has not done the duty of an historian by it.

[17] After this, the following sentence is crossed out: 'This is the further point about the nature of evidence which, as I said at the beginning of the present chapter, could not be made until we had asked what history is about.'

[18] The manuscript leaves room for adding another reference after the Junius letters.

The historian who places before himself on his table a volume
of the Rolls Series, open at a certain charter of Henry I, is looking at what purports to be not the actual language of Henry himself or his clerks, nor even the notation of that language, but a
true copy of the notation, or rather (since the charter is merely
calendared, not reproduced *verbatim*) a true copy of those features in it which the editors of the Rolls Series thought likely to
interest future historians. The chief processes which the historian now has to go through are as follows. First, he must satisfy
himself that the copy, so far as it goes, is a true one. That is
to say, he must rule out the possibility of the charter's sense having been distorted by misprints or by misrepresentation, accidental or deliberate, on the part of the person who calendared it.
Secondly, he must satisfy himself that the original was genuine,
and not one of the forged charters of which there are not a few
in existence. Thirdly, being now satisfied that what he has
before him faithfully represents a genuine original, he must read
it, and find out what it says. Fourthly, having settled in his own
mind what it says, he must decide what it means, that is to say,
what Henry I was 'driving at' when he issued that charter: how
the king envisaged the situation he was dealing with, and how he
intended that it should be altered.

The first process is not a piece of historical thinking at all,
though the successful performance of it may partly depend
upon historical knowledge; not historical knowledge about
medieval kings and tenures, but historical knowledge about
scholars and printers in the nineteenth century. In itself, it is no
more an historical business than the choice of a solicitor is a legal
business. It is an affair of practical judgment, like the decision
to begin that piece of work on Henry I's charters now, instead of
waiting until after tea.

The second process, again, is not an affair of historical thinking. It is an affair of textual scholarship, which is a totally different thing. No doubt, the scholar who works at 'establishing'
a text is, on the whole, likely to do this work better if he knows
what the text means; but that is not even an indispensable condition of establishing it, still less are the two things identical. We
can all recollect cases in which good scholarly work has been
done on texts by persons who gravely misunderstood them. In
the same way, a museum expert may be able to say 'that is not a

52 THE PRINCIPLES OF HISTORY

genuine Bronze Age trunnioned axe, it is a modern forgery', although he has not the remotest notion what a trunnioned axe was for. The textual scholar's function is, in a way, like that of the librarian who has to keep his books in good order and well arranged in case anybody wants to read them, but is too busy to read them himself. Certainly, the scholar has to read his text, carefully and often; but he is under no obligation to bother his head about what the man who wrote it was driving at.

The third process, once more, is not history. It is literature. To carry it out is to do something of exactly the same kind as reading a work of fiction or a warning to trespassers. Investigations concerning the nature of this process are carried out by the science of language, which is not philology but aesthetic. Not philology, because philology does not inquire into the nature of language but into the organization of languages. Now, the first and second processes occur indeed in the case I have taken, but not in all cases of historical work. Even where they do occur, they are no part of the historical process itself, but are only preliminaries to it; and as they do not always occur they are not essential preliminaries. But the third process is an essential preliminary. It occurs in every case of historical thinking. In itself, it is simply an aesthetic activity, which is why a science of aesthetic is an indispensable precondition to any science of historical method; but in its relation to history it can be defined as apprehending or discerning the evidence. The historian's business is to discover what somebody thought: in order to do that, he must first find out what he said (where 'saying' covers not only expressive movements of the speech-organs, but expressive action of whatever kind); and the way to find out what somebody said is to 'read' the notation of it, or the true copy of the notation of it, which you have before you.[19]

To say that the historian's evidence is something which comes within his own perception or observation is therefore to speak not so much in a mistaken way as in a rough-and-ready way. It is not so much untrue as inexact. If he is asking a question whose answer is in fact capable of being supplied by a medieval Latin text at which he is now looking, it is inexact to say that he is actually looking at the evidence. For if he does not

[19] Dated '16.2.39'.

know medieval Latin, or cannot read the script and the abbreviations, the reason why he cannot answer his question is not that
he knows the premises but fails to draw the conclusion from
them; it is that he does not know the premises. The premises
([the] logician's general name for the thing which historians, in
their own special case, call evidence) are not the marks he sees
on the page in front of him, but what these marks say to a man
who is able to read them. What justifies the rough-and-ready
statement that the evidence 'stares him in the face', or is something that comes within his perception or observation, is the
assumption that he is able to read; in which case looking at a
piece of writing comes to the same thing as knowing what it says.

Imprecision would be replaced by error if we were to
comment on this by saying: 'I see; there are two inferential
processes, not one only. The first begins with perceiving certain
marks on paper, or footprints in snow, or sounds made by
speech-organs, which at this stage constitute evidence, and on
the strength of this evidence concludes that something or other
is what the person who makes these marks or noises is saying.
The second process starts with the conclusions of the first: these
now become evidence pointing to (or, if you like, enforcing) a
further conclusion, the one at which the historian has been aiming. But the two processes are of the same kind. Each of them is
an historical inference. The conclusion of the first becomes the
starting point of the second; and this is why, speaking in a
rough-and-ready way, we can treat the two as if they were one,
omit the middle term, and talk as if the premises of the first led
directly to the conclusion of the second.'

This is a blunder of the first magnitude in aesthetic, where it
is a cardinal truth that when one person hears the sounds
another makes when he speaks, or sees the marks he makes when
he writes, and does what we call 'understanding him', that is,
knows what it is that he is saying, the process of thought by
which he comes to know this is not an inferential process. Not
only a cardinal truth, but a notorious one; for we all know that
when somebody who has read a certain book professes that he is
driven to use inferential methods in order to find out what it is
that the author is saying, he does so in order to insinuate that the
author is not fit to write a book at all; though it is alternatively
possible that he, the reader, is not fit to read one. What kind of

process it really is, I have tried to explain at some length else-where;[20] and as this is not a book about aesthetic it would not be proper to repeat it here.

In the course of the preceding chapter, it was said that even where the evidence used by an historian may be said to consist of ready-made statements, the truth is rather that he uses as evidence not these statements themselves, but his own autonomous statement of the fact that they are made. It is now possible to repeat this in a more precise form. The starting-point of any genuinely historical argument is, strictly speaking, not 'this person, or this printed book, or this set of footprints, says so-and-so', but 'I, knowing the language, read this person, or this book, or these footprints, as saying so-and-so.' This is why it could be insisted in the foregoing chapter that in respect of his evidence the historian was autonomous or dependent upon his own authority: for, as we can now see, his evidence is always an experience of his own, an act which he has performed by his own powers and is conscious of having performed by his own powers: the aesthetic act of reading a certain text in a language he knows, and assigning to it a certain sense.

A person who understands this will immediately accept as true what a person who did not understand it would reject as a monstrous falsehood: the doctrine that the historian does not find his evidence but makes it, and makes it inside his own head. A person who does not understand will think, perhaps, that it inculcates or palliates the forgery of documents, or the mendacious claim that documents exist, which prove a desired conclusion. A person who understands will see that it means much the same as saying that an animal makes its own food inside its alimentary canal. An animal's food is not what it finds and takes into its mouth, but what nourishes it; and nothing can nourish it except what has undergone certain processes inside itself. If you said that even to a quite small child, and found later on that it had stopped feeding its rabbits 'because you said that animals made their own food', you would think there was something seriously wrong with the child. Common stupidity would not account for it.[21]

---

[20] † *The Principles of Art* (1938). [Collingwood adds 'especially chapter', but gives no number. It should presumably be ch. XI, on language.]

[21] Dated '17.2.39'.

4. *Action and Event*

Henceforth the word 'action' will be used in the narrower of the two senses distinguished in § 2 of this chapter. It will be used as equivalent to *Res Gestae*, or rather to a tenseless and numberless version of it; for the word 'action' is equally applicable to actions in the past, present, or future, and to a singular action or actions in the plural. 'Action' will henceforth be used to designate only that part of conduct which embodies or expresses thought. The fresh study of historical method reported on in the preceding section has vindicated the traditional view that action is what historians want to know about. It has even added a further point to this traditional view, by showing that what they want to know about, according to the evidence of their own methods, is not only action but action as expressing thought; or that ultimately what they want to know about is the thought it expresses. The action that expresses it has to them the character of language, and the business of language is to reveal thought.

We have not yet gone into the question whether tradition is right in limiting the actions that interest the historian to past actions. Pending that inquiry, we will assume (assumption is all we need for the purpose of this section) that the tradition is right, and further that people are right to think of actions as having each its own irrevocable and unchangeable place in a time-series, so that any action that belongs to the past belongs somewhere in the past and cannot belong anywhere else.

This is as much as to say that we assume, for the purposes of the present argument, that all actions are events. Not only events, of course, but much more; in particular, events that express the thoughts of the agents who are said to 'do' them. But still, events.

On this assumption, history is about a certain kind of events. And, by what logicians call the fallacy *a dicto secundum quid ad dictum simpliciter*, it seems attractive to persons who do not feel like taking the trouble to ask what kind, to leave out the qualification and just say that history is about events.

This temptation has not, so far as I recollect, had much

success with historians. But it has had a good deal with philosophers. Some of these have gone so far as to turn tempter themselves, approaching the historians with honeyed words to cajole them into abandoning their obsolete formula about *Res Gestae*, and coming out all up-to-date under the flag of Events, as flown by modern physics. That great and golden-mouthed philosopher, Samuel Alexander, wrote his last published essay under the title 'The Historicity of Things', and he began it by saying that in his opinion it was time philosophers went to school with historians. The lesson he wished them to learn was, in brief, the all-importance of time, 'the timefulness of things'. Historians had long been inhabiting a world in which there were no 'things', only 'events'; a world in which nothing existed but what was historical, and to be historical meant to be an event or a complex of events. It was Alexander's contention that the historians had been all along in the right of it. They had always maintained that, so far as they knew, nothing existed, or had existed, or would exist, but events. And they were right. Physics had come to their feet, repenting of its old belief in forces, in energy, in bodies, and confessing that what it had meant by these expressions was in reality, as it now saw, nothing but events and complexes of events. Where history and natural science are in agreement, what ails philosophy that she should stand out of the happy party?

The party, as depicted by Alexander, obviously includes one lady and one tiger (two ladies, if philosophy decides to join in); but which is the lady, and which is the tiger? Alexander professes no doubt. The tiger is history, and the first lady is natural science, happy to be absorbed into the all-embracing Science of Events, which is the title justly claimed by history. The only discordant note is the fact, which Alexander nowhere mentions and of which he was probably unaware, that history does not claim that title at all. Somebody else claims it, namely modern physics. So that, before the party can begin, history must break with the immemorial tradition according to which its business is not with events but with *Res Gestae*, and give up all its own principles of method (which, as we have seen, are perfectly adapted to the performance of its traditional business) in order to become what physics already, and very efficiently, is. Alexander's casting has been done quite unambiguously in his

ACTION   57

book;[22] it is only in his list of *Dramatis Personae* that he has got
it wrong; where, for the received text 'Tiger . . . History; First
Lady . . . Physics', a critical reader will accept the absolutely
certain emendation 'Tiger . . . Physics; First Lady . . . History'.

The blunder on a point of fact (what it is that modern historians are studying), which has thus turned Alexander's whole
argument upside-down, is by no means peculiar to him. It is
shared by quite a number of justly distinguished living philosophers. Any one of these might quite easily have avoided it
either by referring the point to his historian friends or by qualifying himself to answer his own question; I do not mean by
reading history-books, but by discovering how they are written
by writing, on his own account, books that historians will recognize to be history, and watching himself at work. If they have
not taken either course, that is because they think that the point
is a 'philosophical' one, and therefore one about which an 'historian' is not entitled to have an opinion, nor one which a 'philosopher' could decide any better for becoming an 'historian'
himself.[23] This, again, is a direct result of the faculty-organiza-
tion in our universities, which automatically breeds nonsense,
the professional 'philosopher' being a person who is debarred
by his academic position from knowing what his academic position nevertheless requires him to talk about. 'And this I say not
as disproving the use of Universities in the commonwealth, but
as pointing out what things in them might be amended; whereof
the frequency of insignificant speech is one.'[24]

---

[22] After 'book' is written 'of the words'. Since this makes little sense, it has
been deleted. Collingwood presumably refers here to Alexander's *Space, Time,
and Deity* (London, 1927); but see also his article, 'The Historicity of Things',
referred to in n. 68 of the Editors' Introduction.

[23] This sentence does not run smoothly and should probably read: '. . . and
therefore not one about which an "historian" is entitled to have an opinion, nor
one which a "philosopher" could decide any better . . .'

[24] † Hobbes, *Leviathan*, chapter I, *ad fin*. [This passage is not correctly
quoted. At the end of chapter I of the *Leviathan* Hobbes says: 'I say not this, as
disapproving the use of Universities: but because I am to speak hereafter of
their office in a Commonwealth, I must let you see on all occasions by the way,
what things would be amended in them; amongst which the frequency of
insignificant Speech is one.' The same passage is correctly quoted by
Collingwood in *The New Leviathan*, 11. The end of this section is dated
'17.2.39'.]

5. *Nature has no History*

So we had been warned, a hundred years ago and more, that the timefulness of natural events is an utterly different thing from historicity. Yes, but only by Hegel; and surely, to a sensible man a warning by Hegel is a tip straight from the horse's mouth to go and do just what Hegel warns him not to. We all know what happens to people who 'drink deep at that poisoned spring'.[25]

If anybody thinks it is only the other day that natural scientists have begun to 'take time seriously', to realize how extremely timeful nature is, I wonder whether he has ever heard of Heraclitus, who is chiefly famous for having said that 'everything moves and nothing stays still'; or of Plato, who was brought up in the school of Heraclitus, and only left it because he thought that the laws according to which events happen are not themselves events; or of Aristotle, who defined nature as that which has the source of its own movement in itself, or whether he thinks that among the European schools of natural science between Aristotle's time and our own there has ever been a single one which differed from Heraclitus where both Plato and Aristotle agreed with him; or whether he thinks that Darwin and Einstein, who are supposed to have made nature more timeful than it was before, teach that the law of natural selection is an event, or that the relations between events which a physicist states in the form of differential equations are themselves events.

There is one way, according to A. N. Whitehead, in which the physics of the twentieth century gives more importance to time than any physics has ever given it before. According to modern physics, as Whitehead puts it, 'there is no nature at an instant'. According to all earlier physicists, motion is something superadded to bodies which already possess the general characteristics of body, and the special characteristics of this and that special kind of body, independently of the fact that they move; so that if all movements in the world could be stopped, the bodies thus brought to rest would still be bodies, and bodies of

---

[25] † I borrow this charming phrase from a new and in many ways admirable book, *The Press*, by H. Wickham Steed (1938), page 73. I do not myself know how people poison springs.

exactly the same kind that they are now. Or if you could take an absolutely instantaneous photograph of the whole world, a view of it from which lapse of time was altogether excluded, it would show you a world containing all the things with which you are familiar, and of course a great deal else besides. But according to modern physicists it takes time to be a body of a special kind, because the special qualities of every special kind are resultants of the patterns in which its constituent parts move: so that within a space of time too short for this pattern to have declared itself the thing would not possess those qualities. And since this applies not only to the special qualities of special kinds of bodies, but to the qualities of bodies in general too, it follows that if you cut the time sufficiently short there would be no physical world at all. For the same reason, if the physical world could be frozen into immobility for a moment, it would for that moment cease to exist.

When Hegel said that nature has no history, it was not because, born too early to participate in this very striking twentieth-century discovery, he underrated the importance of time in nature. On the contrary, no one has ever been more convinced than Hegel of nature's essential timefulness. If anyone had said to him 'I suppose you think that a view of the physical world from which time had been eliminated would show everything existing just as it does now', I would rather not try to guess what his reply would have been, for Hegel was a rude man; but it is certain that he would have repudiated the suggestion with some definiteness; and anybody who has had a drink or two at that poisoned spring can see this for himself, by merely noticing at what point in Hegel's work the 'category' of time is formally discussed. It is the second 'category' in the Philosophy of Nature, the first being space. Space and time between them are thus for Hegel the absolutely fundamental and primary thing in nature.[26] It is difficult to see what more Whitehead himself

---

[26] † It may not be idle to point out that Hegel's doctrine as to the radical timefulness of nature was very far from peculiar to himself. I will add the names of a few other well-known philosophers who held similar doctrines before him. Plato, in that curious passage of the *Timaeus* in which he calls time 'the moving image of eternity', makes timefulness not merely a fundamental characteristic but the fundamental characteristic of the natural world, corresponding to eternity or timelessness as the fundamental characteristic of God. Aristotle emphasizes the timefulness of nature in a rather similar way, by

could have done to emphasize nature's timefulness. And if anybody says 'well, that does not represent the views of physicists
in Hegel's time', the answer is that Hegel was about as anxious
to adopt the views of physicists as Karl Marx was to adopt the
views of capitalists.

Hegel said that nature had no history because he got hold of
the question by the right end. A study of history meant, for him,
first and foremost a study of historical method. He thought that
the historical methods current in his own time were very bad,
but he thought them bad because they did not do what according to all historians they were meant to do: they did not make it
possible to see through the recorded actions to the thoughts
underlying them. He was right about this, though he was wrong
in thinking that his own private historical method would get
over the difficulty. Now, anybody who would take the trouble,
in Hegel's time or our own, to find out what the kind of problem
is that historical methods, as they actually exist, are intended to
solve, would see for himself that it is a kind of problem which
simply does not arise in natural science. It might arise, certainly,
for a scientist who was both pious enough to believe that every
event in nature was a case of direct action by God, all secondary
causes being eliminated (eaten perhaps by the proverbial
chimera, bombinating in the hollow round of his skull), and also
impious enough to repudiate the salutary doctrines that God is
not judged and that his thoughts are past finding out, or superstitious enough to think every such event due to the action of

saying that the essence of nature, the characteristic in virtue of which a thing
belongs to the natural world, is self-movement; and, as he elsewhere says, all
movement takes time. Sampling more modern philosophers, Spinoza, whom I
quote because for some obscure reason he is thought to have spoken disres-
pectfully of time, says the only thing that makes two bodies two and not one is
that they move relatively to each other. From this it follows that the twoness of
two bodies, and therefore not only the manyness of many bodies but the one-
ness of one body, is a thing that takes time to exist. Finally Kant, who seems
anxious to outbid everyone else, makes time not only a universal and fundamental characteristic of the natural world and everything in it, but actually a
precondition of it: for time is a 'form of intuition', and intuition is logically
prior to understanding, and it is understanding that 'makes nature'. Thus all
the four philosophers I have quoted would have shared Hegel's conviction that
anyone who asked what would happen to nature if motion ceased in it, or what
nature was like at an instant, was talking nonsense; though none of them would
have been as nasty about it as Hegel would have been.

some demon, magician, or the like, whose character, motives, and modes of operation he can infer with demonstrative cogency from the events themselves. But it does not arise for anyone who attaches himself to the tradition of natural science which, however much it has changed, has never been broken from the ancient Greeks to the present day.

It is no criticism of this statement to say that modern astronomy, in addition to providing us with a celestial topography or star-map, a celestial mechanics or theory of sidereal motions, and a celestial classification or division of heavenly bodies into their various kinds, white dwarfs and so on, gives us a celestial history or classification according to age, with hints, some people think, for a cosmogony, or account of the universe's beginning, and an eschatology, or account of its ending. It is no criticism to say that modern biology includes among its functions that of a biological history, a division of species according to the time at which they have existed and an account, not yet as conclusive as we could wish, of the way in which one has arisen out of another; or to say that modern geology is among other things a geological history or division of rocks according to their various ages; or to point out that medicine is nowadays interesting itself in the history of disease, showing how the diseases observed at the present time differ from those credibly recorded in the past; or that even physics itself is becoming historical in the mind of a thinker like Whitehead, with his speculation that the laws of the physical world as we know them are only the laws of our own 'cosmic epoch', an epoch preceded and to be followed by others in which different sets of laws held good, or will hold good, each for its own span of time.

It is no criticism, because none of these things is history. Chronology, yes; developments of the age-old idea that nature is essentially process or event, by all means; but history, no. If the methods of thought by which they are arrived at are compared with the methods of history, it becomes at once obvious that they lack just that characteristic which in history is central. A man who was taught history badly when he was at school, and has never worked at it since, may think there is nothing in it except events and dates and places: so that wherever he can find events and dates and places, he will fancy himself in the presence of history. But anyone who has ever worked intelligently at history knows that it is never about mere events, but about actions that express the thoughts of their agents; and that the framework of dates and places is of value to the historian only because, helping to place each action in its context, it helps him to realize what the thoughts of an agent operating in that context must have been like.

In order to illustrate this let us compare two methods which are not only very similar, but have been in fact not unconnected in their history: the stratigraphical methods used respectively in geology and in archaeology. The geologist identifies in one place a number of different rocks, A, B, and C, characterized by fossils of the kind a, b, c, respectively. A is the lowest; B comes next above it, C next above that; and the strata show no signs of having been violently disturbed. Each of them, he judges, must have been originally laid down in water, in the form of silt; and consequently A must be the oldest and C the youngest. Elsewhere he finds fossils of the same kind in strata similarly disposed; so he infers the presence in all these places of an A age, a B age, and a C age. Elsewhere he finds, say, only A and C, next to each other, and infers that in this place there was no B age: in other words, that this place was not under water when organisms of b type were alive. Elsewhere again he finds them in the reverse order, and infers earth-movements by which they have been turned upside down. And so on.

The archaeologist does exactly the same. Floor-deposits in houses or caves, street-levels, and superimposed relics of different buildings take the place of rock-strata. Potsherds, coins, and so forth take the place of fossils. Every detail of the above analysis is repeated point by point; there are even cases where the collapse of an upper floor in a house gives him an example of reversed stratification. But when the methods of geological stratigraphy have been exactly and completely imitated, the archaeologist has not got history; he has only got a chronological and topographical framework within which history is to be constructed. The distinction will become clear if we watch him at work.[27]

[27] Dated '17.2.39'.

6. *Excavations at Highbury, 193–*[28]

The archaeologist determines periods A, B, C, and correlates them with the same periods in other places, exactly as if he were a geologist. He begins to work as an historian only when he begins to see these periods as periods of human history, when people were thinking in characteristic fashions, alike in some ways, unlike in others.

Let us suppose that he is digging a town on a hill known as Highbury, in the county of Wessex; and that in period A he finds house-plans and 'fossils' in the occupation-levels like those which are found in a number of other towns forming a compact group on its west; also that the 'fossils' include utensils of domestic life and agriculture such as characterize a rather primitive peasant society, but no weapons and no coins, and that the relics of buildings include no fortifications. Let us suppose that in period B the character of Highbury is changed by the construction of fortifications round its periphery, and its 'fossils', though still of the same general kind, by the occurrence of weapons in large numbers, and also of a few coins characteristic of another group of towns, larger and wealthier, lying on its eastern side. Let us suppose that on the top of the period B floor-deposits he finds a great deal of charcoal and burnt clay, together with not a few skeletons, their skulls cleft by strokes from sharp implements. Let us suppose that in period C no relics at all are found over the greater part of the town's area, but that in one quarter buildings of a new type are found, whose occupation-soil contains 'fossils' resembling those of the site-group to which the coins of period C belonged; and that this quarter is surrounded by a new set of defences, different in style from the old.

When it is said that from these data the history of the town can be reconstructed, what is meant [is] that they enable the archaeologist to come to conclusions like the following. Highbury was a frontier-town between two peoples, the Westland and Eastland peoples: the Westlanders a relatively poor and peaceful society of farmers, trading by barter when they traded at all

---

[28] Highbury is an imaginary ancient British settlement. Probably to emphasize this, Collingwood left the date of its excavation incomplete.

and having other habits and institutions which are inferred in detail from the 'fossils' of period A; the Eastlanders richer, more given to commerce, and more addicted to warfare. In period A, Highbury was a Westland settlement; and if during this period the Eastlanders were in an aggressive mood, they must have been directing their aggression to another quarter. At the end of period A, something happened to alarm the Westlanders about their neighbours' intentions; they put their frontier in a state of defence, converting Highbury into a fortress; but the Eastlanders, whether because their warlike ardour was cooled by this measure or because it was their habit to let the flag follow trade, attempted no invasion. Instead, they began to trade with the Highbury garrison, who were induced to accept Eastland currency in exchange for their own produce. When this had gone on for some little time, so that Eastland traders had become familiar with the town and its inhabitants, the Eastlanders attacked it, stormed it, mastered its population and burnt it to the ground, subsequently planting a garrison of their own in a small fort upon its site.

I will not labour the point that all these inferences are absolutely compulsive and in no case merely permissive; though it would be interesting to do so by analysing, for example, the evidence which led my excavator to date the fortifications at the end of period A. But I have dealt with this matter in principle elsewhere,[29] and must not trespass on my reader's patience. For the same reason, I refrain from telling him true stories (not fancy ones, like this) about the lengths to which I have known good excavators go in order to make the evidence on a question of this kind absolutely cogent; tearing to pieces, in the process, a permissive proof which their less scrupulous friends would perhaps have willingly allowed to stand.

There is another point that I will try not to labour, because I have dealt pretty fully with it as a matter of general principle in the preceding chapter; but the self-denial costs me a pang, because in its special relation to archaeology it lies very near my

---

[29] Collingwood probably refers here to the chapter on 'Roman Britain' in his *Autobiography*, 120–46. He also discusses there his 'logic of question and answer' as applied to archaeology and the need to interpret archaeological objects in terms of purposes. Besides this, *The Archaeology of Roman Britain* (London, 1930; repr. London, 1996) has a chapter on 'Fortresses and Forts'.

heart. It concerns the function of questioning in work of this kind. Sites can be dug, and have very often been dug in the past, with no questions asked at all: dug because the owner liked digging, or because a local archaeologist wanted a job, or because houses were going to be built over them. And, when digging has once been decided upon, the *mot d'ordre* was, and too often still is, 'let us see what we can find here', and excavation becomes a sport for human terriers, tempered by the possibility that scientific results—who knows?—may be forthcoming. Today, matters have reached a point when it can be said clearly and publicly that no archaeologist ought even to be allowed to excavate at all unless, when he is deciding to work at a certain site, he can answer the question 'what historical problems lead you to that site, why do you think you can solve them there, and how exactly do you mean to go about it?'; unless, every time he orders a new trench to be opened or even a single shovelful of earth to be moved, he is prepared to explain, in terms of historical questions and their possible answers, exactly why he is doing it; unless his record shows that, instead of nibbling away at his site like a small boy with a cake until nothing is left, he is capable of saying 'now I have answered the questions I came here to answer, and we are going home'.

My own experience is that today, in this country, this principle is accepted not indeed by all archaeologists but by all whose record of work done entitles them to be taken seriously. There is still opposition to it; but it is hardly possible nowadays for this opposition to shelter itself beneath a cloak of scientific respectability. It has to reveal itself for what it is: a relic of the good old times when squire-and-parson antiquarianism was a recognized form of sport, like the cockfighting and badger-baiting of what were called the lower classes (not but what I have known cockfighting parsons in my day), and the proposal to dig a site meant the proposal to collect a few chaps, with picks and shovels, when the weather improves, and go up there and have some fun.

And if the reader thinks I have broken my promise not to labour this point, he little knows what I have spared him.

A third point, which I really will not labour, is that Highbury is conventionally called a 'prehistoric' site. This means a site about which there can be no historical knowledge because there are no ready-made statements about it to be found in any sources; but nevertheless a site about which certain people do continue to get historical knowledge, if you can call it historical knowledge, by some means or other not *dans les règles*. The term belongs to the vocabulary of scissors-and-paste history, and is in fact the insult which it hurled at scientific history as it died in the last ditch. There can be no excuse for continuing to use it.[30]

The points on which I wish to insist are two.

(1) Every item in my archaeologist's conclusion concerns the thoughts of the people who are *dramatis personae* in the story. Thus, the descriptions of the Westlanders and Eastlanders are descriptions of the kind of thoughts which mainly occupied their daily lives, pointed by contrast with types of thought that were not habitual to them. The statement that Highbury was a Westland settlement does not mean that its inhabitants, to judge by skeletal measurements, shared a certain group of physical characteristics which marked the Westland race; it means that they shared the Westland culture, that is, whatever physical characteristics they had, they thought like Westlanders. The statement that at the end of period A Highbury was converted into a fortress does not mean that certain changes took place in its visible structures, it means that certain changes took place in the habitual thoughts of its inhabitants. And so on throughout.

(2) Every item in the evidence leading to this detailed conclusion is not simply a perceptible object seen, classified, recorded, photographed, plotted and drawn by the archaeologist and his staff; it is doubtless all this, but it is also (and this is what makes it evidence) an object 'read' by him as a piece of language, that is, something expressing the thought of the men in whom he is interested. For example, among the 'fossils' of period A he finds triangular slabs of clay with a hole in one corner. He might record these, compare them with similar slabs found elsewhere, and thus, arguing like a geologist, assign them to the 'horizon' to which they belong, and so use them as evidence of date; but when he has done that, he has still to begin treating them historically. Granted that they are artifacts, he now has to ask: 'what were they for?' and the answer, of course, is 'loom-weights'. At this point they speak to him as an his-

---

[30] Dated '18–2–39'.

torian. They tell him something about the thoughts of the
Highbury people in period A: they wove. Weaving is not simply
the name for a certain series of movements: it is the name for a
series of movements embodying a plan, the plan to produce tex-
tiles.[31]

7. The History of Thought

The point which has now been reached may be conveniently
indicated by the formula that all history is the history of
thought.[32] To know about events and names and dates, which
for the scissors-and-paste historian is the end of historical inquiry, is for the scientific historian merely its means; merely the
collection of what he hopes will prove capable of being read as
language, and thus lead to the only thing that truly is historical
knowledge: insight into the mind of the person or persons who at
a certain time and in certain circumstances did the action which,
merely as something that has happened, is called an event.[33]

The historian may find that in the course of a certain campaign a certain officer[34] caused a fort of a certain kind to be built
in a certain place. The historian's business is to find out what he
did this for. Was the thing intended merely as a camp in which
a body of soldiers could take up their quarters for a night or
more, sleeping behind defences as was always done for example
by the Romans? Was it a place where supplies could be stored
and transport parked in safety? Was it designed to mask[35] a
stronghold of the enemy or to block one of their lines of
communication? There is no need to exhaust all the possible
alternatives. Whichever alternative the historian adopts, he is

[31] Dated '17.2.39'.
[32] The first fifteen words of this sentence are crossed out in the manuscript,
but have been included here to make the transition clearer.
[33] After this, 'Insight into his mind means insight into his thoughts. Into his
emotions the historian wishes for insight only so far as these emotions are
essentially related to his thoughts. Some are, and some are not. The' is crossed
out.
[34] After this, 'whose name it is quite unnecessary for him to know' is crossed
out.
[35] The meaning of this word in this context is given by *The Oxford English
Dictionary* as 'to hinder (a fortress, army, fleet) from acting on the offensive by
watching it with a sufficient force'.

claiming insight into the mind of the man responsible for building the fort: insight which depends on his understanding the
nature of fortification in general, and of fortification at the time
of that campaign in particular.

Fortification in general is a protection against certain dangers;
any particular type of fortification a protection against some
particular variety of these dangers. And certainly the consciousness that one is providing protection against danger will be
accompanied by certain emotions. If one is conscious that the
protection is of a new and ingenious kind, these emotions will be
complicated by others. These are emotions essentially related to
the thought of the officer responsible for the fortification. And if
we know what his thoughts were, we know what emotions of this
essential kind he experienced.

But in the life of this officer, while the fortification was being
planned and carried out, there were plenty of other emotions for
which we have no evidence. We cannot say, for example, when
we see how strong and elaborate the fortifications were, that he
must have been very frightened of the enemy; any more than we
can say that a man who takes out a domestic insurance policy
must be very much afraid of his house being burnt down, or
that a woman who instructs her solicitor to draw up a marriage
settlement must be very frightened of the man she proposes to
marry. He may certainly have been frightened; or he may have
been unhappy at leaving his newly-married wife, or his child in
the crisis of an illness; he may have been consumed with professional ambition or tortured by money troubles; but so long as
these emotions are neither directly due to his building the fort,
nor the cause of his building it in what a military engineer would
consider a bad or inappropriate way, they have nothing to do
with the fort and relatively to his action in building it are
inessential emotions.

For that matter, many thoughts too find a place in his mind,
while he is planning and building the fort, which affect his
building of it not at all, and therefore have no connexion with
the history of that event. It is matter of biography, not of military history, that Wolfe was thinking about Gray's *Elegy* during
the early stages of his assault on Quebec. It would have been
matter of military history if he had allowed Gray's *Elegy* to
interfere with the assault. Goya's portrait of Wellington has a

place[36] in the history of the Peninsular War; at any rate if it is true that this portrait was one of the things which prevented the victor of Salamanca from reaping the fruits of his victory.

The current distinction between ordinary history and the 'history of thought' is drawn only because it is fancied, absurdly enough, that thinking is the exclusive privilege (or curse) of special persons called thinkers, who are supposed to focus their philosophical microscopes on affairs wherein they do not engage, but which they nevertheless condescend to study; and so we get for example on the one hand a history of politics, and on the other hand a history of political thought or thought about politics: a history of what these thinkers have seen, or fancied themselves to see, through the microscope.

This fancy is absurd because, if anything deserves the name of political thought, it is the kind of thinking that is done by people engaged in politics, the thinking of which their political activities are evidence. Political history is already the history of political thought: the thoughts of Grey and his contemporaries about parliamentary reform, the thoughts of Gladstone and his contemporaries about Irish home rule, and so forth. Whether alongside this history of political thought as directed to individual problems in practical politics, there is room for a history of political thought as directed to universal problems underlying all such practical issues, is a question which I defer to another place; I am only concerned to point out here that even if there is such a distinction, it is not a distinction between the history of politics and the history of political thought, but a distinction between the history of political thought directed to solving individual problems, that is, political thought about cases, and the history of political thought directed to solving general problems, that is, political thought about principles.[37]

8. *Biography*

A distinction was drawn in the preceding section between history and biography; and as all the necessary materials are now at

[36] Collingwood originally wrote, and then crossed out: 'has its place not only in the history of art and the biography of Wellington, but'.

[37] Dated '19.2.39'.

our disposal, this is the place to consider wherein that distinction lies.

The historian's aim is to trace the thought embodied in actions. Within that sphere he admits no other limitation, except so far as he 'specializes' in one group of subjects or another. The distinction set up by his specialization between what belongs to his subject and what does not is in no sense a distinction between what belongs to the proper subjects of historical study and what does not belong there. The biographer, on the contrary, includes in his subject a good deal which does not belong to the object of any historical study whatever. He includes some events which embody no thought on the part of his subject, and others which do no doubt embody thought, but are included not because they embody thought but because they have an interest, or what is better perhaps called an appeal, of a different kind.

The biographer's choice of his materials, though it may be (and ought to be) controlled by other considerations, is determined in the first instance by what I will call their gossip-value. The name is chosen in no derogatory spirit. Human beings, like other animals, take an interest in each other's affairs which has its roots in various parts of their animal nature, sexual, gregarious, aggressive, acquisitive, and so forth. They take a sympathetic pleasure in thinking that desires in their fellow-creatures that spring from these sources are being satisfied, and a malicious pleasure in thinking that they are being thwarted. Biography, though it often uses motives of an historical kind by way of embroidery, is in essence a web woven of these two groups of threads, sympathy and malice. Its function is to arouse these feelings in the reader; essentially therefore it is a device for stimulating emotion, and accordingly[38] it falls into the two main divisions of amusement-biography, which is what the circulating libraries so extensively deal in, and magical biography, or the biography of exhortation and moral-pointing, holding up good examples to be followed or bad ones to be eschewed.

Sympathy and malice must have individual objects. Apart from human sympathy for plants, whose existence I do not deny

---

[38] † *Principles of Art*, [Collingwood gives no specific reference, but on pp. 31–2 and 108 he discusses art as arousing emotion].

although expressions of it are often hypocritical, one animal can feel sympathetic or malicious only towards another animal, which often is, but need not always be, another of its own kind. The domestic cat sympathizes in its master's meals, even though it has no expectation of sharing them; and will sometimes take violent measures to make him obey the dinner-bell. His dog will sympathize in his troubles, though it does not know what they are about: it feels that he is unhappy, and that is enough. Human beings are sympathetic or malicious towards other human beings only when these others are actual to them, perceived or imagined as identifiable and recognizable individuals: the young man next door, the girl in the tram, the stranger on the doorstep, the prisoner who cut this inscription on the damp stones. The more completely the object is envisaged as an individual, the more intense, other things being equal, is the sympathy or malice as the case may be. A man will sympathize with any dog he sees run over in the street; but far more intensely if it is his own dog, or one that he knows well.

The individuality which thus arouses our sympathy is not the individuality of an *animal rationale*; it is the individuality of an animal pure and simple. All that is necessary is that the creature should feel, and that its feelings should arouse an echo in ourselves. Even when we sympathize with rational animals over matters connected with their rationality, it is not their rationality with which we sympathize, but only the feelings in which their pursuit of rational ends has involved them. If a scientist is downcast over his failure to solve a problem, a good wife will sympathize with his dejection although she has no idea what the problem is that has defeated him: her sympathy has nothing to do with his scientific labours, it has to do with his being tired and hungry and unhappy.

Now, because sympathy and its negative counterpart malice are the strings on which a biographer plays, it follows that he must present his reader with a 'subject' that shall be an individual, and an individual animal. He must depict a definite and recognizable person, and emphasize the animal side of this person's existence. He must remind the reader that his subject was born and died; suffered diseases and recovered from them; was at one time a child and at another an old man; desired certain women and succeeded or failed in his attempts to win them, with details about the emotions that failure or success aroused in him; went hungry and endured discomfort in the struggles of his youth, and achieved comfort when later his worth was recognized, or continued to endure poverty and neglect, uncomplainingly or complainingly, to the end of his days. And because it will help the reader to individualize him, the biographer will be wise to include a portrait of him, or several portraits; a photograph of his house; and so on.

The 'other considerations' by which, as I said, the choice of this material must be controlled, mostly arise out of the fact that the purpose of biography is to stimulate emotion. If the person depicted is being held up to admiration, nothing must be inserted which among the readers for whom it is designed would arouse disapproval. If he is being held up to contempt, as in a biography by Lytton Strachey, nothing should be included which according to the conventions of Strachey's Bloomsbury might be ground for admiration. If the purpose of the biography is[39] to amuse subscribers to circulating libraries (and this is proved by abundant evidence to be the object aimed at by the great majority of biographers in English-speaking countries at the present day) great care must be taken to suppress anything that might endanger a certain placid self-satisfaction and confidence in their own security, without which it appears that people of this kind will not allow themselves to be amused.

When history is conceived as an affair of scissors and paste, biography is necessarily regarded as a special *genre* of historical literature; for on that hypothesis their methods are the same. On

[39] After this, the following passage, running to 'When history is conceived', is partly pasted over and crossed out: 'to amuse subscribers to circulating libraries, anything must be suppressed that might endanger that self-satisfied tranquillity of mind whose preservation is necessary to their sense of security; for unless they feel safe it appears that they will not let themselves be amused.

Thus, in the present ["or recent" crossed out] state of English opinion, it is a *prima facie* rule (subject to very carefully selected exceptions) that the hero of a biography should never be allowed a mistress. In respectable society such things are not tolerated, at least not openly: so they are not permissible to a person who is being held up for imitation. In the Bloomsbury of Lytton Strachey, they were thought commendable; so they cannot be allowed in a biography whose victim is being there held up to contempt. And they must not be mentioned in an amusement-biography, because they would remind its readers of problems about which it is no pleasure to think.'

that hypothesis, just as the historian is essentially a person who sticks together ready-made statements about a war or revolution or any other complex of events, so the biographer is essentially a person who sticks together ready-made statements about an individual person's life. Sir Sidney Lee, lecturing on the principles of biography from a strictly scissors-and-paste point of view, was not wholly unjustified in maintaining that history proper differs from biography chiefly in dealing with 'aggregates'—combinations of what, taken separately, are biographies.[40] This is because biography is and always must be a scissors-and-paste affair. The statements it contains are made not for their scientific value but for their gossip-value; they have to arouse emotion, not to command assent; and for the purpose of arousing emotion ready-made statements culled from 'credible' sources are very well suited.

With the discrediting of scissors-and-paste history, biography can hardly expect to maintain its old prestige as a literary form; or even the much diminished prestige it enjoys today; for that, I have no doubt, is mainly due to a delusion on the part of those who read it that they are reading history. Even today, no publisher in any country would make himself responsible for a biography on the scale of Morley's *Gladstone* or Monypenny and Buckle's *Disraeli*. It may be doubted whether[41] any reader ever ploughed through works like these either for the amusement-value to be found in them or for the magic-value of the examples which they held up to his emulation; and my own memory of the time when biographies of overwhelming length were fashionable leads me to believe that they were read because their rather inadequate gossip-value was mistaken by a large number of leisured persons for historical value.

[40] † *The Principles of Biography*, Cambridge, 1911, p. 27. [Collingwood records some critical comments on this book in an initial paragraph of his 'Notes on Historiography' (see the final footnote to the reproduction of this manuscript in the present volume).]

[41] After this, until 'That its attraction', the text is pasted over an original version which runs as follows: 'even magical considerations would lead to a publisher's profit on a biography of that size about Hitler or Mussolini. And this doubt makes me wonder whether biography has not depended in the past and does not in the present still depend for its main attraction less on its gossip-value than on its snobbery-value, the fact that people who read it flatter themselves on being students of history.'

That its attraction is a mixed one and its purposes confused is very evident from reflection on some of the features it presents in current practice. I will mention one only. A biography begins,[42] as a rule, with some account of the subject's family. Now the word family might mean various things. Etymologically, as the Latin *familia*, it means a household or domestic circle. If that is what modern biographers meant by it, they would give under this head a description of the subject's father and mother and brothers and sisters, and the friends and relations who were in the habit of paying long visits, and the old nurse, and the cook who was twenty years in the place. But that is not what we find. Then again, it might be used in a stock-breeder's or eugenist's sense, as a biological term, meaning the subject's pedigree back to, say, his sixty-four great-great grandparents, as evidence of what blood ran in his veins. And this might be of great interest if it were desired to show that the subject was of pure Aryan descent, or began with certain other advantages or disadvantages from a eugenist's point of view. But that again is not what we find. What we find is that the subject 'came of an old Yorkshire family which had been settled in the North Riding ever since the time of Edward I'.

The truth is that this entity, 'family', as commonly recognized and discussed by biographers, is a heraldic entity. To belong to a 'family' in this sense of the word is to be entitled to bear certain arms; and the only point of this stuff about the old Yorkshire family is to serve as a *pièce justificative*[43], proving to

---

[42] After this, until 'The truth is that', the text is pasted over an original version which runs as follows: 'as a rule, with some account of the hero's family. Now the word family might mean various things. It might mean pedigree, in which case the interest of the account would be to show what kind of blood ran in the hero's veins; and this might be of great interest if the biographer desired to show that the hero was of pure Aryan descent, or began with certain advantages or disadvantages from a eugenic point of view. But in ordinary practice it never has this meaning; for if it had, equal importance would be attached to all his eight great-grandparents. But normally we find the subject treated as if the attributes of family were entailed in the male line. Secondly, family might have a cultural meaning, like the Latin *familia*; it might mean the household in which the child grew up, irrespective of blood-relationships. But this is clearly not what is intended. For what we are actually told is that the child "came of an old Yorkshire family which had been settled in the North Riding since the time of Edward I", or the like.'

[43] Collingwood erroneously wrote *pièce justificatif*.

anyone who doubts it that the man was entitled to bear the arms which in fact he did bear. It is a very curious proof of the muddle prevailing in biography, that this matter of the subject's origin and antecedents should ordinarily be reduced to a question of importance only to students of heraldry, which is nevertheless conscientiously asked and answered although hardly any readers know the meaning of it, or would care if they did; and although the person whose biography is being written may not have been entitled to bear any arms at all. The only justification of it at the present day is a kind of make-believe that nobody would either have his biography written, or read anybody else's, without being a member of a circle in which everybody is entitled to bear arms and everybody knows everybody else or would like to; so that a reader will say 'I always wondered if he was one of the Yorkshire lot; uncle John used to tell us such funny things about them.' Gossip-value *plus* snobbery-value, both of them fraudulent.[44]

There is no doubt that the general discredit into which biography has now fallen, assisted by the emergence of those *enfants terribles*, the biographical play and the biographical film, has been of service to history. Nobody, I think, would say nowadays what many people were saying not so long ago, that the account of an ancient civilization based on archaeological sources falls short of genuine history, because of its anonymity: because it cannot give us the names of the persons who were concerned in the vicissitudes of that civilization, and the dates of the years in which they were born and died. Historians, as they clarify their methods and learn to distinguish evidence from testimony, are learning at the same time to distinguish their own problems from those of gossip, and to realize that the history of a thought has nothing to do with the names of the people who think it.

9. *Summary*

§1. The only certain way in which we can ever decide whether a way of thinking is successful or not, is by engaging in it for ourselves and finding out whether from this point of view the answers it gives to its own questions appear as satisfactory. It is

[44] Dated '19.2.39'.

an illusion to think that any point of view (e.g. that of a 'philo-sopher') can give a man the right to form judgments about the validity of a science he has not made his own.[45] Hence only reflection upon historical methods, by persons who have mas-tered those methods for themselves, can tell us what the object is, if any, concerning which history gives us knowledge.

§ 2. Traditionally, historians say that history gives knowledge about *Res Gestae*, understood as human deeds. Behind this for-mula is the notion that history seeks for knowledge of events only in so far as these events are actions embodying and express-ing the rationality which, according to a parallel tradition, is peculiar to man among animals.

§ 3. This is borne out by a further study of historical method. To say that the historian's evidence for his conclusions is some-thing he can see or touch, like a footprint or a charter, is to speak in a rough-and-ready way. To be accurate, the evidence is not the thing he sees or handles, but something which it 'says' to him if he is able to 'read' it. The perceptible 'evidence' is in the nature of language or of a notation of language, and the historian must treat it as such before he can use its message as the start-ing-point of an inference.

§ 4. It follows that the historian's methods are adapted only to solving one kind of problem, namely to deciphering the thought which is expressed in the 'facts' that he studies. It is therefore a serious error to maintain, as some philosophers have main-tained, that he studies 'events' in the sense in which the physi-cist, for example, studies events. Alexander's thesis about 'the historicity of things' is based on a misunderstanding of what constitutes historicity.

§ 5. It is still as true [as] when Hegel said it, that 'Nature has no history'. Many modern sciences place their subject-matter in a chronological framework; but to be placed in a chronological framework is not to be history. In history itself, what makes it history is not the chronological framework but the nature of what it contains: not events as such but *Res Gestae*, actions expressing thought.

§ 6. Comparison and contrast between stratigraphical methods as used in geology and in archaeology respectively lead

---

[45] After this, 'Any person who makes such a claim is in effect claiming the status of an inquisitor' is crossed out.

to an example of modern archaeological method and an analysis of it. As a chronologer, the archaeologist differs in no point of method from the geologist. But he is also an historian; that is, the events to which he argues are events in the thought of his *dramatis personae*, and the evidences from which he argues to these events are not mere 'finds', classified and recorded, but finds which show him, if he can 'read' them, how the people whose activities bequeathed them to him were thinking.

§ 7. All history is the history of thought. This includes the history of emotions so far as these emotions are essentially related to the thoughts in question: not of any emotions that may happen to accompany them; nor, for that matter, of other thoughts that may happen to accompany them. The current distinction between e.g. political history and the history of political thought is illusory; it is based on conceiving 'thought' as something special to 'thinkers', and forgetting that when a politician is working at political matters he is thinking about them and embodying his thoughts in action.

§ 8. Biography is not history, because its methods and interests are different. Its methods are scissors-and-paste; its interest is a 'gossip-interest', based not on the desire to get at the thought embodied in an action, which is the desire underlying historical work, but on a combination of sympathy and malice which are the emotions aroused in one animal by the spectacle of what another animal does and undergoes. Hence the aim of a biographer is to depict his hero not as *animal rationale* but as animal, by insisting on the animal vicissitudes of his life (birth, death, etc.). Under the *régime* of scissors-and-paste history, biography could share the prestige of history and people who read it for amusement could flatter themselves that they were reading history; this is no longer possible; and biography seems to be in a state of decay.[46]

[46] Dated '20.2.39'.

3

NATURE AND ACTION

1. *Historical Naturalism*

Many of the obsessions that have weighed upon historical thought in the past, many of the perplexities that still afflict it today, are due to the fact that history only reached in the present generation a state of maturity comparable to that reached by natural science at the beginning of the seventeenth century. Natural science had three hundred years' start; and during these three hundred years historical thought, in different ways at different times, occupied a position of pupilage.

One expression of this pupilage especially characteristic of the eighteenth century was the doctrine that natural science was not only historically senior to history but was logically prior to it, in the sense that nature, the object studied by natural history, was the determining cause of *Res Gestae*, the object studied by history. Historical research, conceived on scissors-and-paste lines, told us what people had done, what events had happened in the world of men; but that was all; history could not tell us why these events, rather than others, had happened. It only informed us about the facts, not about their causes. But science demands 'knowledge by causes', and if history is to be a science it must instruct us in the causes of the events concerning which at present it only informs us barely that they occurred. Suppose that we could somehow link up history to the already existing body of natural science, in such a way as to demonstrate that the hitherto unexplained events of history are effects of causes already known to exist in nature, then history would become a science.

There is no need to detail the forms which this doctrine assumed in the course of the eighteenth century. They fell into two divisions. According to one school of thought, the subordination of history to natural science must be brought about by the creation of a new science, a science of Man; and you must not spoil the sport by saying 'but we already have one science of Man, history itself'; for in this context 'science' meant a science like the sciences of nature, constructed by means of observation and experiment on inductive lines, tabulating and classifying the components that go to make up human nature and noting the way in which they vary in men of different kinds. And then, when this science had been established, we could explain for the first time why it is that those events have happened which historians have put on record. Just as a botanist can explain why a handful of bulbs, left in a dry place, give no sign of life, but when planted in the moist earth produce flowers, daffodils or snowdrops according to their kinds, for the botanist knows the nature of plants in general and the way in which this nature varies from one kind of plant to another, so the Scientist of Human Nature will be able to explain why it has happened that a number of human communities have at one time stagnated in a quiet primitive life, and at another developed civilizations, each of its own kind. Human Nature is the answer: human nature and the different natures of different breeds of men.

The other school of thought replied 'You are forgetting those all-important features of your own comparison, the moisture and the soil. It is not the differences between different kinds of men that are so important, it is the differences between the environments in which they live. If you took colonies of men from a single stock, and planted them one among the Arctic tundras and one among the islands of the Pacific, how long do you think they would go on having the same kind of human nature? There is a certain constraint that climate and geography exercise on human activities, and where these differ human beings cannot behave in the same ways.' For this school of thought human nature and its variations as between one breed and another became unimportant, if they did not entirely disappear from among the causes of historical events. There was no need for a new science of Man; all we had to do, in order to effect the due subordination of history to natural science, was to take the natural sciences we already possessed, such as geography, meteorology, botany, and so forth, and applying these to the materials given us by history find the causes of historical events in man's natural environment.

The controversy between these two schools, as to whether man's nature or man's environment afforded the truly scientific explanation of his doings; and the various attempts to find a middle course, explaining some historical events by reference to his nature or to this or that special variety of it, and others by reference to his environment; or alternatively finding everywhere a blended causation of natural and environmental factors: these things are of no interest here, though they made a good deal of noise in their time, and the noise still reverberates in faint echoes among people who do not know that history has become a science and fancy that it still occupies the position of pupilage to natural science which it occupied in the eighteenth century. And this ignorance is not a thing that can be corrected by merely calling the attention of the persons concerned to facts they have overlooked. The question at issue is not a question of fact, it is a question of prestige.

During the past three centuries, the natural sciences have established themselves in a position of intellectual authority which is the central fact about modern European civilization. They have won this position by means of a hard struggle. Their representatives, well aware that 'the same arts which did gain power, must it maintain', make it a point of honour that there is no science, no genuine form of organized knowledge, except natural science; from which it follows that history cannot of itself and by the use of its own methods achieve the status of a science; so that if it raises problems for which it wants a scientific solution it must look for that solution in the only place in which it can be found, in natural science. This fight for intellectual dominance is merely disguised beneath the cloak of a metaphysical problem, when it is said that the facts of human nature or of man's environment, or a combination of the two, are the causes of events in human history.

This is not a matter about which there is room for controversy. That was the case only when history, being an affair of scissors and paste, had not yet achieved the status of a science. The plausibility of historical naturalism, or the attempt to find in nature the causes of historical events, rested in its day on a supposed similarity between the 'facts' of history and the 'facts' of natural science. For the natural scientist, a natural 'fact' was something observed, recorded, and therefore believed in by other scientists on the authority of the credible witness who observed and recorded it. The record was accordingly susceptible of scissors-and-paste treatment: it could be copied out into the notebook of anyone who was interested, and then subjected to further treatment of an inductive kind, by which it became corroboration for a theory as to its cause. For the scissors-and-paste historian, an historical 'fact' was similarly something observed and recorded, and thereafter believed in by other historians on the authority of the credible witness who observed and recorded it, and embodied in their works. The exactness of the analogy up to this point suggested a further analogy: it suggested that the next thing to do was to set on foot an inductive inquiry (for which the historian, being a mere scissors-and-paste man, had not the qualifications) to discover its cause.

With the establishment of scientific history, the analogy vanishes. The apparent similarity of status between a natural 'fact' and an historical 'fact' is seen to be the merest hallucination. It is still permissible to describe the things an historian wants to know as 'facts', for example the 'fact' that Aurelian reformed the Roman monetary system; but not to say that such 'facts' are matters of observation and record, accepted on the authority of some observer; for in the first place Aurelian's reform of the coinage was not an observable thing, but a certain complex of thoughts in Aurelian's head and the heads of the persons affected by it, and in the second place it is asserted as a fact by economic historians not on the authority of anyone at all, but as the conclusion of an argument based on analysis of the numismatic evidence. Thus the historian has already vindicated his claim to the title of scientist, provided he is not a scissors-and-paste historian, in the process of arriving at the 'facts' beyond which the naturalistic argument assumes that he must go in order to earn that title.

I do not wish to defend the above statement against any critic who says 'you seem to have a very old-fashioned and obsolete conception of the methods used in natural science'. I know; or rather, I know that I have been describing a very old-fashioned attempt at subordinating history to natural science, in which the implied theory about the methods of natural science was very likely as false as that about history. But that is how people argued: and it is the argument which today still underlies a great deal of what I find people saying and writing in defence of historical naturalism. If it is obsolete, that is not my fault.[47]

2. *The Science of Human Nature*

Let us look separately at the two schools of thought referred to in the preceding section. The first was the 'Human Nature' school, whose proposal was for a new science of man: a naturalistic science, based on observation and experiment and proceeding by way of inductive thinking.

It is important that we should see exactly what the proposal was. It was not what its name seemed to imply. There were already in existence not one only but several inductive sciences of man based on observation and experiment: human anatomy, human physiology, and that science of instinct, sensation, and feeling which had gone ever since the sixteenth century by the name of psychology. The new science of human nature was not meant either to combine or to annex the spheres of these well-established disciplines, whose future advancement it cheerfully left in the hands of their own experts. It aimed at covering a quite different field.

We already know that this was the field of historical facts, because the chief purpose of the new science was to provide scientific commentary on those facts. We already know, too, that those facts had long been identified as *Res Gestae*, actions embodying thought. The new science of human nature was therefore envisaged as a science of human thought, or the rational part of human nature.

There were already sciences of human thought, logic and ethics, more than 2000 years old, and now those eighteenth-century additions to their number, aesthetic[s] and economics; but none of these resembled the natural sciences in method, and the proposal for a new science of human nature was part of a quite deliberate attempt to maintain that, so far as 'matters of fact' were concerned, the method of natural science was the only valid one. The proposal, then, was to replace logic and ethics, and their new kindred economics and aesthetics, by a science

[47] Dated '19.2.39'.

covering the same ground but using naturalistic methods. How would this differ from the sciences it was to supersede?

The answer is simple: by ignoring the distinction between success and failure. Our idea of natural science and its distinction from the human sciences has grown up under the shadow of the idea that nature is the work of God, and that the works of God differ from the works of man in that man is fallible and God is not. The works of man are seldom just what they are meant to be, and whenever we think about them we must bear this fallibility in mind. Here is something which looks like a ship, but it won't float; what does that prove? Does it prove that it is not a ship at all but something else? No; what it proves is that it is an attempt at a ship, but an unsuccessful attempt. Here is something that looks like an argument, but it doesn't prove anything; what then? It is an attempt at an argument, but an unsuccessful attempt. Thus all the human sciences distinguish what a thing is meant to be from what it is, and aim at distinguishing cases where the two coincide (successes) from cases in which they do not (failures). But according to the assumptions of our natural science, assumptions consciously worked out and explicitly stated in the sixteenth and seventeenth centuries and thereafter taken for granted, cases of this kind are not distinguishable in the world of nature, because the world of nature, being God's handiwork, contains no failures. Because God is omnipotent, the 'laws of nature' admit of no exceptions; so that if you find an exception to what you had supposed a law of nature, that only proves there is no such law of nature.

And, once more, it is no use saying 'this is all very obsolete as an account of scientific method', for it was not obsolete in the eighteenth century, which is the time I am talking about. It is true that the first blow had been struck at it by the 'illuminist' revolt against Christian theology; but no one would have admitted this at the time. Similarly in the nineteenth century people who were on the 'scientific' side in the 'quarrel between religion and science' were at pains to protest that they were only attacking Christian 'dogma', and not Christian 'ethics'; although as a matter of fact the two stood or fell together.

In the eighteenth century, then, people believed in the universality and inviolability of 'natural laws' and the impossibility of dividing nature's successes from nature's failures, even if they had parted company with the theology on which these beliefs were based. And so the methodological difference between the natural sciences and the sciences of man came down to this: that the sciences of man distinguished between successes and failures, and tried to give an account of the means used to decide which was which, whereas in the sciences of nature nothing of the sort was to be found, because the distinction on which it was based did not arise.

The means by which a success is distinguished from a failure is called a standard or criterion; a science which investigates criteria I call criteriological. Logic and ethics have always been criteriological sciences, interested in the question how people distinguish successes from failures in the respective fields of theory and practice. Aesthetic[s] and economics had, from the first, the same character. It is clear, therefore, that if these sciences were to be superseded by a naturalistic science of human reason, the chief novelty about the new science would be that it would drop criteriology. And this in fact is what it did, and what has been done ever since by the 'psychology' that has taken over its assets and traded on them ever since.[48]

I do not intend any disrespect to modern psychology in so far as it has continued and developed very successfully the work of the old psychology, the rightful owner of the name, which was originally intended to identify its field as the 'psychic' part of man's nature or activities, as distinct from his 'bodily' structure and activities on the one hand and his 'rational' activities on the other. I am only deploring the fatal error by which, in the course of a misguided attempt to show that natural science is the only kind of science that can exist, the old psychology annexed a territory which was not its own, which its methods did not enable it to manage, and in which to the present day it has never done anything but expose itself to ridicule and contempt.[49] To study

[48] After this, an extensive passage which runs to the paragraph beginning 'Logic divides propositions' has been crossed out. Because of its interest, and despite some repetition on p.88, we have integrated it into the main text here.

[49] † I do not choose to repeat or supplement here the evidence for the bankruptcy of modern 'psychology', in this sense of the word, which I have already adduced in my *Introduction to Metaphysics*, chapter'. [Collingwood refers here to chapters IX–XII of his *Essay on Metaphysics* (101–32), in which the science of psychology is criticized. He worked on this book during his journey to and from the Dutch East Indies, that is, at the same time he worked on 'The

thought without taking into account the fact that people sometimes think truly and sometimes falsely; to study conduct without taking into account the fact that people sometimes act wisely
or effectively or honourably, and sometimes in ways the opposite of these; this is no study of thought or conduct at all, and a
study conducted on these principles can find out anything[50]
about the subject it proposes to illuminate.

Equally futile, and for the same reason, is the attempt to find
causes for different kinds of rational activity in the biological
difference between varieties of the human race. We have seen
this eighteenth-century illusion rise from its grave in our own
time, and stalk abroad in the shape of a vampire, not in one
country alone, but, up till now, in a second also, which has fallen
under the domination of the first.[51] And because there is nobody
in the world who thinks that even the most determined and
highly paid sophist could make out a case for this illusion, the
science in whose light it would vanish is proscribed.

The reference to criteria is not something incidental to
reason, something which a study of reason can afford, even during a small part of its labours, to ignore. Theoretical reason is
operative only so long as it pursues truth and avoids error; it is
the pursuit of truth and the avoidance of error, nothing else.
Practical reason is not something which at times, incidentally,
involves the attempt to do right and avoid doing wrong; it is the
attempt to do right and avoid doing wrong. The writing of a
poem is essentially an attempt to write a good poem. The making of a bargain is essentially an attempt to make a good bargain.
The proposal to study these activities or any part of them while
ignoring the criteriological problem is a proposal to substitute
for the study of them some way of passing the time more in harmony, perhaps, with a fashionable superstition, but not at all
conducive to the advancement of knowledge. It does not call for
criticism. It calls for something else.[52]

Principles of History'. The title *Introduction to Metaphysics* was apparently a
preliminary one.]

[50] Collingwood originally wrote 'nothing'; we are presumably to understand
'anything' as ironical.
[51] Collingwood refers here to the fascist regimes of Germany and Italy, of
which he was an uncompromising opponent. See also the last chapter of his
Autobiography.
[52] Dated '19.2.39'.

Logic divides propositions into true and false, and inferences into valid and invalid: and proceeds to subdivide these main classes with a view to showing what precisely the features about an argument, for example, are which lead a man if he understands argument to say 'this argument is sound' or 'unsound'. A naturalistic or 'psychological' science of human thought ignores these differences and attends to others, such as the differences between propositions that are believed or arguments that are framed by persons of different kinds, or by persons of the same kind under different conditions. Where the logician will say 'that argument is defective, I will show you why', the 'psychologist' will say 'that argument is characteristic of a middle-aged, middle-class Englishman, I will show you why'.

Ethics divides actions into right and wrong, and into virtuous and vicious, and tries to determine what is meant by these terms and by what marks we are guided in their application, whether as agents who are trying to do our duty and wish to be clear about what it is, or as spectators who ask themselves whether this or that agent has succeeded in doing his duty or not. A naturalistic science of conduct will say nothing about all this, but will divide actions according to quite other principles, such as the differences between the kinds of persons who are found, on a statistical investigation, most often doing them.

Aesthetic[s] divides works of art into good and bad, and is interested in a spectator's attitude towards them only so far as this attitude is or includes a 'judgment', correct or incorrect, as to their merits. A naturalistic science professing to cover the same field will approach it quite differently, studying works of art irrespectively of the distinction between good ones and bad ones, and studying spectators' attitude[s] towards them irrespectively of whether their judgment as to their goodness or badness is correct or incorrect, or indeed whether it includes any such judgment at all. It may, for example, be a merely emotional, or even a merely bodily, reaction.

There is one question of fundamental importance to be asked concerning the purpose which these naturalistic sciences are intended to serve. It includes three alternatives.

(1) Are they intended to supersede the traditional criteriological sciences? That is, are they intended to take their business out of their hands, and do it better?

(2) Do they intend, not this, but business of a different kind? And

(2a) Is this because people think that the business of the old criteriological sciences is being on the whole properly carried out by the sciences which profess to do it, and can be safely left in their hands? or

(2b) Is it because people think that it is no good asking the questions asked by the old criteriological sciences, because experience shows that nothing has ever come of asking them, and that if we are to have any science of human thought it must be one which asks questions of a different kind?

Let us consider these alternatives.

(1) Originally, the naturalistic science of human thought was intended to supersede the old criteriological sciences. The proposal for it was made quite explicitly in a revolutionary spirit. The idea was to sweep away a group of pseudo-sciences of mind, and substitute genuine, up-to-date, sciences of mind, by a revolution modelled on that by which the new sciences of nature had replaced the medieval pseudo-sciences of nature.

This view is still widely held today; but it will not stand examination. As I have shown, the problems of the old mental science are not taken up by the new and handled in an up-to-date manner; they are left severely alone.

(2a) This might be because the business of solving them was left in the hands of the people who had always professed to be working at it; but I hardly think anyone will claim that this is so. The attitude of 'psychologists' towards logic or ethics is not one of respect as towards a different but closely-related and reputable science. It is one of outspoken contempt. So we turn to

(2b) This again is not the answer actually implied in the behaviour of 'psychologists'. For not only do these, in their capacity of scientists, habitually distinguish in their own work between true and false statements, sound and unsound arguments, frequently saying for example that the views put forward by rival psychologists are incorrect or confused; but they believe, as any scientist must believe, that they have criteria by which sound arguments and unsound ones can be distinguished, and have been known, like other scientists, to appeal publicly to such criteria, saying that a certain view of a certain rival psychologist must be unsound, 'because . . .'. And if they appeal to criteria, they assume that the nature of these criteria can be investigated and indeed has been investigated, and that what they are doing when they make the appeal is warranted by the result of the investigations.

Thus we get no answer to our question. All the three alternatives are explicitly or implicitly asserted, all three are explicitly or implicitly denied. All we have found, by asking it, is a hopeless confusion of thought, underlying the heads-I-win-tails-you-lose attitude always characteristic of the bully who, professing to appeal to argument, is really appealing to his own big stick. The essence of the original situation, as it arose in the eighteenth century, and of the situation in which 'psychology' stands today, was and is the big stick: the prestige of naturalistic methods, with their well-deserved reputation resting on what they had achieved since the late sixteenth century, being used to enforce exorbitant claims, now against the growing, but immature science of history, now against the ancient sciences of logic and ethics (ancient, and sadly in need of overhaul and repairs), into which that same prestige forbade inquiry, not only as to whether they were justified, but as to what they were.

For anyone who dislikes yielding to the argument of the big stick, the important thing is to bear in mind that the criteriological problem is not only an object of legitimate interest to any science of human thought, it is for any such science the fundamental problem. The reference to criteria is not something incidental to human thought, something which even during a small part of its labours a study of thought can afford to ignore. Theoretical reason is operative only so long as it pursues truth and avoids error; it is the pursuit of truth and the avoidance of error, nothing else. Practical reason is not something which at times and incidentally involves the attempt to distinguish between right and wrong, or virtue and vice: it simply is the making of these distinctions. The making of a poem is nothing but the attempt to make a good poem. The making of a bargain is nothing but the attempt to make a good bargain. The proposal to study these activities, or any part of them, while ignoring the criteriological problem, whatever may be the reason for which that problem is ignored, is a proposal to substitute for the study of human thought some other way of passing the time, more in harmony, perhaps, with the social conventions or fashionable superstitions of a group which may be a powerful group and may have won its power by honourable means, but not at all conducive to the advancement of knowledge.

Such a proposal, based as it is on prestige and not on argument, cannot be touched by criticism. It calls for something else.

3. *Psychology in Lagado*

'There is a sect of philosophers among them' (I quote the words of Philip Gulliver, whose manuscript account of the voyages in which he retraced his grandfather Lemuel's footsteps came to my hands in very strange circumstances that I am not yet at liberty to disclose) 'who hold that whatever exists can be measured and weighed, and that nothing can be known except what is known by these means. Now many persons in that island are much addicted to music; and this is a great annoyance to these philosophers, because as a condition of entering their sect they have been forced to undergo an operation which renders them perfectly deaf, so that they can neither hear the music themselves nor understand what those who talk about it are saying, even though they talk in the deaf-and-dumb alphabet, in which alone members of this sect are able to converse.

'But their admirable good sense has saved them from a fate so shocking as to confess that here is a thing they do not understand, and has devised a way in which they can understand it better than anyone else. They take musicians, and seat them upon certain thrones, having a great many callipers and measuring-tapes arranged upon a kind of scaffolding above them, and weighing machines below. Then they cause others to play music.

'While this is going on, they note with the utmost exactitude every change in the size, shape, position, or weight of each bodily part in those who are seated upon the thrones, and print all these notes in their *Transactions*, together with the conclusions to which they lead. And although their Science of Music is still in its infancy, having been practised only for some seventy years, and with all the newest improvements in the thrones for no more than twenty-three, they have good hopes of bringing it to perfection in time; and point with pride to many pieces of very careful work already done, such as the paper of a certain Sordomute, extending over many numbers of their journal and entitled "Reactions of Fraudulent Solicitors to *Three Blind Mice*", a musical composition much admired in their country.

'This paper I read for myself, and found in it many curious conclusions. I learned, what I never knew before, that a fraudulent solicitor, philosophically defined, is one having a Fraudulence Quotient (F.Q.) of over 50 percent. The author proved to my satisfaction that among those with an F.Q. of between 50 and 70 percent, the chief reaction was a certain drumming of the feet, whereas among those with an F.Q. of between 90 and 100 it was a distinct increase in the size and weight of the generative organs. It seemed to me that in this paper some progress had been made towards determining in a truly Philosophical manner what music is; and I accordingly persuaded a musician of my acquaintance to read it; which when he had done, "why", said he, "there is nothing here about music at all".

'"For you know", he continued, "that music is made up of certain sounds, longer or shorter in duration, louder or softer in volume, higher or lower in pitch, and the like; that what a man is trying to do when he writes or plays music is to arrange the various sounds in such a way that a proper relation is preserved between their several lengths, volumes, pitches and the rest, and improper relations avoided; and that what a man is trying to do when he listens to music (if he knows anything of the matter, which, I beg leave to say, is perhaps not always the case with even the most excessively fraudulent solicitors) is to use what judgment he has to resolve whether those several relations have been properly or improperly ordered. And any man who knows, as you and I know, that this is all there is in the business of music, can see for himself that if books about music are to be read it is better to read those, however bad, in which the right ordering of relations between lengths and volumes and pitches is discussed, than others, however good, in which it is not.

' "As for this Sordomute", he continued, raising his voice a little, "whom I conceive to be infinitely more fraudulent himself than any solicitor he ever seated upon his imbecile engine, if I had my way he would be whipped out of the town at a cart's tail for obtaining money by false pretences, and his stipend made over to some honest man who had projected a machine for perpetual motion or for making silk purses out of sows' ears, or to the impoverished author of a treatise showing that the earth is flat."

'This opinion I repeated, using the deaf-and-dumb alphabet, to the very eminent philosopher who had lent me the paper, as we walked on the next morning towards his Academy. "That", said he, "is what I should have expected of a musician. A man of any other kind would have known that the earth is not flat. But let me tell you that I have some influence with the education authorities, and hope in time to eradicate this obstructive attitude towards a genuine science of music by means of a law compelling all children, before they enter school, to undergo the same operation which we undergo when applying for admission to our sect. The matter is urgent; because unless on this point our views are proved correct, the foundations of our entire philosophical system will . . .". Here, blundering against another foot-passenger, he fell beneath a wagon, of whose approach from behind him he had been unaware; and, to my unspeakable mortification, expired.'[53]

4. *Nature as Environment*

The second eighteenth-century school of thought which attempted to make history shine with a reflected scientific light, if it could not achieve a direct luminosity for itself, proposed to do this by finding explanations for the recorded events of human history in the natural conditions under which those events had taken place.

This was a far more respectable enterprise than the one we have just been considering. The idea of appealing to a 'Science of Human Nature' for an account of the causes which bring about the events of human history, even if it had so far succeeded as to be more than an empty programme, a project never leading to anything but discord among those who pretended to execute it, would always have been exposed to the double

[53] Dated '20.2.39'.

objection that naturalistic methods, based on the distinction between nature and mind, were being used in defiance of the charter under which their use was justified in their own field; and that even its completest success would only have led to the idle and tautologous conclusion that a certain person did a certain thing because he was the kind of person who does that kind of thing; for 'human nature' was only a pseudo-scientific name for the fact that men do the things they do. And admittedly it was the historian, not the scientist of human nature, who had to answer the question 'what do they do?'

In concentrating on man's environment, the natural scientist was at least not forfeiting his title to respect by breaking the fundamental rule of his own game. His fundamental rule was that his methods applied to nature; and that was how he was applying them. Moreover he was not, like the scientist of human nature, devoting his whole energies to building up an argument which, if it could ever be made to go at all, would merely go round in a circle. If differences between different civilizations could be explained by reference to differences in their geographical, climatic, botanical environments, they would be explained by reference to something other than themselves, and the argument would therefore be formally valid. So, at least, it appeared. Was the appearance genuine? It would be rash to say either yes or no, until we have looked into the matter more closely.

The first qualification which this form of historical naturalism would seem to require is this. The effect of environment on a civilization is never direct or immediate. There are many ways in which climate and so forth do directly and immediately affect, in ways to be studied by natural science, the men whose environment they are. Thus, strong sunlight turns men brown. But this is an effect of nature on nature: the physical environment produces physical effects in man's physical organism. Since all history is the history of thought, the historian is not concerned with man's physical organism any more than he is concerned with that organism's physical environment. Anatomical and physiological descriptions of man, or of this or that variety of the human species, are physical anthropology, not history. Books about 'The Races of Man' have no historical interest whatever, except as documents of a propaganda by which natural science has tried, not so much to capture the field of history, as to obstruct the growth of historical thought by distracting public attention towards itself. Not man's physical organism in itself, but what he does with it in order to express his thoughts, is the historian's concern.

I do not doubt, again, that the purely physical effects produced in man's organism by its physical environment are accompanied by corresponding effects in his emotions and appetites; although this is a subject on which information is very difficult to procure, because what has been written about it has mostly been written by men who did not understand the difference between feelings and thoughts, or were doing their best, consciously or unconsciously, to obscure that difference. I will therefore take a hypothetical example. Suppose that there are two varieties of the human species in one of which sexual maturity, with all its emotional accompaniments, is reached earlier than in the other; and that this can be explained physiologically as an effect of climate and the like. Even so, this early sexual development is in itself no more a matter of historical interest than skin-pigmentation. It is not sexual appetite in itself, but man's thought about it, as expressed for example in his marriage-customs, that interests the historian.

It is on these lines that we must criticize the all too familiar commonplaces about the 'influence' of natural environment on civilizations. It is not nature as such and in itself (where nature means the natural environment) that turns man's energies here in one direction, there in another: it is what man makes of nature by his enterprise, his dexterity, his ingenuity, or his lack of these things. The 'unplumbed, salt, estranging sea', as a nineteenth-century poet called it, echoing with some servility this eighteenth-century conception, estranges only people who have not learnt to sail on it. When they have discovered the art of navigation, and become reasonably skilled mariners, the sea no longer estranges, it unites. It ceases to be an obstacle, it becomes a highway. Beset with dangers, no doubt; but the internal combustion engine is not the first thing that has made travel by land a dangerous business. Travelling, however it has been done, has always had its dangers; but no human being has ever put safety first and stayed at home if he thought, as who has ever not thought? that something he wanted was waiting for him at the other end of the road. And if he did, it would still be his thought about the dangers, not the dangers themselves, that kept him at home.

So the attempt to generate the historical characteristics of a civilization out of the natural characteristics of its environment results after all, in a *generatio aequivoca*: for those characteristics of the environment which determine the characteristics of a civilization are not characteristics that the environment possesses in its own right, they are characteristics conferred upon it by the people whose conduct they determine: the navigability of the sea, which is another name for the art of navigation; the fertility of the land, which is a name for the art of agriculture; the penetrability of the mountain range, which is a name for the art of pathfinding; and so forth: or the opposites of these, which are names for the lack of those arts, or more commonly for shortcomings in them.

When this qualification has been made, however, the naturalism that we have qualified is only qualified, not abolished. It has undergone no mortal wound. For although navigability and fertility are now conceived no longer as qualities in varying degrees directly inherent in seas and lands, apart from the rational activity of men, but as resultants of an interaction between lands and seas on the one hand and this rational activity on the other, yet nature as it is in itself is still one of these two interacting terms. The physical constitution of these things is what it is, throughout all changes in the activity which man directs upon them; and being what it is, it makes permanent and unalterable demands on man. Granted that its influence on his civilization is never direct, as the eighteenth century supposed, but is always mediated through his enterprise and skill in dealing with it, yet this only pushes historical naturalism back to another and stronger position; for behind this mediation we find nature as it actually and indefeasibly is, nature in itself, determining the events of history.

This sounds fair enough. But on second thoughts we shall see that if what has already been said about history is taken seriously it is a position that is not likely to remain altogether unqualified. It has been said that history is concerned with *Res Gestae*, with human action as embodying and expressing human thought. It should follow from this that the historian can recognize no 'factors' in history but such as consist in human thought. I am not denying that the phrase 'nature as it actually and indefeasibly is' or 'nature in itself' may have a meaning. I am not even denying, what may or may not be true, but what for the purposes of the present argument we may assume to be true: that the knowledge of nature possessed by natural scientists is a knowledge of nature as it actually and indefeasibly is, a knowledge of nature in itself. What I am denying is that the thing designated by such names can ever be detected by the historian as a factor influencing the course of history.

An example in which 'nature' is not concerned will perhaps help to explain this. Human affairs, some of them or all of them, are sometimes said to be settled by 'brute force'. The troops of a large nation invade the territories of a small one; a decisive battle is fought, in which the troops of the smaller nation are crushed, or alternatively the situation is such that anyone with any knowledge of warfare must be convinced that[54] if fighting takes place that will be the outcome of it; the aggressor announces his desire to annex his victim; and the statesmen of the small nation 'can only yield to brute force'. Certainly the phrase is justified; it is an intelligible way of saying what is true; but it has to be intelligently read. An unintelligent reader might think it was meant to point a contrast between hard facts as they

---

[54] After this, running to 'should the war continue', the text is pasted over an original version, which reads: 'if fighting takes place that will be the outcome of it; the aggressor announces its desire to ruin its victim; and the statesmen of the small nation can do nothing except "yield to brute force". Certainly the phrase is justified; it is an intelligible way of saying something that is true: but it does not mean exactly what a hasty interpreter might think. A hasty interpreter might think it was intended to point a contrast between hard facts as they are in themselves and somebody's mere thoughts about these facts. But this is not so. What causes these statesmen to yield is not the situation "as it actually and indefeasibly is", the situation "in itself", for if the situation had been exactly what it is and they did not know it, but believed it to be otherwise (if for example they had believed that powerful allies, bound by treaty to defend them in just such a contingency, intended to carry out their promises), they would not have yielded. What makes them yield, then, is not the fact of the situation's being what in fact it is but their knowledge that the situation is what in fact it is. And since they would have acted in precisely the same way had they believed the situation to be like that, whereas in fact it was different (if for example the aggressor's army was, unknown to them, on the point of becoming useless through mutiny or the failure of its ammunition supply, or his people on the point of revolution . . .'

are in themselves, and somebody's mere opinion about them. This is not so. What causes these statesmen to yield is not the situation 'as it actually and indefeasibly is', the situation 'in itself'; for if the situation had been exactly what it is, and they had believed it otherwise, if for example they had mistakenly thought that certain powerful allies, bound by treaty to defend them in just such a contingency, meant to carry out their promises, they would not have yielded. What makes them yield, then, is not the situation's being what it is 'in itself', but their knowledge that the situation is like that.

And since they would have acted in precisely the same way had they believed the situation to be like that, whereas in fact it was different; if for example the aggressor's army was, unknown to them, on the point of becoming useless through mutiny or through failure of its ammunition supply, or if his people were on the point of breaking out into revolution should the war continue; we must qualify that again and for 'knowledge that the situation is what it is' read 'belief that the situation is what in fact they believe it to be'. Here at last we get down to hard facts as the historian understands hard facts. The phrase hard facts, in the mouth of an historian, refers to the facts of how certain human beings on certain occasions think. And if we now go back to the original hypothesis and ask what was meant by a decisive battle in which certain troops are crushed, we shall see that here again we were supposing ourselves to be confronted by hard facts of the same kind. A defeated army is an army that thinks it is no use going on fighting. References to brute facts are ways of referring to the belief that certain persons both intend and are able to bring about a situation in which other persons will think 'it is no use our trying to prevent them from treating us as they please'.

With this example before us, let us go back to the case of nature. The thesis I have undertaken to defend is that no historian can ever find 'nature as it actually and indefeasibly is', or 'nature in itself', among the factors that influence the course of history. What influences the course of history is not nature in itself, but the beliefs about nature, true or false, entertained by the human beings whose actions are in question. It was not the eclipse, but his belief that days with eclipses on them were unlucky, that influenced so disastrously Nicias's siege of

Syracuse. It is not the fact that typhoid is endemic there, but our belief that it is, combined with our belief in a certain method of prophylaxis, that influences us to inoculate our troops when they are going to operate there. And the factors which interact with the arts of navigation and agriculture and pathfinding to make the sea navigable and the land fertile and the forest or mountain traversable are not the natures of sea and land, forest and mountain, as they actually and indefeasibly are in themselves, but the beliefs about these various natures entertained by the persons into whose civilization we are inquiring. And this quite irrespectively of whether those beliefs are true or false.

In Java, where I am writing, agriculture means the growing of rice in irrigated sawahs. Among the features of Javanese agriculture that strike every European visitor are these: that sawahs are not manured, and that the rice-seedlings are invariably planted out by women. Europeans would say that the first of these features is based on the true belief that sawahs do not need manure; true, because the irrigation-water brings down a constant supply of silt from the rich volcanic soil of the mountains; and that the second is based on the false belief that rice planted out by men would not bear children in the form of grain; false, because the way in which a plant develops is not affected by the sex of the person who plants it.

Be it so. Let us admit that Javanese sawah-cultivation is based on beliefs about nature which are partly the merest superstitions. Still, that is how it is done: and it is highly successful; and moreover its superstitious character is not exceptional. I at any rate have known at first hand no farmers, just as I have known no sailors, however civilized, whose methods in agriculture and navigation do not show at least a touch of what is called superstition. And there is evidence that the earliest farmers and sailors in Europe were not less superstitious than those of today. It follows that the methods of agriculture and navigation which they developed, and developed very successfully, were not devised and conceived by themselves as methods of coping with a natural environment like that with which we (rightly, no doubt) think of ourselves as coping nowadays, a nature whose processes develop according to impersonal and invariable laws; but as methods of coping with a nature peopled by—or shall we say consisting of?—gods and demons, whose beneficent activities must be promoted, and their maleficent ones fore-stalled or counteracted, by what we call superstitious means.

What man, at any stage of history, thinks of himself as deal-ing with, when we say that he is dealing with nature, is never nature as it is in itself but always nature as at that stage of his-tory he conceives it. All history is the history of thought: and wherever in history anything called nature appears, either this name stands not for nature in itself but for man's thought about nature, or else history has forgotten that it has come of age, and has fallen back into its old state of pupilage to natural science.[55]

5. Freedom[56]

With the disappearance of historical naturalism, the conclusion is reached that the activity by which man builds himself his own constantly-changing historical world is a free activity. There are no forces other than this activity which control it or modify it or compel it to behave in this way or in that, to build one kind of world rather than another.

This does not mean that a man is free to do what he wants. All men, at some moments in their lives, are free to do what they want: to eat, being hungry, for example, or to sleep, being tired. But this has nothing to do with the freedom to which I have referred. Eating and sleeping are animal activities, pursued under the compulsion of animal appetite. With animal appetites and their gratification or frustration history is not concerned. It makes no difference to the historian, as an historian, that there should be no food in a poor man's house; though it may and must make a difference to him as a man with feelings for his fel-low-creatures; and though as an historian he may be intensely concerned with the shifts by which other men have contrived to bring about this state of things in order that they should be rich and the men who take wages from them poor; and equally concerned with the action to which the poor man may be led not by the fact of his children's unsatisfied hunger, the fact, the

<hr>

[55] Dated '20.2.39'.

[56] This section appears in *The Idea of History*, 315–20, under the title 'History and Freedom', but the text there differs in some respects from the ver-sion in the original manuscript.

physiological fact of empty bellies and wizened limbs, but by his thought of that fact.

Nor does it mean that a man is free to do what he chooses: that in the realm of history proper, as distinct from that of animal appetite, people are free to plan their own actions as they think fit and execute their plans, each doing what he set out to do and each assuming full responsibility for the consequences, captain of his soul and all that. Nothing could be more false. Henley's rhyme does no more than utter the fantasy of a sick child who has discovered that he can stop himself crying for the moon by making believe that he has got it. A healthy man knows that the empty space in front of him, which he proposes to fill up with activities for which he accordingly now begins making plans, will be very far from empty by the time he steps into it. It will be crowded with other people all pursuing activities of their own. Even now it is not as empty as it looks. It is filled with a saturate solution of activity, on the point of beginning to crystallize out. There will be no room left for his own activity, unless he can so design this that it will fit into the interstices of the rest.

The rational activity which historians have to study is never free from compulsion: the compulsion to face the facts of its own situation. The more rational it is, the more completely it undergoes this compulsion. To be rational is to think, and for a man who proposes to act, the thing that is important to think about is the situation in which he stands. With regard to this situation he is not free at all. It is what it is, and neither he nor anyone else can ever change that. For though the situation consists altogether of thoughts, his own and other people's, it cannot be changed by a change of mind on the part of himself or anyone else. If minds change, as they do, this merely means that with the lapse of time a new situation has arisen. For a man about to act, the situation is his master, his oracle, his god. Whether his action is to prove successful or not depends on whether he grasps the situation rightly or not. If he is a wise man, it is not until he has consulted his oracle, done everything in his power to find out what the situation is, that he will make even the smallest plan. And if he neglects the situation, the situation will not neglect him. It is not one of those gods that leave an insult unpunished.

The freedom that there is in history consists in the fact that this compulsion is imposed upon the activity of human reason

not by anything else, but by itself. The situation, its master, oracle, and god, is a situation it has itself created. And when I say
this I do not mean that the situation in which one man finds
himself exists only because other men have created it by a rational activity not different in kind from that by which their suc-
cessor finds himself to be in it and acts in it according to his
lights; and that, because human reason is always human reason,
whatever may be the name of the human being in whom it
works, the historian can ignore these personal distinctions and
say that human reason has created the situation in which it finds
itself. I mean something rather different from that. All history
is the history of thought; and when an historian says that a man
is in a situation this is the same as saying that he thinks he is in
a situation. The hard facts of the situation, which it is so important for him to face, are the hard facts of the way in which he
conceives the situation.

If the reason why it is hard for a man to cross the mountains
is because he is frightened of the devils in them, it is folly for the
historian, preaching at him across a gulf of centuries, to say
'This is sheer superstition. There are no devils at all. Face facts,
and realize that there are no dangers in the mountains except
rocks and water and snow, wolves perhaps, and bad men perhaps, but no devils.' The historian says that these are the facts
because that is the way in which he has been taught to think.
The devil-fearer says that the presence of devils is a fact,
because that is the way in which he has been taught to think.
The historian thinks it a wrong way; but wrong ways of thinking are just as much historical facts as right ones, and, no less
than they, determine the situation (always, as we know, a
thought-situation) in which the man who shares them is placed.
The hardness of the fact consists in the man's inability to think
of his situation otherwise. The compulsion which the devil-
haunted state of the mountains exercises on the man who would
cross them consists in the fact that he cannot help believing in
the devils. Sheer superstition, no doubt: but this superstition is
a fact, and the crucial fact in the situation we are considering.
The man who suffers for it when he tries to cross the mountains
is not suffering merely for the sins of his fathers who taught him
to believe in devils, if that is a sin; he is suffering because he has
accepted the belief, because he has shared the sin. If the modern

historian believes that there are no devils in the mountains, that too is only a belief he has accepted in precisely the same way.

The discovery that the men whose actions he studies are in this sense free is a discovery which every historian makes as soon as he arrives at a scientific mastery of his own subject. When that happens, the historian discovers his own freedom: that is, he discovers the autonomous character of historical thought, its power to solve its own problems for itself by its own methods. He discovers how unnecessary it is and how impossible it is for him, as historian, to hand these problems over for solution to natural science; he discovers that in his capacity as historian he both can and must solve them for himself. It is simultaneously with this discovery of his own freedom as historian, that he discovers the freedom of man as an historical agent. Historical thought, thought about rational activity, is free from the domination of natural science, and rational activity is free from the domination of nature.

The intimacy of the connexion between these two discoveries might be expressed by saying that they are the same thing in different words. It might be said that to describe the rational activity of an historical agent as free is only a roundabout and disguised way of saying that history is an autonomous science. Or it might be said that to describe history as an autonomous science is only a disguised way of saying that it is the science which studies free activity. For myself, I should welcome either of these two statements, as providing evidence that the person who made it had seen far enough into the nature of history to have discovered (a) that historical thought is free from the domination of natural science, and is an autonomous science to itself (b) that rational action is free from the domination of nature and builds its own world of human affairs, *Res Gestae*, at its own bidding and in its own way (c) that there is an intimate connexion between these two propositions.

But at the same time I should find in either statement evidence that the person who made it was unable (or for some ulterior purpose had decided to profess himself unable) to distinguish between what a person says and what is implied in what he says: unable, that is, to distinguish the theory of language, or aesthetic, from the theory of thought, or logic; and was therefore committed, for the time being at least, to a verbalistic logic, in which the logical connexion between two thoughts that imply each other is confused with the linguistic connexion between two sets of words which 'stand for the same thing'.

I should see, too, that his attempt to burke the problems of logic by substituting for them problems in linguistics was not based on any very just appreciation of the nature of language; because I should see that, of two synonymous verbal expressions, he was assuming that one really and properly means the thing 'for which it stands', while the other means this only for the insufficient reason that the person who uses it means that by it. All of which is very disputable. Rather than approve such errors, I should prefer to leave the matter where I have left it; to say that these two statements (the statement that history is an autonomous science and the statement that rational activity is free in the sense described) are not synonymous forms of words, but express discoveries neither of which can be made without making the other. And arising out of this, I will observe that the 'free-will controversy' which was so prominent in the seventeenth century had a close connexion with the fact that the seventeenth century was the time when scissors-and-paste history in its simpler forms was beginning to dissatisfy people, and when historians were beginning to see that their own house, as I have elsewhere put it, needed setting in order: that historical studies ought to take example from the study of nature, and raise themselves to the level of a science. The desire to envisage human action as free was bound up with a desire to achieve autonomy for the study of human action.

But I do not leave the matter exactly there; because what I have already said in the first section of the second chapter carries it a stage further. It was said in that section that only by using historical methods could we find out anything about the objects of historical study. It follows that we must first achieve a genuinely scientific and therefore autonomous method in historical study before we can grasp the fact that human activity is free.

This may seem contrary to facts; for surely, it will be said, many people were already aware that human activity is free, long before that revolution took place by which history raised itself to the level of a science. I will offer two answers to this: not mutually exclusive; but the one relatively superficial, the other, I hope, a little more profound.

(1) They were aware, perhaps, of human freedom; but did they grasp it? Was their awareness a knowledge that deserved the name of scientific? Surely not; for in that case they would not only have been convinced of it, they would have known it in a systematic way, and there would have been no room for controversy about it, because those who were convinced of it would have understood the grounds of their conviction and been able to state them convincingly.

(2) Even if the revolution by which history has become a science is only some half-century old, we must not be deceived by the word revolution. Long before Bacon and Descartes revolutionized natural science by expounding publicly the principles on which its method was based, people here and there had been using these same methods, some more often, some more rarely. As Bacon and Descartes so justly pointed out, the effect of their own work was to put these same methods within the grasp of quite ordinary intellects. When it is said that the methods of history have been revolutionized in the last half-century, this is what is meant. It is not meant that examples of scientific history may be sought in vain before that date. It is meant that whereas, earlier, scientific history was a thing of rare occurrence, hardly to be found except in the work of outstanding men, and even in them marking moments of inspiration rather than the even tenor of study, it is now a thing within the compass of everyone; a thing which we demand of everybody who writes history at all, and which is widely enough understood, even among the unlearned, to procure a livelihood for writers of detective stories whose plot is based upon its methods. The sporadic and intermittent way in which the truth of human freedom was grasped in the seventeenth century might, to say the least of it, have been a consequence of this sporadic and intermittent grasp on the method of scientific history.[57]

6. *Heads or Tails?*[58]

When Karl Marx boasted that he had taken Hegel's dialectic and 'stood it on its head', [he] did not mean quite what he said.

[57] Dated '23.2.39'.

[58] This section was inserted by Knox in *The Idea of History*, 122–6, as § 8 of

Hegel's dialectic begins with thought, goes on to nature, and ends with mind. Marx did not invert this order. He did not make his own dialectic begin with mind, go on to nature, and end with thought. Marx was only referring to the first and second terms, not the third. He meant that whereas Hegel's dialectic began with thought and went on to nature, his own dialectic began with nature and went on to thought.

Marx was neither a fool nor a philosophical ignoramus, and he did not for a moment suppose that the priority of thought over nature in Hegel meant that Hegel regarded nature as a product of mind. He knew that Hegel, like himself, regarded mind as a product (a dialectical product) of nature. He knew that the word 'thought', in the sense in which Hegel called logic the science of thought, meant not that which thinks but that which it thinks: so that logic for Hegel is not a science of 'how we think', it is a science of Platonic forms, abstract entities, 'ideas'—if you remember to take seriously Hegel's own warning that you must not suppose 'ideas' to exist only in people's heads. That would be 'subjective idealism', a thing Hegel abominated. They only got into people's heads, according to him, because people were able to think; and if the 'ideas' had not been independent of people's thinking them, there would not have been any people, or for that matter anything else. For these ideas were the logical framework within which alone a world of nature and man, of unthinking beings and thinking beings, was possible.

These ideas not only made a framework for nature, they also made a framework for history. History, as the action in which man expressed his thoughts, had the general outlines of its structure laid down for it in advance by the conditions under which the thinking activity, mind, alone can exist. Among these conditions are two: first, that mind should arise within and continue to inhabit a world of nature; secondly, that it should work by apprehending those necessities which lie behind nature. Accordingly, the historical activities of man, as activities that

part III. In that book, however, the text of p. 122 and the first paragraph of p. 123, up to 'in which bankers think about banking', is taken from p. 116 of Collingwood's lectures on philosophy of history of 1936 (Bodleian Library, Collingwood Papers, dep. 15). The text of the manuscript also differs in some other respects from the version in *The Idea of History*.

take place or go on, take place or go on in a natural environment, and could not go on otherwise; but their 'content', i.e. what in particular people think and what in particular they do by way of expressing this thought, is determined not by nature, but by the 'ideas', the necessities that are studied by logic. Thus logic is the key to history, in the sense that men's thoughts and actions, as studied by history, follow a pattern which is a coloured version of the pattern logic has already drawn in black and white.

This is what Marx was thinking of when he said he had turned Hegel's dialectic upside down. When he made that statement, what he had in mind was history; the only thing in which Marx was much interested, and the thing which, after all, Hegel was probably more interested in than anything else. And the point of his remark was that whereas for Hegel, because logic came before nature, it was for logic to determine the pattern on which history worked, and for nature only to determine the environment in which it worked, for himself nature was more than the environment of history, it was the source from which its pattern was derived. No use, Marx thought, to draw patterns for history out of logic, like the famous Hegelian pattern about the three stages of freedom: 'for the Oriental world, one is free; for the Greco-Roman world, some are free; for the modern world, all are free.' Better to draw your patterns out of the world of nature, like his own no less famous one of primitive communism, capitalism, socialism, where the meaning of the terms is derived not from logical 'ideas' but from natural facts.

What Marx was doing was to reassert the fundamental principle of eighteenth-century historical naturalism, the principle that historical events have natural causes. He reasserted this principle, no doubt, with a difference. The Hegelian side in the pedigree of his thought gave it the right to bear in its arms the term 'dialectical'. The materialism on which he so strongly insisted was not ordinary eighteenth-century materialism, it was 'dialectical materialism'. The difference is not unimportant; but it must not be exaggerated. Dialectical materialism was still materialism. And the whole point of Marx's conjuring-trick with the Hegelian dialectic was accordingly this: that whereas Hegel had broken away from the historical naturalism of the eighteenth century, and had not indeed achieved, except in a partial and limited way, but had at any rate demanded an autonomous history (for an history that recognized no authority except that of logical necessity might not undeservedly claim the title of autonomous), Marx went back on this demand and subjected history once more to that domination by natural science from which Hegel had in principle proclaimed it free.

The step which Marx took was a retrograde one; but, like so many other retrograde steps, it was more retrograde in appearance than it was in reality; for the territory he was evacuating was territory that had never been effectively occupied. Hegel had demanded an autonomous history, but he had not in fact achieved it. He had seen, as it were prophetically, that history ought on principle to be liberated from its pupilage to natural science; but in his own actual historical thinking that liberation had not been achieved. It had not been achieved, that is to say, with regard to history ordinarily so called, that is, political and economic history; a field in which Hegel was not a master, and in which he contented himself with scissors-and-paste methods. There was one kind of history in which he was a master, and a very great one: the history of philosophy. Here, and here alone, he entered into effective occupation of an historical field; and it was here that he must have convinced himself, as he has convinced many a reader, that his claim of autonomy for historical thought is in principle justified. That is why dialectical materialism has always had its greatest successes with political and economic history, and its greatest failures in the history of philosophy.

There is a second reason why Marx's step was more retrograde in appearance than in reality. I said that an history which recognizes no authority but that of logical necessity may fairly claim to be called autonomous; but this is a very mild way of describing the relation which Hegel believed to exist between history and logic. It suggests that Hegel meant no more than that historians must think logically. But in fact Hegel thought that the patterns or types of structure exhibited by complexes of historical fact were identical with the patterns or types of structure exhibited by logical 'ideas', and were derived from these as their originals. Hegel did not take this view without thinking out its implications and seeing what he thought good reasons for taking it; and these are not reasons which can be disposed of, or even stated, in a few words. I shall therefore not try to deal with

them, or even to state them, here. I will content myself with
observing that to accept them is to place history in the same kind
of pupilage to logic in which Marx, following the eighteenth-
century historical naturalists, placed it to natural science; and
that this position is not tolerable to a person who knows, as any
educated twentieth-century reader knows, that history is an
autonomous science and does not stand in that relation to anything whatever. The point I am making at the moment is that
here, in respect of its relation to logic, Hegel did not even claim
autonomy for history, far less achieve it; and that made it easier
for Marx to 'correct' him by going back to the eighteenth-
century view.

For these reasons Marx's reversal of the Hegelian dialectic
was[59] something more than a mere backward step; it was based
in the realities of the situation Hegel had bequeathed to his
pupils; and for the same reasons, it led to a very great advance in
the handling of that particular kind of history, economic history, in which Marx was especially interested. If all modern
treatment of the history of philosophy goes back to Hegel as the
great modern master of the subject, all modern treatment of
economic history goes back in the same sense to Marx.
Nevertheless, the practice of research can no more be left today
where Hegel left it for the history of philosophy, or where Marx
left it for economic history, than the theory of history can be left
where Hegel left it with his 'philosophy of history' based on
transcendental logic or where Marx left it with his 'dialectical
materialism'. These were expedients whereby a type of history
which had not passed beyond the scissors-and-paste stage
attempted to conceal the defects inherent in that stage by the
adoption of non-historical methods. They belong to the embry-
ology of historical thought. The conditions which justified and
indeed necessitated them no longer exist.

7. *Summary*

§ 1. 'Historical naturalism' was the attempt, characteristic of the
eighteenth century, to elevate history to the level of a science by

---

[59] In the manuscript, 'was' is followed by 'not only', but the latter has been
bracketed, i.e. marked for deletion, probably at a later date.

external means: by referring questions which arise about its subject-matter for any scientifically-minded man, not to history itself for their answer, because the answers are such as history cannot give, but to natural science. The reason why history cannot give the answers is that the only business of history is to 'record events', whereas the questions are in the form 'what caused these facts?' In other words, historical naturalism presupposes that history is a scissors-and-paste affair and can never be anything else. For an history which has ceased to be a scissors-and-paste affair the problem which historical naturalism professes to solve does not arise; because scientific history does not deal in 'recorded events'. Historical naturalism was therefore a by-product of a certain immature stage in the development of historical thought. It is further considered in this chapter only because relics of it survive today, among persons who are working (consciously or unconsciously) to keep history in its old position of pupilage to natural science, which arrived at scientific maturity three centuries earlier than history.

§ 2. One form of historical naturalism was the attempt at a 'science of human nature', to establish generalized conclusions about how human beings act. The word 'act' here referred to historical action, i.e. to action as expressing thought; so the proposed science did not interfere with psychology, which had existed under that name since the sixteenth century as the science of sensation and feeling. What it did interfere with was the old sciences of logic and ethics, and the new ones of economics and aesthetics, which it proposed in effect to abolish and hand over their territory to an enlarged psychology; and psychology is the name under which this enlarged science is today known. The meaning of this transference of territory was that the activities of human reason were to be treated 'non-criteriologically', that is, without reference to the self-critical element in them (the way in which a thinker aims at applying certain standards or 'criteria' and thereby finding out whether he is thinking rightly or wrongly). But this element is really the essence of a rational activity, so that a 'science of reason' which ignores it is not a science of reason and throws no light on its nature.

§ 3. It is like a 'science of music' invented by some sect of crazy philosophers in *Gulliver's Travels*, who should try to discover what music was by measuring and weighing persons listening to it, irrespectively of whether their 'subjects' knew anything about music or not.

§ 4. The second form of historical naturalism was that which attempted to find the causes of historical events in the geographical, climatic, etc. conditions under which they happened. Such physical conditions certainly do produce direct and immediate effects upon man, in ways explicable by natural science; but only on man as a physical and psycho-physical organism, not on the thoughts which alone constitute him an historical agent. When it is said that they affect his history, it is not meant that they affect it in this direct manner. What is meant is that they affect it through the medium of his own thoughts and actions. His history is never affected by natural things in themselves, but only by what he makes of them; e.g. the sea affects his history because, to him, it is or is not navigable: which means that he has or has not, by dint of his own enterprise, dexterity, and ingenuity, developed the art of navigation to a certain point. Moreover, the difficulties which he overcomes in learning to sail, to farm, etc., are not difficulties arising out of the physical nature of sea or land, they are difficulties arising out of his ways of thinking about sea or land, irrespectively of whether these are true or false. Problems for man's thought about nature to solve are not set to it by nature, they are set to it by man's thought about nature. The 'influence of nature on history' is an influence of history upon history (human reason on human reason).

§ 5. Thus the action which history studies is 'free', not determined by natural conditions but determined by itself. The discovery that this is so is a discovery intimately related to the discovery that historical thought is 'free' or autonomous, i.e. not dependent upon natural science for the solutions of the problems that arise out of its subject-matter, but able and obliged to solve all such problems for itself. The so-called problem of human freedom solves itself, the moment history becomes a science.

§ 6. Karl Marx, when he said that he had made Hegel's dialectic stand on its head, meant that whereas Hegel's dialectic led to mind through a sequence of thought (logic) and nature, his own led to mind through the same terms in the reverse order. The importance of the reversal lay in the theory of history. Neither for Hegel nor for Marx could history be a science, for in their days historical thought had not yet achieved its autonomy. But whereas Hegel placed history in pupilage to logic, Marx reasserted in the style of the eighteenth century its pupilage to natural science. Marx's view of history is historical naturalism in its second form (cf. § 4) but with the difference that the causal efficacy of the natural world over the historical is understood 'dialectically'. Marx thus abandoned a position by which Hegel had made an advance on the eighteenth century; but this retrograde step was more apparent than real, because (except in the history of philosophy) Hegel had not effectively occupied the territory he claimed to have conquered. With the rise of scientific history, 'dialectical materialism', which was only an expedient to compensate for the defects of scissors-and-paste history without overcoming them, became obsolete.

4

THE PAST[59]

Res Gestae, or deeds, are not only actions, they are past actions. That history is about the past is no less an established and traditional opinion among historians, than that it is about action. And this opinion is in agreement with the results hitherto arrived at in the present study of historical method: for historical thinking, we have seen, proceeds by interpreting evidence, and in the first chapter evidence was described as consisting of traces which past action had left in the present world, so that reference to the past is necessarily contained in any piece of historical thinking. It is true that this account of evidence was reconsidered and elaborated in the second chapter, where we found that the traces left by past action in the present world are not themselves evidence, but are only a linguistic notation which the historian converts in his own mind into evidence by reading them. But this does not affect the conclusion that the actions an historian studies are actions which have left perceptible traces in the world he inhabits, and that in order to have left such traces they must be actions which have happened. They must be past actions.

This does not mean that they belong to the past in all the senses in which that word is used. Often, when we speak of the past, we contrast it with the present as something distant in time from something close in time, or (which comes to the same thing; for today's dinner, as the Autocrat of the Breakfast-Table remarked,[60] subtends a larger visual angle than yesterday's revolution) as something which no longer interests us from something in which our interest is still fresh. The past in that sense of

[59] This section is a mere fragment. Its subject does not accord with the one assigned to the fourth chapter of Book I in the Scheme for 'The Principles of History' (see p. 245), but it appears to be relevant to the proposed subject-matter for Book II.

[60] The allusion is apparently to *The Autocrat of the Breakfast-Table* (Boston, 1858), by Oliver Wendell Holmes.

the word, which may be called the 'emotional past', may acquire a certain attractiveness from the very fact that it has ceased to interest us. Weak and timid minds, afraid of the present (the emotional present, that is to say) because they are unequal to the emotional strains it imposes on them, find a welcome calm awaiting them when they step outside it into the emotional past, where all passion is spent, all strife ended, and action that once was alive and dangerous is stilled in the calm of death. To such minds there is great attraction in the study of history, because it seems to offer them an escape from the urgencies and perplexities of actual life into a realm of peace. And for the same reason, people who feel that temptation and know that it must be resisted have been known to denounce historical studies as a cowardly refuge from reality.

Attraction and denunciation alike are based on a misunderstanding. They are based on confusing two different senses of the word past. The historian's past is not the emotional past, it is the past pure and simple. It is not that part of the past in which we are no longer interested, it is the past as such. A man who takes refuge in medieval charters from his thoughts about a threatening letter from a solicitor or a notice printed in red from the collector of taxes, brought him by the morning's post, or from disquieting news in the daily paper, is not taking refuge from the present in the past. He is not taking refuge from actual life in history. For the letter or newspaper about which he refuses to think is an historical document. That is why he refuses to think about it. It is a matter of history that the solicitor has threatened him, that the tax-collector has demanded more money than he has in the bank, or that the affairs of his country have entered upon a dangerous crisis. What he is doing is to pick and choose among various trains of historical thought, repressing some which are unpleasant to him and concentrating upon others which involve him in no such discomfort.

The disquieting letter or newspaper, it is true, belongs not only to the past, in the sense that the events it reports are yesterday's events, but also to the present, in the sense that it serves as a medium through which those events have an impact here and now on the reader's mind. But this does not remove it from the sphere of history. It only confirms its historical character.

All historical evidence is a medium through which past events have an impact on the mind of the historian; medieval charters no less than solicitors' letters.

HISTORY AND PHILOSOPHY[61]

It is commonly thought that history and philosophy are not only different forms of thought but, in certain ways at least, opposite forms of thought, each characterized by features which it is characteristic of the other to lack. With regard to their methods, philosophy has been conceived as working by means of demonstration, staking its very life on its ability to prove with conclusive force the doctrines it asserts, and accomplishing nothing unless that is accomplished: history as working by the acceptance of what authorities have to say, or alternatively (since the notion of an authority has long been obsolete among working historians) as unable to reach demonstrative certainty from interpretation of its evidence, and content with something variously called probability or 'moral certainty'. With regard to their objects, philosophy has been conceived as thought about the universal, the timeless, the eternal: history as thought about the individual, the temporal, the transient.

This way of contrasting history with philosophy cannot survive the study of historical thought already made in the earlier chapters of the present book. With regard to its method, we have seen that history has nothing to do with probabilities. Or rather, it has no more to do with probabilities than any other science. Probability is a methodological conception applicable to any sphere of knowledge. To say that something is probable is to say that it requires proof. If I come across an English word whose meaning I do not know, I say that it is probable I could find its meaning by looking it up in the *Oxford English Dictionary*. To prove this probability is to look the word up

---

[61] This is also a separate fragment, not belonging to Ch. 4 of Book I. It should be considered rather as a sketch of what would be said at an appropriate point in Ch. 3 of Book II (see the Scheme for 'The Principles of History'). Collingwood also discusses the relationship between philosophy and history, but in a quite different context, at the beginning of 'The Principles of History', Ch. 2.

there. If I go to meet a train on a foggy day and the train does not turn up to time, I say that it has probably been delayed by the fog. To prove this probability is to find out whether it has been thus delayed. When somebody stumbles upon a truth by accident, there is no stage in the process of discovery at which it is a probability; but when he finds a truth for which he is looking, there is such a stage: namely when he is looking for it and has not yet found it, but expects to find it. What are called degrees of probability are degrees of confidence in this expectation; and what is called the mathematical theory of probability is the mathematical analysis of the grounds on which a given degree of confidence rests, or rather, may rest; for these grounds do not always admit of mathematical analysis, and therefore a mathematical theory of probability as such is not conceivable.

PART II

ESSAYS AND NOTES ON
PHILOSOPHY OF HISTORY 1933–1939

NOTES TOWARDS A METAPHYSIC

Causation and Development[1]

. . . We speak of causes in history, e.g. the causes of the French Revolution, or of the decay of the feudal system. The word is not equivocal: here too it means a necessary antecedent.[2] This use is longer established in fact than the other: Caesar (*Bell. Gall.* I. 1. 4) says that the geographical situation of the Helvetii was the *causa* of their warlike disposition, and cf. the use of αἴτιον in Thucydides. But it is a different kind of necessity. Mill calls a cause an unconditional antecedent; but this kind is a

This manuscript, written in five 'Woolworth' notebooks lettered A to E, consists of jottings recorded from September 1933 to May 1934. On the cover is written Περὶ Φύσεως ['on nature'], but Collingwood calls the subject he discusses 'cosmology'. The general position towards which the text moves, which has as its background the evolutionary philosophies of Alexander, Lloyd Morgan, Smuts, and Whitehead, and is reached by an application of the theory of the scale of forms expounded in the *Essay on Philosophical Method*, is presented more systematically in the 1934 Conclusion to Collingwood's Lectures on Nature and Mind. From the manuscript's 522 pages we have selected a few passages which seem especially relevant to the themes of the present volume. The title page has the following opening passage: 'If these notebooks fall into the hands of anyone but myself, let him take notice that they are intended as receptacles for purely experimental, disjointed and desultory notes and attempts to "think on paper" at problems whose solutions are not in my mind when I begin to write on them. Much of what I have written here is mere groping down blind alleys. At best, these notebooks can be regarded as quarries containing, together with much rubbish, materials out of which I hope to build a metaphysical treatise' (Bodleian Library, Collingwood Papers, dep. 18).

[1] This section and the three following are from Book A, fos. 66–71, 84–91.

[2] The reference is to a passage of a preceding paragraph which runs thus: 'The ordinary scientific idea of cause as the necessary antecedent (as stated by Hume and Kant) certainly implies, as Kant saw, that only particular phenomena can be called causes or effects, and that the category cannot be applied to the thing in itself . . .' This 'scientific' sense is presumably the 'other' sense referred to in the sentence which follows, a sense which Collingwood now begins to contrast with a specifically historical one, a position he was to develop further in *EM*.

conditional (necessary) antecedent. An historical cause is a fact or assembly of facts which, when an agent is aware that he stands in them as his circumstances, determine him through this awareness to act in a certain way. The causality is doubly conditional: (i) he cannot be acted upon by the facts unless he is aware of them as his circumstances (ii) nor unless he freely and intelligently thinks out a line of appropriate response to them. He can truthfully say 'I *had* to retreat *because* of the enemy's strength', where *because* carries its full meaning: but (i) if he hadn't known the enemy's strength it wouldn't have thus affected him (ii) nor if he had been a sufficiently incompetent officer to neglect it.[3]

There are also biological causes, like the warmth and the egg. Here awareness is not required, but active response is: here, too, therefore, causality is conditional on the active co-operation of that in which the effect is produced.

There remain mechanical causes as alone unconditional. But if a billiard ball hits another and sets it in motion, this surely demands active co-operation on the part of the second ball; it must go on being itself and acting according to the laws of its own nature, conserve the motion imparted to it, etc.

Thus the idea of transeunt causality seems nowhere adequate; all causality has a double aspect (a) an agent acts on a patient (b) the patient is itself active, and the change produced in it is conditional on this and is itself a change of activity in it, an earlier activity changing into something which it 'has it *in* it' to change into. The idea of the patient as purely patient is a mere abstraction from the facts, or, if a dogma, a mere mistake.

In this way what from an external point of view appears as transeunt causality from an internal point of view appears as a change of activity occasioned by a stimulus from without; or, since a stimulus is not a stimulus except it be reacted to, a change of activity *tout court*, i.e. development.

λόγῳ, χρόνῳ πρότερον ['*prior in logic, in time*']

Concepts have among themselves an order, i.e. a *prius* and a *posterius*: this is a logical order. It is irreversible and is such that the

---

[3] In § 4 ('Nature as Environment') of Ch. 3 ('Nature and Action') of 'The Principles of History' the same argument is used.

later cannot be without the earlier as *pre*supposed, or rather pre-being or forebeing (Sir Thos. Browne's good word), and the earlier cannot be without leading to the later.

This notion is full of difficulties. Hegel thought that *all* genuine concepts fell into a single unilinear order: I do not know if he was right, but I suppose it probable. Croce of course agrees, though he thinks there are very few genuine concepts, which makes it more plausible.[4] I would only say, for the present, that order is constantly found among concepts, cropping up as it were. So far, I think I am on safe ground.

Events also have among themselves an order. This is a temporal order. It likewise is irreversible, and according to the ordinary idea of causation it likewise is necessary, i.e. the later cannot be without the earlier, nor the earlier without leading to the later.

There are difficulties here too—even worse ones, I think; they are pretty familiar. But in spite of them no one seems able entirely to dispense with the notion.

What I want to suggest here is that history is the coincidence of logical with temporal order. I mean that the successive events of history form an order which, so far as it is genuinely historical (not all chronological sequences of events in human life are so), is a logical order as well as a temporal one. If it is temporal but not logical, the sequence is not historical but merely chronological—it is what Croce calls annals, or a mere series of events. History begins when we see these events as leading by necessary connexions one to another: and not only that—for history demands more than that—but as the γένεσις ['coming to be'] of something, the history *of* something which is coming to be in this temporal process. Now, in a mere temporal process, necessary though it is, nothing comes to be; there is only change, not development. What imparts to an historical process its character of development is that the phases of this process are the phases in the self-development of a concept—e.g. that parliamentary government is coming into existence, which can only happen if the concept parliamentary government is articulated into elements or moments which (a) are capable of arrangement

[4] Collingwood here refers to Croce's doctrine of the pure concept. On this see his *Logic as the Science of the Pure Concept*, tr. Douglas Ainslie (London, 1917), 20–3, 37–9. See also Collingwood's discussion of Croce in *IH*, 194–8.

in logical order, the first being what historians call the germ of
it (b) are capable of being brought into temporal existence *in
that order*.

Thus history is the deployment of a concept in a process that
is at once logical and temporal.

Alexander's Categories

Rationalism and empiricism, I suppose, are one-sided attempts
to derive reality from logical and temporal sources respectively.

(a) If you ignore time and think *after* simply means *because*,
you get Spinoza. You will then get a world of purely logical entities with purely logical connexions: *tout est donné* and there is no
freedom or development. You get a kind of pseudo-time in the
shape of the logical sequence described in language calculated to
appease your desire for a temporal sequence.

(b) If you ignore logic and think *because* simply means *after*,
you get something like Hume. Your world is now a world of
point-instants between which there are no relations except
spatio-temporal ones. You will have a kind of pseudo-logic consisting of these relations posing as logical relations—in Kantian
terms, you will have the schemata of the categories masquerad-
ing as the categories themselves.

At present it seems to me that Gentile represents (a) (for he
reduces history to a purely logical sequence)[5] whereas
Alexander represents (b) . . .

---

[5] Collingwood here refers to Gentile's dialectic of *pensante* and *pensato* (act
of thought and content of thought). According to Gentile the *pensante* is out of
time because it creates time, whereas the *pensato*, as the product of *pensante*, is
always in time. In 'Can the New Idealism Dispense with Mysticism?', which
Collingwood read in 1923 to the Aristotelian Society (*Proceedings of the
Aristotelian Society*, Suppl. 3 (1923), 161–75; repr. in *Faith and Reason*, ed.
Lionel Rubinoff (Chicago, 1968), 270–82), he explains that the mind, which is
his term for Gentile's *pensante*, is both in and out of time, because it '*originates
change in itself*'. 'For then', Collingwood maintains, 'as the source and ground
of change, it will not be *subject* to change; while on the other hand, as undergoing change through its own free act, it will exhibit change' (*Faith and Reason*,
275). In the 'Libellus de Generatione' of 1920, however, Collingwood had criticized Gentile for identifying the *pensante* with the pure act of thought, thus
reducing all experience to thought, in particular philosophical thought, a position he identified with that of Spinoza. On this subject, see also Rik Peters,

'Nature has no history'

All existence has, or is, a history. This statement sharply conflicts with the view of Hegel, who divides existence[6] into (a)
nature, a static *Stufensystem* in which everything is arranged
outside everything else (b) spirit, a dynamic *Stufensystem* in
which everything turns into everything else. These are the
realms of Science and History respectively. Science as developed by Galileo and Newton certainly *did* seem to be the study
of something which though temporal was not historical: i.e. in
nature as so conceived there was no development, there was only
change: and the object of science was not the changes but the
unchanging laws that governed them. History, on the contrary,
was plainly the study of something (*Geist*) *in fieri*: something
whose changes, being governed not by law but by consciousness
of law, could never be reduced to expressions of unvarying formulae.

Hegel is patently a very able historian with a lively sense of
historical reality and historical method, and a not very able natural scientist; if he is radically wrong about one or other sphere,
it is likeliest to be Nature.[7] Moreover, as Leibniz said, philosophers are generally right when they affirm and wrong when
they deny. Well then: has nature a history?[8]

'Croce, Gentile and Collingwood on the Relation between History and
Philosophy', in David Boucher, James Connelly, and Tariq Modood (eds.),
*Philosophy, History and Civilization: Interdisciplinary Perspectives on R. G.
Collingwood* (Cardiff, 1995), 152–67.

[6] Added on the opposite page: 'Yet this is not right. It is not a division of
existence, for nature and spirit don't exist in the same sense; nature exists for
another, spirit for itself. Ultimately, spirit exists and nature doesn't. Nature is
so to speak a framework of abstractions against which the historical development of spirit registers itself, very much as within nature space and time are a
framework against which the movement of bodies registers itself. And this
removes much of the objection to Hegel's view. We have only to add, this
framework is not really rigid. And very likely Hegel would reply "of course it
is not *really* rigid: that is what I mean!"'.

[7] Collingwood does not capitalize 'Nature' consistently in this section, but
we have left the text as it is.

[8] Added on the opposite page: 'Croce, *Storiografia* ix, agrees with Hegel. He
pours scorn on the cosmological romances of vulgarized semi-scientific
thought, and regards these as mere mythology in which abstractions are strung
out on a time-scale. He realizes firmly that at best they are not "la storia degli

(a) There is too much solid basis in Hegel's position to allow an easy denial. *Prima facie* it is true that nature changes but does not develop, and that development is the prerogative of mind— So Joseph in his Spencer lecture, reaffirming Hegel's main position.

(b) But the whole Darwinian view of the world lies in the opposite scale. Unless Darwinian science is totally misdirected, it is a fact that in the nineteenth century a great and fertile revolution was effected in natural science by adopting the view that nature *has* a history. It remains to reconcile these positions by showing in what sense nature has a history and in what sense it has not.

Here it may be of use to point out that even within the Hegelian realm of Spirit there is a department which has no history and forms a quasi-nature, 'human nature' as psyche or subjective spirit. This is a curious anomaly: Croce has pointed it out (*Ciò che è vivo*, p. 155).[9]

Further, there are even peoples who 'have no history'— *Naturvölker* etc.—according to a current conception. And Hegel seems to accept this: a great deal of the life of the human world he regards as 'unhistorical', for history is only the history of the State, in his view, and before that begins man is devoid of self-consciousness and of freedom. And cf. what he says of the Inca and Aztec states as collapsing at their first contact with Spirit—implying that they are Nature.

storici", because that has its object individually determined and proceeds by internal reconstruction while this concerns itself with types and abstractions and proceeds by analogy (114). But he also realizes that the "living dialectic of the genesis" of geological strata or primitive vegetable life are objects for historical thought (119), but closes on a note of hesitation, inconclusively calling this *pseudostoria* (120).' Collingwood here refers to ch. IX, 'La "storia della natura" e la storia' ('"History of Nature" and History Proper'), in Croce's *Teoria e storiografia* (Bari, 1917), in his possession since 1917. He discusses Croce's idea of the relation between nature and history in *The Idea of History*, 198–200, concluding that Croce's resolution of nature into spirit is incomplete.

[9] Collingwood refers here to Croce's *Ciò che è vivo e ciò che è morto della filosofia di Hegel* (Bari, 1907), 155. The third edition was translated by Douglas Ainslie as *What is Living and What is Dead of the Philosophy of Hegel* (London, 1915), and reprinted with an introduction by Pete A. Y. Gunter (Lanham, Md., 1985), 160–1. The editors thank Rik Peters for generous assistance with nn. 5, end of 8, and 9.

I. Can one reconcile (a) and (b) by saying that whereas Spirit has a rapid historical movement—macroscopic so to speak—Nature has one, but a microscopic one? This would be a half-truth. Geological time belongs to the history of Nature and it is obviously far slower than historical time. The habits of ants and bees do not change within what we call history, just as human nature does not, but all must have changed vastly in the time-scale of palaeontology. And this difference of velocity is discernible as between (i) Nature and the *Naturvölker*, for palaeolithic man developed much faster than ants or bees (ii) *Naturvölker* and *Kulturvölker*, and the velocity increases as civilization increases. One might suggest that all history shows a variable velocity-factor: at the beginning time all but stands still, as it goes on its velocity increases until at some ideal point in the future it would have become infinite, thus packing any amount, however large, of development into any amount, however small, of time. At this stage one day would be as a thousand years, and the self-externality of time would be overcome—events would take *no* time.

This speculation may possibly prove of interest later; but for the present there are objections to the attempted reconciliation of (a) and (b).

(i) The difference between Nature and Spirit cannot be a mere difference of degree. They are opposites, rather.

(ii) Where will you draw the line? Any such distinction is merely arbitrary. A may say 'palaeolithic time moves too slowly for me to regard it as history', B may say 'but not for me'.

(iii) *Why* should time move with an accelerating velocity? Only because of some change or development undefined which permits the acceleration: e.g. the electric telegraph enables us to transmit news more quickly, it *is* not merely the quicker transmission.

(iv) There is danger of optical illusion. Do we not merely *think* more recent history more eventful than the remoter past? Is there *really* any acceleration of velocity?

(v) What anyway is *meant* by time moving faster? What moves faster, moves faster relatively to a framework, and this framework is time itself, so *time* can't move faster—indeed doesn't move at all, nor yet stand still. We are of course using the language of Rosalind (I'll tell you who time stands still withal . . .)[10] but it badly needs explaining.

II. Can one reconcile (a) and (b) by saying that Nature has a history but doesn't know it, whereas Spirit knows it (self-consciousness being the differentia of Spirit) and thus has it in a new and intensified way? This too would be a half-truth. Broadly and in general, Spirit knows it *has* a history but knows very little and in varying degrees what that history is: Nature doesn't know it at all (or anything else)—So here the division is too abrupt, the continuity element seems lacking: the proposed solution merely applies, rather mechanically, a ready-made formula whose real applicability is to a rather different kind of subject-matter (e.g. A wants x, B wants + knows that he wants it).

III. I seem driven back to the scale of forms[11] (is this another ready-made formula? No, not in any bad sense, for it was made to fit exactly such cases as this). Existence is history, but the scale of existences is a scale in which the historical character is at first rudimentary and then gradually emerges. It will be necessary to trace the stages of this emergence.

History in the fullest sense—historian's history—is a thing whose nature and methods I know well. It is always the history of man; specifically the history of man as active spirit, organizing his own life and reshaping it at will. It proceeds by interpreting documents, these documents being man's works regarded as the expression of his spirit. Its aim is the reconstruction, in a present act of thought, of the past thought which has made the present what it is: hence it is always focussed on the present and working at the explanation of the present. And the present does not, here, mean a timeless present like $2 + 2 = 4$, it means the actual present, what is now, was not yesterday, and will not be tomorrow.

Before there can be history—I do not say before there can be historical thought, but before there can be anything for it to

---

[10] The allusion is to Shakespeare's *As You Like It*, Act III, Scene 2.

[11] Collingwood refers here to his theory of the scale of forms as explained in his *Essay on Philosophical Method*. At the beginning of his 'Notes' he says that he hopes that this theory may help to clear up the difficulties regarding the relation between matter, life, and mind by seeing it, in accordance with the theory of the scale of forms, as exemplifying various kinds and degrees of reality, distinct from and opposed to each other.

think about—man must realize both in fact and in consciousness his power to re-shape his own life by his own will. He must know his freedom and know that this freedom is unlimited. He must know, that is to say, that the rules of the game under which he lives are rules not simply to be discovered and obeyed, but to be *altered*, by himself. That was known (thought doubtless in a very dim and insecure way) by the first man who chipped a flint or pointed a stick in the fire: so with him human history in the strict or highest sense begins.

But in order that there should be history in this highest sense there must first be history in a vaguer and lower sense.

Now in general, history is development: I mean, a process in which the form as well as the matter changes, namely becomes itself. In non-historical change, forms are imposed on matter and it loses them again; there is change, one thing changes into another (day into night etc.), but the form does not change: that which makes this a day is not different from that which made it day a million years ago. This is change as it occurs in Hegelian Nature with its absence of history. In historical change, the form, in the course of its reappearance in matter, itself changes; e.g. as the tide ebbs and flows on the coast it gradually erodes the coast and alters its own ebb and flow, so that we can speak of the geological history of that coast; or as pigeons reproduce their kind the kind itself undergoes change, so that for the first time we can speak of a history of the species or origin of the species.

In this secondary sense, nature *has* a history—Perhaps one may distinguish the two as (a) *Development*, or history in the wider sense (b) history in the narrower (which is also the stricter or more proper) sense, i.e. *History*. So far as (b) is the proper sense, Hegel is right. So far as (a) also is history, he is wrong.

Gentile on History[12]

The time has not yet come when I, at any rate, can make a total judgment of Croce's philosophy, and therefore of Gentile's, which on the whole I regard as a fossilized or arthritic version—

[12] This section and the following are from Book B, fos. 8–18.

containing in general the same ideas, but working them out with blind disregard of all not in the immediate field of vision—of Croce's. But I am obliged here to comment on *one* aspect of their fertile and many-sided discussion of History.

Croce, whose antagonism to Hegel has served in a highly instructive way to mark his own limitations (as he says himself, in beginning to read Hegel he came 'to grips with his own consciousness'), opposing the universal to the individual, contends that philosophy thinks the former, history the latter: that Hegel was utterly mistaken in supposing that there could be a philosophy of history, because historical reality (the individual) can be cognized only in one way (viz. by historical thinking) and simply escapes the philosophical point of view (*Ciò che è vivo*, vii). The individual contains the universal as its predicate, and hence history contains philosophy as a subordinate moment (the methodological moment: *Storiografia*, appendix III). And it easily follows that every historical fact, being concrete, has as predicates *all* the categories known to philosophy. Hence all the categories are present equally, *en bloc* as it were, in every historical fact, and the distinction between one and another fact cannot ever be expressed by referring one to one category and another to another. This view Gentile shares with him, and this is what I am considering here.

The past is, on this view, an abstraction from the present, which alone is actual; history is a projection of thought backwards into time, like a jet of water thrown backwards by some marine animal to push it forwards. There is therefore no real development: only an eternal present, which does not enrich itself by taking up the past, but defecates a past out of itself. This seems to me to be subjective idealism. It follows from the indifference of logical structure between fact and fact: since in everything that matters every fact is identical with every other, all presents are the same present, differing 'merely empirically', i.e. not at all. The past being a mere abstraction from the present, past facts cannot be known in their concreteness, and there is no series of facts; there is no transition from one to another, nothing becomes, everything *is* in a timeless present. Gentile seems to me to have concentrated his attention on the epistemological notion of the historian building up his history into the past and so forming his perspective of past time, but to have neglected the problem of the relation between perspectives; and each man's perspective is for him a subjective-idealistic world, in which the object is not spirit (*pensiero pensante*) but idea (*pensiero pensato*). The problem of development, which had been pushed out of sight by Croce's polemic against Hegel, has been wholly overlooked by Gentile, with the result that Fascist thought, egocentric and subjective, can rightly be called by Croce *antistoricismo*.

Tout passe

To exist is to be in time. That which is in time comes into being at one time and, if it endures for a while, ceases to exist at another. The mind, according to my hypothesis, is in time: it therefore comes into being and passes away.

If this really follows from the hypothesis, there is a conflict between the hypothesis and all those hopes of immortality which have so persistently haunted mankind. It is supposed to be the part of an enlightened spirit to welcome such a conflict as this, and without hesitation to take the part of 'science' against 'religion', of the hypothesis, that is, against the hope. But this crusade against superstition is at best completely unphilosophical, and at worst only another superstition; to me a persistent emotion like this is quite as important a fact as the scientific spirit that condemns it—more important indeed, because far more deeply rooted in human nature and more searchingly tested by the course of evolution. What has only been played with for the last few centuries by a few men is likelier to be a false scent than something all men have lived by, or lived on at least, as far back as man was man. Therefore I attach no importance whatever to pseudo-scientific explanations of this hope as a 'projection of desire' or the like. It remains a fact, and resists all such disintegrative attacks.

'But it is a mere *fact*, whereas the scientific view of the world is an *idea*; that is *feeling*, this is *thought*; its mere status as belonging to the emotional nature of man marks it as something primitive, which the growth of reason must destroy.' I reply: the antithesis is false. A fact of the spirit *is* an idea. An emotion which we find by reflection to persist as part of the furniture of our mind is a thought, or contains thought. Emotion as such is

not destroyed by reason; it is clarified, it comes to know itself, it
rids itself of many strange errors; but it survives all these
changes . . .

Nature is the realm of change, Spirit is the realm of becoming. The life of the spirit is a history: i.e. not a process in which
everything comes to be and passes away, but a process in which
the past is conserved as an element in the present. The past is
not merely a *pre*condition of the present but a condition of
it. Whereas in nature the past *was* necessary in order that the
present may *now* exist (e.g. there must have been an egg that
there may now be a hen) the past being thus left behind when
the present comes into being, in history, so far as this is real history and not mere time-sequence, the past conserves itself in the
present, and the present could not be there unless it did. Thus,
if there is a history of thought, Newton's physics still stands as
a necessary element in Einstein's: if it does not, there is no history but only change. The historian does not simply argue back
from the present to what the past must have been: he finds the
past living on *in* the present. The immediate form of this is *memory*, where the past lives on *as past* in consciousness, constituting an element without which the present consciousness would
not be what it is.

So far as spirit is spirit, therefore, and so far as its life is a history, it does not die with the death of its body. Somehow it *must*
survive that. So far, the common human feeling is right and well
founded. But how? That is a question which πολλῆς δεῖται
σκέψεως ['needs a great deal of examination'].

Put it otherwise. If A is χρόνῳ πρότερον ['prior in time'] to B,
then A ceases to exist when B comes to exist. If A is λόγῳ
πρότερον ['prior in logic'] to B, then A continues to be when (in
the logical sense of this phrase) B comes to be. Thus in an argument where a later step depends on an earlier, the earlier is a
proposition whose being propounded must endure while the
later is being propounded, for otherwise this could not happen.
Consequently in an historical series, where A is καὶ λόγῳ καὶ
χρόνῳ πρότερον ['prior both in logic and in time'] to B,[13] there
is γένεσις in time *but no* φθορά ['ceasing to be'] in time. Instead
of a series of events like this

<hr/>

[13] † See Book A, 68–70 [Collingwood refers to the section λόγῳ, χρόνῳ
πρότερον].

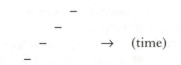

there will be a series in which the earlier continue, thus

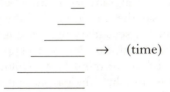

with accumulation or enrichment of the existent by the sum of its own past. For mind in general, this accumulation is called experience; for consciousness, it is called memory; for a social unity, it is called tradition; for knowledge, it is called history.

The result of this is that in a series defined as above we get for the first time pattern-qualities of a new order, viz. one to which the past contributes elements. Now, this transcendence of time seems not to happen at the level of life. A conditioned reflex does not fulfil the requirements: for there, what we have is not the past, enduring, but only a *result* of a past event enduring, though enduring in a peculiar way viz. so as to bring about a present event, or a sequence of events, all similar to the past one. This seems to be, not so much a series of the required type, as a kind of forecast or foreboding of that series at a level of existence too low to bear the thing itself ('bear' in the sense in which a tree bears fruits). But the series *does* seem to occur at the lowest levels at which we recognize mind. In the 'unconscious' of the psychologist it is true that past events, in a sense, go on happening: nothing is lost: there *is* no past, except in the sense that there has been γένεσις in the past: what comes to an end is not mental states, ideas, etc., but only the *initiations* of these. It needs further consideration whether the facts revealed by this kind of psychological inquiry constitute a *real* series of the kind (historical series), or whether we are at this level only getting very much 'warmer' in our search for it. I *think* the former, but I am not sure. In any case consciousness does provide us with exactly this series, in the shape of memory.

N.B. I would here demur to a subjectivist theory of memory, viz. that we *make* the past by remembering it. Memory has all the same marks of givenness or discovery that perception has. I would also demur to a representationist theory viz. that the immediate object of memory is not the past experience but a present image or trace or engram or anything but the experience itself. I would rather say that the survival of the past in the present, like the existence of secondary qualities, is something that really happens in the world, but does not happen except when the world reaches the level of mind in its evolutionary process. Till then, it is a mere virtuality: the past is as it were *killed* by a destructive force—Time in its negative aspect—it doesn't die a natural death—it dies fighting—it discovers how to triumph over Time and make itself immortal by becoming Mind or creating Mind as its preserver.

Because I deny a subjectivist theory of memory, I deny the consciousness theory of identity. My identity with my own past does not depend on my memory, in memory I partially *discover* that identity. 'The mind thinks not always': remember Leibniz's pregnant reply to that, pointing out that consciousness is a far narrower field than what he recognizes as *pensée*, though Locke identified the two. . . .

The Differentia of Consciousness[14]

. . . Consciousness is the ability to eat your cake and have it too: eat it, in the sense of enjoying the after-effects of past experience fused into present immediate quality; have it, in the sense of remembering that past experience as something distinct from the present. Elsewhere, as I have shown, externality is overcome in a perpetual fusion; in consciousness this fusion does indeed take place (only a sentient being is conscious) but the fused elements are held apart as well as being held together.

An example from music may make this clearer . . . I have pointed out[15] that a piece of music is a pattern of elements whose

[14] This section is from Book D, fos. 40–2.
[15] Collingwood refers back to fo. 45 of Book A.

An example from music may make this clearer . . . I have pointed out[15] that a piece of music is a pattern of elements whose pervasive pattern-quality is the aesthetic quality of that piece of music: and that each element, each note, is also a pattern whose elements are air-vibrations and whose pervasive quality is the pitch of the note. I pointed out that the difference is this: we *hear* the elements of the piece of music (notes) which is thus a pattern of *heard* elements: we *don't* hear the elements of the note (individual vibrations) which is thus a heard pattern of unheard elements (unheard, but in Aristotle's phrase 'received' by our auditory mechanism).

On this I now comment as follows: we hear the *note* by an act of *sensation*, in which the elements of the pattern are fused into a unity where their distinction is lost. If the vibrations are slowed down until we can hear them separately, at that same instant we cease to hear them as composing a note: we can't have it both ways: either we have our cake (perceive the separate vibrations) or we eat it (lose the separate vibrations and perceive only their pattern-quality). But we hear the *symphony* by an act of *consciousness*, in which we apprehend the quality of a pattern whose elements are *both* fused into a unity *and* distinguished as so many separate objects. Observe the inference from this, that birds (e.g.) which sing definite tunes enjoy not only sentience but consciousness[16] though no doubt a consciousness in many ways unlike ours and (for reasons not here to be considered) much less highly developed. . . .

Objectivity[17]

I have insisted on the correlativity of reason to experience: but I do not mean that reason is a mere shadow of experience. Concepts determine facts as their formal cause, as the essence of which they are existence. Now, essence is one where existence is manifold; one form is therefore capable of embodiment in a plurality of instances. Therefore, whereas my experience can only be mine, and nobody else's, the concepts exemplified in it may

[16] Collingwood refers here in parentheses to fo. 28 of Book D.
[17] This section and the three following are from Book E, fos. 33–5, 58, 109–14, 156–7.

be exemplified in other experiences. No two people can have the same tooth-ache, but they may both have tooth-ache. Thus concepts provide a common ground on which diverse experiences can meet. Any world of thought is a public world, accessible not indeed to every mind in common, but accessible in common to any two minds which enjoy similar experiences. It is because they have similar experiences that they can share the same thoughts, and it is through sharing the same thoughts that they can know their experiences to be similar.

I have already argued that there may be a plurality of worlds, all derived from the same root and all therefore exhibiting the same pure essence; in the same way, there may be a plurality of finite experiences, all derived from the same finite essence and all exhibiting this essence in various forms. Philosophers have wondered why experience should be as it were shattered into the experiences of finite experients; but it seems to me that the necessity for this is clear enough, and arises out of the nature of existence. Experience is nothing but the existence-term of that dyad whose essence-term is thought; consequently what is unified in thought must be dispersed in experience.

Objectivity is that characteristic of the concept by which it transcends experience. In so far as what is given in my experience is something that exists outside my experience, it is objective. It need not transcend all experience: to call the French Revolution an objective historical fact does not imply that it really existed quite apart from the experience of the people who took part in it; nor does it imply that in that experience the revolution appeared exactly as it appears to me in my historical study of it; what is implied is that the French Revolution is an object of thought, or concept, which appears in different ways to the different persons into whose experience it enters. Everyone, whether contemporary observer or historical student, who has genuine knowledge of the French Revolution knows what it really or essentially was, that is, conceives its essence, and this essence is a concept which is public and objective, accessible to any thinking mind into whose experience it enters.

This example is intended to show that concepts or essences are not eternal objects; historical thought has as its objects individual events; biological thought, types of structure limited to this world since the emergence of life; physical thought, types of structure limited to this world; mathematical thought, those common to all possible worlds; only in pure metaphysics do we encounter concepts which are truly eternal objects. Objectivity does not imply eternity; only community as between similar experiences; and there are many different reasons why two experiences may be alike. . . .

Modes of Reason: Theoretical

. . . *History* is the process of this essence into existence.[18] Reality here is not the abstract concept but the existentializing of this concept into individual spatio-temporal form. To be real, for history, is to be a *fact*, i.e. objectivity is sought (for thought is still abstract and seeks reality in an object) in *pastness*: so reality is envisaged *sub specie praeteriti*.

N.B. the object of historical thought, though individual, is not concrete. It is still, like that of science, an abstraction, a mere *schema* of the past, not the past in its full concrete existence. No historian ever tried to conceive *that*: but only to get the answers to certain determinate questions about the past.[19] . . .

History[20]

. . . History, like science, starts from experience: not from the merely here-and-now (pure perception) but from consciousness of an enduring and changing given world. This world already contains in itself its own past, experienced as that which we remember; so that the past as such is not discovered by history, which as it were prolongs and elaborates a phase of experience whose roots are already present to consciousness. But history is not memory. What I remember, I have no need to discover by historical research; and the mere fact that a certain mind applies

[18] In the preceding paragraph Collingwood had said: 'Reality, for the scientific mind, consists in this absolutely public world of concepts, entirely objective and removed above all relativity to the thinking mind.'

[19] After this, Collingwood refers forward to the section on 'History'. The passage beginning with 'N.B.' has been added on the left page.

[20] Dated '7.v.34'.

historical thought to a certain event proves that the event does
not fall within its memory. It is nearer the truth to say, as Bacon
and seventeenth-century thinkers in general said, that the historian collects and adds together the memories of other persons,
whether living in his own time or recorded in writing; but even
that statement misses the real essence of historical thought,
which is that it aims at discovering a past which no one remembers or ever did remember, for the reason that no one ever knew
it.[21] The historian who sketches the economic history of the
Roman Empire depicts a state of things which no contemporary
ever saw as a whole; and this whole is not built up in the historian's mind out of parts, each separately seen and reported by a
contemporary; because the whole which is the object of the historian's thought is not the sum of these parts but the system of
relations uniting them, and it is because he grasps this system of
relations that he is able to reject certain contemporary statements of alleged fact as inaccurate or misleading, and to inter-
polate inferences of his own concerning matters on which his
own sources are silent.

The historical past then is not a remembered past, nor a sum
of individual remembered pasts; it is an ideal past, arrived at in
his mind by a process of theorizing or thinking, and to that
extent resembles the ideal world of concepts arrived at by the
theorizing or thinking of the scientist. As the scientist begins
with observations and experiments falling within his own experience, so the historian begins with records and evidences falling
within his; and the connexion of historical thought with present
experience lies in the fact that nothing can be a 'source' for the
historian which does not come into the sphere of his personal
experience. If he relies on another's description of a document
which he has not seen, his source is not that document itself but
the description of it.

Like the scientist's world of concepts, again, the historian's past

---

[21] On the following page is added: 'This principle gives the answer to the
question, why ought the historian not to foretell the future? Everyone with a
sound historical sense knows that he ought not: but why? Because the idea that
the historian ought to foretell the future means that he ought to tell us in
advance what we shall experience when it happens: e.g. that *I* shall be the person who falls out of a window and is killed at the king's coronation. But this is
just the kind of thing that the historian doesn't know about the past, even.'

is objective. No one can share in every detail his experience of his sources; but the view of the past to which he is led by that experience can be shared by others, and, if valid for him, is valid for them; so that their criticisms of it are conversely valid for him.

Lastly, the historian's world resembles the scientist's in being a world of abstractions. It may seem to a very hasty view, that the historian's business is to describe the past exactly as it happened; but to describe the smallest historical incident exactly as it happened, complete with every detail and circumstance, every shade of emotion in the actors and every link of development in the action, would be far beyond the skill of the most learned, and no historian has ever attempted it. What the historian always tries to do is something very different: to answer certain definite questions concerning the past; that is, to confine himself to certain selected aspects of it. Consequently the most he ever wishes to do is to give an abstract or schematic account of the events he is studying, from which are omitted vast quantities of fact which for one reason or another—perhaps because he thinks them unimportant, perhaps because he has no evidence throwing light on them—he chooses, or finds himself compelled, to ignore. It is a corollary from this, that just as the scientist's abstract concepts cannot wholly explain the world of concrete experience, because no multiplication of such concepts can show why every detail in that concrete world is exactly what it is, so the historian's abstract past cannot wholly explain the concrete given present, which is the outcome not of an abstract past but of that concrete past which the historian does not attempt to reconstruct.

So much for the resemblances between history and science. The main difference is that whereas the scientist is in search of abstract generalities, the historian is in search of abstract individualities. The scientist's concept is an essence detached from all localization in space and time, and therefore able to realize itself in an instance located at any time and at any place; the historian's concept (for concept it is, since reached by thinking) is an essence that has achieved existence, that is, an essence localized in space and time—gravitation happens, and always has happened, everywhere: the Norman Conquest only happened once, and in one place. The objectivity of the historical concept, its segregation from the flux of subjective experience, is achieved by its location in the past. This protects it against the intrusion of practical interests, and places it in a region where all passion is spent and where, accordingly, thought can be purely theoretical. History inhabits the present only as an astronomer inhabits his observatory. Its business is not with the present, though that is where its data are situated. So long as a problem in politics, economics, religion, art, or the like, is an actual problem, calling for solution by practical activity, it is unripe for historical treatment. Only when the *faciendum* has become a *factum* can history begin to take cognizance of it.

History is therefore, no less than science, a partial and incomplete view of the world, aiming not at knowledge *de omni scibili* but at knowledge of a certain special field, detached from the actuality of what is given in experience, and leaving certain essential elements in that actuality deliberately ignored. In confining himself to the study of the past, the historian is certainly finding himself an objective, intelligible, and so far rewarding object for thought; in realizing that object not as the concept in its pure essence but as the concept existentialized, he has advanced his aim one step beyond that of the scientist in the order of metaphysical development; but in so far as his programme is based on a fundamental abstraction separating the world of concepts from the world of actual experience—in his case, the past from the present—he has, not by any failure to realize his programme but by the terms of that programme itself, prevented himself from giving a full and sufficient answer to the question which thought as such is always asking, the question 'why is my experience *this*, and not anything else?' A partial answer the historian, like the scientist, can and does give; but a complete answer he cannot give; not because he is a bad historian, but because he is an historian.

Postscript to Causation[22]

Having written my Aristotelian Society paper on causation,[23] I am left in this situation: Whereas the seventeenth-century physicists thought that to predicate *final* causation of nature was an illegitimate anthropomorphism, but that nature in itself really does operate according to efficient causality and that in so far as we think of nature in terms of efficient causality we are thinking about it truly; and whereas I believe I have shown that this second kind of natural science is just as anthropomorphic as the first and just as little entitled to claim objective validity: *what is the upshot?* Here are two great efforts at a science of nature, from the Greeks to ourselves: they are both false (it appears) because anthropomorphizing. The alternatives before me seem to be:

(a) *all* our science of nature is anthropomorphic. Our only knowledge is historical knowledge, i.e. man's self-knowledge. Our attempts to know nature result only in thinking of nature as if it were man.

(b) *causal* science of nature is anthropomorphic; but there is or might be a non-causal science of nature which would not be.

(c) though anthropomorphic it is not false, for nature is not really heterogeneous to man. What we call matter is mind.

(a) I suspect that this is going to turn out the right alternative. The difficulty is how to answer the question 'What, however, *is* this thing called nature which we know only as if it were man?' Answer: 'If I could tell you, I should have just that kind of knowledge which I say no one has.' Question: '*Why* have we not that kind of knowledge?' Answer: '*Ex hypothesi* no one knows.'

(b) What would this non-causal knowledge be? A *mathematical* science of nature? I imagine this would be equally subjective—but that would have to be demonstrated.

(c) Won't do. For in order that it should be true 'nature' would have to be mind at a quite high level—not *mens momentanea*, which is all one could afford to allow.

[22] Dated '27.xii.1937'. It was therefore added three years after completing the rest of the 'Notes towards a Metaphysic'.

[23] Collingwood refers here to his article 'On the So-Called Idea of Causation', *Proceedings of the Aristotelian Society*, 38 (1937–8), 85–112, the substance of which was subsequently incorporated into his *Essay on Metaphysics* (Oxford, 1940), 285–343.

HISTORY AS THE UNDERSTANDING
OF THE PRESENT

The ultimate aim of history is not to know the past but to understand the present. What the historian does is to find himself confronted with a certain state of things and to say 'this is mere fact;
I don't understand *why* things are so'. This sets him thinking
historically about it, and giving an account of its origin, which is
its explanation.

(1) *Nature of this process*. The past is the explanation of the
present: but the past is only known by analysing its traces (evidence) in the present. The common-sense view seems to be that
the historian *first* discovers these traces (what they are) and *then*
discovers what inferences can be drawn from them to the past:
distinguishing τὸ τί ἐστιν ['the what it is'] (ascertaining what
the facts are) and then deciding τὸ διότι ['the why'] (discovering
the past as their explanation).

This seems to be wrong. Crusoe did not *first* ascertain that
this was a human footprint and *then* infer that it had been made
by a human visitor. Neither do I *first* discover certain stratified
remains (La Graufesenque Samian,[1] Flavian coarse pottery,
mint coins of Vespasian) and *then* infer a Flavian occupation. To
discover *what* the evidence is, is already to interpret it. By recognizing it as a human footprint Crusoe has already concluded
to a visitor, etc.

This short manuscript is not dated, but the reference to a doctrine of
Oakeshott's in *Experience and its Modes* (Cambridge, 1933) indicates that it
must have been written after that date. Donald S. Taylor dates it 1934
(*Bibliography*, 70) and Christopher Dreisbach '1934 or later' (*Checklist*, 27).
Both authors regard it as dealing with Oakeshott's view of history, but, in fact,
it treats its subject, 'history as the understanding of the present', quite inde-
pendently, Oakeshott's position being mentioned only at the end. (Bodleian
Library, Collingwood Papers, dep. 15.)

[1] See ch. XIII on 'Samian Ware or Terra Sigillata' in Collingwood's *The
Archaeology of Roman Britain* (London, 1930; repr. London, 1996), 200–15.

I infer that τὸ τί ἐστιν of the present *is* the past—the past is the substantial being of the present: to know the past is to know not *how* the present came to be what it is but *what* it is. 'This document before me is a charter of king John granting such and such lands to such and such abbey'—that is a description of *what* the object is, and that says *why* it is what it is.

One must be careful then not to assert an *inferential relation* between the 'evidence' and the 'conclusion to which it leads'. The relation between the two things is more like the relation between seeing a surface and seeing a body. To see the surface intelligently *is* to see the body: and if *not* seen intelligently the surface doesn't provide data from which a body can be inferred.

(2) *Limits of this process.* The past doesn't *actually* ever explain the present in its entirety. It only gives *part* of the present—not a complete determination of it. E.g. the peace treaty and German defeat partially explain Nazi mentality: but even if you add conditions *ad infinitum* (German socialism, fear of Russian influence, etc.) you never get a complete explanation.

The reason, I think, is that the given historical fact is always *more than what it is*. It is this (i.e. the past) as to content: as to form, it is free activity. To understand it = understand what it is, its contents. The form is not understood, it escapes the understanding.

Putting this *a parte subjecti*: the historian sets himself to understand his own world of ideas and does so: but the act in virtue of which he possesses this world of ideas he does not set himself to understand; he merely 'enjoys' it and takes his enjoyment for granted. Why should he have any historical ideas at all? He does not know: it is no part of his business. But so long as he does not understand *that*, the whole of his historical experience presents itself to him as a mere datum, which he can analyse indefinitely but can never explain in its totality. He just finds himself here, possessed of this problem and this means of attacking it (the two are correlative: a problem not capable of being attacked by me is for me no problem).

Putting it *a parte objecti*: the past does not possess the present, the present possesses its own past. The possessive act by which the present affirms itself affirms its own past. This *positedness* of the past is part of the selfpositingness of the present. This selfpositing of the present is what always and necessarily escapes the historian.

For the historian, this limitation appears as *contingency*: i.e. an incomplete determination of the present by the past. The past event which he cites as explaining why the present is what it is does not determine the present: it only determines *possibilities* between which the present may choose. No historian can claim to have shown that a certain sequence of events *must* have fallen out thus and no otherwise. The fall of a man's income may lead him to retrenchment or to bankruptcy: which it does, depends certainly on what kind of man he is, but what kind of man he is can never be finally determined: he determines it himself *in* his own action as he goes on. He goes on to bankruptcy and we say he *was* an extravagant and thriftless man, but this does not explain *why* he chose that alternative, it is only a way of saying that he *did* choose it. The 'free will' which chose this course only becomes a reality to the historian when it has ceased to be an act and has passed into fact. When it *has* done so, the historian is no better off; because the free will is now in another situation and is confronted by another choice.

This is Oakeshott's doctrine that history is only a mode of experience, not experience itself. It is not 'completely self-conscious' because in conceiving reality *sub specie praeteritorum* it omits the reality of the present or rather mutilates it by omitting that in virtue of which the past is past.

INAUGURAL: ROUGH NOTES

'Common-sense' theory (memory plus authority). There is what
I will call a common-sense theory of historical knowledge: by
which I mean that it is the theory most people believe, or imagine themselves to believe, whenever they reflect on the matter.
Like most common-sense theories, it is not entirely mistaken.
It gives a rough-and-ready account of the more elementary
forms of historical thinking. It describes the superficial aspects
of these, but fails to go deeply even into them. In the case of
the subtler and more advanced types of historical thought it
does not even get so far as to be superficially true; it is merely
irrelevant. None the less I will begin with it, partly because
common-sense theories like this so deeply affect our ordinary
thinking that the only way of becoming immune to their errors
is by inoculating ourselves against them with deliberate injec-
tions; partly because I believe that they are never wholly erroneous, but that there is always something of value to be learnt
from them.

The common-sense theory of history represents it as a matter
of tradition. It is a co-operative business requiring at least two
partners. The event or state of things which is to be known historically must first of all be remembered by a person who has
been acquainted with it; then he must state his recollection of it
to another person; and then this other person must accept his
statement as true. The historian is the second of these two persons. The first is not an historian, he is the historian's authority.
If for example Cicero writes to a friend that he met Caesar at a
certain place on a certain date, Cicero is stating what, at the

This essay is a draft of Collingwood's inaugural lecture as Waynflete
Professor of Metaphysical Philosophy at Oxford, which he delivered on 28 Oct.
1935 under the title 'The Historical Imagination'. The lecture was printed at
the time by the University and was later reprinted in *The Idea of History*,
231–49. The draft is included in this volume because it differs in interesting
ways from the final version. (Bodleian Library, Collingwood Papers, dep. 13.)

moment of writing, he recollects; and the historian who is trying to reconstruct a biography of Caesar, accepting Cicero as his authority, incorporates in his narrative the fact that Caesar was there at that time.

According to the theory, this is a fair sample of all historical thinking. Thus, on the theory, history is not the same as memory; the person who writes his memoirs is not an historian, although he is providing raw materials for the use of other historians; history is the believing of what other people remember and have confessed to remembering.

Corollary 1: dependence *on authority (no originality).* There are certain corollaries and difficulties which follow so obviously from this theory that they need not be insisted upon. One is the complete dependence of the historian upon his authorities. If their memory is at fault, or if they omit to record something that they remember, or if they conceal or distort what they remember, or (worst of all) if they tell deliberate lies, the historian has no remedy; he falls through no fault of his own into irremediable ignorance or error. It is strange that there should be a kind of knowledge where error cannot possibly be guarded against and where for that reason it reflects no discredit upon the man who falls into it; yet that is exactly what is implied in the conception of authority, for it is the essence of that conception, that if I take a drug out of deference to the authority of my doctor or make a statement out of deference to the authority of Cicero, it is the doctor or Cicero, and not myself, that is responsible if the drug or the statement is wrong.

Corollary 2: need of selection; historical importance. A more serious difficulty arises from the fact that the historian's authorities often tell him not only too little but too much: they deluge him with all kinds of information which he does not need and in which he is not interested; and if he transcribes into the pages of his own work everything that they tell him, his work will be a mere chaos of disconnected details. Hence, just as the painter, sketching from nature, must select what he thinks to be essential and portray that, neglecting an infinite mass of detail which he regards as unimportant, so the historian must select from out of the welter of facts presented to him by his authorities those which he regards as having historical importance, and reproduce these, omitting the rest as trivial.

This difficulty is more serious than the other because there is no way of escaping it except by inflicting irreparable damage on the conception of authority. The difficulty of supplementing or correcting the statements made by one's authorities may be met, provisionally and temporarily, by a mere act of resignation: there is no help for it, we may say, and we must accept it as a condition and limitation of historical knowledge, that we can only know what our authorities tell us. But the difficulty of selecting, out of all that they tell us, those statements which we regard as important is a difficulty which we cannot evade. We can only seem to escape it when we are using as authorities men like Thucydides or Tacitus—men who, being themselves historians of the first rank, have already done for us the work of selection, and have recorded only what they regard as historically important. Even then, the reason why a Grote finds himself obliged to write his own history by transcribing as closely as he can whole pages of Thucydides is not because Thucydides regarded the details of his narrative as having historical importance but because Grote regards them as having historical importance.

This fatal to authority. The question what it is that gives a fact historical importance is one which has often perplexed those historians who have tried to philosophize about their own work. It is a question that cannot be answered, but it is important that it should be asked; because the asking it reveals one fatal flaw in the common-sense theory of history. According to that theory, the historian's work consists in studying his authorities, finding out what they have to say, and accepting this because they say it. His attitude towards what they say is on this theory a purely receptive attitude. But now it appears that he must take up towards it another and a very different attitude, a discriminative or selective one, where he exercises his own independent judgment and divides what his authorities tell him into things which matter and things which don't. The question whether a certain fact matters or not is a question which his authorities have not answered for him; therefore he cannot answer it for himself by merely accepting what they tell him; he must therefore, whenever he raises this question, deliberately abandon that receptive attitude, cease to regard his authorities as providing whatever is needed for his instruction, and draw upon some other source.

What this source is, the common-sense theory cannot tell us: in fact, it stands committed to the doctrine that no such source can exist.

Critical history. (1) conflict of authorities. Difficulties of a more urgent kind begin to crowd upon us when we turn to what I may call the higher branches of historical study. First I will touch very briefly on the problem of critical history. When, for the same facts, we have two or more authorities, it happens not only sometimes but almost always that their testimony conflicts. Sometimes the conflict arises only over small points which we can regard (though, once more, it would be hard to defend our opinion) as unimportant; and we can simply set these points aside as unsettled. Sometimes we can regard the various authorities as contributing each his own quota to our mosaic, and we can fit in every piece without contradicting ourselves. But often it happens that we cannot avoid flatly rejecting the testimony of one authority because it flatly contradicts that of another. The historian who has reached any degree of expertness and is dealing with a complicated mass of evidence is constantly doing this, and yet on the common-sense theory he can have no right to do it. The fact that he does it is proof that there are elements in historical thought of which that theory gives no account.

Critical history. (2) the impossible and οἶα ἂν γένοιτο *['such things as might happen'].* Further, even when there is no conflict of authorities, the critical historian will sometimes find himself forced to reject a statement because it asserts that something has happened which he believes to be impossible. The portents described by Livy are passed over in silence by historians of Rome, not because they are judged unimportant, but because on what I may broadly call philosophical grounds these historians believe that Livy was mistaken in thinking that they happened. Huxley professed himself ready to believe anything whatever, granted that the evidence for it were sufficiently strong; but argued that in the nature of the case no evidence could be strong enough to convince him that the miracles recorded in the Bible really took place. These are extreme cases; but they reveal the fact that in spite of his apparently passive acceptance of whatever his authorities tell him, the historian is always checking this testimony by reference to a criterion of his own, by which he distinguishes what could happen from what could not.

Critical history: questioning witnesses. The importance of critical history for the theory of historical knowledge lies in the fact that the critical historian (and every historian in so far as he is critical: for there is not and never has been any such thing as wholly uncritical history) has explicitly abandoned a merely receptive attitude towards what his authorities tell him, and thus no longer regards them in the proper sense of the word as authorities. They are now treated not as authorities but as witnesses; and just as natural science begins when the scientist, in Bacon's famous metaphor, puts Nature to the question, tortures her in order to force from her an answer to his questions, so critical history begins when the historian puts his authorities in the witness-box and extorts from them information which in their original and freely-given statements they have withheld, either because they knew it but did not wish to give it, or because they did not know it and therefore could not give it.

Example (1) where the witness conceals facts. I will take an example of a case where the historian can extract from his authorities information which they possessed but have endeavoured to conceal. In studying Caesar's narrative of his invasion of Britain, the historian, if his mind is at all alert, will find himself asking 'what exactly did Caesar intend to bring about by this invasion?' He will notice that Caesar has kept silence on this point; a silence curiously contrasting with his candour about his invasion of Germany, about which he says that it achieved everything it was meant to achieve. The inference is that his intentions in Britain were not fulfilled. He obtained from his opponents submission, hostages and tribute; therefore he meant to obtain more. That more can only have been permanent conquest. Having reached this point, the historian goes again over all the evidence in the light of his new idea; he finds that the new idea illuminates the evidence and makes it fall into a coherent whole; and he concludes that the idea was right.

Example (2) where the witness does not know facts. Authorities can also be made to give the historian information which they themselves did not possess. This is an easy matter. A physician questioning a patient discovers from his answers that he has a disease of which he has never heard; a mechanic, from a car-owner's account of his car's breakdown, may recognize what it is that has gone wrong. So from reading Dio's account of the

Claudian invasion of Britain the historian can discover what Dio himself did not know: that the Britons intended to fight a decisive battle on the Medway, and thus disappointed the Romans, who expected their chief stand to be made on the Thames.

Thus treated, Caesar or Dio is no longer an authority, because what we learn from reading him is no longer believed simply because he says it; we believe it because it is somehow implied in what he says. The precise nature of this implication I shall consider later on.[1]

Authorities become sources. For the moment, I must point out that with this change of attitude towards what were once called our authorities but must henceforth be called our sources, there comes a change of great importance in our answer to the question what things are qualified to be used as sources. When we imagined that history depended on authorities, and that the historian could learn of an event only through being told, by a credible witness, that it had happened, the only things that could be used as authorities were explicit statements to the effect that certain events had happened. But it now appears that the statements which it is the historian's business to make need not be repetitions of any statements which he finds ready made in his sources and that when he is doing his work well he is constantly making statements on his own authority which no one has made before him.

Sources need not be statements. It follows that his sources need not consist of statements at all. If he says that a certain person has handled this revolver, his ground for saying so need not be that a witness has sworn to seeing it in that person's hand; it may be that he has discovered upon it that person's finger-prints.

Written and unwritten sources. Historians often distinguish between written and unwritten sources. So far as this distinction has anything more than a merely empirical significance, it is equivalent to a distinction between sources which consist of ready-made statements and sources which do not. The point I am here making may be put by saying that to the critical historian no source consists wholly of ready-made statements. For example, a coin bears an inscription stating that it was issued by a certain ruler; but what the historian gets out of the coin is not

[1] After this, the following is crossed out: 'here it must suffice to say that it in no way resembles the way in which a conclusion is implied in premisses.'

that fact—it is for him, as an historian, of no interest that this particular coin was issued by this particular ruler—but the very different fact that coins issued by that ruler were used at a certain place, and this is not stated by the inscription on the coin; it is an original and self-authorized statement by the historian, depending on his satisfying himself that the coin is not a forgery, that it was found at that place, that it was not dropped there by a modern collector, and so on. Again, a tombstone states that a certain person, whose name is stated together with, perhaps, his age, parentage, occupation and so forth, was buried here. What the historian gets out of it is none of these facts, but most likely something not stated on the tombstone at all, e.g. the date, implied by the tombstone's style in workmanship, at which people of that kind resided in that place. Are these to be classified as written or as unwritten sources? Literally, of course, they are written sources; but the use which the historian makes of them differs in no way from the use which he might make of an uninscribed coin or a piece of sculpture. He knows something about the object which the inscription upon it does not tell him, and it is *this* that he is using as historical evidence. So with the vast mass of implements, utensils, and so forth which constitute the material for what is commonly called archaeology.

The originality of history. It is, in fact, precisely in archaeology that the originality or self-authorizing character of historical thought is most obviously manifested, because here it is most obvious that the statements made by the historian are underived from the *ipse dixit* of any authority. Here too it becomes obvious that the historian has the power of rediscovering facts which have been completely forgotten, although there is no continuous tradition to inform him of them: which of course is fatal to the common-sense theory of history with its complete reliance on memory and authority. Still stranger, but very important for the theory of history, is the fact that the historian can in this way recover facts which until he ascertained them no one ever knew at all. For example, the Gaulish potters of the second century A.D. supplied most of the western Roman Empire with their products; and at that time there was probably no one engaged in the trade who knew, as every student knows today, how widely its products were distributed over Europe. The historian of today who sketches in broad outline the economic condition of the Roman Empire is doing something which certainly no Roman was able to do.

It may be said, in reply to this contention, that all the modern historian can do is to put together a mosaic of facts each one of which was known to contemporaries, and that no one fact in his mosaic can have been unknown to them. This is like Hume's contention that every idea must be derived from an impression and that all imagination can do is to redistribute materials derived from sensation. But Hume himself discovered that this was not so; he saw that, between two shades of blue both derived through memory from sensation, imagination had the power of interpolating a third not so derived. Similarly, the facts which the historian knows, even though they include many that were known to the actors on the stage of history, include others that were not so known: facts at which he arrives by studying the implications of what he has been told.

Constructive history: originality. This brings me to a branch of historical thought which is still higher and more important than critical history; it is what I shall call constructive history. Its essence is that it takes the statements made by its authorities, after these have been subjected to criticism, not as so many pieces of fact to be fitted into a mosaic, but as so many clues from which the required fact is to be reached inferentially. The finished product, the historical narrative or description, is here not a collection of statements each directly drawn from an authority and merely selected and fitted together by the historian, but something which the historian has arrived at by thinking out the implications of what his authorities have told him. It is not something he has been told, it is something which he has thought out for himself.

Constructive element never absent. I have called this a branch of historical thought; but what I wish to insist upon is that all historical thought is in reality of this kind. Historians may imagine that they are merely accepting what they have been told; or that they are merely doing this in a critical spirit, choosing those authorities whom they find most worthy of credence; but they are never doing either of these things only: they are always to some extent thinking for themselves, using the statements of their authorities as clues to the discovery of what really happened. But this constructive or inferential element, which is present in all history, is often present in a poor and as it were rudimentary form; it is the higher development of this element that marks off good historical work from that which is merely mediocre.

If never absent, why ignored? Cf. perception. It may seem strange, if this element is present in all historical thinking, that the common-sense theory should so completely ignore it. But it is not really strange; at least in the sense that things of the same kind are not uncommon. Everyone who has read printer's proofs knows how difficult it is to find misprints. Take a familiar word, replace one letter in it by another letter, and ninety-nine times out of a hundred persons reading the page will imagine themselves to be seeing the letter that ought to be there. This could only happen if, in our ordinary reading, we habitually perceive only a part of what is printed, and use this as a clue from which we construct the rest in our imagination. What is true of reading is true of all perception. What we commonly say that we perceive we really always to a great extent do not perceive but only imagine. It requires an effort to discover that we are not seeing but only imagining the outline of a hill where it passes behind a tree, or the leg of a table where a shadow obscures it; often the fact escapes our notice altogether until by some mischance we imagine what was not really there, and then find the discrepancy.

Interpolative imagination. As in our daily perception, so in historical thinking, the work of constructive imagination plays an indispensable though commonly unrecognized part. If our authorities tell us that in June Caesar was at Rome and in July at Boulogne, we make no scruple to believe that in the meantime he travelled from one place to the other, although we are not told this; very much as, if we perceive a ship in one place when we look out to sea and in another when we look again five minutes later, we do not hesitate to believe that it has occupied intermediate positions when we were not looking. In both cases the source of our belief is the activity of our imagination. What we know or believe ourselves to know concerning the world around us consists mainly of such imaginings, interpolated as it were between scattered perceptions. Similarly, what we know or believe about history consists mostly of imaginings, similarly interpolated between and among the facts recorded by our authorities.

History and historical fiction. This may seem dangerous doctrine. Historical knowledge, if we may still call it by that name,
seems now to be a mere tissue of imagination, pegged down as it
were to the world of reality only at the fixed points provided by
recorded fact. If that is so, what distinguishes the work of the
historian from that of the historical novelist? Is not the novelist
only doing consciously what every historian is doing unconsciously, and what good historians know that they are doing and
thus know themselves to be only historical novelists?

A priori *imagination.* The answer, I think, is that the historical imagination is (if I may borrow a Kantian phrase) *a priori.* It
is characterized by universality and necessity. What the historian imagines, in so far as he does his work aright, is what he must
imagine, not simply what he may imagine; and not simply what
in fact he does imagine, and imagines here and now, but what
any historian in possession of his evidence would imagine, and
what he would imagine if he considered the same evidence on
another occasion and in another mood. The historical novelist's
imagination is (in terms of that Kantian antithesis) an empirical
imagination; starting from the same fixed points of recorded
fact, he interpolates between them events which, granted those
facts might have happened, need not have happened. Let me
take an example. When news of Boudicca's rebellion reached
the governor Suetonius Paulinus in Anglesey, Tacitus says that
he hurried to London and when there, seeing how few soldiers
he had, decided not to defend it but to abandon it to destruction.
Later, he fought a pitched battle on ground of his own choosing
and destroyed Boudicca's host. The historian who is using his
imagination when reading this narrative is obliged to ask himself why Paulinus did not defend London. Haverfield suggested
that it was because he had ridden there with his cavalry, and that
he could not meet Boudicca until his infantry came up. I think
Haverfield was certainly right; at any rate, after the most careful
scrutiny of Tacitus's narrative I cannot resist his suggestion.
But this ride of Suetonius from Anglesey to London, I cannot
but recognize, is to me, as to Haverfield, purely imaginary: as
imaginary as the back of the moon or the inside of an unopened
egg. It is a necessary or *a priori* imagination. If, on the other
hand, someone wrote an historical novel about the Boudiccan
rebellion, and made his hero a young Briton, a grandson of

Cymbeline, who had at first enthusiastically adopted Roman ways and had become a bosom friend of the governor's son, but had by degrees been revolted by Roman rapacity and misgovernment and had finally joined the rebels after a severe struggle of conscience in the conflict of loyalties, and so forth; all this would be neither less nor more imaginary than the ride of Suetonius, and it would be a thing which might very well have happened, but it would be fiction and not history because if our writer were asked: 'what is there in the evidence which obliges you to imagine this person as existing, and as acting in this and that way?' he could only reply that there is nothing.

Nothing is given. Let us pause for a moment to see where we stand. Critical history accepts nothing on mere authority; it cross-questions its witnesses, amends their statements, and extracts from them knowledge which they endeavoured to conceal or did not possess. Constructive history interpolates between the facts that it has discovered from its sources others supplied by the historian's own imagination. Now, if the historian's work were only constructive, without being critical, the web of imaginative construction would remain firmly pegged down to objective fact at the points where it rested on authority; and if these points were frequent enough the imaginative flights interpolated between them would never rise very far from the ground, and would be in little danger of losing touch with the reality which they endeavour to represent. And if the cross-questioning of witnesses could be verified by actually putting them in the witness-box and wringing from them the admission that their original statements had been false, the amended statements would rest on their authority and all would be well. We could still accept the common-sense theory of historical knowledge from which my inquiry began, modifying it by pointing to the necessity of examining witnesses and of completing their story by the merely subsidiary use of the constructive imagination.

History and the detective. And this is a fair description of what happens in detective stories, where the detective, instead of relying on confessions or the testimony of eye-witnesses, uses every known device of historical method in solving what is strictly an historical problem, but in the last resort, according to the conventions of that literary form, has the satisfaction of receiving a confession of guilt from the person to whom he has brought home the crime. But this is precisely where the detective differs from the historian, whose conclusions can never be thus verified. I say never, because if an autograph document were discovered proving that Bacon wrote Shakespeare, or that Henry VII murdered the princes in the Tower, this would only give rise to a new problem, the problem of its own authenticity.

Our result, then, is this. Where the historian's web of imaginative construction is, as I have put it, pegged down to his sources, it is pegged down not to matters of fact given by his authorities, but to the conclusions at which he has arrived by criticizing his authorities, or rather, interpreting his sources. The element of given fact has disappeared altogether. Our common-sense theory maintained that in history everything is given; the conclusion which we have now reached is that nothing is given. I do not mean that nothing is certain; that is another question altogether; I mean that there is no single historical fact which the historian can accept simply and solely on the authority of his informant without taking upon himself the responsibility for asserting it. If I find a certain statement of fact in a certain book, I cannot accept the statement until I have made up my own mind on a whole host of questions, for example, whether the alleged event could have happened; how trustworthy the writer is, and in what directions he is prejudiced or misinformed, and so on.[2] Thus there are in history no data. It is not a datum for the historian even that certain words occur in a certain charter; to ascertain that they do occur is a task for a trained palaeographer. It is not a datum that a certain potsherd was found in a certain sealed deposit; that is a statement which we accept from some archaeologists, and not from others, having our own ideas about their ability to carry out the difficult work of excavation. The crucial thing is not that I am told this or that, but that I believe it; and for believing it I and I alone am responsible.[3]

[2] After this, the following is crossed out: 'The crucial thing is not that he says it, but that I believe him when he says it: and for believing him I and I alone am responsible.'

[3] After this, the following is crossed out: 'Of course I have reasons either for belief or for disbelief. Criticism implies a criterion; and we must ask what the criterion is. It might be thought that somewhere an absolute datum must be

Analogy of historian and authority with moral agent and giver of advice. In this way the historian is related to his so-called authority as a man engaged in some course of conduct is related to another who advises him how to act. That I am advised to act in a certain way does not alter the fact that it lies upon me, and upon me alone, to decide whether I shall take the advice. The advice may have, at least in my own eyes, the emotional colour-ing of a temptation or a threat; or it may offer me an easy escape from a situation in which I am too little interested to take the trouble of making up my mind independently; and in these cases I may weakly yield to it instead of exercising my own choice and deciding for myself that what I am advised to do is the right thing, or the wrong one. Similarly, if a writer whom I am using as a source tells me that someone did a certain action, nothing is easier than to let my critical faculty go to sleep, either to save myself the trouble of thinking (and this is the special temptation of professional historians, who are often obliged to go on work-ing at a subject when their interest in it has flagged), or because I desire to believe the statement or am afraid to challenge the prestige of the writer who makes it. When the historian yields to this temptation, then and only then his sources become to him authorities and their statements become data. Thus there can be such things as authorities and data in history only when history is not history: when the historical spirit that should be active and alert in the historian's mind fails to act and sinks into uncrit-ical slumber.[4]

Relative sense of data and authority. This is not to say that words like authorities and data cannot be legitimately applied in a purely relative sense to certain features of historical study. At any given moment in the course of his work, the historian's attention is concentrated upon a certain definite question. While he is trying to answer this question, he is working on the assumption that certain others which are relevant to it have been

found: that, for example, if I disbelieve in the authenticity of an alleged Saxon charter, that is because it is to me an absolute datum that the formulae occur-ring in it are formulae not used until after its alleged date.'

[4] After this, the following is crossed out: 'The analogy extends further. There is an uncritical perversity of disbelieving as well as an uncritical supine-ness of believing; and just as people will decide not to do something, merely because they are advised to do it, so'.

answered, whether by himself or by other people. These answers are his data, and if they have been arrived at by other people these other people are his authorities. The datum is a datum relatively to the present inquiry, because within the limits of this inquiry the question whether our belief in it is justified is a question that we are not reopening. It is not an absolute datum, because this question has been an open one at some time in the past, and always may be reopened in the future. To the historical spirit in its universality all questions are open questions; but as it operates here and now in the person of this individual historian, many questions are of necessity judged and for the time being closed. But no historical question is closed in perpetuity. If that were the case, historical knowledge would advance by the gradual accumulation of ascertained facts; and nothing can be more certain than that this is not so. If I am compiling a map of Roman roads, I take it as a datum, on the authority of some archaeologist, that a Roman road exists at such and such a place; but the authority is not an absolute authority, nor the datum an absolute datum, because I have already formed an opinion of my own as to the trustworthiness of this archaeologist, and as to whether, though trustworthy in general, he may not have been making a mistake on this occasion. And I reserve the right to reopen these questions at any moment: being indeed forced to do so if the road which he records does not seem to fit convincingly into my map as a whole.

But a question which may be at any moment reopened is a question that has never been really closed. What is only provisionally settled is not settled at all. If the authority of my informant depends on his information's fitting convincingly into the historical picture I am constructing, it is that picture which validates his information, not his information that validates the picture. Thus we get the result, paradoxical from the point of view of the common-sense theory, that the historian's authorities and data are so called not because they have a claim on his belief but only because they have a claim on his consideration: they abide a verdict which he and only he can give. And for that very reason this verdict can never be given once for all: not only must future historians reopen the question, but the same historian must reopen it every time his inquiries lead him back to reconsider the same problem.

Aliter.[5] Although in a strict and absolute sense there can never be for historical thought either authorities or data, because the so-called authorities, to the critical historian, abide a verdict which only he can give, and the so-called data are alleged facts whose genuineness only he can decide, yet in a relative sense both these things can and must exist. Unlike the novelist, who sets himself the task of describing a subject never before described, the historian is commonly if not always working at a subject which others have studied before him. These others were historians like himself; and this is why they have a claim on his attention; for they have been doing what he is trying to do, and it is from them that he must learn how to do it. In proportion as he is more of a novice, either in this particular subject or in historical work as a whole, his forerunners are, relatively to him, authorities, and their judgments data; that is to say, he is relatively incompetent either to criticize their methods or to challenge their conclusions. As he becomes more and more master of his craft and his subject, he releases himself by degrees from this attitude of pupilage. The writers that were once authorities, to be humbly followed, now become fellow-students, to be criticized and judged good, bad or indifferent. The best among them will be treated with increasing respect as the historian becomes more and more able to appreciate their greatness; but this will be the critical respect of one master for another, not the blind respect given to authority. The statements they make, which were once data to be accepted, now become assertions to be challenged and either verified or refuted.

It is this relative sense of the terms authorities and data that justifies, so far as it can be justified, the common-sense theory of historical knowledge. That theory is a description of historical knowledge as it appears in its embryonic stages, when it is trying to orientate itself by mere imitation of historical work already done, and before it has reached the maturity of critical and constructive thinking. So far, it is a true enough theory; its error is in taking the features characteristic of this immaturity and erecting them into characteristics of historical thought as such. And this error falsifies it even as a description of immature

---

[5] The paragraph entitled 'Aliter' (meaning 'in another way') was probably inserted at a later date.

historical thinking, for immaturity can never be described simply in terms of what it is, but only in terms of what it is trying to become.

What is the criterion? This brings me to the central and most difficult point of my inquiry. What is the criterion of historical truth? As long as we were content to think of history in terms of the common-sense theory it was easy to answer this question. The truth about history, we assumed, so far as it could be ascertained at all, was already possessed by our authorities, who were constituted authorities by already knowing the facts in question. The criterion of truth for an historian's statements was consequently their agreement with the statements made by his authorities. This simple faith is now destroyed, not on one ground alone but on several: first, because the historian interpolates between the fixed points of his authorities' statements others made on his own authority, implied somehow (he thinks) by these but not in any obvious sense agreeing with them; secondly, because he has turned the tables on his authorities by deciding for himself whether this or that statement which they make is true or false, and if false how it is to be corrected. By what right does he take upon himself this responsibility?

N.B. The philosopher must not question the fact of historical knowledge. In parenthesis, I would observe that my question cannot be answered by saying that the historian has no right to do these things. The philosopher who finds him doing them, and elects to ask why he does them, is not entitled to raise the question whether historical knowledge is possible, but only how it is possible. Whether there can be historical knowledge is a question that [can] be answered only by trying to attain it, that is to say, by engaging in historical work. Success in this endeavour proves that the thing is possible, though failure does not prove the opposite; and by success I mean not the final or definitive solution of historical problems, for that, as I have already explained, is not what the historian achieves, but something which can be recognizably, if somewhat vaguely, described as the advancement of historical knowledge. When I have worked long and hard at an historical problem I find, not that I have solved it, but that I see further into it than I did. This is all that, as an historian, I ever hope to do. But this I know that I can do; and as a philosopher I ask myself not whether I do it but how I do it.

Bradley's Presuppositions. In order to approach this question I will begin by reminding you that it was asked, and an answer to it offered, by the greatest English philosopher of our time, in an essay which has now at last become accessible to the general public. Bradley's essay on *The Presuppositions of Critical History* was an early work, with which in his own maturity he was dissatisfied; but, unsatisfactory though it certainly is, it bears the stamp of his genius. In it, Bradley faced the question how it is possible for the historian to do what I have called turning the tables on his authorities and saying with confidence 'this is what our authorities record, but what really happened must have been not this but that.' Briefly, his answer to this question was that our experience of the world teaches us that some kinds of thing happen and others do not; this experience, then, is the criterion which the historian brings to bear on the statements of his authorities. If they tell us that things happened of a kind which according [to] our experience do[es] not happen, we are obliged to disbelieve them; but if the things which they report are of a kind which according to our experience does happen, then we are free to accept their statements.

There are many obvious objections to this doctrine, on which I shall not insist. It is deeply tinged with the empiricist philosophy against which Bradley was soon so effectively to rebel. That experience of particular facts is the source of knowledge; that the course of nature is uniform; that the unknown must resemble the known; all these familiar dogmas are implied in it and are characteristic of the philosophy against which Bradley's later work was, as he said, a 'sustained polemic'. But apart from all this I would call your attention to three points in which his argument seems to me defective.

Criticism of Bradley. First, the proposed criterion is a criterion not of what did happen but of what might happen; it is in fact nothing but Aristotle's criterion of what is admissible in drama. Hence it does not serve to discriminate history from fiction. And the historian would fare ill if in his own work he had no standards more rigorous than those of the historical novelist.

Secondly, because it can never tell us what did happen, we are left to rely, for that, upon the authority of our informant. We undertake to believe everything that our informant tells us so long as it satisfies the merely negative condition of not falling outside the bounds of possibility. But this means that we are not really criticizing our authorities at all; we have not turned the tables upon them; we are blindly accepting whatever they tell us, merely because they tell it.[6]

Thirdly, the historian's experience of the world in which he lives can only help to check the statements of his authorities in so far as these statements are concerned not with history, but with nature, which has no history. The laws of nature have always been the same, and what is against nature now has always been against nature; but the historical as distinct from the natural conditions of man's life differ so much at different times that no argument from analogy will hold. That the subjects of the Roman Empire worshipped their emperors as gods is no less true for being unlike anything that happens in the British dominions, and[7] if the evidence for emperor-worship had been small in quantity and poor in quality no analogy from our own experience would have helped us to decide whether to believe it or not. In point of fact, Bradley's criterion grew out of his interest in the credibility of the New Testament narratives, and in particular their miraculous element; but a criterion which only serves in the case of miracles is of sadly little use to the ordinary historian.

Bradley's merit. Bradley's essay, inconclusive though it is, remains memorable for the fact that in it the[8] Copernican revolution, so to call it, in the theory of historical knowledge has been in principle accomplished. Whereas according to the common-sense theory historical truth consists in the historian's

[6] After this, the following is crossed out: 'Thirdly, the proposed criterion has nothing to do with history. My experience of the world in which I live gives me no information about the kind of things that might have happened in a fourteenth-century Border raid or in the market-place of a Hellenistic city. The world of which Bradley is thinking is not the world of history, but the world of nature which has no history; and his criterion, which in fact grew out of his interest in the credibility of the New Testament narratives, might help someone to decide that water was not turned into wine at Cana of Galilee, but could never help him'.

[7] After this, the following is crossed out: 'where a genuine historical point is at issue, as for example whether the Phoenicians traded with ancient Britain, no analogy from experience will help us to decide it. We must study the sources and by'.

[8] After this, 'fundamental problem of the theory of history is correctly' is crossed out.

beliefs conforming with the statements of his authorities, Bradley has seen that in fact the historian brings with him to the study of his authorities a criterion of his own, and that by this criterion the authorities themselves are judged. What this criterion is, Bradley failed to discover.[9] It remains to be seen whether, sixty years later, the problem, which since his time I think no English-speaking philosopher has discussed, can be advanced beyond the point at which he left it.

The historian and the artist: their resemblance. The historian's aim is in one way like that of the artist; and for convenience I will compare him with that artist whom he most obviously resembles, the novelist. The historian and the novelist are alike in that each of them tells a story. That, I know, is a crude and incomplete account of what they do; but the qualifications of it which are needed in either case are needed in the other too. The novelist, as Mr. E. M. Forster has eloquently reminded us, does much more than tell a story: he analyses character, he describes situations, he displays motives. And the same generation which has revolted against the idea of the novelist as a mere storyteller has revolted against the idea of history as mere narrative. Here too, situations are described, character is analysed, motives are displayed. The totality of all these things I shall call the picture.

The novelist's picture. The novelist's aim is to compose his picture as a single coherent whole, where every character and every incident and every situation[10] is so bound up with every other that we cannot imagine this character in this situation doing anything except what he is depicted as doing. Or rather, since what is in question is not an impotence to imagine things being otherwise, but an ability to see the necessity of things being thus, we see that Conrad's Peyrol would necessarily accept the task offered him by the lieutenant, or that Dostoevski's murderer cannot but confess his crime. But it is in our imagination that we see these characters and their actions; hence this vision of a necessity in their development is what I have called *a priori* imagination. (In the middle of the last century, a school of novelists whose leader, I suppose, was Zola, rightly grasping the *a priori* character of their own constructive

[9] After this, 'the reason, I think, being his own lack of experience in first-hand historical work' is crossed out.
[10] After this, 'is needed by the whole and' is crossed out.

work, but thinking that nothing could be *a priori* except the universal propositions of science, were led to revive with a new motive the old error that the characters of fiction are not individuals but types, and must behave in certain ways because any example of their type must behave in that way. But Peyrol accepts his task not because he is a patriotic French seaman but because he is Peyrol; Alyosha confesses his crime not because he is a neurotic Russian student but because he is Alyosha.)

The historian's picture. The historian's picture, like that of the novelist, is a picture displayed by the imagination to the imagination.[11] The historian's world, the world of past events, is a world absolutely closed to perception; no part of it can in any circumstances be perceived by him, nor can his beliefs about it be in any circumstances verified by his perception. It is equally closed to memory; for although he may choose to deal with subjects of which he can recollect some part, this is a mere accident of his work as an historian; and so far as he is a critical historian he does not even rely on the memory of others. It is equally closed to scientific thinking in the ordinary sense of that term, which deals with what is constant and universal, whereas the historian as such deals with what is transitory and unique. But although he cannot perceive it, or remember it, or in the scientific sense think it, he can and does imagine it, and this is all he can do. Not only is it by imagining them that he interpolates additional facts in between the fixed points supplied by his authorities; it is also by imagining them that he envisages the facts recorded by those authorities themselves, or the facts which, again by the use of his imagination, he finds that his authorities have concealed or did not know. Thus the critical work of the historian, as well as his interpolative work, is done in and by his imagination. In both cases the imagination is *a priori* imagination.[12] The entire aim of the historian is so to compose his picture that in any part of it, whether that part is a

---

[11] After this, the following is crossed out: 'This is true not only of those parts which are, as I called it, interpolated between the fixed points supplied by his authorities; it is true also of what is taken over, however directly, however uncritically, from those authorities themselves. When we speak of believing, whether critically or uncritically, what our authorities tell us, we mean by believing simply imagining.'

[12] After this, 'and this reduces what at first appeared as two separate parts of his work to a unity' is crossed out.

narrative of events, or an analysis of social and economic conditions, or a sketch of some historical character, all the elements
hang together in such a way that each of necessity leads on to or
arises out of the rest.

ὑποκειμένη ὕλη ['subject(ed) matter (substrate)'] in both. This
aim is only achieved within certain limits. Neither the novelist
nor the historian can ever present a picture wholly transparent
to the *a priori* imagination. In both cases there is always an element of brute fact which is the presupposition of there being any
story to tell. In Conrad's story there happened to be a derelict
boat ready for the old sailor to play with; the existence of this
boat is necessary for the story but, within the limits of the story,
as inexplicable as the length of Cleopatra's nose in Pascal's
aphorism.

This ὕλη ['matter'] does not determine history. But it is not the
boat that makes the story, and not Cleopatra's nose that makes
history; it is what human agents did[13] in relation to these things.
The fault of what they did, if fault it is, is not in their stars but
in themselves. However important it may be for the historian to
obtain a correct idea of the natural surroundings—geographical,
climatic, biological and so forth—in which historical events took
place, it is even more important for him to understand that these
things are only the stage upon which historical events are
enacted, and which provides them with a raw material offering
alternative directions for development. These natural facts condition the course of history but do not determine it; nothing
determines it except itself; and hence the historian in seeking a
reason for its proceeding in this direction and not in that can
never find such a reason in its natural stage or background. The
course of history is self-determining; and therefore the historian's picture of it must be self-explanatory in the same sense in
which the novelist's picture of his subject is self-explanatory.[14]

So far, the historian and the novelist are doing the same thing
and doing it in the same way. And the same task of composing a
picture by and for the *a priori* imagination is, I need hardly add,
the task of the poet or painter or musician. How then does the
historian differ from the artist? The obvious difference is that
his picture is meant to be true, a picture of things as they really

---

13 After this, 'and suffered' is crossed out.
14 From this point Collingwood does not insert any section titles.

were and of events as they really happened. But how are we to know that it is true, or, if knowing is too presumptuous a word, to form even an opinion that it is probably true? There is only one way: by doing his work over again for ourselves, that is, by reconsidering the evidence upon which his picture is based and, exercising upon this evidence our own historical imagination, finding that we are led to the same result. This, then, seems to be the difference between the historian and the artist: each of them produces a picture which, in its self-explanatory coherence, is the work of the *a priori* imagination, but the historian's picture stands in a peculiar relation to something called evidence. What is this, and what is the relation between it and the finished work?

We already know what evidence is not: it is not ready-made historical knowledge, to be swallowed and regurgitated by the historian's mind. It is only the raw material of historical knowledge. If we ask what kind of things are qualified to serve as evidence, the answer is that they must be things perceptible to the historian, such as a printed page, a written document, a spoken utterance, a ruined building, a finger-print. What is only perceptible to another is no evidence to him; if only one historian has seen a document, it is his written or spoken account of it, not the document itself, that constitutes evidence for other historians. If we ask what special kinds of perceptible things are capable of being used as evidence, the answer is, all kinds. There is no single thing which we see, hear, touch, taste, or smell, which might not be used as evidence bearing on some historical question, if we came to it with the right question in mind and had the wit to see how the perceived object bears on it. And in fact the advancement of historical knowledge and the improvement of historical method comes about mainly through discovering the evidential value of certain kinds of perceived fact which hitherto historians have thought worthless to them. The discovery of new kinds of evidence may have two functions: it may help to answer old questions, or it may solve new problems about which, if only because there was no evidence bearing upon them, historians have not previously thought.

The whole perceptible world, then, is potentially and in principle evidence to the historian. It becomes actual evidence in so far as it is used as such. And it cannot be used as such except by a person having the appropriate kind of historical knowledge. The printed marks on paper which represent Greek letters are perceptible to anyone; but they are evidence of the activity of the printing-press only to a person who knows about printing, and evidence about Greek history only to a person who knows Greek. Perceptible things only become historical evidence when looked at historically. The more historical knowledge we have, the more we learn from any piece of historical evidence; if we had none, we could learn nothing. It follows that historical knowledge can only grow out of historical knowledge; in other words, that the activity of historical thinking is an original and fundamental activity of the human mind, or, as Descartes might have said, that the idea of the past is an innate idea.

What, then, is the relation between the historian's evidence and the conclusions he draws from it? It is, no doubt, an inferential relation; but it is one of a peculiar kind. The historian does not simply ask 'what does it prove?' He is interested only in one kind of conclusion which it may yield: namely a conclusion which shall help him to build up his imaginary picture of the past. Into the drawing of this conclusion everything that the historian knows may enter either as additional premisses or as controlling principles: knowledge about nature and man, mathematical knowledge, philosophical knowledge and so forth. The whole sum of his mental habits and possessions is active in determining the way in which he shall draw his conclusion; and since these are never quite the same in any two men, it is not to be expected that two men will necessarily draw exactly the same conclusion from the same evidence.

This no more proves the arbitrariness or irrationality of historical thinking than the difference in apparent shape of the same body seen from various directions and distances proves the irrationality of visual perception. Because we are bodies situated in the world of bodies, our bodily situation is a factor in the way in which other bodies appear to us; because we are historical individuals having our own place in the historical process, the varying endowments which that process has conferred upon us make it inevitable that we should envisage that process itself each from his own point of view. This is why every generation and every people must rewrite history in its own fashion and can never be content with second-hand historical knowledge.

Everything that the historian knows thus serves him as aids to the interpretation of his evidence; and that evidence consists in the last resort of everything he perceives. But neither the raw material given in perception, nor the knowledge that serves him to interpret it, can give him the criterion of historical truth. That criterion can only be the idea of history itself: that is to say, the idea of an imaginary picture of the past. This idea is, in Cartesian language, innate; in Kantian language, *a priori*. It is not a chance product of psychological causes; it is an idea which every man possesses as part of the fundamental endowment of his mind, and discovers himself to possess in so far as he becomes conscious of what it is to have a mind. Like others of the same kind, it is an idea to which nothing in experience wholly corresponds. The historian, however long and faithfully he labours, can never say that his work is done and his picture of the past adequate to his idea of what it ought to be. But however fragmentary and faulty the results of his work may be, the idea which has governed its course is clear, rational, and universal. It is the idea of the historical imagination as a self-dependent, self-determining and self-justifying form of thought.

It will be useful to distinguish three forms of imagination. First, there is the wholly free or pure imagination whose specialized development is seen in the activity of the artist. Secondly, there is the perceptual imagination, as I shall call it, which presents to us objects of possible perception which are not actually perceived; the under-side of this table, the back of the moon, the inside of an unopened egg. How important this 'blind but indispensable' faculty is, Kant has shown in a famous passage. Thirdly, there is what I shall call the historical imagination, which presents to us the past: not an object of possible perception, since it does not exist to be perceived, but none the less able, through the activity of imagination, to become an object of our thought.[15]

The problems with which philosophy concerns itself are in part unchanging from age to age; in part they are determined by the special characteristics of human life and thought at different[16]

[15] The five paragraphs following do not fit into the preceding argument and seem to be an afterthought. They correspond with the opening section of 'The Historical Imagination', *The Idea of History*, 231–4.

[16] After this, 'periods of history' is crossed out.

times. These two elements in the subject-matter of philosophy, the permanent and the changing, cannot be sharply divided from one another. It might with equal truth be said that the philosophy of any given age deals with permanent problems[17] *sub specie saeculi*, or that it deals with the special problems of the age *sub specie aeternitatis*. And every age, in revising for its own use the philosophy of the last, endeavours to purge away from it the dross of time, and discover in it and behind it a truth which is both new and old: both permanent and in a special sense suited for, and elicited by, its own present needs.

For the thinkers of the Middle Ages, the interest that gave a special colouring to their treatment of the permanent problems of philosophy was theology. For those of the seventeenth century, it was physical science. We reckon these seventeenth-century thinkers as the founders of modern philosophy, by which we mean that the scientific interests which dominated their thought still dominate ours. But if we compare the general orientation and tendencies of seventeenth-century thought and literature with those of our own, we find at least one important difference. Since the time of Descartes, and even since the time of Kant, mankind has acquired the habit of thinking historically. Not only has the total bulk of historical knowledge increased out of all recognition in the last century and a half; not only has the relation in quantity between historical and other literature undergone a similar change; not only have historians elaborated a technique of their own, no less definite in its character and certain in its results than the older-established technique of natural science; but the spirit of historical thought has permeated and to some extent transformed every department of human life. Among others, it has profoundly influenced philosophy; but although philosophers in all countries are aware of this influence, some welcoming it and some deploring and attempting to resist it, comparatively few have seen in it a philosophical problem. Some, in Germany and Italy, have attempted to answer the questions: what is historical thinking, and what light does its existence throw on the central and familiar problems of philosophy?—questions which, if anyone could answer them adequately, would do for the historical consciousness of

---

[17] After this, 'in the special shape proper to that age' is crossed out.

today what Kant's transcendental analytic did for the scientific consciousness of the eighteenth century; but in this country such questions seem to be by common consent ignored, and the most part of our philosophers continue to discuss the problems of knowledge in seeming unawareness that there is such a thing as history, which conforms to none of their canons and tallies with none of their theories.[18]

For this reason, having spent much time in the study of history and having, in a narrow field specially chosen for the purpose, made myself familiar with its methods of research and discovery, I propose in this lecture, not indeed to embark upon the larger question of the light thrown by the theory of history upon philosophy in general, but to indicate as simply as I can what kind of thing historical thinking is. I will begin by describing how it differs from certain other things, more familiar to students of philosophical literature, which in some ways it resembles.

The historian's thought—and here I am using the word thought in the wide or Cartesian sense—is like the activity of perception in that each has as its proper object something individual. What I perceive is a horse, not horseness; a piece of white paper, not whiteness. So in my historical thinking I study not the general nature of war or policy, statesmen or generals, but the Peloponnesian War or the policy of Augustus, the individual figures of Richelieu or Marlborough. But in one way history and perception are poles apart. Perception is always of the this, the here, the now. However long it may take for a sound or a light-signal to reach the perceiver, the moment of its arrival is the moment of his perceiving; if he misses that moment he has missed the perception for ever. Historical thought is always of the past, of something which can never be to the historian a this, because it is never a here and a now. The events which he studies are events no longer happening, the conditions he describes are conditions no longer in existence. History is a standing refutation of all theories which describe knowledge as the apprehension of an object which, to be apprehended, must exist, or

---

[18] After this, the following is crossed out: 'This may seem a sweeping statement; yet I have tried in vain to discover a single English philosophical book of the last 50 years in which historical thought has been made the central object of study.'

think of subject and object as somehow compresent in one environment.

Again, the historian's thought is like scientific thought in being inferential or reasoned. But whereas science finds itself at home in a world of abstract universals, which are in one sense everywhere and in another sense nowhere, in one sense at all times and in another at no time, the things about which the historian reasons are not abstract but concrete, not universal but individual, not indifferent to space and time but having a where and a when of their own, though the where need not be here and the when cannot be now. History is thus a standing refutation of all theories which maintain that there can be reasoned knowledge only of the abstract and universal, the realm of essences or eternal objects.[19]

[19] After this, the following passage is crossed out: 'I will not spend time in enumerating the current philosophical doctrines into which history cannot be fitted. I will only remark that of those who maintain them, when their attention is somehow drawn to the existence of history, some are content, like less philosophical persons, to denounce what they cannot understand and to give this very unphilosophical attitude a cloak of pseudo-philosophy by arguing that, though history does exist, it has no right to exist. Others maintain that though it doubtless exists it is not knowledge; thereby salving their conscience for refusing to deal further with it and forgetting that, knowledge or not, *eppur si muove*; it is an organized and sustained effort to solve certain problems.'

REALITY AS HISTORY

1. *Introduction*

One of the most important features of metaphysical thought in our own time is the attempt to give an account of reality in terms of process. Bergson has given us a theory according to which reality is a creative evolution, a movement which presupposes nothing that moves, and which in the course of its development creates matter, organisms, and minds out of itself as its own vehicles. The Italian idealists have worked out a metaphysic (if they will pardon me for using a word which they regard as the shibboleth of their opponents) according to which mind is the only reality, and the nature of mind is not merely exhibited in its history but is that history itself. Whitehead and Alexander, among ourselves, have contributed powerfully to the same movement with their vast and imposing systems presenting, in varying but not disharmonious ways, the concept of a world not only in development but of development, where successive orders of being are progressively built up, each out of material provided by the next before it.

The purpose of this essay is to make some small contribution to this movement by starting from the conception of history. Alexander himself has given the lead which I am following (happy and proud, here as often in my thinking, to follow so inspired a master) by writing an essay on 'The Historicity of

This essay, dated December 1935, is a sustained attempt by Collingwood to work through a problem that was engaging his attention at that time, partly in response to an article by Alexander entitled 'The Historicity of Things' which, as a reader for Oxford University Press, he had seen before publication. Below the title is written: 'An experimental essay designed to test how far the thesis can be maintained that all reality is history and all knowledge historical knowledge.' The essay should be considered along with Collingwood's 'Notes towards a Metaphysic', written in 1933–4, and the first two Conclusions to his Lectures on Nature and Mind, written in 1934 and 1935. (Bodleian Library, Collingwood Papers, dep. 12.)

Things'; what I propose to do here is to ask myself how far I can accept the implications of that title and apply the conception of history, as he there suggests it should be applied, 'not only to the affairs of man but to Nature itself', and to all that exists.[1]

The method I propose to follow is to lay down experimentally the thesis that all reality is historical, and all knowledge historical knowledge. I shall begin by considering what, in a general way, such a thesis implies; not the whole of its implications, but some of the more obvious ones. In this part of the essay I am throwing in my lot whole-heartedly with the movement some of whose leaders I have already named, and working out certain doctrines which, I imagine, would be accepted more or less as common ground by them all. Then I shall go on to consider more particularly what I understand by the historicity of human affairs; and here certain implications of the idea of historicity will come to light which at first were not obvious. After that, I shall ask how far the idea of historicity, as now further defined, can be applied to Nature.

2. The Terms of the Problem

The thesis with which I am experimenting lays down that reality is history and that knowledge is historical knowledge. Now history, whatever else it may be, is a sequence of events or process; and therefore the thesis implies that reality is process and that knowledge of process is not only possible (which has often been doubted or denied) but actually all the knowledge there is.

No one has ever denied, I suppose, that in some sense there is such a thing as process. It has always been recognized that process is, generally speaking, what we are actually acquainted with. The Greeks very early came to the conclusion that what directly presents itself to us, what we perceive around us and experience within us, is a flux of events where nothing is stable

---

[1] The full sentence in Alexander's article reads: 'The thoroughgoing conception of history in its application, not only to the affairs of man but to nature itself, is due, as I suppose, chiefly to Darwin' (Samuel Alexander, 'The Historicity of Things', in Raymond Klibansky and H. J. Paton (eds.), *Philosophy and History: Essays Presented to Ernst Cassirer* (Oxford, 1936), 11).

or permanent; and that conclusion has never, I think, been seriously challenged. But the Greeks also laid it down that a flux of this kind, though it can be perceived and experienced, cannot be known. It is given as fact, but it is not intelligible. We perceive and experience events, but we cannot understand them. They saw, however, that we should not enjoy this perception and experience unless we were intelligent beings; there must be something which we know, though that something is not the flux itself nor anything contained in it. What we know is therefore something other than the flux. It is not events with their ceaseless coming into existence and perishing; it is something that neither comes into existence nor passes away; it is something timeless and changeless. To work out the conception of this timeless, changeless object of knowledge was the main task of Greek philosophy. The result reached (to express it roughly and crudely) was that the object of knowledge is form or structure, in itself and apart from that whose form or structure it is.

The Greeks, with their extraordinary genius for essentials, not only worked out this philosophical doctrine but propounded the test by which this or any other system of knowledge is to be judged: the maxim know thyself. The meaning of this command, as addressed to Greeks with their conviction that πάντες ἄνθρωποι τοῦ εἰδέναι ὀρέγονται φύσει ['all human beings reach out for knowledge by nature'], is not an answer to the question 'what am I to do with myself?' but an answer to the question 'what am I to know?' Thus it means: 'you, who crave knowledge above everything else, turn your intellectual powers upon that strange object yourself.' It is the answer to the riddle of the Sphinx. It is the test of any system of knowledge, because all other alleged knowledge can impose upon us by professing to be mere statement of brute fact, and demanding acceptance as such; but whatever professes to be knowledge of myself is brought to an immediate and direct trial: am I really like that? If the alleged knowledge of myself is genuine, it cannot be mere information, a mere addition to my stock of ideas; it will illuminate my path, solve problems that actually weigh upon my spirit, launch me out into new action where hitherto I halted perplexed. And by the same test is proved the falsity of false knowledge: if you have built up your system of knowledge badly, and test it by turning it upon yourself, you destroy yourself. Oedipus was destroyed not because he failed to answer the riddle, but because he succeeded: he knew that man was the answer, and so became king of Thebes; but because that knowledge did not solve the mystery of his own identity, its very success destroyed him.

The Oedipus of Greek philosophy is Socrates. Bringing philosophy down from heaven to earth, he turned the apparatus of Greek thought upon the study of man. Where earlier thinkers had discovered, behind the flux of outward things, a hierarchy of forms, Socrates discovered behind the flux of inward experience a hierarchy of virtues, standing over against man's chaotic life as the forms of Nature stand over against the flux of the world. And in applying this method to the inner life, Socrates in effect gave up that life itself as something inherently unintelligible, allowed its actuality to slip through his fingers, and perished after seeing his city perish, like Oedipus before him. The great age of Greece was at an end.

The same problem confronted thought at the beginning of the modern age, but the solution now attempted was very different. Once more it seemed clear that what we actually perceive and experience is a flux of things within us and without; and that although this is actually present to us (nothing else, indeed, is present) it is not intelligible. But where the Greeks had found intelligibility in something wholly outside the flux, the men of the seventeenth century found it in the flux itself, not in its fleeting moments, but in their *ordo et conexio*, the constant relations between them. These relations are permanent and therefore knowable precisely because they hold good not between individual terms, but between any terms of certain kinds. The fact of A's being followed by B is a fact as impermanent as A and B themselves; but the fact that any A is followed by some B is a 'law of nature', a permanent truth about the structure of the flux, whether it is a law of things outside us or a law of ideas within—if indeed the two are different.

This is the account which seventeenth- and eighteenth-century thinkers give of the meaning of the word to understand. Everything in the flux of actual experience, as such, is merely perceived and not understood at all; but every such thing is a thing of a determinate kind, and to understand it is to think of it as belonging to that kind and as having whatever is implied in so belonging: e.g. coexistence with something of this kind, following something of that, preceding something of another. The individual as such, on this view, is unknowable; we experience it, but that is all; to the intellect, it is inscrutable. All we can do towards understanding it is to enclose it more and more narrowly in a network of classifications: for all its features, taken singly, or even in groups, may be shared with other things, and are thus general characteristics about which laws may be formulated. The practical test by which you can see whether you understand a thing in this sense of the word is to try replacing it with something else like it and see whether you understand that. Do you understand why your clock keeps time? Try thinking of it with a different pendulum of the same length. If you realize that it is not the pendulum but the length of the pendulum that counts, you understand the clock's keeping time.

This theory was, of course, a perfectly general theory of knowledge; and it is a curious testimony to the use of Latin as the learned language of the period, that the word 'science' came into use for a kind of knowledge constructed in conformity with the theory. Traditionally, science in modern usage simply means a kind of knowledge which, abandoning as unintelligible the flux and multiplicity of things as they present themselves to us in actual perception and experience, conceives its task to be 'understanding' things in the sense above defined: that is, establishing the laws of coexistence and succession for the kinds of things that the flux exemplifies.

As the Greek phase of thought, before it perished, gave us mathematics, so this modern phase gave us what is called natural science. But once more, as any system of knowledge must do sooner or later, it found itself confronted with the Delphic test and obliged to turn its scientific methods upon the mind of man. Greek thought, true to its general character, here produced ethics, a theory of virtues as transcendent patterns for conduct; modern thought produced psychology, a theory of laws governing the association of ideas or elements of the mental flux.

There is a certain parallelism even in the mythology of the two worlds. The Greek myth is that of Oedipus, destroyed through knowledge; corresponding to this in the modern world is the myth of Faust (Spengler has seen how faithfully that myth portrays the modern mind) burdened with a load of knowledge it cannot use, and finally flinging it aside to embark on the adventure of life without it. The burden of modern science, strangely enough, is its uselessness: strangely, because utility is just what it claims to possess as constituting its special merit.

Psychology is an attempt to understand man by the same methods by which modern man understood Nature. These methods, as applied to the study and consequent control of Nature, were built on the double assumption that man, the knower and controller, is intelligent; Nature, the known and controlled, unintelligent: mere mechanism, blind force. When these same methods are turned upon man, they preserve their character unchanged. They therefore assume that human nature, as the object upon which they are exercised, is unintelligent. The result is that intelligence itself is converted into unintelligence. For mind, we are given mechanisms which merely enjoy the honorary title of mental; for activity we are given passive reaction to stimulus; for thought, ideas associated automatically in accordance with fixed laws. Since the wealth and dignity of modern man are constituted by his superiority as mind to the mere Nature over which he rules, this reduction of his own mental nature to the level of unintelligent mechanism marks his bankruptcy and degradation. This application of scientific method to the problem of self-knowledge is consequently, not a demonstration that there are regions where the unit of science does not run: the claims of scientific thought could never allow such a possibility: but a *reductio ad absurdum* of science itself. The situation is therefore that science has taught us how to manipulate nature; it has given us extraordinary technological powers and enabled us to make anything we please in any quantities we like; and at the same time it has not only failed to give us that instructed wisdom which might be based on a true self-knowledge, but it has taken away the unreflective virtue and simple faith in ourselves which we possessed before psychology dispelled our belief in our own rationality. We have therefore, directly through the work of science, lost at once our honour, or habit of acting rationally, and our nerve, or belief that we can so act. Every increase in the power which science gives us over Nature has been attended by a decrease in our ability to use that power wisely; and if the process could go on long enough it is hardly to be doubted that mankind would all but annihilate itself in a series of mutually destructive wars, while the scientists stood by lamenting over the folly of human beings. What the scientist fails to understand, when he finds himself an impotent spectator of movements he can neither control nor arrest, is that the folly and wickedness which he deplores, the Mephistopheles of this rake's progress, are of his own creating; it is he that raised the devil by inventing psychology and teaching man that he is neither virtuous nor rational but a mere bundle of instincts with nothing in himself either to respect or to obey. But this is understood strongly enough, though confusedly, among mankind at large; and that is why, among the various movements of the modern world, none is more widespread and more characteristic than a certain anti-intellectualism, irrationalism, hatred of thinking, which is simply the revolt of man against the modern scientific tradition.

If this were all, the state of man would be desperate. But while the fabric of civilized society as built upon the foundation of seventeenth-century scientific theory is everywhere collapsing, the first stages of a new scientific movement are everywhere vigorously asserting themselves. In physics, the so-called classical conceptions and methods—which means those laid down in the seventeenth century—have been abandoned, and a new system of thought is being built up, based on radically different principles. In psychology, the old aim of classifying instincts and establishing laws of association is a thing of the past, and a new psychology has arisen based on the idea of a single stream of psychical energy developing through a type of process peculiar to itself; and, directed as it primarily is to coping with the problems of mental disease, this new psychology seems a providential gift to a world whose only trouble is that it has lost its nerve and its sense of direction. These new sciences have little in common with the science that ruled the world from the sixteenth century to the nineteenth. They are based on the conception, first worked out for a scientific subject-matter by Darwinian biology, of process or development as creating its own vehicles. The profound novelty of this conception lies in the fact that here, for the first time, the principle is laid down that the flux or changing process of things is intelligible in itself and in its own right. The dominance of this principle over that of traditional science is not yet complete; even in Freudian psychology, for example, we are still encumbered with talk about instincts and mechanisms, and rival schools of thought, less emancipated, classify psychological types each with laws of its own; and therefore it is an urgent matter for metaphysics to disentangle the principle itself, to clear the ground for its free development, and to show how it applies to the various fields of thought in which its application is most needed.

3. Historical Understanding

The thesis I am here proposing to maintain, in order to examine how far and with what modifications it holds good, is that reality is history and that knowledge is historical knowledge. The first step, then, is to accept the doctrine common to Greek and modern thought, that what we actually experience is a flux or multiplicity in space and time of changing events around us and within us: and that the direct or immediate experience of these things is not yet knowledge, or, what is the same thing, that what we immediately experience at any given place and at any given time is something less than reality. What then is reality, and what is knowledge?

Two answers to this double question are now before us, as answers that have been tried and have been found to fail. It is necessary to know what they are, in order to avoid falling back into them; for established habits of thought are hard to break; the inertia of the mind is a formidable thing, and any attempt to think in a new way is bound to seem unnatural, perverse and therefore misguided.

The Greek answer is that reality must be sought altogether outside the flux of things, in something abstract and changeless. That idea now seems strange to us; we have learnt to accept a different answer; but we must remember it, because having been already stated and worked out in the past, it is the first into which we shall tend to fall back if we are dislodged from the one to which we have become accustomed.

The seventeenth-century answer is that reality must be sought in the laws or uniformities according to which the

elements of the flux are connected. This, the conception of traditional science, is the conception from which we are immediately trying to liberate ourselves.

The answer which we are here experimenting with is that
reality is to be found in the flux itself; neither in something outside it altogether nor in constant or recurring uniformities that
control it, but in the actual sequence of the elements which make
it up. This is the principle of history, in the wider sense of that
word; where history means process in time.

According to this principle, everything is what it has become.
To be something is to have become that thing. To know what a
thing is, is to know what it has become. To understand what a
thing is, is to understand how it has become that thing. The
problem of knowledge is therefore everywhere and always the
same in its general form: when we are presented with something
which we do not understand (that is, whenever the problem of
knowledge arises; for the terms of that problem are, that we
should be presented with something we do not understand) we
are to reach an understanding of it by finding out how it has
come to be what it is: that is to say, by learning its history. The
standing problem of knowledge is the given, the here-and-now,
something experienced without being understood; the solution
of that problem is the discovery of its past, and the way to this
solution is historical thinking.

Up to a point, this is commonplace. Everyone has always
known that to understand things is to know why they are what
they are, and that in this sense *vere scire est per causas scire*.
Greek thought maintained that it was doing this by conceiving
any given thing as coming into existence by the imposition of a
certain form upon a certain matter: I am healthy, said Socrates,
because of the presence of health in myself. But this way of
thinking led to the conclusion that what I understand is health,
and of the way in which it comes to be in myself I understand
nothing. The abstract world of forms is intelligible; the flux
remains unintelligible. Scientific thought maintained that it was
knowing *per causas* when it argued that, in the flux of things, A
is followed by B because it is a general law that any A is followed
by some B. But this, however far it was pressed, served only to
explain why *some* B had come to exist, never why *this* B. Any
other B would have satisfied the requirements of the law equally

well; and therefore the actual thing itself, this B and no other B, remains unintelligible. Scientific thought does not answer the question asked. Instead of explaining why this and nothing else happens, it explains why something of this kind happens. And scientific thought only succeeds so long as we are content with thus altering the question. If we fix our minds resolutely on the original question, we see that any scientific explanation of facts, that is, any explanation of them in terms of general laws, is not so much untrue as irrelevant, an *ignoratio elenchi*. Both Greek thought and scientific thought, therefore, methodically evade the real question, the question how *this* came to be what it is. The only kind of thinking that does not evade the question is historical thinking.

The true scope of historical thinking has been much misunderstood. It has been supposed to be a special kind of thinking appropriate to a special kind of object. Attempts made by German philosophers to define it during the last century were conditioned by the assumption that its special object was humanity, or, as it was called, mind; and that the best way of expounding its peculiarities was to think of it as a complex of *Geisteswissenschaften* or sciences of mind, having a general character of their own distinguishing them from the *Naturwissenschaften*, the sciences of nature. According to this doctrine, historicity was peculiar to mind; nature had no history; thinking historically was therefore right and proper when we were thinking about mind, but about nature it was right to think scientifically as distinct from historically.

This conception had the advantage—a political advantage, as it were—of pleading for the recognition of historical thought in a world where the prestige of science was unshaken and its dominance unquestioned. At the same time, it rested on a fundamental mistake. Scientific thought is in reality based not on a recognition that certain peculiar kinds of things need to be thought of in that peculiar way, but on a belief that this is the way in which thinking is to be done. It therefore claims absolute and universal validity and cannot tolerate the existence, alongside itself, of any thought different in character. Consequently, as long as the validity of scientific thought in its own allotted field of nature was left unquestioned, its prestige reacted on historical thought and twisted it into pseudo-scientific forms. Thus arose a number of hybrid sciences such as anthropology, *Völkerpsychologie*, comparative philology, etc., whose general principle lies in extracting historical facts from the context in which alone they are truly, that is historically, intelligible, reassembling them in a classificatory system according to their likenesses and unlikenesses, and attempting to lay down general laws governing their relations. These sciences have always been regarded with distaste by historians, because the historian, trained as he is to think of facts in their concrete actuality, cannot tolerate the substitution for any one fact whatever of another more or less like it. He knows—that indeed is what makes him an historian—that no explanation of the French Revolution can be the right one which will fit any other revolution; whereas these pseudo-historical sciences work uniformly on the assumption that any explanation of the French Revolution, if correct, will fit every other revolution equally well, and will in fact be an explanation of revolutions as such. Hence the attempt to reduce history to a science (as it was called), which means to renounce history as such and substitute sociology in the wide Comtian sense of that word, was an attempt whose futility and viciousness every historian recognized, but one whose existence was a testimony to the dominance of the scientific spirit and the precarious position of historical thought in the world.

This is not to deny the utility of the studies which in general may be called sociological. They are vicious only when they invert their own true relation to historical studies. History can find room within itself for studies of a scientific kind; indeed, the relation between historical and scientific thought is in this way not unlike that between scientific and mathematical. Nature cannot be described without residue in mathematical terms, and therefore the mathematician as such is not yet a scientist; but mathematical thinking is the indispensable groundwork of all scientific thought. Human activity as it takes place in history (assuming for the moment, as the theorists of the *Geisteswissenschaften* assumed, that there is no history except the history of human activity) cannot be described without residue in scientific terms, yet the ability to think scientifically is indispensable to the historian. All the sociological sciences are useful to him; what he cannot allow, if he understands anything about his own work, is that this relation should be inverted and that the sociological sciences should represent themselves as the end to which historical thought is the means.

When this relation between a scientific and an historical study of human affairs is established, the question arises whether the same relation does not hold good in the study of nature. When it is said that nature has no history, does not this mean simply that the scientist, in studying nature, ignores its history, just as the sociologist ignores the history of man? It must be obvious that the answer to both questions is in the affirmative. The dandelion-head whose seeds I now watch a sparrow eating is as individual and unique a thing as the French Revolution. The sparrow is this sparrow, not any sparrow. Its appetite for the seed I now see it eating is, no doubt, an example of a kind of appetite common in sparrows; but if I cannot be content to say that the French Revolution happened because oppressed populations rebel against rulers too weak to control them, I cannot be content to say that this sparrow eats this seed because sparrows like dandelion-seeds. In both cases, the ground of my discontent is the same: it is, that the general rule, just because it explains every case of the kind indifferently, does not explain this case in its concrete actuality, but only those features of it in which it resembles the rest. In short, if I am content with a scientific explanation of a natural fact, the reason is that I am content to think of it not as the unique fact which it is, but merely as an example of a certain kind of fact.

It often happens that our interest in things falls thus short of their concrete actuality, and would be satisfied with the substitution of another thing not conspicuously unlike them. I care that my razor-blade should be sharp and so shaped that it will fit the razor; these features, which another blade might equally possess, may very well be all that I notice in it; and consequently, so far as my ordinary attitude to the razor-blade is concerned, scientific thought about it is all I desire to have. Similarly, all I notice about a particular man might be that he can dig my garden, and can be induced to do it by paying him a shilling an hour. In both cases I am attending to features shared by many pieces of metal and many human beings; in so far as these features are all I wish to understand, a scientific understanding is all I want. The scientific attitude is thus no less natural, no less adequate, when we think about human beings and their actions than when we think about anything else. To say that there can be no science of mind but only of nature is thus untrue unless by nature we mean anything in which our interest is exhausted when we have decided to what kind it belongs, and by mind that in which our interest is inexhaustible.

There is, therefore, no such division as was suggested by the theorists of *Geisteswissenschaft*, between mind as the proper object of historical thought and nature as that of scientific. In both cases, scientific thought is the way in which we understand why a thing of a certain kind is of that kind and not of another; historical thought is the way in which we understand why this thing is the thing it is and not anything else.[2]

But the matter cannot be left here; for the term understanding seems to be used in these two phrases in two somewhat different senses. In science, understanding a thing is simply thinking of it as an example of a certain general law: explaining it is showing it as an example of such a law. According to the theory of knowledge on which science is based, this is more than the way in which science explains or understands (which would permit the possibility of other ways of doing it); it is what explaining or understanding is; nothing that is not subsumption under a general law can be rightly called explaining or understanding at all.

From the point of view of a theory such as this, history, it is clear, cannot explain or understand things. All it can do is to ascertain that certain events have happened in a certain order. It narrates these facts, that is, it exhibits them in their succession; but exhibiting a succession is one thing, exhibiting its necessity is another; and to explain a thing is to exhibit its necessity.

This argument begs the question at issue. It contains two statements as to what explanation is: first, that it is to exhibit the necessity of something, secondly, that it is to subsume it under a general law. The question is whether there is any way of exhibiting a thing's necessity except by subsuming it under a

---

[2] After this, the following is crossed out: 'At this point it is well to consider some obvious objections. (1) It will be said: "History as such does not explain anything at all. It only ascertains that a certain thing or state of things has been preceded by another. It merely exhibits successions; and to exhibit a succession is not to demonstrate the necessity of that succession". To this I reply: certainly there is a difference between exhibiting a'.

general law. If there is, scientific explanation is not the only possible kind of explanation. The argument assumes that there is
not. We have to consider whether this assumption is justified.

There is no doubt a difference between exhibiting a succession and exhibiting its necessity; but where does this difference
lie? If it is said: 'on September 25 Great Britain went off the gold
standard; on September 26 there was an earthquake in Japan',
that statement exhibits a succession but not its necessity. If it is
said: 'on September 25 Great Britain went off the gold standard;
on September 26 we changed what was left of our francs back
into pounds and recovered the whole cost of our holiday in
France',[3] not merely a succession, but the necessity of that succession, is exhibited: the second event could not have happened
unless the first had happened already. The function of history is
to make statements of this second kind; in so far as the historian
merely exhibits successions without thus exhibiting their necessity, he has failed in his proper task; instead of being an historian he is being a mere annalist. No doubt there is much that goes
by the name of history which in reality is just annals; but that
does not affect the question what history is.

A person who believes that all explanation is scientific explanation will have no difficulty in dealing with my example. He
will say: 'the difference between exhibiting a succession, and
understanding it, is that to understand it is to see it as an
instance of a general law. The reason why we understand the
connexion between Great Britain's going off the gold standard
and your recovering the cost of your travels in France is that we
know certain economic laws, and see that your recovery of the
cost of your journey is an instance of these laws. The difference
between the historian and the annalist, then, is that the historian
is annalist and scientist in one: he narrates the facts in their
order, and at the same time he sees them as instances of a general law, while the annalist only narrates them in their order.'

But if for the moment we refuse to share that belief, we shall
see that a very different method of dealing with the example is
open to us. We shall see that what makes the second statement
history, and the first merely annals, is that in the first statement
events are put together which in the actual flux of things do not

[3] After this, 'anyone who understands the nature of the events in question
can see that' is crossed out.

come together; the one does not in any way lead to the second, and in thus stating them successively we are making a *suggestio falsi*, if no more, about the facts themselves; whereas in the second statement we are exhibiting a portion of the flux as it really happened, and this is the reason why we understand it; or rather, this is what historical understanding is: it is simply seeing how events happened, and to do this is to see why they happened. Our thought follows the movement of the events themselves, and in so doing finds them intelligible. The difference between the historian and the annalist is not that the historian adds something to the annalist's mere sequences; it is that the annalist takes something away from the historian's mere sequences.[4] The flow of events in itself is intelligible; the annalist makes it unintelligible by dropping bits out of it and making it discontinuous.

The difference, then, between exhibiting a succession and exhibiting its necessity, or making it intelligible, is that a succession so exhibited as to be unintelligible is a succession discontinuously exhibited. What makes a succession intelligible is its continuity. And to understand, in the most general sense, is simply to see continuities. Scientific understanding is one way of doing this: it is seeing general types of continuity, the continuity between anything of one general kind with something of another general kind. Historical understanding is another way of doing it: seeing the continuity of this individual thing with this other individual thing.

This account of what understanding in general means may be further illustrated by considering what it means to say that we understand a poem or a novel or a piece of music. In all these cases there is a flow or movement of events, and to understand this is simply to see its continuity, to see how the events flow each into the next. A listener who complains that he cannot understand a piece of music is not complaining that he cannot refer the various sequences of sound that it contains to general types; he is complaining that, just as they stand and quite apart from any such subsumption, he cannot apprehend them as sequences at all: he cannot hear one sound as leading to the next. He is in the position of the annalist who knows that one event is

[4] The sentence should probably run: '. . . the historian's more than mere sequences.'

in fact followed by another but does not see the connexion between them: the trouble being due to his failure to perceive their continuity.

These non-scientific forms of understanding—historical, literary, musical—are in general what Bergson has so well described under the heading of intuition, a kind of thought which 'installs itself in the movement' of its object, follows that movement, and thus gives insight into the flux of events itself. Bergson contrasts this with scientific understanding, which, he says, arrests the flow of events, cuts it up into artificial blocks, and manipulates these blocks, rearranging them in an arbitrary order. The value of Bergson's distinction between intuition and intelligence, great though it is, is somewhat diminished by over-emphasis on the difference between them and failure to insist on the truth that each is a kind of understanding. Paradoxically, Bergson holds that 'intelligence' does not, in the proper sense of the word, understand at all; it has, according to him, no insight whatever into the nature of things; that is reserved for intuition; and if we ask what exactly intuition is and how it works, we get vague and unhelpful answers simply because, divorced as it is from intelligence with its logical apparatus and systematic methods, intuition can have no logic, no system, no method at all. The source of this weakness, a weakness that runs all through Bergson's philosophy, is that instead of asking whether scientific understanding is really the only possible kind of understanding he has uncritically acquiesced in the traditional view that it is; and consequently he finds himself obliged to build his concept of intuition in a no man's land outside the realm of science, instead of showing how that concept is capable, as it assuredly is, of embracing scientific thought as one element in its own structure.

The principle of historical understanding in the widest sense, then, as a form of understanding distinct from scientific, is that the flux of things in itself and as it actually flows is intelligible. If I take the whole sequence of events which I call my visit to France, the story of those events is intelligible as it stands. It does not first appear or become intelligible when I extract from it this or that feature which it shares or might share with other sequences and subsume this feature under its general law. So far from its being true that the single sequence in itself is unintelligible, and only becomes intelligible when thus sub-sumed,[5] in fact the opposite is true: unless the sequence in itself, as a single and unrepeated sequence of events, were already intelligible, it could not be made intelligible by showing it to be an example of a general law. For in that case the general law would merely be a statement that events of this unintelligible kind frequently happen, or might happen, elsewhere in space and time; and what is intrinsically unintelligible does not become any more intelligible for being repeated, whereas if something is intrinsically intelligible we may very well come to understand it better for seeing it, or something like it, again.

From this position it is possible to deliver a counter-attack against the doctrine that there is no understanding except scien-tific understanding, and to show that scientific understanding would not be understanding at all unless there were also, and first, what I am here calling historical understanding.

Suppose it were the case that scientific understanding is the only possible kind. On that view, any given sequence of events as it actually happens is wholly unintelligible. We take opium and go to sleep. We experience this sequence, but no more: as it stands, we can find no necessity in it; we have no idea why the first event should lead to the second. Molière ridiculed the doc-tors, justly enough, for answering that question by saying 'because there is in opium a *virtus dormitiva*'. Is it any better to say 'because taking opium is always followed by sleep'? If the single instance is wholly unintelligible, any number of such instances are equally so; if it is a mere brute fact that this taking of opium is followed by sleep, it is no less a mere brute fact that every taking of opium is followed by sleep, for that is only a statement in which the original fact and all others of the same kind are summarized. A logician may say, this is to confuse an enumerative proposition with a true universal. An enumerative proposition merely summarizes a number of individual instances; the laws of science are true universals, they state nec-essary connexions. No doubt; but if there is a necessary connex-ion between taking opium as such and going to sleep, there is a necessary connexion between taking opium here and now and going to sleep. If the law, in its generality, expresses a necessary

5 Collingwood writes mistakenly: 'subsumed, that'.

connexion, that same necessary connexion exists in the individual instance. If we deny it in the individual case, we are obliged to deny it in the general law. Consequently, unless there is necessary connexion in the flux of events as it actually happens, the so-called laws of nature are not true universal propositions: they are merely enumerative.

Someone who remembers his Hume may say: there may be necessary connexions between events as they happen, but we cannot detect it. 'We never perceive any connexion between distinct and separate existences.' That doctrine certainly rules out the possibility of historical understanding: but is it not equally fatal to scientific understanding? For if we can really see no connexion between this taking of opium and this going to sleep, how are we entitled to believe that another antecedent of the same kind will lead to a like consequent? The very basis of induction is destroyed, and our belief in the laws of nature becomes wholly irrational. Unless it is admitted that sometimes, at least, we do see the connexion between this and that individual event; unless it is admitted that there is such a thing as historical understanding; scientific understanding itself disappears and we are left with a blind and baseless set of beliefs which, in virtue of some providential pre-established harmony, happen to correspond not too badly with the actual flow of events. And even that is a fatal admission: for it implies that there is a pre-established order of events, and that, however mysteriously, we do to some extent understand it historically, though not scientifically.

It may still be urged that history does not really explain anything, and that what I have called historical understanding is not real understanding, because at best it only explains one event by showing its connexion with another. Either that other is explained in the same way, or in some other way, or not at all. If it is explained in the same way, we are embarked on an infinite regress and nothing is explained at all, for the real explanation of the whole series is postponed until we get to the first term, which in history we can never do. If it is explained in a different way, that only shows that historical explanation is powerless unless it depends on some other and better kind. And if it is not explained at all, how are we the better off for appealing to it as the explanation of the first?

We had better grasp our nettle by taking the difficulty in its acutest form. Let us suppose that one event is explained by reference to another, preceding, event, and that this other is left wholly unexplained. Ultimately, we may admit, all historical explanation comes to this. Whatever it explains, it can explain only in terms of something else which is itself unexplained. All that can be done by any historical researcher is to advance knowledge by solving the particular problem that lies before him; and as soon as that is solved, another is sure to confront him, posited by the very solution of the last. The criticism amounts to this: that because any such advance ends in leaving upon our hands an unsolved problem, which in a sense is the old problem over again in a new form, it is worthless. And this amounts to saying that unless we know all history we know none. Is this position tenable?

I do not know if anyone is prepared to maintain it seriously. If he does, he must apply it not only to historical knowledge (which the critic I have imagined is evidently distinguishing from some other kind or kinds) but to knowledge in general.[6] For it is true not only of history, but of every field of knowledge, that it is inexhaustible; not merely in the sense that, however far we explore it, some past remains unexplored, but in the sense that the very advance of knowledge brings us into contact with new problems which had not arisen before. Wherever thought is active and is achieving solid results, the solution of one problem leads to the statement of others. It is only when minds are sluggish and dull, or lack a lively interest in the subject about which they are thinking, that the knowledge they possess fails to arouse in them a consciousness of new and as yet unsolved problems.

The point made in this criticism, therefore, has no special relevance to the case of historical knowledge. Nevertheless, it may be considered now that it has been made. The suggestion is that, unless we know everything, we know nothing. This would be true, if there were only one thing to know, and if this one thing were of such a kind that within it there were no distinctions whatever: an absolutely undifferentiated unity, outside which there is nothing at all, and inside which nothing is in any way

---

[6] After this, the following is crossed out: 'In that case, however, it has no special relevance to history and, as a criticism of historical knowledge, is a piece of empty sophistry.'

distinguishable or distinct from anything else. The history of philosophy contains no record of anyone's maintaining so fanatical a monism; and, obviously, nothing of the kind is likely to appeal to a student of history, whose object of study, the historical process, is richly diversified in all manner of ways into events which, however genuinely interconnected, are no less genuinely distinct. It has certainly been maintained by some idealists that knowledge is a whole where everything is related to everything else; if that is so, the addition of any new knowledge must to some extent alter the knowledge we had already; but even on that view it cannot be said that until we know everything we know nothing; for that view implies that, however little we know out of all that might be known, there is something here already to which additions can be made.

There is no finality in any knowledge whatever. There is nothing about which we have any knowledge at all, about which there is not more to know. If anybody thinks that in any field, however narrow, he has exhausted the possibilities of knowledge, he is not only under a dangerous delusion, he is demonstrating the feebleness and sterility of his thought concerning that field itself. If it is truer in history than elsewhere (which I doubt) that here the incompleteness of all we know is peculiarly manifest, it follows, not that history is a peculiarly futile form of thought, but that it is a peculiarly privileged one, where the thinker is more than commonly aware of what he is doing and more than commonly exempt from delusions about the nature and extent of his achievement.

4. *Human Nature and Human History*

In the foregoing chapter it has been contended that, contrary to the traditional theory of knowledge handed down to us from the seventeenth century, scientific understanding is not the only kind of understanding that exists: there is another kind, which I have called historical understanding, whose function is to understand the flux of events as they actually happen, seeing them in their actual connexion with one another. To such an understanding, this flux or process is not merely a matter of immediate experience and perception, it is intelligible or knowable: and the term history has been used in a wide sense to stand for this knowledge of process.

If reality is in the nature of process, it is necessary to reconsider the distinction which we are in the habit of making between what a thing is and what it does or what happens to it. For what it does and what happens to it constitute its process; and if its reality is process, there will be nothing left when these are taken away. We habitually think that in that case there would be something left, namely what we call the nature of the thing, what it is; and this we conceive as something permanent which underlies its activities and the changes it undergoes, and serves as a condition or limit of these things. What it can do, and what can be done to it, we think, depends on its nature: for neither its own activity nor the action of anything else on it can change its nature, and it can only do what its nature permits it to do, and only be acted upon in ways which its nature makes possible. In this chapter I shall consider this distinction with special reference to the nature and history of man.

To say that the reality of man consists simply and solely in the process of human history, implies that in the case of man at least this familiar distinction is a metaphysical error, and that what is ordinarily called human nature can be resolved into terms of human history. This sounds paradoxical; not only because it is unfamiliar, but because it seems to carry implications which we think false. A person who argued in this way would seem to be maintaining the doctrine of the extreme libertarians in ethics, who believe that a man is perfectly free to choose between alternative courses of action, irrespectively of what kind of man he is, and of the relation between his 'character' and the kind of actions that are open to him. To such a position in ethics we should reply, I think, that however much we may sympathize with its motive, which is no doubt the desire to assert the reality of freedom and moral responsibility, we cannot agree with its substance; on the contrary, we believe that a man is never more free than when he acts in accordance with his character, and think it absurd to maintain that an honest man shows his freedom by acting dishonestly but not by acting honestly. Indeed, character, so far from hampering freedom, confers it: or rather, confers not freedom in general but the special freedom to act in this or that way. Certain actions are possible only to a man whose character is of a certain kind; so that his possession of such a character, instead of shutting him out from a particular field of activity, opens that field to him. If, however, a man's character is a fixed and unchangeable thing from which his actions flow automatically, there would be no freedom and no responsibility in his doing those actions. In fact, it is not fixed and unchangeable; it is modified by the actions he does. Because he has a certain character, certain choices are open to him which to a man of different character would not be open. When he has acted in a determinate way on such an occasion, the fresh action leaves (as it were) a deposit in his character, develops it in this way or that: so that, when he comes to his next action, his character has been, however slightly, modified. This constant modification or development of character is brought about not only by his actions, the things he does of his own free will, but also by the things that happen to him; so that at any given moment his character is partly something which he has made, and for which he is responsible, partly something which has been made in him by force of circumstances.

This may be expressed by saying that a man's character is something constructed or built up by his history; what character he has, depends on what history he has had. And when we say that on a given occasion he acts in a certain way because such is his character, we are either uttering a tautology, saying that he acts thus because he acts thus, or else we are saying that he acts thus now because of the ways in which he has acted, and been acted upon, in the past. We are, in fact, explaining his present action historically, adducing the past as the *vera causa* of the present.

Two warnings may be given here. First, it is not to be supposed that character means habit, i.e. that by doing an act of a certain kind a man becomes such as to do others of the same kind. On the contrary, it may be doing an act of a certain kind that makes him such as to do an act of a different kind.

Secondly, when it is said that the past is the *vera causa* of the present, the term cause must not be understood as meaning that which by itself is sufficient to produce its effect. Even a spark causing an explosion in gunpowder only causes that if the gunpowder lies ready to be exploded; and when it is said that the past causes the present it must be remembered that the present in question is a spontaneous and self-maintaining activity, upon which the past confers not its existence but only the special shape which it takes. A man's past does not make him act; granted that he does act, it makes him act thus and not thus.

We have to distinguish, not three terms—a man's history or his past; his present character as determined by that past; and his present action as determined by that character—but two only: his past, and his present action. His past and his character are the same thing. His character is the name we give to his past as existing here and now, in so far as it determines his present action. As past, it is dead and does not exist at all. What exists here and now is neither his past as such (for that is dead and gone) nor his character (for that is a mere figment, a mythological entity invented to explain why he acts as he does) but solely his present action or total present complex of actions. Within this present action, determinate as it is, we can distinguish by analysis two factors: the indeterminate activity or will, and the determinant which fixes the will into this particular action. This determinant is what we call his character, and we are now in a position to identify this with his past: what a man is, is what he has made himself and been made in his history.

This resolution of a man's character into his history, or statement of what he is in terms of what he has done and what has happened to him, is convertible: what a man has done and what has happened to him is what he is. If there were anything that he had done, or anything that had happened to him, which was not present here and now in the shape of something that he is, it would be what I have called a dead past. But a dead past is nothing at all. There can be no act, no experience, however trifling and however remotely connected with others, of which it cannot be said that the person who did it or underwent it is now the person who did it or underwent it, and is, however slightly, different for having done so. But how exactly he is different depends not on the nature of that act or experience by itself, but on its relation to others: two men, for example, who committed similar crimes ten years ago, still carry that past act about with them as a present fact in their characters; but the present fact is very different according as one was caught and mangled in a blundering penal system, the other wisely reclaimed and brought to see the value of honesty.

It might perhaps be admitted that what we generally call character, or the nature of the individual man as such, is in this way a product of his history and is indeed nothing but that history itself now living in the shape of fact; and yet still maintained that, in addition to this developing and historically-conditioned character, every man has an unalterable nature which he shares with all men, or perhaps with all men of a certain type—a racial or psychological or other type. In support of this it will perhaps be argued that there is in every man something which can never be changed, whatever is done to him; and that all development of character takes place against this unalterable background, the 'nature' which proverbially, if thrown out with a pitchfork, will always reassert itself: against which there is no striving, and with which the only wise course is to come to terms.

But however true these contentions may be in themselves, they do not prove the point at issue. For suppose it to be true that the so-called nature of a certain racial type of man is nothing but the product of that race's history, and that the so-called nature of man at large is in the same way the living past of the human species: surely it is true that the past is unchangeable, and that nothing can now alter the fact of our descent from ancestors who lived lives of a certain kind and consequently left a certain heritage to their posterity. What are nowadays called racial types in the psychological sense are in fact certain cultural traditions built up, not unlike the character of an individual, through a history of many centuries; what are called in the stricter sense psychological types are the product of that historical process which biologists call the evolution of man.

What is the difference between this view, according to which everything in human nature is the product of historical processes, the past living in the present, and the view which would make of it a permanent and fixed 'nature'? If in either case it is unalterable, what point is there, other than purely academic, in replacing one view by the other?

The practical and very unacademic difference is this: that what history has produced is mere fact—unalterable, as fact must be, but nothing more than fact—whereas 'nature' is something more than fact, it is compulsion. If I do actions of a certain kind because, as a matter of historical fact, I have acquired the habit of doing them, it is an unalterable fact that I acquired that habit: but it does not follow that, in the further course of my history, the habit cannot be modified or broken. On the contrary, since the habit is a mere fact, it falls away, like any other fact, into the past, unless it is constantly renewed by fresh action. I have acquired the habit of smoking; because of this habit, I have a craving for tobacco; but if for some days I refuse to satisfy it, it disappears. If, forgetting that I had acquired the habit within my own remembered lifetime, I regarded the craving as 'natural', I should not believe in the possibility of thus overcoming it, and I should become what is called a 'drug addict'. For if I do actions of a certain kind because it is my 'nature' to do them, I may indeed by an effort of will refuse to do an action of that kind on a given occasion, but the tendency to do them, and the shock to my 'nature' every time I refuse to, will be permanent; consequently, unless my life is to be a slow suicide, I must find out what it is natural for me to do, and do it.

Thus, if the habitual 'sets' or recurrent patterns of action in a given man or people are historically produced, the gates of the future are open; if natural, they are shut. For example, if war as we know it is an institution that has grown up in the course of human history, and if its recurrent appearance as a fact in our world is due to the way in which our political systems have been organized and our political habits shaped, it follows that since history (in this case the history of corporate human action) has created war, history can abolish it; and since in principle it is a thing that can be abolished, the task of men who think it an evil is to discover some way of reorganizing our political life so as to do without it. If war is due to some natural instinct of pugnacity, it cannot be abolished, and the attempt to abolish it will be attended by mischievous consequences.

The converse does not hold. The failure of one, or two, or a hundred attempts to abolish war goes no way towards proving that war is due to a natural instinct, any more than a man's failure to give up smoking proves that the craving for tobacco is natural. I make this observation because the fallacy against which it is directed enjoys a good deal of popularity at the moment; and further, because it seems that no other type of argument exists to support the traditional belief in what is called human nature. I do not deny that the phrase may be loosely used as a collective name for those sets or patterns of human activity which we regard, at any given moment, as permanent, and accept as things beyond our power to change. I do not deny that there are many things of this kind which we are wise so to regard; forms of activity, like eating, sleeping, reproduction, without which man could not even be an animal, and others, like talking or thinking, without which he could not be man. Still less do I deny the wisdom of reflecting carefully on what is called human nature when we wish in this way or that to alter the general lines of established human conduct, so as to avoid, for example, imposing certain political forms on peoples whose past history has not trained them for such a manner of life, or abolishing the institutions of public religion in such a way as to drive men to the practice of private superstition. But the right reason for avoiding these errors is not a respect for a mythical entity called human nature: it is a respect for facts, for human history.

In denying that there is such a thing as human nature, I am thus not denying the reality of what goes by that name: I am denying the implications of the name, and asserting that what is so called is the historic past of mankind as conditioning, and in turn modified by, mankind's present activity. Metaphysically, this contention implies that the reality of man is an historical reality, to be resolved without residue into terms of historical process. There is not, first, a substantial and changeless entity called human nature, and then a series of historical activities and changes somehow performed and undergone by this changeless substance: the substance is nothing else than the activity itself, determining itself and developing itself in time.

I have asserted this view of man's nature as identical with man's past, in opposition to what I have called the traditional view. So far I have given no grounds for the preference. I will begin therefore by pointing out certain difficulties which may perhaps induce an open-minded person to doubt whether the traditional view is tenable.

(1) If there is a substantial and unchanging block of characteristics constituting human nature, of what is it composed? Psychologists will offer various answers. But I beg them not to be content with arbitrary catalogues of instincts and the like, but to produce an agreed catalogue, even if not an exhaustive one. It is not an unreasonable demand; chemistry has long had

a table of the elements, agreed so far as it went; and it was only when such a table was established and chemists had ceased to select arbitrary elements like sulphur, salt, and mercury, and to invent imaginary ones, like phlogiston, that chemistry began to be a science. Psychology can produce nothing of the kind. It is vain to ask for time, on the plea that the science is yet in its infancy; the question is whether, in attempting to support the traditional conception of human nature, it is not wholly on the wrong lines. One thing is, I think, clear: that the progress which psychology is making at the present time is altogether independent of any such conception, and is leading further and further away from it. For the old table of instincts we now have the notion of a single undifferentiated energy, whose differentiations are worked out, well or ill, in the course of its own historical activity. Modern psychology is thus, on its more progressive side, a witness against the conception of human nature, and for the conception of human history, as fundamental to the study of man.

(2) If there is such a thing as human nature, when did it begin to exist? Was it possessed, a quarter of a million years ago, by Neanderthal man; or half a million years ago by Pithecanthropus Erectus? If so, did it already exist in the humanoid apes of the Miocene period? but if not, at what point in the last quarter of a million years was it bestowed on their descendants? I ask these questions not in order to win an easy victory through showing that we do not know the answers, but in order to show that the whole conception of human nature is a relic of pre-Darwinian biology. It is simply a survival, in popular psychology, of the ancient idea of special creations, species fixed immutably and furnished with fixed characteristics. Classical studies of human nature by Locke, Hume, and others have come down to us from pre-Darwinian ages; in reading them today, we ought to remember that they described man as keen observers found him in Western Europe two centuries ago, and it never occurred to their authors to ask whether the nature they were describing was fixed and eternal, or the product of a long historical process. To us, the second alternative is the only one open.

(3) If there is such a thing as human nature, how is it related to the nature of the various races—European, African, Asiatic,

Australian—which form the varieties of the human species? Is it identical in all these? and if so, are their differences merely physical and not mental? or are they somehow superadded to the common stock of qualities without affecting them? Or—since neither of these answers is very plausible—is it differently realized in each race? If so, it will be differently realized again in their various subdivisions and mixtures, and the conception of a single unchanging and universal human nature is gone for ever. And here again, modern science is a witness against that conception: for it is believed by students of genetics that the psychical, no less than the physical, characteristics of a given man, so far from conforming to an invariable pattern, vary according to his pedigree and to the combination of Mendelian factors, genes, chromosomes or what not in the fertilized ovum where his life began.

(4) In short, if there is any such thing as a history of man, there can be no such thing as human nature, in the sense here defined. So long as it was denied by philosophers that history was real, it could be maintained that there was an ἰδέα ἀνθρώπου, [a] 'form' of man which, as immanent in this and that man, was what is called human nature. The conception of human nature is thus a relic of ancient metaphysics, and irreconcileable with the doctrine that there is such a thing as history. If man's existence is an historical existence, as distinct from a mere γένεσις ['coming to be'] in which a form is indifferently imposed on this or that piece of matter, its being as historical involves the consequence that human nature itself, and not merely the instances of it, comes to be in the process of historical development. In the three preceding paragraphs I have pointed out how modern psychology, modern biology, and modern genetics are committed to this historical view of man; here it only remains to state the dilemma: either this historical view must be absolutely rejected, with the rejection not only of these three sciences but of history as a whole, or else the historical view must be carried to its logical conclusion by asserting that the thing whose history we are tracing, namely mankind, has its being only in, and as a product of, that process.

5. *Process in the World of Nature*

I have urged that, in treating of man, human nature should be consistently regarded as the product of an historical process which is itself the progressive development of man's activity. At any given moment in the process man is what he has come to be; that, all that, and only that; and he does what is necessitated by what he is. That he acts at all, that the process of his development continues, is his freedom; what he does is what, by various kinds of necessity commensurate with the stature of his being, he finds it laid upon him to do (ἀνάγκαις ['by necessity'], for example, οὐ μαθηματικαῖς ἀλλ' ἐρωτικαῖς ['not mathematical but erotic']).[7]

If this will serve as a thumbnail sketch for a philosophy of man, what is to be said towards a philosophy of Nature? Some will deny that there can be such a thing; yet even they will give an account in their own philosophical terms of what Nature is or is not; and that is all I mean by a philosophy of Nature. And in passing I will point out that whereas, when I speak of the nature of something, I spell it with a small letter, I spell Nature with a capital when I mean by it the totality or system of what are called natural things.

Whether Man is or is not a part of Nature is a question that may be despised as merely verbal. I shall therefore not linger over it. To a Descartes, identifying Man with man's mind and Nature with sheer body, the answer is no; to a materialist, it is yes. To myself neither answer seems quite satisfactory. To be frankly metaphorical, Man seems a child of Nature but a

[7] Professor David Gallop has suggested to the editors that Collingwood may be alluding here, slightly inaccurately, to *Republic* 458d5, where Plato contrasts 'geometrical' necessities with 'sexual' ones—in context, the sexual urge which will drive male and female guardians to mate with one another. Since the Greeks, as a modern translator, R. Waterfield, has noted (Plato, *Republic* (Oxford, 1994), Oxford World's Classics, p. 409), commonly spoke of 'geometrical' necessity where we should speak of 'logical' or 'deductive' necessity, one can read Collingwood here as jokingly contrasting the compelling power of deductive argument with the compelling power of sex. It is also possible, of course, that he had in mind a broader sort of force compelling man to do whatever he has to do, in which case a vaguer term like 'passionate' might better convey his meaning.

rebellious child: prodigal son, or perhaps youngest son sent out, as in the fairy-tale, to seek his fortune. In some moods he prides himself on having severed all family connexions; in others, he rediscovers his mother with vast satisfaction and sinks on her bosom until he has there recovered strength for another access of rebellion. But I will go no further at present into the thoughts half-expressed by images like these. For the moment I will assume that Man and Nature are not one but two, and that the principles above laid down for the study of Man do not automatically apply to the study of Nature.

Man has, or rather is, history: but Hegel's dictum has become a commonplace, that Nature has no history. If that is right, in the wider sense of the term history, the philosophy of Nature must be very different from the philosophy of Man. There, the appearance of an unchanging nature was resolved into the reality of history; here, conversely, the appearance of history must be resolved into the reality of an unchanging nature. On this view, what history is to Man, nature is to Nature: and natural things are well called so, because they are what they are through having natures, fixed and unchangeable characters, of their own.

If we are to accept this doctrine, we must begin by qualifying it. Human history has a beginning in the history of the anthropoids; and this implies that the anthropoids and all the hierarchies of living things have, or rather are, history. History therefore, at least, stops nowhere short of life. Here we are on ground prepared for us by palaeontology and familiar to everyone since Darwin. If there is anywhere a non-historical reality, we must not seek it anywhere in the kingdom of biology.

We turn therefore to the inorganic world. But how can we draw the line here? A time certainly was when no life existed on our planet. At a later time, life had begun to exist. I do not ask how or why that strange event took place; my point is that it took place at a time, and that this time was thereby marked out in the annals of the earth's being as a unique time: a time when something happened which could have happened only once. Now the difference, I suppose, between the clock-time of a non-historical world and the time of history is that in clock-time there *is* repetition: things happen again and again, and are no way different for having happened before; whereas in historical time things happen only once. There might be time without history, I suppose, in a world where we could never say *nova rerum nascitur ordo*: where nothing grew old and nothing came into existence; where atoms danced eternally, eternally young, on the infinite floor of space. But if a moment came in that dance when a new figure, never before seen there, appeared among the dancers, henceforth to grow and multiply itself and live a changing and developing life, that moment would be the beginning of history; and if it was a moment in a time-series already running, the whole series could be reckoned from it, forwards and backwards alike, as a series of times each unique and non-recurrent—times A.D. and B.C., so to speak, each with its unique reference-number.

Put it another way. If there was one particular time when life began to exist on the earth, the earth at that particular time must have been in a state (or, if you like, in a relation) in which it never was before, and never has been again. It was a moment in the earth's being which must have been arrived at by a process of preparation; the state in question must have established itself through certain determinate changes; and, as leading to a unique and non-recurrent culmination, each of these changes must have been itself unique and non-recurrent. In other words, the changes which the earth was passing through before the appearance of life on it were themselves historical in character.

It does not seem possible to avoid the conclusion that even inorganic Nature, in its temporal changes, undergoes a process that is historical: were it not so, life could not have begun. But this brings us again face to face with the old dilemma. Is the historical process of Nature something superadded to its changeless being, or is it the genesis of a being which at every moment is but the presence of its own past?

The first answer might seem to be the right one, because it seems implied by the doctrines of the conservation of matter and energy; and because (to put it generally) the whole of physics seems to imply that every piece of matter is identical with itself however it moves or subdivides or is agglomerated with others; and because to give the second would seem to imply that matter can develop or become, whereas it seems obvious that this is a privilege of higher orders of being.

It is worth pointing out that these answers, however cogent they may seem to what we call common sense, would not be endorsed by modern physicists; who have abandoned the conservation of matter, have reinterpreted the conservation of energy until it no longer means what it used to mean for the last generation, have lost faith in their ability to say what is meant by the self-identity of a piece of matter, and are by no means willing to say that matter cannot come into or pass out of existence. The so-called common sense which rejects these doubts as fantastic is nothing else than the established habit of conceiving matter in the way which the seventeenth century borrowed from the Greek atomists. If the chief merit of modern psychology lies in getting rid of the conception of human nature and replacing it by that of a self-developing and self-shaping energy, it may well be the chief merit of modern physics to have got rid of this old conception of matter and to have asserted that the whole being of matter is made up of what it does. For that seems to be, at bottom, what modern physicists think about matter; whereas the Greek view which underlies what is called the classical physics is based on the assumption that, whatever a given piece of matter is, it is quite independently of what it does.

Up to a point, the identification of what matter is with what it does presents no difficulty. Everything which can be said about the nature of, for example, iron, resolves itself into description of the activities of atoms having a certain constitution; and this constitution, so far as it is in any way peculiar, consists not in the atom's being made of something peculiar but in the fact that its component parts move and arrange themselves in peculiar ways. Thus the nature of iron as such resolves itself into a special form of activity.

Moreover, this activity resembles the historical activity of an organism in two further ways. First, what a given atom is doing now depends on what it has done in the past, in the sense that it is where it is, and its exact structure is what it is, at any given moment because in the course of its internal and external motions it has arrived at that place and state. This is still true even if the motions of its component electrons are in certain ways and at certain times discontinuous: there is discontinuity, it seems, in all historical processes, such as the evolution of organisms or the conscious life of a mind. Secondly, it is possible for an atom of iron to come into or pass out of existence, through the alteration of another atom by the addition or removal of electrons. In both these ways it is as true of an atom as it is of a human being that it is what it has become, and that its specific nature, which is its specific form of activity, is what its past has made it.

But it seems that, even so, its historicity is not complete. There seems no reason to believe that an atom of iron, if it came into existence through the loss of electrons by a heavier atom, would carry that past with it in the sense of acting differently from an atom of iron otherwise produced. If it does not in fact behave differently, we must express this by saying that atoms, and other pieces of inorganic matter, do not conserve in their present being the whole of their past: or, from a[n] historian's point of view, that their present being, even to an ideally perfect historian, would not afford evidence of their whole past. This again might be put by saying that whereas in the full-blown historicity of mind there is only one possible past which is a *vera causa* of any given present, in the case of matter there are for any given present a number of possible pasts, or in other words that different causes may produce the same effect. Similarly, we have no reason to think that a given atom would behave differently if one of its electrons were removed and replaced by another.

These are points that must not be too much emphasized. We know very little about the behaviour of individual electrons, or even of individual atoms; physicists assure us that the generalized descriptions they give of such behaviour are only 'statistical laws', like the law stating the percentage of unaddressed letters posted in a year; and, if that is so, these laws tell us nothing about the behaviour of any one atom or electron. Some people, owing to training and a habit of accuracy, probably never post an unaddressed letter; perhaps no two fail to address the same percentage of their total correspondence. Possibly, then, in spite of the regularity of statistical law, the historicity of the smallest particles of matter is to that extent absolute.

But there is another way in which it seems doubtful if the existence of matter is fully historical. That which is genuinely historical not only develops its nature progressively in the course of its own history, but actually began to exist at a determinate time. The conception of historical beginnings is a very

difficult one. It is relatively easy to give a date to the beginnings
of the steamboat or the League of Nations, though even in cases
like these there is always an embryonic or prehistoric period,
when the thing itself did not exist, but something else existed
out of which it grew and which cannot, except by a somewhat
arbitrary line, be distinguished from it. The Roman principate
existed, we are agreed, by the end of the last century B.C., but we
cannot describe its beginnings without reference to Caesar,
Pompey, Sulla and even the Gracchi. Yet it remains true to say
that it came into existence, however hesitatingly and tentatively,
during the last century and a half before Christ, though the
question what it was that was then coming into existence could
never be answered until the constitutional work of Augustus
had been done. It is far harder to say when man came into existence. Even if our palaeontological record were as complete as
we could wish, we could not say that this event took place at any
given date; rather we should have to describe it, like the genesis
of the Roman principate, as an event which took time, and
indeed, relatively to what we commonly call history, a very long
time. Nevertheless, it fell within certain limits and can be in that
sense dated. In this way (it may be observed in passing) it
resembles all events: for any event whatever falls not at a time
but in a time; there is a time which it takes, and at an instant
there are no events.

   If the existence of matter is an historical existence, it had a
beginning, and the beginning can (theoretically) be dated. This
proposition is the 'thesis' of Kant's First Antinomy; and his
reply to it on behalf of the 'antithesis' is that if the world had a
beginning in time there must have been an empty time before it
(a time, that is to say, devoid of events), and that in such a time
there would be nothing to distinguish one moment from
another and therefore no possibility of the world's coming to
exist at any one moment rather than at any other. Plato, as if to
answer this argument, maintained that time began with the
world; and if this could be accepted, the complete historicity of
material existence would at least be an hypothesis exposed to no
insuperable objection. Here I shall not pursue this problem: for
the sake of the present essay I shall assume that a solution on
Plato's lines is possible. My immediate subject leads me in a
different direction.

I think that modern physics, and the philosophical cosmologies
based on it by Alexander and Whitehead, have established the
point that, just as so-called human 'nature' resolves into history,
so the 'nature' of inorganic matter resolves into process. The
result is a metaphysical achievement of the first importance.
Roughly, it consists in the resolution of existing into happening.
But we must not jump to the conclusion that because all is process
therefore all is history. In the preceding chapter of this essay,
when I was trying to expound the reduction of human nature to
terms of human history, I identified what a man is with what he
has done (and what has happened to him). Later, discussing the
reduction of material existence to process, I identified what a
piece of matter is with what it does (and what happens to it). The
difference between these two phrases marks the difference
between history and a process which is not strictly historical.

It is not possible to resolve what a man is into what he does.
To say that his character is only a collective name for the ways in
which he behaves is to say too little. His character is not the way
in which he acts, it is something which leads him to act in that
way; it is a principle of continuity in his actions, a power which
he draws from the past, which enables him to act thus in the present. To neglect this power of the past, a power at once liberat-
ing and constraining—enabling him to act as otherwise he could
not have acted, and making it impossible for him to do what
otherwise he could and would have done—is the error of abstract
libertarianism. Thus when we say that a man acts thus because
he is this kind of man, his being this kind of man (his character)
is his having acted in certain ways in the past. History is this
gathering-up of the whole past into the present, as determining
that novelty which the present, by thus being itself, creates.

When history is thus accurately distinguished from process,
the question whether Nature has a history must be reopened.
Certainly Nature's process is more than change. Change, as
such, is wholly uncreative. It gives with one hand and takes
away with the other just so much as it gives. In change, the past
perishes without residue. No doubt, there cannot be change
without permanence; but the permanent which change implies
need be nothing more than the fact of change itself. For mere
change does not imply conservation, and the discovery that
changes in Nature do imply conservation (for example, that the

coals burnt in the fire do not perish, but turn into gases) is a discovery of importance for the theory of Nature: a synthetic
proposition, in Kantian language.

Nature's process is not mere change. It is a creative process.
It resembles history in leading to the existence not only of new
individual things but of new orders of being, and using things of
one order as materials out of which to build the next. In that
sense, like history, it is progressive: the past survives in the
process as the foundation of the present. But, even here, there is
a difference between Natural process and historical process.
The sense in which the past survives is different. Suppose a
number of scattered atoms unite to form a molecule, which if
you like may be a molecule having chemical properties that
never existed before: a new creation in the sense of being not
only individually but specifically new. Here the past is preserved in the present only in the sense that the atoms, which
existed in the past, still exist, individually and specifically the
same, in the present. But their past scatteredness does not still
exist. The process has this element of changefulness about it,
that the past scatteredness perishes altogether. The new molecule, once formed, forgets the past, is no longer possessed of
that past as the substance of its present being, and is only what
it now does, not what it has done.

To say this is not to return to the ancient error, against which
Whitehead has warned us, of attempting to conceive 'Nature at
an instant'. By 'now' I do not mean 'at this instant'; I mean 'in
this specious present'; for if we adopt, as a useful metaphor, the
Leibnitian description of matter as *mens momentanea*, the
'moment' in question must always be conceived as a stretch of
time long enough to establish the character of the process taking
place in it. If we ask how long this is, the answer is that it
depends on what we are talking about. The specious present of
an electron is very short; that of an atom is longer; that of a molecule, still longer; that of an organism, very much longer again.
We seem forced to conclude that matter possesses nothing but
its own specious present: that, which is its activity, is its being
also; its past is only what it was, not what it is. Whereas mind not
only possesses its own specious present, it possesses its own past
as well, in the shape of character or substance. It is this contrast
which is expressed by the phrase *mens momentanea*.

The existence of matter as such is therefore not, after all, fully historical. Hegel is so far right. He is even right in speaking of the *Ohnmacht der Natur*, as a way of describing the fact that Nature differs from Mind in being thus devoid of a certain power: the power to conserve its own past alive in the present. In saying this, I abate nothing of my agreement with what Whitehead has taught about the identity of reality with process or Alexander about the historicity of things: I am only saying that the historicity of things as expounded by Alexander falls in certain ways, which I have tried to describe, short of complete historicity, and that process, as understood by Whitehead, is akin to the process of an organism's life (he calls his own philosophy the philosophy of organism, as if to emphasize this fact) rather than the process of history. In this way, while fully admitting the resemblance between the two, I find it necessary to distinguish natural or physical development from historical development.

There is another way in which an attempt might be made (unsuccessfully, I think) to bring Nature under the concept of history. It is by arguing that Nature is a system of ideas or concepts, and that these concepts are themselves historical in the sense that they have their effective being as phases in the history of human thought. Nature, according to this view, means that which natural scientists think about; but, it is argued, the theories of nature which scientists construct are not descriptions of an independent reality, differing from one another as, for example, the various maps of Africa have differed according as ignorance and unbridled fancy were gradually replaced by knowledge based on exploration; they form the links in an historical chain of self-developing thought, related to one another somewhat as different legal or political systems are interrelated. In support of such a view it is pointed out that the science of a given age is just as obviously a product of that age's spirit as its music or its architecture; and further, that from the point of view of one age the science of a past age may seem so utterly different from its own, that no sense can be made of the assertion that these are two descriptions of the same reality.

From this, which may be called the idealistic point of view, there is certainly such a thing as natural science; and this thing, as a necessary form of thought, has its own value and its own place in human life; but there is no such thing as Nature: when we speak as if there were, we are only projecting into the mist of ignorance by which we are surrounded the shadow of our own ways of thinking and acting.

I do not here propose either to accept this idealistic account of natural science or to dismiss it as obviously fantastic. Plainly it is paradoxical and under the onus of proving its case; but plainly, too, what it alleges to happen in the case of science is a thing that does happen often enough, as a matter of common knowledge, when we attribute to things around us what really belongs to ourselves and our own attitude towards them.

For my present purpose I can leave this an open question; it is beside the point. Whether the idealist is right or wrong, two things are clear.

First, the succession of scientific theories, in their actual development, is obviously historical. Whether or not science is the knowledge by man of an independently existing Nature, the extent to which he attains such knowledge, the means which he devises for acquiring it, the extent to which the search for it is furthered or impeded, or turned into this or that special track, by his general interests and habits and prejudices—all this is a matter of history.

Secondly, if at any given phase in the history of scientific thought a scientist conceives Nature itself as containing, or consisting in, temporal development, the development of phases in Nature as so conceived in no way corresponds with the development of theories in the history of science. As Kant pointed out once for all, the sequence of our acts of thinking is one sequence: the sequence of the events which we think about is quite another. Whether we take a realist or idealist or any other view of knowledge, this remains true. Whatever view of knowledge we take, the admittedly historical character of scientific thinking (the historicity of scientific theory) does not prove a similar character in the object of scientific thinking (the historicity of Nature).

It is therefore by a confusion of thought akin to that which deceived Hume, when he identified a succession of cognized events with a succession of cognitions, that the view which I am here examining argues from the historicity of science to the historicity of Nature. If such a view were correct, it would follow (for example) that, since life is a later creation than matter, the science of matter is worked out first, and followed by the science of life. No doubt there is some ground for saying that physics was the great achievement of the seventeenth century, and biology of the nineteenth; but one result of the general re-orientation of thought which biological studies brought about in the nineteenth century was a reconsideration and very drastic revision of physics itself. Thus every new phase in the history of science involves the revision of all the sciences, that is, of the conception of Nature as a whole.

And if anyone, taking refuge in a familiar *argumentum ad igno-rantiam*, suggests that as yet our knowledge of Nature is very small, and that in the future we may discover that natural processes are not so different from historical processes as we now think them, the answer is easy. Anyone can draw cheques in his own favour on the account of posterity; but only a fool will accept them in payment of present debts.

CAN HISTORIANS BE IMPARTIAL?

If I had begun this paper by asking whether historians ought to be impartial, I suppose most of us would have thought we knew the answer. We have been trained to think that all intellectual inquiry should be impartial, animated by no practical end and no desire except to discover the truth, whatever the truth may be. That, at least, is the notion which I find myself inheriting from the tradition of scholarship and science to which I belong. But I am often uneasy about it, and wonder whether this complete separation of theory from practice is possible. I want therefore, in this paper, to raise the question in the single instance of historical research; and instead of asking whether historians ought to be impartial I am asking whether they can be impartial, because that is the question that comes first. If a person can't do something, the question whether he ought to do it does not arise.

We cannot discuss this question without first deciding what we mean by impartiality and its opposite, partiality. I think we can usefully distinguish two kinds of partiality, one depending on what we want, the other on what we think right. Our partialities, that is to say, may either be simple prejudices, or they may be judgments of value. I admit that the two shade off into one another, but it will be clearer to consider them separately.[1]

(1) Impartiality may mean absence of prejudice. By prejudice I mean a tendency to prejudge questions or settle them in advance of the evidence. Thus, a man may begin a course of research into the question whether Oxford or Cambridge began its life as a university first; and if he thinks that mere age is honourable to an institution and wants to think his own university

Under the title is added: 'Paper read to the Stubbs Historical Society, 27 January 1936'. (Bodleian Library, Collingwood Papers, dep. 12.)

[1] After this, the following is crossed out: 'We cannot very well discuss this question without asking what impartiality means. I think it may mean either of two different things, which I shall distinguish and treat separately.'

the more honourable of the two, he will begin with a prejudice in favour of the view that Oxford is older than Cambridge. Similarly, he may begin an inquiry into the causes of the war in 1914 with a prejudice in favour of the view that it was all Germany's fault, or an inquiry into the Norman Conquest with a prejudice in favour of the view that it was a bad thing for Englishmen to be conquered by Frenchmen, or an inquiry into the Peloponnesian War with a prejudice in favour of the view that since Athens stood for democracy, which means liberty, the downfall of Athens was a disaster for civilization. I have chosen my instances to show how widely prejudice may sow its seeds over the field of historical knowledge. It infects, not only questions with which the historian is personally concerned, but questions concerning his family, his town, his country, his nation, his class, his profession, his religion, his race; and when these loyalties are lacking in their immediate shape, he finds reflections of them in the subjects of his study, as Grote found a reflection of nineteenth-century liberalism in Athenian democracy, or as Rostovtseff finds a reflection of Bolshevism in the soldiers and workers of the later Roman Empire.

I should define prejudice as a desire to find that a certain answer to the question one is asking is the right one. If you are trying to settle a particular historical question, whose answer may be either A or B, I assume that you desire to find out which answer is the right one; but quite often you have in your mind another desire as well, namely the desire that the right answer should be A. To have the first desire only is to be an unprejudiced inquirer; to have them both is to be a prejudiced inquirer; to have the second only is to be prejudiced without being an inquirer—a very common state.

Anybody can see that prejudices are dangerous things for a man who wants to discover the truth. If he wants A to be true, this desire will lead him to emphasize all the evidence in favour of A and slur over the evidence in favour of B. If the prejudice is strong enough, it can brush aside conclusive evidence for B and manufacture evidence for A out of nothing. Obviously, it follows that prejudice is a nasty thing and that you mustn't have it.

But this argument has taken two fences at one jump. I said that we must ask the question whether historians *can* be impartial before we asked whether they *ought* to be. It is all very well to say: 'If I were God, making historians, I should make them without prejudices'; but that question doesn't arise. Let us stick to the point. *Can* historians be unprejudiced?

Clearly they can't be, when discussing questions that either touch or even reflect their interests as practical men. People like Grote, Macaulay, Mommsen, with active political lives and policies of their own, reflect their own political experiences and ideals into the history they write. Philosophers (I have seen it argued) oughtn't to write the history of philosophy, because they are prejudiced in favour of philosophies resembling their own; and so on. The principle that emerges from all this is straightforward enough. In order to avoid prejudice, the rule must be laid down that no one who is personally interested in a subject may write the history of that subject. The only unprejudiced historian of politics is the person with no political views of his own; the historian of art must be a person with no artistic taste; the historian of warfare is disqualified for his work if he has ever taken part in a battle; and so on, until you come to this, that the only competent judge of female beauty is the eunuch. I shall venture to call this principle the doctrine of the historian as eunuch.

However attractive this doctrine may be in theory, it encounters difficulties in practice. In the first place, it is just the historians who have not been eunuchs, but have had good hearty passions of their own, who have contributed the most memorable things to historical literature. What could be sillier than to deplore the prejudices of a Gibbon, a Grote, a Macaulay, a Rostovtseff, when any reader can see that these very prejudices have brought their minds up to a heat which made them think more intensely and fruitfully about historical problems? The fact that Rostovtseff hates the Communists who have ruined himself and his friends is the fact which has enriched us all with a new interpretation of third-century history, and so with the other cases. And in the second place, how is the eunuch-theory of history to be worked? All historical thought is a re-enactment in the historian's mind of certain experiences which happened to people in the past. How is the historian to enter into the mind of a statesman like Richelieu or a soldier like Marlborough, if he has no experience whatever of politics and war? If I love a fair

woman, I may find it odd that anyone should love a dark one;
but I have a better chance of understanding his experience than
if I had never loved a woman at all.

I should thus express my objection to the eunuch-theory in
two ways. (i) What the theory aims at is impossible. Prejudice
casts its net so widely and so subtly that there is no escaping it.
The historian who evades it in one direction falls into it in
another. If, writing political history, he has no prejudices based
on his own political views, he will have others based on his
desire to prove right the views of historians he admires, or, more
subtly, a desire to prove them wrong. Our own eponymus, the
great Stubbs, said that no historical work could be done without
an element of spite in it. In short: we may take it as an axiom that
the unprejudiced historian does not exist. (ii) What the theory
aims at, though strictly impossible, is damaging to the real
worth of historical research just in the degree to which it is
attained. The nearer an historian comes to being unprejudiced,
the further he is from being really competent to deal with his
subject-matter, because he is defective in the experience which
would equip him for understanding it.

The difficulty, of course, remains. Undeniably, a prejudice
leads one to magnify the evidence on one side and to ignore it on
the other. What then? Well, there are two observations which I
have to make. First, instead of hypocritically flattering ourselves
that we have no prejudices, or vainly trying to rid ourselves of
them, we ought to examine our own minds and find out what
our prejudices are. We may be certain that they exist; very well,
let us discover them and discipline ourselves to attend with special care to the evidence in favour of the views against which we
are prejudiced. This is to abandon the attitude of the advocate,
and take up that of the judge. And if we think that we can do this
successfully, this is what we ought to do.

But, secondly, if we can't do this, because our prejudices are
so strong that we feel ourselves unable to overcome them, we
ought still to discover what they are, and in this case we ought to
make a public confession of them. The result will be a candidly
and honestly partisan reading of history: and there is no reason
why it should not be historically valuable. On the contrary, the
very strength of the prejudices may increase its value. A desire
that one particular answer to a question should be the right one,

if it is a very strong desire, will lead the historian to a closer and more intense study of his subject in the hope of proving his point, and thus the prejudice itself will serve as steam in the engine of historical research.

Let me take a parallel. The controversy in the early Middle Ages between Christian and Mohammedan philosophers, each trying to prove philosophically the truth of their own creeds, began as a controversy between two rival interpretations of Aristotle; but the importance of the practical issues involved drove the Christian philosophers to investigate logical and metaphysical questions far too abstruse and difficult for anyone to engage in without some powerful incentive, and it was this research that created the great systems of the later Middle Ages and laid the foundations of all modern thought.

And this brings me to my point. I see going on around me conscious attempts to study history from, say, a Communist point of view, setting out with the avowed intention of forcing upon it a particular interpretation. I applaud these attempts. The people who make them have seized on the great truth that all genuine historical thought begins with prejudice, and that people who deny this are either too stupid to recognize their own prejudices or else ashamed to avow them. I agree that the so-called unprejudiced historical inquiry of orthodox historians falls between two stools: either it is riddled with national prejudice, class prejudice, the prejudice of a school of thought and so on, or else, in so far as it is really devoid of important prejudice, it is eunuch-history, written by people with no insight into its subject-matter. I agree that since all real historical thought must begin from prejudice, it is vitally important to one's own work to know what one's prejudices are and to make no secret of them. And I have sufficient faith in the power of historical thinking to believe that the mere embarking upon a course of historical research, even if done with no aim in view except to support a certain political thesis, will lead to historical results far transcending that thesis itself.

I will venture to indicate the direction in which I think these results may be hoped for.

It seems to me that the frankly prejudiced historical thinking which we see growing up around us today is already having the very valuable result that it is driving people, in the endeavour to support their prejudices, up against very difficult problems concerning the interpretation of history, which would not otherwise be raised; and I believe that if the inquiry into these problems continues it will lead to a strengthening of historical thought in just that place where at present it is weakest. For although the nineteenth century worked out and has bequeathed to us a magnificent technique for the discovery of isolated historical facts, a technique of historical scholarship and criticism, it has left us rather at a loss to know what to do with the facts we have discovered; it has not taught us how to see what Henry James called the pattern in the carpet. When I find Marxist historians laying down the law about this pattern, I often think that they are doing it badly; but it seems to me that although the badness of the results is due to their prejudice, it is only because of that same prejudice that they undertake the job at all, and the important thing is that it should be undertaken.

(2) So much for one sense of the word impartiality.[2] The other sense which I want to consider means refraining from making moral judgments or judgments of value about historical facts. In this sense, the impartial historian is one who simply discovers and states what happened, what people did, without allowing himself to say that this was a good thing and that a bad, this person was right and that person wrong. The idea that the historian ought to be impartial, in this sense of the word, means that he ought to accept facts simply as facts, look at them with a detached scientific curiosity in which his nature as a moral being must not interfere. The only moral law which he recognizes is a moral law incumbent upon himself, dictating to him the duty of impartial research.

The question which I have to ask is not whether people ought to look at history in this way but whether they can. I know that people can look at some things in this way. Notably, this is the way in which the scientist can and does look at nature. This is, in fact, part of the great discovery which modern science has made about nature. Whereas Plato and Aristotle looked at it

---

[2] After this, the following is crossed out: 'If to be impartial means to be without prejudice, I do not think the historian can be impartial; and I think that his prejudices, so far from disqualifying him for historical thinking, give his thought a driving force, and provide a motive for tackling difficulties, which he could not get from any other source.'

teleologically, by asking what was the best way in which nature could have been arranged, and assuming that whatever way was the best was the way in which nature must actually exist, modern science has achieved its triumphs by discarding that point of view and concentrating on what is, without any attention to what ought to be. The technique of natural science thus consists, in part, of learning to look at things without making any judgments of value about them.[3] The technique of modern historical research has been worked out in the last 150 years under the shadow of its elder sister, the technique of natural science; and it has very often been assumed that the more historical thought can be brought to resemble scientific, the better it will be. Consequently it has been thought that the suppression of all judgments of value is as possible and as desirable in history as it is in natural science, and this is what has often been meant by saying that the historian ought to be impartial.

There is one misunderstanding which I must here forestall. By moral judgments I do not mean only judgments that acts are moral and immoral in the narrower sense of the words. Expediency too is a form of value, and to describe a man as acting prudently or imprudently is no less a value-judgment than to describe him as acting rightly or wrongly. Whenever we say that someone is acting wisely, firmly, consistently, courageously, skilfully, scrupulously, generously, justly, and so on, or their opposites, we are making a judgment of value about the man and his action. No judgments of any of these kinds appear or ought to appear in a well-ordered piece of scientific thinking: so far as we are thinking as scientists we do not say that the liver-fluke behaves unscrupulously to the sheep upon which it becomes parasitic, or the ichneumon-fly skilfully in selecting a place to lay its eggs in a caterpillar where its ovipositor will paralyse the caterpillar without killing it. Certainly the man who always

---

[3] After this, the following is crossed out: 'Actually, this technique grew up under the influence of the theological principle that the ways of God are inscrutable and that therefore, since Nature is the work of God, man is not competent to judge its value and must accept it simply as so much given fact: rational and therefore intelligible because God made it, but also and for the same reason perfect, and not amenable to our judgment. But history is concerned with human actions, and its subject-matter has all the defectiveness that attaches to all works of man; the historian therefore cannot tell his story without calling attention to this and that defect, showing how . . .'

judges the acts of historical characters by asking if they are right
or wrong is a nuisance; but no more of a nuisance than the man
who always asks the same question about his actual neighbours.
Where he goes wrong is not in making judgments of value, but in
recognizing only one form of value. To call a man a fool is just as
much a negative value-judgment as calling him a knave.

Is it possible, then, to be an historian and discuss the past
affairs of men without, in this wide sense, making judgments of
value? In one sense it is possible. You might narrate a sequence
of events, getting them in the right order and at the right dates,
and saying what kind of event each was, and yet never make any
judgments of value at all. Thus, I read in the *Annales Cambriae*
that in the 126th year Gildas died, in the 129th year the battle of
Ardderyd took place, in the 130th year abbot Brendan died, and
so on. I am sure that the author attached value-judgments to all
these events, but he has not told us what they were; so, to us, the
thing comes as a bare recital of devalued events: and, as we can
learn them and remember them in that shape, it is possible to
have a kind of knowledge about events thus devalued.

But what we have now to ask is whether such knowledge is
historical knowledge. Take the death of Gildas in A.D. 570, the
126th year of the *Annales*. Is it historical knowledge, to know
that Gildas died in that year without knowing who Gildas was?
I think not; it seems to me to be only a kind of pigeon-hole ready
to receive historical knowledge, the latitude and longitude, so to
speak, of an event, not the event itself. The event itself was the
death of a famous monk, a saint of the Celtic church, a turgid
but forcible stylist, a notable pamphleteer who scourged the
vices of the petty kings of Wales, the man who has given us a
description, the best we possess, of Britain in the fifth and early
sixth centuries, and so on. But, in saying all this, I am making
value-judgments; and I can no more put genuine historical
knowledge into the pigeon-hole marked Gildas without making
judgments of value about the man, his strange mixture of
insight and stupidity, of knowledge and ignorance, of eloquence
and barbarism and so on, than I can put historical knowledge
into the pigeon-hole marked Napoleon without making judgments of value about the man's military genius. I distinguish,
then, between knowing about the names of historical events and
knowing about the events themselves: and although I admit that

you can know about the names of events without making judgments of value I submit that you can't, on that condition, know
about the events themselves.

Take an example. Julius Caesar was assassinated on the Ides
of March, B.C. 44. That is the latitude and longitude of a labelled
event. But what was the event? In as few words as I can put it,
the event was this: Julius Caesar was a man of brilliant gifts who
realized more clearly than any of his contemporaries that the
Roman Republic was dead past hope of revival. He saw, and saw
quite rightly, that Rome needed a new constitution. The best
idea he could think of was to give it one modelled on that of a
Hellenistic monarchy. But others, far stupider men than he, had
yet the sense to realize that this would not work, and their only
way of preventing it was to make a plot and murder Caesar.
That statement of the facts is full of value-judgments. Caesar is
applauded for his insight, his initiative, his boldness; and yet he
is condemned for his failure to gauge correctly the strain which
his plan was putting on the human materials with which he had
to work. All these are judgments of value. Without judgments of
value, there is no history.

Why is this? Judgments of value are nothing but the ways in
which we apprehend the thought which is the inner side of
human action. Outwardly, a human action is a mere event of a
certain kind happening at a certain place and time. Inwardly, it
is the realization of a thought: it is thought itself, expressing
itself outwardly in the world around it. Outwardly, Caesar's
death was merely the spilling of some blood on a floor and the
cessation of organic functions in a human body. Inwardly, it was
the breakdown of Caesar's policy, the proof that he had made a
mistake. The historian who wishes to penetrate into the inside
of the events he describes must therefore commit himself to
making judgments of value: in this case he must dare to accuse
Caesar of having blundered. But, it may be asked, why should
he venture into this dangerous region and not be content with
the outside of events? The answer is easy. It is only because of
the drama of Caesar's mind that the spilling of his blood interests the historian more than that of thousands of other men who
have died violently. It is the historian's judgments of value that
select from the infinite welter of things that have happened the
things that are worth thinking about.

What kind of value-judgments the historian makes will depend on what kind of historian he wishes to be. Historians of twentieth-century poetry will probably agree in saying a good deal about T. S. Eliot and nothing about Ella Wheeler Wilcox. Why? What is it that makes one a[n] historical character and the other not? Simply the poetic value of what they write. The historian of poetry must be first and foremost a man with definite views about what constitutes good poetry, and the whole of his history will be a detailed presentation of those views. Take away the value-judgment 'this is good poetry and that is bad', and you are left with no possibility of writing any history of poetry at all. The historian of philosophy must similarly know good philosophy when he sees it; the historian of politics must recognize political ability; and so on.

A corollary follows. Scales of value change; not perhaps very quickly; man is changed by his living, but not fast enough; *eppur si muove*. If one generation feels its scale of values to differ from that of its fathers, it will have to rewrite history; what used to be thought failures it will think successes, what used to be thought lapses into barbarism it will think the victory of higher ideals, what used to be thought progress it will think degeneracy. This revaluation and consequent rewriting of history may seem a confession of failure; it may suggest that in history there is no sure and permanent advancement of knowledge; but that is not so. The advancement of knowledge is there; but it is not a mere advancement of knowledge; it is an advancement in the whole moral attitude of humanity.

I conclude by urging that we, as historians, must not shrink from this responsibility. Let us realize that, as historians, we have taken upon ourselves the serious task, not only of discovering what actually happened, but of judging it in the light of our own moral ideals. We are the present of man, passing judgment on his own corporate past. If we dislike shouldering that responsibility, we have none the less accepted it in so far as we are historians at all. If we feel that we cannot shoulder it, we ought to drop historical studies and do something else. What we cannot do, is to continue playing with historical research and yet shirk the responsibility of judging the actions we narrate: saying this was wise, that foolish; this courageous, that cowardly; this well done, that ill.

NOTES ON THE HISTORY OF HISTORIOGRAPHY AND PHILOSOPHY OF HISTORY

Human Nature and Human History[1]

The eighteenth-century philosophers proposed a theory of human nature: the locus classicus is Hume's treatise, where it is claimed that all sciences are either *parts* of this (morals, politics, logic, etc.) or *functions* of it (mathematics, physics, etc.). The idea behind the proposal is that our intellectual and other faculties are *given*, a permanent framework conditioning whatever comes under their cognizance (we *can* think etc. only in the way in which human beings can do so) hence analysis of human nature can give us the explanation why the world appears to us as it does appear. The *a priori* elements in knowledge, according to Kant's development of Hume's doctrine, are subjective, *liegen bereit* in human nature itself. This is the innatism which Kant starts with. But Kant modified this: in his mature (critical) view the faculty only comes into existence with the exercise of it. Even so, human rationality is the predetermined end of the teleological process of human development. Because it has a predetermined end, the process is not really historical, because not genuinely creative.

This manuscript was written in the spring of 1936, apparently in preparation for the lectures on philosophy of history which Collingwood gave from January to June of that year, and which Knox later edited as parts I–IV and Epilegomena 4, 5, and 7 of *The Idea of History*. The first and third items appear also to be preparations for the lecture 'Human Nature and Human History' which Collingwood gave to the British Academy in 1936, which was printed in its *Proceedings*, 22 (1937), 97–127, and reprinted in *The Idea of History*, 205–31. Only five of the manuscript's ten items and part of a sixth have been included here. A list of the ones omitted is given in a final note. (Bodleian Library, Collingwood Papers, dep. 13.)

[1] Dated '9.iii.36'.

I want to press this view further. I want to hold that *what is falsely called human nature is really human history*. The fundamental theses of such a view would be something of this kind:

(1) *Human nature is mind*. We are not talking about bodily nature: only of mental (with the proviso that mind always means embodied mind).

(2) *Mind is pure act*. Mind *is* not anything apart from what it *does*. The so-called powers or faculties (δυνάμεις) of mind are really activities (ἐνέργειαι). Activity does not (a) *exhibit* or *reveal* the nature of mind, or (b) *develop* or *explicate* its unrealized potentialities: it *is* mind.

(3) *The pure act posits itself and its own presupposition at once*. The past belongs to the present, not the present to the past. Whereas in nature the present is the caused effect of the past, in mind the past is the analysed content of the present. Thus what the mind is and what it does are its past and present respectively.

(4) *Past time therefore is the schema of mind's self-knowledge*. It *can* know itself only *sub specie praeteritorum*. To know oneself is simply to know one's past and vice versa. The philosophy or science of the human mind thus = history.

My present difficulty is this. I think I can make good the above theses without difficulty in the case where human nature = rationality: it is easy, as Hegel showed, in the extreme case where what you are studying is history of philosophy. But how far down the scale can you go? Hegel thought you could go down as far as objective mind, but not as far down as subjective mind.

If so, subjective mind is nonhistorical (though its *esse* is certainly *fieri*: but not *historicè fieri*). Psychology (in the objective sense) has no history. In this part of his being, man is simply an animal. His instincts, that is, are not historically conditioned. Is this so? I think it probably is. Subjective mind might be said to = unconscious mind, and historicity = consciousness = self-consciousness. This must be worked out.

Historical Events as Eternal Objects

The event is *ex vi terminorum* the transient. The whole difficulty of historical epistemology lies here: for historical knowledge is for this reason not only degraded from the level of *vérité de rai-*

son to that of *vérité de fait* and so merely empirical, but it is degraded a stage beyond this, inasmuch as the flowing has here flowed *away*, to the level of empirical 'knowledge' of the no longer existent—*une fable convenue*.

I propose to argue that even on the assumptions of the kind of philosophy which gives us these results, they can be refuted.

On these assumptions, the best and most perfect knowledge is that of pure forms. The form may be either embodied (ἔνυλος λόγος) or disembodied (ἄνευ ὕλης). The eternal objects of Whitehead are embodied (ingredient in events, where the events are actual events). But in order to be an eternal object a form need not be embodied. Its being embodied has nothing to do with either its eternity or its objectivity. Nor is its essence *qua* form dependent on the plurality of its embodiments—to be a form is not to be a generalization or 'universal'. A form without matter is an individual, not a universal.

In contending that pure (= disembodied) forms are individuals I am (a) making contact with Aristotle (b) arguing that history as knowledge of the individual is not necessarily acquaintance with one instance of an embodied form. I am rejecting the view that grasping the concept *man* is science, being acquainted with *this* man is history. History is not acquaintance at all. The *this* is present only in the data (evidence) of historical knowledge not in historical knowledge itself (its object).

History is knowledge of the individual (e.g. the Norman Conquest) but (a) subjectively this is not empirical knowledge (acquaintance) (b) objectively it is not knowledge of an embodied form (which would have to be acquaintance). It is knowledge of a disembodied form: but (a) subjectively it is not generalizing knowledge (science) (b) objectively it is not knowledge of a universal (which would have to be science).

The form in question, a structure-pattern called the Norman Conquest, is disembodied because the matter in which it was once embodied has perished, i.e. there is no longer anything organized in that way. It is individual because there never could be anything *else* organized in that way. It is eternal because (a) subjectively it remains as a possible object of knowledge (b) objectively it remains as a presupposition of the present state of historical affairs—the effects of the Norman Conquest, as we say, are permanent, never wiped out. To this last point it may be replied: '*it* passes away, and has passed away; what lasts is not it but its effects. You are blundering into the foolish maxim *cessante causa cessat et effectus*, forgetting that the cause is *antecedent* to its effect.' I answer: The objectivity of historical fact is this: that *there was* such a fact. Historical fact has its objectivity precisely in being past. To be past here means to be past in the historical sense of the word past. The *mere* past is that which merely was; the historical past is that which not only was, but remains historically knowable, which it does only because it remains: remains not in its actuality (as form embodied in matter) but in its ideality (as pure form).

History is creative in the sense that it brings into being that which, once brought into being, is eternal. The eternal, in history, has this peculiarity, that it begins in time. The historical is eternal as *in aeternum*, not as *ex aeterno*. Historical being triumphs over time in the sense that it *becomes eternal*: but it becomes eternal not in its actuality (as embodied form), for here, because embodied, it perishes: but in its ideality (as disembodied form).[2]

On the other hand: it may be said that the historical form is never disembodied; for if it were, it would not be historically knowable.

The condition of its being thus knowable is that it lives on in ourselves. We can know the Norman Conquest because, being its heirs, we have it in our own minds (in our actual political consciousness) as an integral element. Its eternity is therefore nothing but a grandiloquent (and inaccurate) way of stating its survival as an effective force down to the present. On this showing the eternity of historical fact is only the continuity of historical tradition: the continued embodiment of the past in the present.

Note however that this does not mean that the *esse* of the past is to be historically known. Tradition here does not mean conscious knowledge of the past. Our present political consciousness has been formed by such events (experiences) as the Norman Conquest, but not on condition of our consciously remembering them. On the contrary: this consciousness is a

---

[2] After this, a 'II' appears in the manuscript, apparently in error, since there is no 'I'.

given fact, it is the way in which we now think politically. It is only when we ask *why* we thus think that, analysing this consciousness, we discover it to have been formed by such past experiences.

This brings me to the conception of history (= historical thought) as the re-enacting of the past in the present.[3] In so far as all history is the history of thought, this must be so: for one can only apprehend a thought by thinking it, and apprehend a past thought by re-thinking it.

But the formula needs a good deal of clearing up.

It may be said: the word thought is equivocal. It may mean τὸ νοεῖν ['the act of thinking'] or τὸ νοούμενον ['the thing being thought'] (νόησις ['act of thinking']) (νόημα ['thing thought']). Now, you can re-think a νόημα, for two acts of thought may have the same object. But you can't re-enact a νόησις, for the new νόησις is different from the old. If history means thinking thoughts (νοήματα) that have been thought already, it is only a name for any thinking that isn't a discovery, isn't original. The learner in Euclid is re-thinking a thought of Pythagoras, i.e. investigating the history of mathematics. Which is absurd.

Obviously we must qualify. History means not re-thinking what has been thought before, but thinking of yourself as re-thinking it. The learner of mathematics is an historian of mathematics also just so far as he thinks: I am here thinking what Pythagoras thought before me.

But whereas the thought (νόημα) in *this* case is a *pure νόημα*, in the case of the Norman Conquest it is a *νόησις-νόημα*. I mean: Pythagoras was thinking about the triangle: William the Conqueror was thinking about a political situation, and this situation was not merely *apprehended* but *constituted* by certain acts of thinking. For Pythagoras, knowing how other people thought about the triangle was no necessary part of thinking about the triangle; for William, knowing what other people thought about the political situation was not only an integral

---

[3] Collingwood dealt with this subject in his lectures on philosophy of history, given in the spring of 1936, under the title 'Re-enactment of Past Experience the Essence of History' as part of their 'Metaphysical Epilegomena'. When Knox included this piece in part V of *The Idea of History* (282–302), he changed the title to 'History as Re-enactment of Past Experience'.

part of thinking about the situation, it was *the essential* part of it.
There *was* no political situation distinct from what people
thought about it.

Thus there are not *two* but *four* senses of thought: (a) the act
(νόησις) (b) the object (νόημα) (c) a peculiar kind of act whose
object is an act (νοήσεως νόησις ['thinking of thinking']) (d) a
peculiar kind of object which is itself an act (νόησις νοουμένη
['thinking that is thought']). What we are dealing with in history
is this third sense. History is νοήσεως νόησις.

Why do I say that (c) is a peculiar kind of act? Someone will
say that it differs in no way from (a): it is just thought over again,
its peculiarity being only in its object.

I say this because it is the peculiar character of this act that it
does not *contemplate* its object. It is not θεωρία ['contemplation']. It alters the situation which it apprehends. The mind of
William is a factor in the situation, and it is this because William
understands the other minds which are also factors. The
thought of Harold, his view of the situation, is for Harold not a
factor in the situation but the *whole* situation. When William
knows what Harold is thinking, that thought (νόησις) is for
William a *factor* and no more. It is an *object* to him: one of the
objects about which he thinks: at the same time it is a *factorial
way in which he thinks*, for he 'enters into' Harold's thought,
thinks as Harold thinks, but thinks other things as well. Thus
νοήσεως νόησις is not merely a peculiar *case* of νόησις, it is a
peculiar *kind* of νόησις, where not the object merely but the act's
relation to its object (and therefore the character of the act) is
peculiar; for the act in this special case absorbs the object into
itself, makes it a factor in itself.

But conversely, *any* νοήσεως νόησις goes beyond its object.
The *mere* re-thinking of a νόησις is the transcending of that
νόησις and the reduction of it to the status of a factor. This is a
crucial point in all theory of history. It has e.g. consequences in
the history of philosophy, where the philosophical understanding of someone else's philosophy is already the transcendence of
that philosophy and its reduction to the status of a past or
absorbed moment in one's own thinking.

Human Nature and Human History[4]

(1) All processes are not historical processes. (2) That alone has historical processes which is rational. (3) That which is irrational has a natural process. (4) To have an historical process = having a history = being historical. (5) To have a natural process = having a nature = being natural. (6) That which is historical therefore has no nature, and to speak of its nature is already to falsify it by placing it on the wrong side of this frontier. (7) But here, as elsewhere, there is overlap of classes. *Man* occupies an ambiguous position. He stands with one foot in nature and one in history. (8) I am not here distinguishing body and mind. Man *qua* mere body (matter) is a subject of physics and chemistry and these take no account of man as such: the carbon in the human body is not human carbon but carbon merely. (9) The distinction is within the human mind (i.e. man *qua* mind). It is the distinction between τὸ ἄλογον ['the irrational'] (brute-mind in man) and τὸ λόγον ἔχον ['that which has reason']. (10) τὸ ἄλογον includes senses, instincts, impulses and in general the subject-matter of psychology. (11) τὸ λόγον ἔχον includes the intellect, will, and their synonyms and implicates: 'intellectual and imaginative faculties' (Hume). (12) The idea of a naturalistic psychology is well-founded, but it runs into error if it is identified with a science of mind. It is a science of τὸ ἄλογον ἐν ἡμῖν ['the irrational in us'], human brute-mind or horse-sense. To speak of 'the psychology of the moral self' or 'the psychology of reasoning' (the titles of books by Bosanquet and Rignano)[5] is to embrace this error. (13) The idea of a special science of the human understanding (Locke) or of human nature (Hume) is well-founded, but the right name of this science is history. Locke and Hume went wrong by modelling their new science on natural science. (14) The conception of a philosophical science is thus a very dangerous one: by using the phrase, we may be committing ourselves unawares to thinking of such a science as a special kind of naturalistic science, and this will produce

---

[4] The title is followed by 'iterum' and the date '26.iii.36'.
[5] Collingwood refers here to Bernard Bosanquet, *Psychology of the Moral Self* (London, 1897) and Eugenio Rignano, *Psychology of Reasoning* (London, 1923) (tr. of *Psychologie du raisonnement* (Paris, 1920)).

strange paradoxes, *either* falsifying the conception of spirit *or* reducing the phrase philosophical science to a case of *contradictio in adjecto*.

The Idea of Historical Efficacity[6]

Among the countless events which have happened, and which we can know to have happened, not all are worthy of our study. We need to select, to concentrate our attention on those that are worth attending to. Selection implies a criterion of value or importance. On what principle then are we to select?

The difficulty of stating any principle arises from the following dilemma. If what makes a certain event worthy of the historian's attention is anything *other than* its historicity, this other thing will be a non-historical conception superimposed on that of historicity, and history ceases to be an autonomous form of thought: principles not themselves historical will dictate what is of importance to the historian as such, and this is a contradiction in terms. But if what makes an event deserve attention is its historicity or something bound up with this, selection is at an end: everything that really happened becomes of importance.

In order to meet this dilemma, it might be suggested that the term historicity is equivocal: (1) it designates events that really happened (2) it designates events that are historically important. What we need is an inquiry into this second sense of the word.

---

[6] This section, drawn from fos. 46–57 of the manuscript, where the title here used appears as a subtitle, is the second half of a longer one that begins with notes and some critical observations on Eduard Meyer's *Zur Theorie und Methodik der Geschichte* (Halle, 1902). Meyer's theory of history is discussed in *The Idea of History*, 176–81. The present section may be considered as an elaboration of the idea of historical efficacy as discussed by Meyer. On fo. 40 of the manuscript Collingwood says of Meyer's position: 'The material for a given historical period is very large and of very varying value. Of the events for which we have evidence, which are *historical*?—In general, whatever is *wirksam* (effectual).' He then adds the comment: '[H]e seems to mean that whatever has no consequences is unhistorical. This is ambiguous. (a) What has strictly no consequences has left no evidence of itself and is therefore not knowable. (b) What has no consequences other than the evidence of itself is not therefore necessarily unhistorical, e.g. a minority policy that was not acted upon, or an idea neglected by contemporary thought.'

In passing, I note that this suggestion will not really overcome the dilemma. But to return to the suggestion.

When we call an event historical in sense (2), we mean that its occurrence turned the course of events into a new direction: it was a determining cause of subsequent events. Historicity (2) means *efficacity* (*Wirksamkeit*). The historian, then, is to concentrate his attention on those historical events (historical in sense (1)) which are historical in sense (2), big with consequences.

It is easy to bring empirical arguments forward to justify this contention. I will assume that as done, and explore the objections to it.

(1) It is circular. An event E_I is called important because it had consequences. But *all* events have consequences: e.g. my filling my pen ten minutes ago had the consequence that the ink in my pot is a quarter inch lower, and this again will lead to my refilling the pot, buying a new bottle of ink, borrowing a corkscrew, and so forth. This however does not make my filling my pen an historical (2) event, in the sense in which the signing of Magna Carta was historical (2): for the consequents E_2 E_3 E_4 are as unimportant as E_I. Therefore the historicity (2) of E_I is conditional on the historicity (2) of E_2 E_3 E_4 etc. or at least of some one term in that series. The historically important (this now emerges as the real meaning of the principle) is important because it leads to important consequences.

This principle is either circular or empty. If the importance of any event whatever is to be judged by its consequences, and if it depends on the importance of those consequences, we are involved in a vicious regress: E_I is important because its consequence E_2 is important, E_2 because its consequence E_3 is important, and so on *ad infinitum*. We never get to anything that is important in itself, and consequently the derivative importance of the whole series is derived from *nothing*, and disappears. This is not a merely 'logical' objection which 'in practice' can be ignored. The historian who in practice uses this criterion of importance finds that to use it robs everything of importance.

But if it is admitted that some things are intrinsically important, we have at once to ask: what constitutes this intrinsic importance? and as we cannot answer that question we are no better off.

(2) It is based on the false assumption that the historical process consists of events in causal series: that the event E_1 *causes* the event E_2. But this is a very doubtful doctrine. The cause of my buying ink (if it is insisted that I use that phrase at all) is not the fact that I have none left, but my resolve to buy new instead of borrowing, using a pencil, etc. The cause of my being involved in a traffic accident is not the fact of my being on the scene at the time, but my carelessness when there. A series of historical events is never a causal series in the sense of a series in which the earlier determine the later.

In spite of these objections, the theory deserves sympathetic consideration and has important merits. It is a great thing to reject the idea of intrinsic importance, which is really a nonsense idea, and to insist that when we speak of an event as important we should recognize the responsibility of showing *why* we call it important. It is also a great thing to insist that historicity in the full sense means something more than mere having-happened, and that this more has to be described in terms of value. What is needed is a restatement of these two ideas in a way not exposed to the dilemma which I stated at the beginning.

When the historian says that an event was important, he *seems* (and the theory under examination is deceived by this appearance) to be talking about it as a thing in itself apart from his own thought about it. But he is really talking about its relation to his own thought. 'Important' here means 'important to me'. Not, of course, to himself in any *role* except as historian. In that *role* he speaks of an event as important, in so far as it illuminates his thinking, throws light on a problem with which he is concerned. But this does not exclude the alternative, that the importance of an historical event may also have been its importance to the persons concerned in it and in its results. So far as the historian's thought is a re-thinking of past thought, what was important for the persons whose thought he re-thinks is important for his own too. The state of the weather at the battle of Trafalgar is important to the naval historian because it was important to Villeneuve and Nelson. For them, it determined the conditions under which they had to fight: for him, the knowledge of it is essential to any understanding of the battle. Still, what was unimportant to the historical agent may be important to the historian, and then he is right to say that it *was* important although no one saw its importance at the time. A statesman may think it unimportant that his policy is opposed by a small minority; to the historian, the existence of this minority may be an important fact because of the light it throws on later developments.

Fundamentally, then, the importance of events is their importance to the historian. But what makes them important to him is his being concerned with problems on which they throw light. Their importance is not intrinsic, but relative to the line pursued by his inquiries. The special case in which the theory under examination fits the facts is the case where the historian's problem is stated by such a question as: 'what were the events leading up to a given event E?'—for example the Peloponnesian War or the French Revolution. In such a case he may dwell on the importance of the Megarian Decrees: but the importance of the Megarian Decrees consists not in their having caused the Peloponnesian War, but in their providing the answer (or part of the answer) to his question. That type of positivistic history which conceives its main task as the 'discovery of causes' for given events will, of course, tend to identify the historical importance of an event with its relevance to that task, i.e. its efficacy.

I turn to the relation between importance and selection. When we speak of selecting, we imply that we could answer two questions that may be asked of us: 'selection from what?' and 'selection for what?' When the historian is said to select, it is implied that he begins by having before him a certain assemblage of things from which a selection is made, and that the selected objects are then submitted to some further process. From what, then, is the selection made? It cannot be the sphere of the historically known; for that would leave no further process to be carried out; this further process can only be one of historical study. It cannot be the merely knowable; for that is not present to the historian's mind at all. It cannot be the totality of historical problems, out of which some are selected for attempted solution; for there is no such totality; a problem neglected or shelved ceases to be a problem. For the same reason it cannot be the totality of historical evidence, out of which some is selected for interpretation. Evidence becomes evidence only in so far as it is interpreted. There seems in fact to be only one sense in which the historian can select. He can think of himself as free to pursue at choice this or that line of research, and as choosing to pursue one and not another. The field of choice is the field of possible historical inquiries. It is not a field of alternative objects, it is a field of alternative activities. The idea of selection belongs not to the theory of historical knowledge but to the ethics of historical research.

So understood, it is to be qualified in the kind of way in which the ethical conception of choice is always to be qualified. The situation to which the name choice is applied is a situation neither so common nor so significant as we often believe. As a rule (and the rule applies with special stringency to the more momentous of our decisions) we do not find ourselves standing at a halt, confronted by two or more clearly-envisaged alternatives between which we choose with complete indifference. We find, rather, that one of the alternatives arises out of something that we are doing already, and thus presents itself as a course to which we are already committed: it is not a wholly new departure, it is only a new stage on a journey long ago begun. We might, no doubt, change our minds, repudiate our commitments, and begin travelling in a new direction; but even that would not be done after a halt: it would be a new development whose roots could be traced somewhere in the past course of our activity. Zeno's argument about the arrow applies with double force to the story of Herakles' Choice: if he was ever really standing at the crossroads, he could never move either along the right-hand road or along the left. Thus, in historical inquiries, the choice of our direction is never made by an indifferent *liberum arbitrium*: the course of our studies shapes itself as we pursue it, always taking on new shapes and developing new aspects, but never involving a choice between two indifferent courses. We work as best we can; pursuing possibilities that open up before us, developing our past inquiries in whatever way we are able, never making a completely new start. We always have problems in our minds, which are never completely blank, virgin to every suggestion of the evidence: such a virginity could never be fertilized, for it would be a complete lack of interest in history. The direction, then, in which at any given moment we decide to move is the direction in which we see a chance of throwing light on the problem now occupying our minds. If the important means what is important to us, as historians, because it throws light on our problems, and if selection means pursuing a certain line of inquiry, it is certainly true that the historian, in proportion as he is a good historian, selects the important, that is, pursues the line of inquiry which he judges likely to solve the problems that are in his mind. But that is all the statement can legitimately mean.

Croce has well pointed out that selection, although strictly it has no place in history, has an important one in antiquarian and philological work: here it means picking out from among the relics of antiquity those which are useful for our present purpose and rejecting (it may be, destroying) the rest. He observes that only a madman would treasure *all* the relics of antiquity, which is very true: and as, for him, philology is not a form of knowledge but a case of economic activity, the choice of the useful (hallmark of economic activity) is of course characteristic of it. Thus, on his view, the ascription of a selective act to the historian belongs to philologism or the substitution of scholarship for history, and has no grounds apart from that error. I accept his point but think that there is actually a further ground, viz. the conception of historical thinking itself as a free activity involving a choice not between *scibilia* (which would be absurd) but between possible courses of inquiry. The error here, so far as it is an error, is an error in general moral theory, referring to choice what is really will (i.e. conceiving the freedom of will in an arbitrary sense as excluding necessitation).

A Note on Evidence and Certitude

The term evidence is used with reference to both historical and legal procedure. The sense in the two cases is so far the same that the historian's evidence is that given fact which obliges him to conclude that a certain event has happened: the law-court's evidence, that given fact which obliges the court to conclude that a person did or did not do a certain act. But there is a difference between the two cases. The court is under an obligation to decide, here and now, between the alternatives presented to it. Sometimes the evidence is conclusive one way or the other, and in that case legal evidence approaches the condition of historical evidence: but often it is not conclusive either way, and in that case a decision is only arrived at by applying a rule whose validity is purely practical—e.g. the rule that unless the prosecution has established the guilt of the accused he must be deemed not guilty. The fact that such a rule is even contemplated shows that a great gulf divides the procedure of the court from that of the historian. The court has to have rules of this type because it is a function of the community's *active* life. In the situation where someone is accused of a crime the community must do *something*: there is no third alternative between treating him as guilty and treating him as innocent. The question which the court has to decide, though called a *quaestio facti*, is not really a question of fact, it is a question of *faciendum*, a question of how we are to treat this man. If we treat him neither as guilty nor as innocent but only as *suspect*, so treating him would merely consist in committing him for trial. The point of trying him is to eliminate this third alternative: if the court perpetuated it, such a conclusion would be a mere declaration of bankruptcy on the part of legal institutions.

The historian is under no obligation to settle any question here and now. He is concerned not to *act* towards the past but to *know* it. If (through lack of evidence or any other cause) he finds himself unable to reach a conclusion, he must suspend judgment and rest content with his ignorance on the question at issue. The three alternatives *yes*, *no* and *non liquet*, are for him all equally open and genuinely distinct: *non liquet* is not (as for a court of law it must be) a mere way of saying either *yes* or *no*.

Probability is a conception alarmingly involved in controversial issues: but (with due timidity) I suggest that when we say 'S is probably P' we mean 'we do not know whether S is P or not, but we assume in practice that it is'. This suggestion amounts to saying that the theory of probability belongs not to logic but to ethics. To think of something as probable is not to make a judgment or assert a proposition about it, but to take up a practical attitude towards it—an attitude consisting essentially in the intention to treat *non liquet* as if it were *yes*. Thus when I say the train will probably be punctual I mean, 'I don't know whether it will be or not, but I propose to act as if I knew it would be.' Someone may object: I might say 'the train will probably be late, but all the same we had better be at the station in time'. But I reply that a person using such language would not be saying quite what he meant—if he *really* thought it probable that the train would be late he wouldn't turn up in time except on the principle of *ex abundanti cautela*.

I think that discussions of probability often go on the wrong lines by substituting for a discussion of what probability is a discussion of the grounds on which we say that something is probable. If there are 99 black balls in a bag and 1 white, the odds (i.e. the proportion of black balls to white) do not *constitute* probability, they *found* it. It is *because* the odds are 99 to 1 that it is expedient to act as if, out of every 100 times you dip into the bag for a ball, 99 times you will get a black one. I think that arithmetical probability (as it is called) is not a kind of probability but a kind of reason for treating possible events as probable.

There is thus a clear distinction between uncertainty and probability. When in a strictly scientific (I mean *wissenschaftlich*) context someone says 'S is probably P' he is not referring to probability, only to uncertainty. The historian as such has therefore nothing to do with probability.

I know this is a paradox. Most people would say that historians are constantly dealing with probabilities: some, that they never deal with anything else. It is a commonplace that historical evidence very often falls short of demonstration, and that in such cases the careful historian claims no more than he can claim justly. But *what* can he justly claim in such cases? If my suggestion is right he can only claim *possibility*. What then are historians doing when they say 'so and so probably happened'? Croce says they are perpetrating romantic or poetic history—believing what they like to believe instead of what the evidence proves. My view would suggest a similar criticism: that they are taking up a practical instead of a merely theoretical attitude to the facts, and neglecting the duty of saying 'we do not know'. There is another alternative: that they are taking up a practical attitude towards the course of their own inquiries, saying in effect 'we should be wise to expect that the future course of research will prove A or disprove B'. It is as if the historian were making a bet, e.g. betting that Early Iron Age remains would be found on such and such a site. And this is quite legitimate, though it must not be confused with historical knowledge.

This confusion might happen in either of two opposite ways. Historical probability might be taken for historical certainty:

the bet that something would be discovered might be confused with knowledge that it was there. Or historical certainty might be taken for historical probability: i.e. the knowledge that the evidence does prove something might be taken for a mere bet that further evidence would prove it.

The latter confusion is found, I think, in the minds of those who maintain that historical knowledge is never more than merely probable. I should object to that doctrine on the ground of self-contradiction. Genuine probability, I think, implies the possibility of verification. It would mean nothing to say the train will probably be punctual unless, by presenting myself at the station, I could ultimately decide whether it was or not. Where verification is ruled out, probability is an empty word. It is meaningless to say 'There is probably a God', unless one is prepared to define the conditions under which we shall know whether there is one. Hence the fallacy of Pascal's wager.

Similarly it is meaningless to say 'Caesar was probably assassinated', unless one is prepared to define the nature of the evidence which, for us here and now, would verify the probability and entitle us to say 'now we know that he *was*'. But *all* our knowledge of the past is reached through evidence—it is never empirical, just because the past is past and not therefore perceptible. Our experience of the past is altogether historical experience, mediated through inference. Therefore the condition under which alone we can call it probable is lacking.[7]

---

[7] Further items contained in this manuscript but not included here are: 'Notes from Fueter' on a part (334–485) of Eduard Fueter, *Geschichte der neueren Historiographie* (Munich, 1936), dealing with historiography from the Enlightenment to Ranke; 'Hegel on History', some scattered notes on his philosophy of history; 'Notes on Spengler', a critical discussion of *Der Untergang des Abendlandes* (1918–22), probably using the English translation *The Decline of the West* (London, 1926–8), since English quotations are given; a page of desultory notes on *Exploratio Philosophica* (first part 1865, second, posthumously, 1900) by John Grote, philosopher brother of the historian George Grote, mentioned by Collingwood in *The Idea of History*, 208; an extensive critique of Eduard Meyer, *Zur Theorie und Methodik der Geschichte* (Halle, 1902), probably in preparation for Collingwood's discussion of Meyer in *The Idea of History*, 176–81; a few notes on C. Jullian, *Histoire de la Gaule* (Paris, 1920).

NOTES ON HISTORIOGRAPHY

Historical Naturalism[1]

I use this term as a name for that kind of failure to think histor-ically which ends in either (a) *substituting* natural facts for the historical facts about which one is trying to think (losing the dis-tinction between them altogether), or else (b) *superordinating* natural facts to historical facts, as the causes of which these his-torical facts are the effects (here the distinction is, superficially, preserved intact; but only superficially, because it is, to a more penetrating eye, destroyed by the μετάβασις εἰς ἄλλο γένος ['change into another kind'] which makes a fact of one order the cause of a fact in another order. Only historical facts can be causes of historical facts). The *cause* of this failure, in both its forms, is the thinker's relative immaturity and incompetence in historical thinking, as compared with his greater freedom and ease in the pursuit of natural science: this gives him a constant motive for switching over from a kind of thinking in which he feels ill at ease, to one in which he feels more at home. The *cure* for it is, of course, historical methodology.

Examples of historical naturalism: (1) *Geographical (and climatic) history*, where geographical facts (I include meteor-ology in geography) are taken as the causes of historical facts (Montesquieu and other eighteenth-century writers). Here a long view would soon dissolve the illusion, by showing that the

This manuscript, which bears the subtitle 'written on a voyage to the East Indies 1938–9', was written by Collingwood during a trip he made to the Dutch East Indies from 21 October 1938 to 5 April 1939 to recover from ill health. It is of special interest as a preparation for writing 'The Principles of History', on which he began working on 9 February 1939. The manuscript contains not only paragraphs addressing problems that were to be dealt with in the book, but also Collingwood's overall plan for it. Eighteen of the 'Notes' are included in the present volume; those omitted are described in a final note. Because of the omissions, the numbers Collingwood assigned to particular paragraphs have not been reproduced. (Bodleian Library, Collingwood Papers, dep. 13.)

[1] Collingwood adds: '16.i.39, steaming into Amboina [an island in the Dutch East Indies]'.

same geographical facts which are said to cause one type of historical development are compatible with developments of a
quite different kind; so that what causes a development of that
type is not the geographical facts in question but the way in
which people think of these facts and of themselves in relation to
them. (2) *Biological history* (including psychological, so far as
psychology is a naturalistic science of man). Here the causal
relation is between what certain men *are* (this conceived as a
biological matter) and what they *do* (history). Perhaps the most
famous example of this error is the confusion in ancient Jewish
thought between the special function of the Jewish people as a
factor in history, especially the history of religion, which is traditionally represented by calling them the 'chosen people', and
their real or fancied biological character as a group of persons
related by blood and descended from a common ancestor. Here
we have: (α) a genuine historical fact, the 'mission' of a certain
historical community, i.e. its own consciousness of its own
uniqueness or individuality; (β) a mythical expression of this
fact viz. the myth of common descent from Abraham. By calling
it a myth, I do not mean that it was a fiction; for I do not know,
any more than anybody else does, whether at any given time all
the people who called themselves the 'children of Israel' were
descended from a common ancestor or not; I mean that it was a
belief whose importance for those who believed it lay not in its
literal sense as depending on the biological meaning of the term
children, but in its symbolic sense, as depending on the use of
that same term to indicate a common way of life and a common
inheritance of traditions; (γ) an acted myth, the careful preservation of the Jewish stock in a condition of biological purity by
forbidding mixed marriages. This prohibition expresses in a
practical way the confusion between the historical fact, the
Jewish people's consciousness of its individuality, and the biological myth of common descent from Abraham.

In a world which had learnt to accept Roman law with its
practice of adoption, this myth was obsolete; and the declaration
of its bankruptcy was one of the greatest triumphs of
Christianity (and incidentally one of the proofs that Christianity
was not, as it has often been fancied, a deposit of brilliant *aperçus*
by an individual genius, later obscured by his unintelligent followers. The founder of Christianity is not recorded to have

made this point; there is even some evidence of his being personally a little hostile towards it. Certainly it was implied in the logic of his position; but the person who made it explicit was Paul). Paul's discovery that the Jewish law was obsolete was (partially, not exclusively) his recognition of the truth that the unity of a common way of life and the unity of a common pedigree are different things between which there is no necessary connexion.

The survival of a separate Jewish community in the Christian world has carried with it the survival of historical biologism. The recent outbreak of persecution against the Jews in Germany is conditioned not by the persecutors' desire to stamp out historical biologism, but by their acceptance of that error. The official doctrine of the persecutors is a so-called *Rassentheorie* according to which the facts of history are subordinated, as effects to their causes, to certain biological facts, namely the differentiation of the human species into those varieties which are called the 'races' of man. This *Rassentheorie* is an eighteenth-century thing—the eighteenth century was characteristically the age when the still immature historical consciousness of the modern European world was experimenting with every form of historical naturalism—being in fact Herder's special version of the general type of pseudo-history then prevalent. (Query: is there any *direct* evidence that Herder was influenced by Jewish thought? he was, of course, as an eighteenth-century German, a Bible-reader and presumably given to taking his Bible very seriously: you would *expect* him, in a matter such as this, to regurgitate fragments of Biblical doctrine; but I should like proof.) Modern Germany thus stands officially committed to the same error which infected ancient Jewish thought, and which Paul exploded—the error of regarding a given community's historical function as bound up with its biological character, i.e. with the common pedigree of its members—and thus persecutes the Jews *because it agrees with them*. Intellectually, the Jew is the victor in the present-day conflict (if you can call it that) in Germany. He has succeeded in imposing his idea of a chosen people (in the biological sense of the word people) on modern Germany: and this may explain why the victims of this persecution take it so calmly.

No Beginnings in History[2]

You can trace institutions back into *earlier forms of themselves* (relative beginnings, a_2 arising out of a_1) but only that. You can't ever find an absolute beginning. The desire for an account of absolute beginnings is a desire not for history but for *myth*. Examples: Livy and the origin of Rome. Hobbes and the origin of Civil Society. Freud and the origin of morals. History is *about* something that doesn't begin and doesn't end. It is *connected* with things (e.g. individual human lives) that begin and end, but there is no history of these things.

The Comparative Method

This is the apotheosis of anti-historicism in a positivistic interest. You cease to care about what a thing *is*, and amuse yourself by saying what it is *like*. (A critical discussion of the idea of *similarity* would be useful here.) Imagine a 'comparative pathology'. This condition is *like* nasal catarrh (but it *is* scarlet fever).

That History is the Only Kind of Knowledge

I have already shown that metaphysics is what I have called an historical science, i.e. that the problems of metaphysics are without exception historical problems.[3] It is easy to show that this is true of every so-called philosophical science. Thus philosophy as a separate discipline is liquidated by being converted into history. To deny this proposition is legitimate only so long as the person who denies it has a false view of history, which he feels it necessary to amend by *adding* to it what he has left out (and *correcting* the errors he has put in) by calling a conception of *Philosophy* into existence to redress the balance of his conception of History. The problems of *Natural Science* are not historical problems and cannot like those of philosophy be resolved

---

[2] Dated '17.i.39'.

[3] Collingwood refers here to his *Essay on Metaphysics*, the first draft of which he had written on the ship sailing to the Dutch East Indies.

into such. Its methods again are radically different. But it is an *abstraction from* history. Its chief methodical principle is to start from certain presuppositions and think out their consequences. These presuppositions are not true (or false) and therefore thinking them together with their consequences is not know-ledge (or error). What is knowledge is the knowledge that such presuppositions, with such consequences, are made, and this is historical knowledge. Such historical knowledge is not merely knowledge about scientists possessed by other persons, histori-ans. It is possessed by the scientists themselves, *qua* scientists. If a man did not know that he was making certain presupposi-tions he would not be a scientist.

No Endings in History[4]

The story which an historian tells is never a story which has come to an end when he tells it. He may call his subject 'the decline and fall of the Roman Empire', as if it was something that had happened and had finished happening; but when he comes to define the subject more accurately you will find him defining it as 'the triumph of barbarism and religion', i.e. assuming that what he is really narrating is how *these* barefoot fryars came to be in the temple of Jupiter Capitolinus.[5]

Formerly, believing that the historian narrated past events that have finished happening, I expressed the idea of no endings in history by saying that all history was *also* history of the sec-ond order, and that second order history always came down to the present day and reached into the future.[6] I now want to say *more* than that. I want to say that Grote was writing the history of the Liberal party, and Mommsen the history of Prussia—that all genuine historians interest themselves in the past just so far

[4] Dated '5.2.39'.
[5] Gibbon records: 'It was in Rome, on the fifteenth of October, 1764, as I sat musing amidst the ruins of the Capitol, while the barefooted fryars were singing Vespers in the temple of Jupiter, that the idea of writing the decline and fall of the City first started to my mind.' *The Autobiographies of Edward Gibbon*, ed. John Murray (London, 1897), 302; see also 405–6.
[6] For the idea of history of the second order, also called by Collingwood the history of history, see L26, 379–82, 407–10, and L28, 461–9.

as they find in it what they, as practical men, regard as living issues. Not merely issues *resembling* these: but *the same* issues (theory of historical interest as depending on *resemblance* between past and present, a mere disguise for this truth). And this must be so, if history is the re-enactment of the past in the present: for a past so re-enacted is not a past that has finished happening, it is happening over again.

Historical Importance[7]

People have been quite right to say that the historian's business is not to narrate the past in its entirety, nor even, it might be added, the past for which evidence is available (which of course would have been impossible anyhow), but to narrate such of the past as has historical importance. But what do such people mean by historical importance? It has sometimes been thought that to call something historically important means that it 'influenced' other things happening subsequently. This is only a muddled way of saying that historical importance means importance *for us*. And to call a thing important for us means that *we* are interested in it, i.e. that it is a past which we desire to re-enact in our present.

In cases coming under this head, the questions would be possible, and in fact often easy, to answer, if they arose: but owing to our lack of interest they don't arise. There are other cases, of course, in which lack of evidence would make it difficult or impossible to answer a question if it arose, but in which this doesn't matter because the question doesn't arise. Where a question does arise, and the force of our interest is sufficient, evidence will always be forthcoming, in the sense that the search for it never encounters obstacles which are in principle insuperable. This of course is Locke's great point, that we know 'sufficient for our needs'. The limitations of what we know are derived from the limitations of what we want to know (where want = need, not = desire).

[7] Dated '5.2.39'.

No Completeness in History[8]

No piece of historical work ever exhausts either its subject, however small, or the evidence for its subject, however exiguous. (1)
Its subject, because every profitable reconsideration of an historical subject re-defines the limits of the subject. Every competent historian who comes to the consideration of an old
historical theme finds himself asking afresh what the theme is
that he is dealing with, and giving a new and individual answer
to this question. (2) Its evidence, because every advance in historical method is an advance in the power of historians to cite
new kinds of evidence.

The idea of 'definitiveness' in history owes its hidden motive
to a kind of jealousy like that which caused Mithridates to kill
his mistresses; and its ostensible motive to the scissors-and-
paste idea of history according to which 'the evidence' for e.g.
Marathon is a finite number of words in the texts which are 'the
authorities'. It is possible to be argued out of the second; but the
former is an emotional condition or 'state of sin' which is hard
to cure. To think that one's book will one day be superseded is
as much against the grain as to think one's body will one day be
eaten by worms. No book is a *monumentum aere perennius*.
Habent sua fata.

But must not the historian *try* to be complete even though he
knows he can't be? Is not historical completeness an 'idea of
Reason'? No. The historian should not aim at completeness, he
should aim at relevance. He should aim at providing an answer
that really is an answer to the question he is asking. (It is often
only in answering it that he can find out what it is, of course).

This conception, especially when the discovery is made that
philosophy resolves itself into history, clashes sharply with
Kant's famous demand for completeness in his exposition of
the Categories and his quotation *Nil actum reputans si quid
superesset agendum*.[9] It must be made clear that Kant's ideal of

8 Dated '5.2.39'.
9 Collingwood refers here to a passage in Kant's *Critique of Pure Reason*, B
xxiii–xxiv, where he says of metaphysics: 'Consequently, metaphysics has also
this singular advantage, such as falls to the lot of no other science which deals
with objects (for *logic* is concerned only with the form of thought in general),

completeness was a relic of his early Cartesianism, in fact of the fallacy he so eloquently attacked, that philosophical method was in essentials the same as mathematical.

Logic an Historical Science[10]

The aim of logic is to expound the principles of valid thought. It is idly fancied that validity in thought is at all times one and the same, no matter how people are at various times actually in the habit of thinking; and that in consequence the truths which it is logic's business to discover are eternal truths. But all that any logician has ever done, or tried to do, is to expound the principles of what in his own day passed for valid thought among those whom he regarded as reputable thinkers. This enterprise is strictly historical. It is a study in what is called contemporary history = history of the recent past in a society which the historian regards as his own society. (Thus people like Mill, Jevons etc. in their 'inductive logics' are giving as good an account as they can of the conditions under which 'modern scientists' regard a piece of 'scientific thinking' as valid, or consider a 'scientific theory' well founded.) Often this kind of historical study is accompanied by a good deal of confusion or error as to whether the principles of 'contemporary' thought have been recognized at other times also, and if not, what follows. Actually, the kind of thinking which was investigated by the nineteenth-century inductive logicians hardly existed before about the sixteenth century. Logic as 'theory of scientific

---

that should it, through this critique, be set upon the secure path of a science, it is capable of acquiring exhaustive knowledge of its entire field. Metaphysics has to deal only with principles, and with the limits of their employment as determined by these principles themselves, and it can therefore finish its work and bequeath it to posterity as a capital to which no addition can be made. Since it is a fundamental science, it is under obligation to achieve this completeness. We must be able to say of it: *nil actum reputans, si quid superesset agendum*' ['He considered nothing done, so long as anything remained to be done']. (*Immanuel Kant's Critique of Pure Reason*, tr. Norman Kemp Smith (2nd edn. London, 1933), 26).

[10] Dated '7.2.39'. Collingwood adds the observation that this section is a continuation of the section entitled 'That History is the Only Kind of Knowledge'.

method' is in effect, at any given time, a fragment of a history of scientific method.

Ethics as an Historical Science[11]

(a) Ethics as an account of the principles of action depends for its content on the structure of the moral world of which it tries to give an account. Thus ancient Greek ideas of conduct are different from Christian ideas and consequently Aristotle's ethics (say) differ[s] widely from any seventeenth- to twentieth-century ethics, without this implying error on either side. Any ethical theory is an attempt to state what kind of a life is considered worth aiming at, and the question always arises—by whom? (b) There are departmental ethical sciences like politics, economics. These, at any given time and place, describe the political and economic principles accepted at that time and place. For economics, this has been seen by the Marxists, and it has been admitted by J. M. Keynes, with the odd result that he has tried to construct a 'general' economic theory, stating the supposedly permanent general principles of which any 'special' economic theory, like Adam Smith's, is a special case. This of course is illusory. (c) Even the distinction between logic and ethics is an historical one and no more. As we inherit it from the Greeks, it certainly has no permanent validity: the Indians or the Chinese do not make the distinction between thought and conduct in any such way as that which we presuppose when we make it.

Crypto-history[12]

This word may prove useful as a name for sciences which *are* historical sciences but profess not to be. Thus, tactics is taught in military academies with reference to the 'contemporary'

---

[11] Dated '7.2.39'. Collingwood observes that this section, too, is a continuation of the one entitled 'That History is the Only Kind of Knowledge'. The titles of the sections on logic and ethics, which are as they appear in the manuscript, are not phrased identically; but this does not appear to be intended to make a philosophical point.

[12] Dated '7.2.39'.

kinds of weapons and methods of fighting (where 'contemporary' means 'belonging to the recent past'—cf. the remark that 'soldiers are always preparing for the *last* war') but it need not be taught, and is not always taught, in such a way as to impress this fact upon the pupils' minds. It may even be taught with this fact concealed or denied. It is then a crypto-historical science. The so-called classical economists have written of an 'iron law of wages', meaning that a certain theorem about wages must always be true under any kind of social system. Actually, this theorem was true of the social system under which they wrote: but under a different social system it would not necessarily remain true. The so-called classical economics is thus a crypto-historical science, describing a certain set of transient historical conditions under the belief that it was stating eternal truths—anthropology is crypto-history. A number of different historical complexes are lumped together under the name of 'primitive life' or something like that: and their characteristics, all of which have their own historical contexts, are thus by a fiction abstracted from these contexts and treated as a kind of matrix (I use the word metaphorically in its geological, not its mathematical, sense) within which historical formations arise.

Pseudo-history[13]

ἐσθλοὶ μὲν γὰρ ἁπλῶς, παντοδαπῶς δὲ κακοί ['for men are good in only one way, but bad in all sorts of ways']. All the same, there is *one* thing which is so pre-eminently pseudo-history that it may be awarded that name κατ᾽ ἐξοχήν [*par excellence*]: namely *change*. People are always talking as if history were the same thing as transience or timefulness: 'this has a merely historical interest' means 'this interests only people who are interested in things that have passed away'. I myself have insisted that history is the story of 'events that have finished happening', and must be careful about this in future. But I have also insisted that all history is the history of thought, and that the historian knows a past thought by re-enacting it in the present. As so re-enactable, it is not something that has finished happening. Is it

[13] Dated '7.2.39'.

a *condition* of the past's being historically knowable, that it should be still something actual, not something dead? Or is this a *consequence* of its being historically known? Neither: it is the same thing as its being historically known. There are (of course) no 'conditions' of a thing's being knowable—that is the error of realism. Pseudo-historicity then shall be my name for what Alexander, Whitehead, etc. call historicity. A pseudo-history is an account of changes, whether geological, astronomical, social, or any other kind, where the person giving the account does not re-enact in his own mind the thoughts of the person or persons by whose action these changes come about.

Scheme for a Book: 'The Principles of History'[14]

Main topics will include (1) a single account of the most obvious characteristics of history as a special science (2) Relations between this and others (3) Relation of history as thought to practical life. These could be Books I, II, III.

I. 1. State and expound the conception of *Evidence*. Contrast this with the conception of *Testimony* and the *Scissors-and-paste history* which that implies. I. 2. State and expound the conception of *Action* (*res gestae*). Contrast this with the conception of *Process* or *Change* and the pseudo-history[15] which that implies. I. 3. Conception of *Re-enactment*, and contrast the *Dead Past* and *Completeness*. I. 4. History as the *self-knowledge of mind*. Exclusion of other sciences of mind.

(There might be an *introduction* on the word '*history*', showing how originally it = investigation of *any* kind, e.g. *historia naturalis*: and how it gradually focussed itself on the kind of meaning which it had for Herodotus, Thucydides, and Polybius. Survivals of the original generalized sense in modern usages. This book deals with the specialized sense.)

II. 1. History and natural science. A. difference between them irreducible: A1. history not to be reduced to natural science: A2. natural science not to be reduced to history. B. relation between them: any given natural science an historical

---

[14] Dated '9.2.39'.
[15] Within brackets Collingwood refers back to the section on 'Pseudo-history'.

achievement: its dependence on 'facts' and 'principles', i.e. the *historical* fact that someone has observed something and thinks in a certain way about it.

II. 2. History and the human sciences. These are crypto-history or just history.

II. 3. History and philosophy.[16]

III. The main idea here is that history is the negation of the traditional distinction between theory and practice. That distinction depends on taking, as our typical case of knowledge, the contemplation of nature, where the object is presupposed. In history the object is enacted and is therefore not an *ob*ject at all. If this is worked out carefully, then should follow without difficulty a characterization of an historical morality and an historical civilization, contrasting with our 'scientific' one. Where 'science' = of or belonging to *natural* science. A scientific morality will start from the idea of *human nature* as a thing to be conquered or obeyed: a[n] historical one will deny that there is such a thing, and will resolve what we are into what we do. A scientific society will turn on the idea of *mastering* people (by money or war or the like) or alternatively *serving* them (philanthropy). A[n] historical society will turn on the idea of *understanding* them.

History and Positivism[17]

(a) Positivism = thesis that natural science is the only knowledge. This involves a direct attack on history as such. (b) Positivistic history in its crudest form (Buckle) *is* such an attack. (c) In an attenuated form it conceals this attack beneath a pretence of solving historical problems by methods analogous to those of natural science (Bury). These will be pseudo-historical problems: history proper is not thereby advanced. (d) In a third, modern, form it = subsumption of history under nature as *Process* or *Event* (Alexander, Whitehead, Rickert). This involves the reduction of history to pseudo-history. This is dis-

---

[16] Using his own paragraph numbering, Collingwood appends a reference here to the sections on 'Logic an Historical Science' and 'Ethics as an Historical Science' which he had written two days earlier.

[17] Dated '9.2.39'.

guised as a reduction of natural science to history through the idea of *Evolution*, falsely supposed an historical idea. So it frequently (especially in Germany) goes by the name of *historicism*, which should in such a case be read *Pseudo-historicism*.

Accident

An accident, in Aristotelian logic, is that which is predicated of a subject without being either part of, or a consequence of, its essence. In modern European languages this sense is obsolete, and the word belongs to the vocabulary of history. An accident is an event which happens to a person without his intending that it shall happen to him. If a second person intends that it shall happen, it is still an accident relatively to the first person; but relatively to them both together it is not an accident. (The practice of confining the use of the term to cases where the event is untoward is a vulgarism which has established itself only in certain contexts, e.g. in the vocabulary of insurance.)[18]

History and Contingence

If history has to do with events, then of course accident plays an enormous part in history (Bury's treatment of this subject, e.g., betrays two confusions, one about what history is (he thought it was about events) the other about what contingency is (he thought it was the opposite, not of being intended, but of being caused)). Actually, accidental or contingent events do not occur *in* history at all: they form the background or scenery of history. A mariner is caught in a storm: this is an accident: but that storm appears in the history of navigation only if the historian is interested in the mariner's handling of the situation to which this accident gave rise (or someone else's, e.g. the Board of Trade or the Meteorological Office). Nature as such is contingent.[19]

---

[18] Dated '10.2.39'.   [19] Dated '10.2.39'.

Nature and History

Nature may be called a background or scenery for history, but it does not figure in history as a constant. It affects the course of history in different ways according as man copes with it differently. Nature as the background of history is what man makes it. One would infer that behind this changing thing called 'what man makes of nature' there is an unchanging thing, namely what nature is in itself; but if so, we have no knowledge of it. Natural science at any rate does not reveal it, for natural science is always concerned with what man makes of nature: thus, when man makes machines, his natural science regards nature as consisting of machinery; when he discovers how to use chemical action, his science regards nature as consisting of chemical apparatus: in short, the 'forces of nature' described at any given time by natural science are the ways in which man has learned to manipulate nature.[20]

Introduction to Book I[21]

'History', said Bury, 'is a science; no less and no more.' Let us grant that it is no less. But anything that is a science at all is more than merely a science: it is a science of some special kind. A science means simply an organized body of knowledge; but a body of knowledge is never merely organized, it is always organized in some special way. Some, like meteorology, are organized by collecting observations concerned with events of a certain kind which the scientist can watch as they happen, though he cannot produce them at will. Others, like chemistry, are organized by deliberately producing events of a certain kind under strictly-controlled conditions, and others are organized by making certain assumptions and proceeding with the utmost exactitude to argue out their consequences.

[20] Dated '10.2.39'.
[21] This apparently is the beginning of the introduction to Book I of 'The Principles of History', which is included in the Epilegomena to *The Idea of History* under 'Historical Evidence' (249–50). Since the text of *The Idea of History* differs in some respects from that of the manuscript, the latter is reproduced here.

History is not organized in any of those ways. Wars and rev-olutions, and the other events with which it deals, are not delib-erately produced by historians under laboratory conditions, in order to be studied with scientific precision. Nor are they even observed, if the word observation implies that accuracy and detachment which it implies in the mouth of a natural scientist. Meteorologists and astronomers will make long and arduous journeys in order to observe for themselves events of the kinds in which they are interested, because their standards of obser-vation are such that they cannot be satisfied with descriptions by inexpert witnesses: but historians do not fit out expeditions to countries where wars and revolutions are going on. And this is not because historians are less energetic or courageous than nat-ural scientists, or less able to obtain the money such expeditions would cost. It is because the fruits of these expeditions would be of no scientific value to them. The sciences of observation and experiment are alike in this, that their aim is to detect the con-stant or recurring features in all events of a certain kind. But the historian has no such aim. If he is studying the Hundred Years War or the Revolution of 1688, this is not for him a preliminary stage in an inquiry whose ultimate object is to . . .[22]

Revolutionary Inventions[23]

[These] are impossible because if they are to be revolutionary they must be successful in supplying a demand; and there is no demand for what is quite unrelated to experience. What people want is an invention enabling them to do just a *little* better or easier or cheaper something they are already doing (according as they are interested in doing the work, saving trouble, or saving money), e.g. shaving without stropping your razor, or having music in your house without learning an instrument, or writing without dipping your pen in the ink. You may be sure that no

[22] The text ends here, with the note: 'Copied out and continued elsewhere'. Dated '10.2.39'.

[23] Dated '8.3.39'. This means that it was written by Collingwood on the ship returning home. The paragraph was untitled. We have used the first two words of the first sentence, which are italicized, as the title.

mariner would have taken to the compass unless mariners had
already been able to steer a course.[24]

[24] Not included in the above selections from 'Notes on Historiography' are
some desultory and critical observations on Sidney Lee's *Principles of
Biography* (Cambridge, 1911) and on the prefaces to a few historical plays by
Racine. Collingwood ends his criticism of Lee with the remark: 'What he is trying to do is (a) to erect into permanent Rules of Biography the working rules he
has found convenient in editing the D.N.B. [*Dictionary of National Biography*]
(b) to base these imaginary Rules on a permanent factor (equally imaginary) in
human nature, the "Commemorative Instinct". Wash out all the silly pompous
nonsense and pseudo-philosophy and the lecture is a quite nice and interesting
account of "how I go to work on D.N.B. material".' Collingwood's observations on Racine end with the comment: 'What Racine is doing might be
described as working out rules for the game of historical fiction or romance,
which is thus an older thing than history as now understood. N.B. historical fiction is not really a mixture of history and fiction, because it cannot exist where
the distinction between the two things is clearly understood. Historical fiction
is a false form of history. (This is worth stating in detail. People will refuse to
believe it, but they ought to be made inexcusable for refusing.)' These observations may usefully be read with what Collingwood says of biography in 'The
Principles of History'. The 'Notes' end with some desultory observations,
mostly written on the ship sailing home. Of these, only the ones on 'revolutionary inventions' are included here.

CONCLUSIONS TO LECTURES ON NATURE AND MIND

The Conclusion of 1935

I have brought this historical survey of the development of the idea of nature down to the present time, and the general conclusions which I should wish to draw from it are, I hope, clear from the survey itself. I will finish these lectures by simply pointing out the chief features of the situation in which we now stand.

Alexander has lately written an essay, not yet published, called *The Historicity of Things* (it is to be published in a volume of essays presented to Professor Cassirer).[1] I will take that title as the text of these concluding remarks.

History is a process which, as it goes on in time, creates its own vehicles. All history is the history of something—e.g. the history of England, the history of Chinese art, the history of naval tactics—and the history of anything is the history of the

---

This manuscript consists of two Conclusions to the Lectures on Nature and Mind which Collingwood delivered at Oxford in 1934, 1935, 1937, 1939, and, after substantial revision, with the title 'The Idea of Nature in Modern Science', again in 1940. Knox put them aside in favour of a third Conclusion, written in 1940, when he edited the lectures as *The Idea of Nature* in 1945 (174–7), and they then dropped out of sight until discovered in January 1995, along with the manuscript of 'The Principles of History'. The shorter Conclusion probably dates from 1935, and the longer one from 1934, as indicated by the titles we have inserted. On the title page of the manuscript is written: 'The Idea of Nature (originally called: Nature and Mind). Lectures written Sept.–Oct. 1934 for delivery in Mich. Term, 1934. Delivered again, 1937 (Based on the work, occupying the whole period Aug. 1933–Sept. 1934, which is recorded in the five notebooks labelled περὶ φύσεως, α–ε). Revised extensively Sept. 1939, and rewritten in the form of a book'. The notebooks referred to contain Collingwood's 'Notes towards a Metaphysic'. The manuscript also contains a table of contents for *The Idea of Nature* which has not been reproduced here. (The manuscript can be examined in the Archives of Oxford University Press.)

[1] † *Philosophy and History*, ed. Klibansky & Paton, Clarendon Press, 1936, pp. 11–25. [This note was added at a later date. Collingwood had seen the manuscript as a reader for OUP. The same article is referred to at the beginning of 'Reality as History', PH, Ch. 2, §4, and in *The Idea of History*, 210.]

ways in which that thing itself changes. History is not a series of superficial changes which, flowing over the surface of something, leave its inner essence unchanged: the changes of which the historical process consists are changes that reach right down into the heart of things. In the history of England, for example, there is not one part of England that changes and another part that does not change: the whole thing which is England changes, and yet in this change it remains itself, because the change is continuous and involves no breaks. If we find this difficult to grasp, if we find ourselves clinging to the belief that there is an essential and substantial England that remains unchanged behind the shifting veil of historical events, the way to disabuse ourselves of the error is to recollect that England itself, if we look far enough back in history, did not exist: England itself, in other words, is the product of historical processes. This, then, is the general nature of history: a process which brings into existence everything which it contains, a movement creating that which moves.

This conception as applied to human affairs is, I will not say a commonplace, but reasonably familiar to everyone who has thought what human history implies. I will not call it a commonplace, because if it were we should not find ourselves tempted, as we so often are, to think that something exists called human nature, which underlies historical process and is unaffected by it. In order really to grasp the implications of the idea of human history we must realize that human nature at any given moment is what it is because human history has made it so, and that to speak of human nature at all is only a way of referring to the summed results of human history down to the present time.

The conception of nature which has been worked out by philosophers like Bergson, Alexander and Whitehead applies the idea of historicity in the sense I have defined not only to man, but to nature. During the later nineteenth century, this idea of historicity was already applied to man but not to nature: this was the ground of the distinction, familiar in the writings of German philosophers at that time, like Dilthey, between Sciences of Nature (*Naturwissenschaften*) and Sciences of Spirit (*Geisteswissenschaften*) where the sciences of spirit were conceived as historical sciences, resolving the conception of reality into the conception of process, and the sciences of nature were non-historical sciences dealing with the permanent and unchanging essences of things. What this new philosophy of nature has done is to extend the conception of historicity from its restricted field of human affairs to the universal field of metaphysics in general. Matter itself, which the dominant tradition of thought from the seventeenth to the nineteenth century regarded as essentially inert, changeless, preserving its self-identity behind all the movements and combinations which it undergoes, thus came to be regarded on the analogy of human nature as something brought into existence by these very movements and combinations. Not only is mental being conceived as identical with mental process, but physical being is conceived by this new philosophy as identical with physical process.

This new conception of nature or the material world is not simply a philosopher's conception, propounded over the heads or behind the backs of scientists. It is a conception which those who propound it regard as no more philosophical than scientific, no more scientific than philosophical. As in the time of Descartes, so again today physics and metaphysics are working hand in hand, and one of the most remarkable features of this new cosmology is just that fact: the fact that the separation of philosophy from science, of which we have so long been conscious that we have come to regard it almost as a necessary evil, has disappeared. The results of this new situation ought to be extremely fertile both for science and for philosophy, strengthening and enriching both of them: and perhaps it is not too much to hope that the alliance and cross-fertilization of these two streams of thought will have a beneficial effect on the future of civilization, which has suffered greatly in the last few generations from the fact that those who ought to be its intellectual leaders have spent much of their time in a mutual warfare, damaging to the prestige of both sides and of no advantage to either.

One question remains. I have referred to Alexander's phrase, the historicity of things, as describing the main conception of this new philosophy. The question that remains is how far this phrase is strictly justified. It is intended to express the fact that natural reality, like human reality, is now regarded as consisting altogether in process. But is there one kind of process or two? Is there any difference between the process of human affairs, which is strictly and properly called historical process, and the process of nature? That the two things, if they are two things, are very much alike, has been amply demonstrated by these new theories of nature. It remains to be seen whether in spite of this great resemblance there is any difference between them: whether, in other words, the phrase historicity of things is completely and literally justified or is only partially and analogically true.

This is too large a question to consider now. It will be the underlying theme of my lectures next term, in which I shall be trying to give an account of history, to describe exactly what it is and how it is known.[2] When that is done, we shall be in a position to consider the question how far the process of nature and the process of history are identical in character, and how far they differ, if they differ at all.

The Conclusion of 1934

In conclusion, I must now give some brief account of the view of nature which in my opinion is indicated or demanded by the development of thought I have described.

1. The old conceptions of inert matter having a situation in space and undergoing movements in time have disappeared, and we are left with the conception of all that exists—not only mind but life and even matter—as not only permeated by activity but as identical with this activity.

2. This activity is a process or development, creating new forms of itself; for example, it proceeds from a first stage as inorganic nature through a second stage as life to a third stage as mind. These stages must therefore be both continuous and differentiated; each must be in one way the same as its predecessor and also in another way really different from it.

3. The starting-point of the process, space-time or the extensive continuum, is a phase of existence in which externality is the supreme ruling principle. Everything is outside everything else (points in space) and one phase of any given thing's existence is outside every other phase (moments in time).

[2] The reference is to Collingwood's lectures of 1936, which were later to form the basis of *The Idea of History*.

4. The culmination of the process is a phase of existence in which internality or inwardness is the ruling principle. This phase of existence is to be identified with mind at its highest development. The phases of one mind's life, so far as it is a mind, are not juxtaposed in time; the past is present as memory, the future is present as purpose. Different minds, so far as they are minds, are not outside one another; they share in each other's activities, know the same things and pursue the same ends, so that, since their activity is their being, they actually share in each other's being. The more perfectly mind becomes mind, the more perfectly this ideal of absolute mutual inwardness is realized in fact.

5. Mutual inwardness does not imply obliteration of distinctions (e.g. the remembered past is really past). Consequently, within the realm of perfectly-developed mind there are distinctions of various kinds, but these distinctions do not involve, still less are they identical with, divisions of substance.

6. The entire evolution of the world may therefore be conceived as a passage from outwardness to inwardness. Each phase of that evolution is consequently a special case of such a passage. At any given stage there is a certain degree and kind of inwardness already achieved, and there is also a residue in the shape of a certain degree and kind of outwardness. The next stage in the process will therefore be the overcoming of this particular kind of outwardness and the substitution of the corresponding inwardness.

7. In the case of things moving through space, such as electrons, each has its own inwardness as what Whitehead calls self-enjoyment, i.e. the possession by each electron of its own mass, velocity, determinate path etc. Each is absolutely external to all the rest. This mutual outwardness is overcome by their combination into atoms; for this combination gives rise to a new set of qualities belonging not to any of the electrons but only to the atom as a whole; these qualities pervade the entire atom, and are not located in anything less than the atom. Hence the atom represents an overcoming of the special outwardness belonging to the electron; it is only because electrons situated outside one another are fused into a single unity in the atom that the specific qualities of the atom appear at all. The outwardness of the electrons does not disappear, but it is overcome. Similarly with the molecule and all chemical combinations.

8. The evolution of matter consists entirely in the discovery of new patterns, and patterns of patterns, and so on, which electrons, protons and so forth can progressively form. This line of evolution if produced to infinity would never lead to life. The peculiarity of life, in the biologist's sense of the word, is that activity here takes the form of a life-cycle through birth to youth, maturity or ability to reproduce itself, senescence, and death. Each organism traverses this cycle once only.

9. Why should there be forms of existence having this peculiarity? If our hypothesis is correct, it must be because herein some special form of externality pervading the entire physico-chemical world is overcome.[3]

10. This form of externality consists in the relation between a thing and its environment. However elaborate the physico-chemical organization of matter may be, each thing in the material world is absolutely outside every other, and remains permanently outside it. Bodies may and do act on each other, but in no case can one become another. The mutual externality of any given body and its environment is complete.

11. A living organism lives by nourishing itself. At any given moment, the organism simply is the material particles of which it is composed; but the activities which constitute its life are directed towards maintaining its existence not, as in the case of purely material objects, by resisting forces directed upon it from without, and merely holding itself together, but by taking portions of this environment into itself, and incorporating them in its own structure. In eating, drinking and breathing, the organism perpetually converts its environment into itself; a process whose other aspect consists in a perpetual conversion of itself into its environment by the waste of its tissues.

12. The self-identity or self-enjoyment of a living organism thus not merely survives, but actually depends upon, or even consists in, a constant change in the material particles of which the organism is composed. This is a totally new way of overcoming the mutual outwardness of these particles; they are now united in a pattern whose peculiarity consists in re-making itself at every moment out of new materials. The environment may be

[3] After this, the following sentence is crossed out: 'If so, it would follow that the material or physico-chemical world has in it an inherent nisus towards the creation of life, i.e. the overcoming of that special form of externality.'

represented as streaming constantly into the organism, taking up a specific pattern there, and passing off to become mere environment once more.

13. The principle of life being the constant overcoming by the organism of the mutual externality of itself and the environment, life can only appear when the organization of matter has reached a point where such metabolism is rendered possible by chemical and other conditions. But it would never take place, even when that point had been arrived at, unless there had been from the first a nisus towards the production, not exactly of life as we know it, but of some form of existence in which the mutual externality of a thing and its environment should be overcome.

14. The evolution of progressively higher forms of life should therefore represent a progressive overcoming of this mutual externality. The higher organisms cannot indeed nourish themselves on anything and everything; the chemical differentiations of matter make it necessary for them to nourish themselves on what is chemically appropriate; but the highest organisms, those which are most intensely alive, will find means of using those material bodies on which they cannot feed as means for the discovery of those on which they can; they will move about in search of food and by degrees discover food which is peculiarly adapted by its chemical constitution to the needs of life as such. This is probably the general nature of the principle which has led from merely vegetable life to animal life and thus to the higher species of animal.

15. As this evolution has proceeded, the autonomous character of the life-cycle has been accentuated. The lowest organisms have a comparatively variable span of life and their characteristics differ only vaguely according to their individual age; in the highest, there is a comparatively fixed span of life and a regular and orderly development of these characteristics. A tree differs much more in its vital characteristics according to the seasons of the year than it differs according as it is ten or twenty years old; its life, that is to say, is comparatively speaking tied down to the rhythmical life of the inorganic world. A dog shows little change in its biological functions according to the seasons, but much according to whether it is one year old, or five, or ten. Thus the evolution of life seems directed to the establishment of peculiar cyclical periods of its own, independent of all inorganic

periodicities and each coextensive with the entire existence of the individual concerned. Thus conceived, life is nature's way of discovering a wholly new form of process or activity, passing through phases peculiar to itself, where each individual embodiment of the process traverses these phases once and only once.

16. The peculiarity of mind, as distinct from life, is best described in general by the word sensation. Mind has higher functions, but no other functions coextensive with the entire range of its being. By the word sensation I mean (a) the act of seeing, feeling, etc., i.e. the sense-perception of objects (b) the act of feeling one's so-called feelings e.g. of warmth or cold, pleasure or pain. This function is connected with the possession of a nervous system, which in its most rudimentary form represents a type of sensation not yet differentiated into seeing, hearing and the like; in higher organisms the nervous system elaborates itself into specifically different parts, and the act of sensation differentiates itself correspondingly.

17. This new stage of evolution, like the origin of life, must represent the overcoming of some form of externality which life, however far it develops along its own line, can never overcome. If so, the whole biological world is pervaded by a nisus towards the evolution of mind.

18. The special characteristic of sensation is that material patterns and rhythms external to the organism are absorbed into the organism (e.g. the ear is a mechanism for reproducing certain air-vibrations in the brain; the eye, one for producing a retinal image reproducing the organism's perspective of its environment); but that in this absorption they are not destroyed or converted into anything else, as are the patterns and rhythms constituting the chemical qualities of food. When it eats, the organism absorbs food into itself and destroys the food; when it hears, it absorbs the sound-waves into itself but does not destroy them.

19. This constitutes a new relation between the organism and its environment. In becoming part of an organism's body, its food ceases to be environment; in entering an organism's perceptual field, the objects it perceives do not cease to be environment. The grass that a cow eats is no longer grass; the grass it sees is still grass; yet, although still grass and still situated outside the cow, it actually enters into the cow's being, in so far as

those rhythmical disturbances in it which are the physical basis of light reproduce themselves in the cow's brain.

20. This new relation overcomes a specific type of outward-ness: namely the separation between two states of the environment, according as it is outside or inside the organism. This is overcome by the emergence of a relation in which one and the same part of its environment is at once external to the organism and internal to it.

21. To avoid misapprehension, we must beware of saying that the object remains outside the perceiving and that what is inside it is a mere copy or reproduction of it. The patterns and rhythms which are the physical basis of light, sound, etc. as they exist in the percipient nervous system are the very same patterns and rhythms which exist in the object; and since these are in both cases activities, and activity is the essence of both subject and object, they form points of actual identity between the being of the two. Of course the grass does not enter into the eye in its entirety: only one part of it does so; but what enters the eye is not a copy of the grass but one part of its actual being.

22. We must also beware of separating, though we must carefully distinguish, the complex patterns and rhythms which are the physical basis of colour or sound from the simple colour or sound which we actually see or hear. The two things are related precisely as the electron-pattern of an atom is related to its chemical qualities: in each case there is a determinate pattern which when fused into a unity presents peculiar qualitative characteristics pervading it as a whole. A certain rhythm of air-vibrations communicates itself through the tympanum to the ear; physically it consists of impacts having a regular time-interval between them; as heard, it is a single continuous sound lasting uniformly as long as the vibrations go on.

23. The difference between the quality of the atom and the quality of the sound is that whereas the atom possesses its own chemical quality in itself, the vibration-pattern in the air comes to possess its sonority only so far as it is fused into unity by the nervous system of the percipient organism. In the physical world, sound-patterns and light-patterns are simply series of discrete events; it is the function of the percipient organism to fuse them into unities and thus to elicit from them the qualities which in themselves they possessed only potentially.

24. Thus the perceptive act of the sentient organism makes a difference to its objects, though it does not destroy them. The difference which it makes to them is that it fuses certain of their patterns and rhythms into a new unity, and calls forth the qualities which result from this fusion. Hence, just as the life of the organism may be conceived from the environment's point of view as a peculiar way in which this environment can pass over into a new mode of existence, so the sentient activity of mind may be conceived from the point of view of the objective world as a peculiar way in which this world can fuse itself into a new unity and come to possess qualities which before this fusion it did not possess.

25. Every new stage in evolution has two aspects: (a) it produces a new form of existence of a specific kind (b) it initiates a new stage in the existence of all the other forms, in virtue of the new relation in which they stand to this new form. The whole world is thus involved in each one of its creative advances.

26. Hence the emergence of mind not only affects the organism in which the sentient activity is located as subject, by giving it a new attitude towards its world; it also affects that part of its world, the perceptual field, over which this activity is distributed; for the activity which in one sense is located within the organism as subject is in another sense located all over the objects which are its field. All activity has this double character. It is diffused all over its field, and is also focussed at a centre (e.g. the activity of a managing director is in one sense situated in his office; that is its focus; in another sense it is diffused throughout the employees of the company; that is its field).

27. It follows that the emergence of mind not only satisfies a nisus contained in the organism which becomes its subject, it also satisfies a nisus in the world which becomes its object. Just as life implies an environment preadapted to its maintenance (L. J. Henderson, *The Fitness of the Environment*) so that the environment conspires, as it were, to promote life and therefore realizes potentialities of its own through the existence of living organisms in contact with it; so mind implies an environment of a special kind, namely an environment possessing sensible qualities in potentiality, and comes to enjoy the actualization of this potentiality when it becomes the perceptual field of a sentient organism. Figuratively speaking, we may say that the world

already wants to be seen, heard and in general perceived, and that by satisfying this want through the creation of mind it raises its whole self to a higher level of existence, that is, to a new inwardness of self-enjoyment.

28. At its first appearance mind is closely tied down to life. The organism does not perceive anything and everything, it perceives only what is of interest to it as a living thing endeavouring to complete its proper life-cycle. Hence it perceives only what may help or hinder the activities constituting this life-cycle, and its perceptions are all coloured by its desire to pursue these activities; that is, it perceives food with hunger, enemies with fear or rage, a possible mate with sexual desire, and so forth. Whatever cannot be a proper object for such emotions it does not perceive at all.

29. From the first, however, mind has in it a principle of autonomy; seeing food is one thing, eating it is another. And since mind is a higher form of existence than life (by which I mean that it stands higher in the evolutionary scale, as a form of existence overcoming the specific form of externality which life leaves untranscended), in reality mind is not a means to the existence of life, life is a means to the existence of mind. Consequently mind, once it has established itself as a new form of existence, develops not by emphasizing this initial servitude to life but by gradually abolishing it. Mind in its evolution progressively insists on being itself.

30. The higher forms of mind are therefore more and more disinterested in their attitude to the vital functions out of which they have grown. To know the world, which includes knowing itself as at once part of the world and knower of the world, becomes the purpose upon which the activities of mind concentrate themselves. This does not mean leaving behind all interests, all efforts, and all emotion; it means that these things take new forms; a highly-developed mind chiefly desires to know itself and the world, and its main interests and emotions are bound up with the satisfaction of that desire. Since its activity is its being, this desire to know itself and the world is at the same time a desire to be itself.

31. This desire on the part of mind, to be itself by knowing itself and the world, is at the same time a desire on the part of the world to be known, and by being known to enter into the

enjoyment of qualities which exist in it potentially before it is known, but actually only in so far as the patterns and rhythms and processes of nature are fused into unity, with resulting emergence of their appropriate qualities, in the focus of mind. Somewhat as a lower mind like that of a dog desires the company of a higher mind like that of a man, in the light of whose presence it feels itself completed by being understood in a way in which it cannot understand itself, so in the objective world as merely intelligible or potentially known, apart from the intellect which should know it, there is an element of incompleteness or unrealized potentiality that can be perfectly satisfied or resolved into actuality only when the intellect has done its work. This is why the creative process of nature has evolved mind.

32. Mind is thus in one way dependent on body and in another way independent of it. Dependent on it, because mind can only arise as the mental activities of living organisms, and can only work upon a field which consists of the world, a world which is always physical and vital as well as mental; independent of it, because when it has arisen it provides itself with its own interests and purposes.

33. The question here arises, whether this independence goes to the length of what is usually called immortality, or the mind's eternal survival of the death of the body in which it has arisen. As a preliminary to answering this question it should be recollected that mind in its most perfect development, as reason conscious of itself and devoted to being itself, achieves the highest conceivable overcoming of externality; its field extends over all time and all space, the whole world being fused into new qualities at its focus, and even the separateness of mind from mind is in principle overcome. But on the other hand the focus has always a place and a time of its own, and a mind which is not in this sense located somewhere in space, and which does not traverse a life-history in some part of time, does not seem to be conceivable. Here I shall leave this question, to return to it in the future.

I now turn to the problem of eternal objects (Whitehead's term). According to Whitehead's view all qualities are eternal objects, having a double function (a) as lures for the process of development, or final-efficient causes (b) as ingredient in actual occasions, or formal causes. But I have explained that

Whitehead gives us no thought-out view of the world of eternal objects; and its relation, as a world of unchanging abstractions, to the natural world of change, I venture to think does not admit of being formulated at all. The result is a metaphysical dualism between two worlds—a world of unchanging abstractions and a world of changing events—and Whitehead leaves this dualism unresolved. His view has, however, the merit of facing the problem of eternal or necessary being which Alexander evades by reducing everything to space-time. Our problem is: if nature is all process, how can there be anything eternal? Whitehead replies that there can be a realm of eternal objects prior to and therefore outside nature; this is certainly true; but he has no right to include in this realm such purely natural and empirical qualities as blueness or toothache.

The concept of process implies, if properly considered, that one and the same thing can be the product of a process and also an eternal object. Thus the dualism which Whitehead thinks the only way out of his problem is avoided, and we can say that the world of process *is* the world of eternal objects. Whitehead does not realize this, possibly because he has not considered the nature and implications of history.[4]

34. History is a process. The substance of it is human activity; the process of this substance is the change which human activity undergoes, not in virtue of external causes working upon it, but in virtue of its own autonomous self-development. Thus the constitutional history of England has been a more or less constant change in the manner in which England has governed itself; this change has been a development, because each step in it could have occurred only where it did occur—the Reform Bill of 1832 could not have happened in 1688, and the Revolution of 1688 could not have happened in 1215. Moreover, England itself has changed with the changes of its constitutional history; and so has the idea of government, which has undergone enormous developments since the Norman Conquest, or even since the time, say, of Henry VIII. Thus modern England and modern government have actually come into existence in the process of English constitutional history. This kind of

---

[4] In the manuscript this paragraph is numbered 33 in error. To avoid confusion with the previous paragraph, which is also numbered 33, we have deleted the number.

process in which the thing undergoing the process forms itself, or comes into existence, as the process goes on, is called *becoming*.

35. It is characteristic of becoming that it is creative or rather self-creative. What it has brought into existence passes out of *existence* again, but does not pass out of *being*. Thus, the Revolution of 1688 was produced by the self-development of the English constitution in the seventeenth century; as an event in time, it happened, and then stopped happening; since the existence of an event is its happening, that revolution does not now exist, it is an event which is not going on now. But historians can still think about it; that is to say, it is still an object for historical thought. Its being, in this sense, is timeless; that is to say, it is in the strict sense of the words an eternal object. Thus all historical events become eternal objects; and if this is the case with history, it is the case with all self-creative processes. If the entire process of nature is a becoming, as Whitehead sees that it is, then this becoming must generate eternal objects. It does not presuppose them all, as Whitehead thinks, nor does it generate merely transient objects, as both he and Alexander assume.

36. The eternal objects of historical thought are concrete eternal objects, e.g. the Revolution of 1688; Whitehead's eternal objects are abstract eternal objects, e.g. a certain kind of blueness, or (returning to 1688) the exact configuration of the splash made when James II threw the Great Seal into the Thames. What is the relation between these? I suggest that the abstract eternal object is merely one element in a concrete eternal object taken by itself in abstraction. The real eternal object here is the event as a whole, James II throwing the Great Seal into the Thames; the configuration of the splash owes its eternity not to the fact that a splash with exactly the same configuration might happen again at any time, if that *is* a fact (which I suspect it is not), but to the fact that it was part and parcel of the event.

37. The eternal being of an historical event does not consist in or depend on its being known to historians. The Revolution of 1688 enjoys its eternity through being a permanent element in the political experience of the English people; even if they forgot the event itself, the fact that they have lived through it would continue to colour their political outlook and influence

their political activity. It is only because historical events leave permanent traces in the subsequent course of history that historians can find out anything about them: for the historian begins his work from documents and sources of various kinds, and all these must be things existing in the world contemporaneously with himself.

38. Historical knowledge is not empirical knowledge, it is not perception or observation: it is essentially inferential. The historian argues to his conceptions; he argues that because the data are thus and not otherwise the past event must have been of such and such a kind. His object, therefore, the past event, is not only an eternal object but also a necessary object, an object that must be what it is, and is known rationally in apprehending this necessity.

39. Applying these results to our knowledge of nature: we regard nature as a self-creative process and therefore creative of eternal objects. One such eternal object is the physical world as it was before the emergence of life, the purely physical world, the world as conceived by the physicist. For Whitehead this world is an abstraction; the actually existing physical world as we find it here and now is a physical world profoundly affected by its relations with life and mind, and the physicist making abstraction from these relations in order to conceive a purely physical world is conceiving a mere *ens rationis*. I reply: it is not an *ens rationis*; it is a real past stage in the evolution of nature, reconstructed in his thought by the physicist as the surgeon reconstructs a past attack of appendicitis from the present shape and colour of an appendix. Thus the residual element of subjectivism in Whitehead's conception of matter is overcome, and it becomes clear how we can think of the physical world as it would be if we were not there to observe it.

40. There is however one kind of eternal object which cannot be the product of the cosmic process: namely that which is the ground or presupposition of any process whatever. In saying this I am not referring to space-time or the extensive continuum. There is no empty time before events begin to happen, and no empty space before things begin to occupy it. I am referring to certain fundamental conceptions like being, unity, necessity, and so forth, which are logically presupposed by the very idea of process; or, in cosmological terms, to the fact that

all process is essentially finite and must depend upon something other than itself.

41. This other may therefore be conceived in two ways. Logically, it is the ultimate concepts which I have mentioned; cosmologically, it is the ultimate creative force which underlies the existence of anything whatever; that is to say it is what we call God.

42. Our ordinary conception of God is at bottom the conception of something (a) infinite and (b) creative. When we say that God is a spirit, that God is love, that God is our heavenly father, we are expressing not the ultimate and fundamental elements in our conception of him but what I may call new discoveries about him, ideas which have come to characterize and qualify the original idea. And it is bad theology to interpret these qualifications in such a way that they contradict the original and fundamental conception: e.g. when we argue that because God is a spirit he is a person and therefore finite, or when we argue that because he is love he cannot have created a world full of evils.

43. God is infinite in himself, creative in his relation to the world. In himself he is not creative, only infinite. He is pure and absolute being, unqualified and undifferentiated: if we ask what particular kind of being, the answer is no particular kind—not mental or physical, not even creating or created, but no kind at all; the ocean or abyss of being which is indistinguishable from an abyss of nothingness. This conception is at once the starting-point of logic and the starting-point of theology, and for both reasons it must be the starting-point of cosmology.

44. Pure being is not a mere abstraction, an *ens rationis*, the empty form that is left in our minds when we have thought away everything particular; it is a real object of thought, and (as Hegel pointed out) by no means difficult to think. Nor is it, as certain modern logicians believe, the product of a verbal quibble, the copula of a judgment whose predicate has been cut off; it is a necessary thought, which no theory about logic can explain away.

45. This pure being has in itself no determinations; but it is not only the ground of determinations in other things, it is also a source of determinations belonging to itself. In terms of logic, pure being determines itself not only negatively but positively: it is one, it is self-identical, it is necessary. These determinations arise out of it and so qualify it; but nevertheless it is in itself, as

unqualified, logically prior to them all. Thus it undergoes a process, from pure indeterminacy to determination; and this process, which is a logical process, belongs to it essentially, and is not imposed upon it accidentally or by the operation upon it of anything else. Strictly therefore it does not undergo the process, it is or determines itself as the process.

46. In terms of theology, or cosmology, God in himself is pure being, but he is also, in his relation to himself, a process generating a variety of determinations, ὑποστάσεις or *personae* in theological language. Each ὑπόστασις is what it is and not the others; in thinking of them therefore we must, in the words of the Athanasian Creed, not confound the persons; but they are not independent beings, they are determinations of the one being, growing out of itself; hence in thinking of them we must not divide the substance, the οὐσία or essence, being itself.

47. These determinations of being are the eternal objects logically prior to and in that sense independent of the cosmic process. The cosmic process is a process in space and time; but the determinations of being have a process of their own, which is not a spatio-temporal process but a logical process. In theology this process is called the generation of God as son by God as father: the father is in himself pure being, the πηγὴ θεότητος or fountain-head of deity in the words of a Greek theologian, out of which comes the Son who in himself is the logos or concept, the structure of categories like unity, identity, necessity; the relation between pure being and the logos is the πνεῦμα or breath of life, which is nothing else than process itself. Thus we have pure being, the categories, and becoming, all three asserted by Christian theology as prior to the creation of the world. In logic, this means that a world of categories or eternal objects, all determinations of pure being and all pervaded by logical process, is logically prior to the existence of anything whatever.

48. We must next ask, what is the relation between this primordial world of eternal objects and the changing world of nature? In relation to the world, God is conceived as creator; that is to say, in terms of logic, pure being, with its determinations and their process, is not only the necessary presupposition of actual existence but its sufficient ground. The existence of nature must somehow be a necessary logical consequence of pure being.

49. Theologians have said that light is the shadow of God; and this gives a clue to answering our question. The process of the world begins with the extensive continuum or space-time; and this means a state of things entirely dominated by the principle of outwardness or externality, a state in which all you can say about any one thing (let us call it with Alexander a point-instant) is that it is not any of the others. It is a world wholly composed of plurality, difference, contingency. Now these are the logical opposites of unity, identity, necessity, which we found among the attributes or determinations of God. Every concept has an opposite, and there is a necessary logical process leading from it to this opposite; hence, when we find that space-time is the sum of all the opposites of the determinations of pure being, we can see that, granted these determinations, space-time necessarily follows from them.

50. Space-time is thus the opposite of the categories; but it is not the opposite of pure being, for it has being. If it were the opposite of pure being it would be nothing and could not exist, for it would have no characteristics. In cosmological terms, therefore, space-time is not something wholly other than God; it is a necessary stage in the logical process which is the life of God. God is immanent in nature from the first, and the life of nature is the life of God in nature.

51. The process of nature as a whole is therefore one part or phase of the process by which God works out new determinations of his being. Every creative advance in nature is an increment or enrichment of the being of God. This is why nature, although it is wholly composed of transient events, can create eternal objects: the events of nature are eternal because they are taken up into the being of God.

52. Every stage in the advance of nature consists in overcoming some form of externality, advancing from one form of outwardness to the corresponding form of inwardness. The perfect development of mind, as I have explained, would lead to a form of existence in which there was no outwardness left unresolved: where not only mind and nature, but even one mind and another mind, were not merely different but fused this difference into a real unity. Consequently the perfect development of mind would seem to be a real culmination of the process of nature; not leading on to any further development, but closing the course of

natural evolution. The world of nature would then have fulfilled its function in the life of God, and it would cease to exist.

53. This is why in trying to define God we find it best to define him in terms of mind or spirit. For, in so far as God lives in and through nature, spirit is what he is becoming. But it is only through nature that God becomes mind. In himself, as creator of the world, he is not mind, but pure being.

54. This leads back to the question of immortality. All events in the course of nature have a kind of immortality in so far as they come to qualify the eternal being of God; but the immortality of a mind implies something more than this. A mind is not only an object but a subject, it is not only knowable, it is also a knower. Consequently the actions and experiences of minds, if they are really taken up into the being of God, must be taken up not merely as facts that have happened, which might be called an objective immortality, but also as acts that are being done; that is to say, they must enjoy a subjective immortality. Not only the deed but the doer must become an eternal increment to the being of God. Thus all minds must be immortal; but they can only be immortal in so far as they are really minds, that is to say, so far as they overcome the outwardness or sheer difference that separates them from nature and each one of them from the rest. This eternal life of mind as taken up into the being of God can best be symbolized, though it is only a symbol, by the life of a human society in which the differences between person and person are welded into a unity by honourable dealing and loving intercourse.

55. Lastly, nature as we know it, *the* world, as we call it, need not be and can hardly be the only field for this kind of evolution. The fundamental physical characteristics of our world, as Whitehead has pointed out, have in them an element of arbitrariness. Imagine a world in which the velocity of light was different; every detail in the structure and history of that world would be different from anything in ours. But one thing we can be sure of: the process of its evolution would be governed by the same general law, that every stage involved the overcoming of externality. Consequently it too would lead up to the creation of something analogous to what we call mind; a kind of mind to which our textbooks of psychology would have no application whatever, but one which could understand what we meant by

knowing the truth, doing right, fearing God and loving one's fellow-creatures. There may be an infinite number of such worlds; if there are, owing to differences of physical constitution it is certain that we cannot see them, so that it does not matter whether we like to imagine them as remote from ours in space or time, or as actually interpenetrating the world in which we live; for, just as we could never see them, so there could be no physical interaction between them and our own. Whether they exist we shall only know when we meet, in the bosom of God, the minds for whose creation they have existed.

BIBLIOGRAPHY OF WORKS CITED

Collingwood: published works

Religion and Philosophy (Oxford, 1916).

'Hadrian's Wall: A History of the Problem', *Journal of Roman Studies*, 11 (1921), 37–66.

Roman Britain (Oxford, 1923; rev. edn. 1932).

'Can the New Idealism Dispense with Mysticism?', *Proceedings of the Aristotelian Society*, Suppl. 3 (1923), 161–75; reprinted in *Faith and Reason: Essays in the Philosophy of Religion by R. G. Collingwood*, ed. Lionel Rubinoff (Chicago, 1968), 270–82.

Speculum Mentis (Oxford, 1924).

'The Roman Frontier in Britain', *Antiquity*, 1 (1927), 15–30.

'Oswald Spengler and the Theory of Historical Cycles', *Antiquity*, 1 (1927), 311–25; reprinted in *Essays in the Philosophy of History*, ed. William Debbins (Austin, Tex., 1965), 57–75.

The Archaeology of Roman Britain (London, 1930; republished London, 1996).

The Philosophy of History, Historical Association Leaflet No. 79 (London, 1930); reprinted in *Essays in the Philosophy of History*, ed. William Debbins (Austin, Tex., 1965), 121–39.

An Essay on Philosophical Method (Oxford, 1933).

Roman Britain and the English Settlements, with J. N. L. Myres (Oxford, 1936).

'On the So-called Idea of Causation', *Proceedings of the Aristotelian Society*, 38 (1937–8), 85–112.

The Principles of Art (Oxford, 1938).

An Autobiography (Oxford, 1939).

An Essay on Metaphysics (Oxford, 1940; rev. edn. 1998).

The First Mate's Log of a Voyage to Greece in the Schooner Yacht 'Fleur de Lys' (London, 1940; republished Bristol, 1994).

'Fascism and Nazism', *Philosophy*, 15 (1940), 168–76; included in *Essays in Political Philosophy*, ed. David Boucher (Oxford, 1989), 187–96.

'Goodness, Rightness, Utility', Lectures, 1940, appended to *The New Leviathan*, rev. edn., ed. David Boucher (Oxford, 1992), 391–479.

The Three Laws of Politics, 1941, Hobhouse Memorial Lectures, 1941–50 (London, 1952); included in *Essays in Political Philosophy*, ed. David Boucher (Oxford, 1989), 207–23.

The New Leviathan (Oxford, 1942; rev. edn. 1992).
The Idea of Nature (Oxford, 1945).
The Idea of History (Oxford, 1946; rev. edn. 1993).
The Roman Inscriptions of Britain, i: *Inscriptions on Stone*, with R. P. Wright (Oxford, 1965).
Essays in the Philosophy of History, ed. William Debbins (Austin, Tex., 1965).
Faith and Reason: Essays in the Philosophy of Religion by R. G. Collingwood, ed. Lionel Rubinoff (Chicago, 1968).
Essays in Political Philosophy, ed. David Boucher (Oxford, 1989).

Collingwood: unpublished manuscripts

'Libellus de Generatione', 1920, Collingwood Manuscripts, Bodleian Library, dep. 28.
'History as the Understanding of the Present', 1933, Collingwood Manuscripts, Bodleian Library, dep. 15.
'Lectures on Moral Philosophy', 1933, Collingwood Manuscripts, Bodleian Library, dep. 8.
'Notes towards a Metaphysic', 1933–4, Collingwood Manuscripts, Bodleian Library, dep. 18.
'Conclusions to Lectures on Nature and Mind', 1934, 1935, Archives, Oxford University Press.
'Inaugural: Rough Notes', 1935, Collingwood Manuscripts, Bodleian Library, dep. 13.
'Reality as History', 1935, Collingwood Manuscripts, Bodleian Library, dep. 12.
'Can Historians be Impartial?', 1936, Collingwood Manuscripts, Bodleian Library, dep. 12.
'Notes on the History of Historiography and Philosophy of History', 1936, Collingwood Manuscripts, Bodleian Library, dep. 13.
'Folklore', 1936–7, Collingwood Manuscripts, Bodleian Library, dep. 21.
'Notes on Historiography', 1939, Collingwood Manuscripts, Bodleian Library, dep. 13.
'The Principles of History', 1939, Archives, Oxford University Press.

Secondary works

ALEXANDER, SAMUEL, 'The Historicity of Things', in Raymond Klibansky and H. J. Paton (eds.), *Philosophy and History* (Oxford, 1936), 11–25.

BOUCHER, DAVID, *The Social and Political Thought of R. G. Collingwood* (Cambridge, 1989).

—— 'The Principles of History and the Cosmology Conclusion to The Idea of Nature', *Collingwood Studies*, 2, (Swansea, 1995), 140–74.

—— 'The Significance of R. G. Collingwood's *Principles of History*', *Journal of the History of Ideas*, 58 (1997), 309–30.

—— CONNELLY, JAMES, and MODOOD, TARIQ (eds.), *Philosophy, History and Civilization: Interdisciplinary Perspectives on R. G. Collingwood* (Cardiff, 1995).

BRINTON, CRANE, *A Decade of Revolution* (New York, 1934).

BURY, J. B., *Selected Essays*, ed. Harold Temperley (Cambridge, 1930).

CEBIK, L. B., 'Collingwood: Action, Re-enactment, and Evidence', *Philosophical Forum*, 2 (1970), 68–90.

DONAGAN, ALAN, *The Later Philosophy of R. G. Collingwood* (Oxford, 1962; republished Chicago, 1985).

DRAY, W. H., *History as Re-enactment: R. G. Collingwood's Idea of History* (Oxford, 1995).

—— 'Broadening the Subject-Matter in *The Principles of History*', *Collingwood Studies*, 4 (1997), 2–33.

DREISBACH, CHRISTOPHER, *R. G. Collingwood: A Bibliographic Checklist* (Bowling Green, Oh., 1993).

GOLDSTEIN, LEON, *The What and the Why of History* (Leiden, 1996).

KLIBANSKY, RAYMOND, and PATON, H. J. (eds.), *Philosophy and History: Essays Presented to Ernst Cassirer* (Oxford, 1936).

MARTIN, REX, *Historical Explanation: Re-enactment and Practical Inference* (Ithaca, NY, 1977).

—— 'Collingwood's Doctrine of Absolute Presuppositions and the Possibility of Historical Knowledge', in Leon Pompa and W. H. Dray (eds.), *Substance and Form in History* (Edinburgh, 1981).

—— 'Collingwood's Claim that Metaphysics is a Historical Discipline', *Monist*, 72 (1989), 489–525.

MINK, L. O., *Mind, History, and Dialectic: The Philosophy of R. G. Collingwood* (Bloomington, Ind., 1969; republished Middletown, Conn., 1987).

NIELSEN, MARGIT HURUP, 'Re-enactment and Reconstruction in Collingwood's Philosophy of History', *History and Theory*, 20 (1981), 1–31.

OAKESHOTT, MICHAEL, *Experience and its Modes* (Cambridge, 1933).

PETERS, RIK, 'Croce, Gentile and Collingwood on the Relation between History and Philosophy', in David Boucher, James Connelly, and Tariq Modood (eds.), *Philosophy, History and Civilization: Interdisciplinary Perspectives on R. G. Collingwood* (Cardiff, 1995), 152–67.

Pompa, Leon, and Dray, W. H. (eds.), *Substance and Form in History* (Edinburgh, 1981).

Ritter, Harry (ed.), *Dictionary of Concepts in History* (New York, 1986).

Rubinoff, Lionel, *Collingwood and the Reform of Metaphysics: A Study in the Philosophy of Mind* (Toronto, 1970).

Saari, Heikki, *Re-enactment: A Study in R. G. Collingwood's Philosophy of History* (Åbo, 1984).

Simissen, Herman, 'On Understanding Disaster', *Philosophy of the Social Sciences*, 23 (1993), 352–67.

Skagestad, Peter, *Making Sense of History: The Philosophies of Popper and Collingwood* (Oslo, 1975).

Taylor, D. S., *R. G. Collingwood: A Bibliography* (New York, 1988).

van der Dussen, W. J., 'Collingwood's Unpublished Manuscripts', *History and Theory*, 18 (1979), 287–315.

—— *History as a Science: The Philosophy of R. G. Collingwood* (The Hague, 1981).

—— 'Collingwood's "Lost" Manuscript of *The Principles of History*', *History and Theory*, 36 (1997), 32–62.

Weingartner, R. H., 'Historical Explanation', in Paul Edwards (ed.), *The Encyclopedia of Philosophy*, vol. iv (New York, 1962), 7–12.

GENERAL INDEX

Abraham 236
absolute presuppositions lxiv n. 108,
    239, 267
abstraction 123–4 n. 8, 177–8, 204,
    239, 263–6
  of eternal objects lxxxv–lxxxvi
  of historical object lxix, 128, 169
  of thought 135, 137, 138
accident lxxix, 247
acquaintance 143, 221
action xxxvii, xli, li n. 87, lxxiii–lxxiv,
    49–50, 76, 111, 163
  as caused xlvii, l
  compulsion of, see compulsion of
    action
  corporate 194
  as event xli, 55–6, 70, 76, 217
  as expression of thought, see thought
    as expressed in action
  inside/outside of 217
  senses of xviii, 44, 46–7, 55
  as subject-matter of history xviii,
    xx, xxxiv–xxxvi, li n. 87, 45, 111,
    245
  see also cause of actions; events as
    actions; res gestae
Acton, Lord 37
aesthetic as science of language
    xxxi–xxxii, 52–4, 101
aesthetics xxxix n. 62, xlvi, 82, 84, 86,
    108, 133
Africa 45 n., 206
agriculture, art of 94, 97
Alexander, Samuel xli–xlii,
    lxxii–lxxiii, lxxxi, 56–7, 76, 119 n.,
    122, 170, 171 n., 204, 206, 245,
    246, 251–3, 268
Alyosha 162
American frontier lxxxiii
Anglesey 152
Anglo-Saxon Britain lxxxi n. 143
Annales Cambriae 216

annals 121, 183–4
anonymous individuals xl, 75
anthropology xxv, 43, 92, 180, 244
anthropomorphism 139
antiquarianism 65, 231
Antonine Wall xxx n. 40
appetites xxxv–xxxvi, 45–6, 93, 98–9,
    225
a priori li, lii, 19, 152, 161–4, 166, 219
archaeology xiv, 154, 156
  methods of, see method, archaeologi-
    cal
  resemblance to history xxx–xxxi,
    xxxii n. 46, 15–16, 75, 76–7
  see also practice, archaeological; sites,
    archaeological; sources, archaeo-
    logical
architecture 206
Ardderyd, battle of 216
argument, practical xxxv
Aristotelian logic 9–10, 247
Aristotle 8, 58, 59 n., 133, 159,
    213–14, 221, 243
art:
  amusement and magical xxxix
    n. 62
  history of 211
artefacts xxxiv
Aryan descent 74
astronomy xliv n. 74, 4, 61, 138, 245,
    249
Athanasian Creed 267
Athens 210
Augustan constitution lxxxvi
Augustus, emperor 168, 203
Aurelian, emperor 81
authority lxxi, 12–14, 21, 25, 114,
    143–50, 153, 156–62
  of the historian 16, 31, 149
  limited lxxi, 155–7
  of memory 45
Autocrat of the Breakfast-Table 111

history (*cont.*):
  likeness to natural science xxix, xli
  as non-explanatory 78, 182
  in pupilage to natural science 78, 80,
    98, 106–7, 108, 110, 215
  scientific xxiii, xxviii–xxix, xlix–l,
    liii, lxxi, lxxix, 3–6, 12, 13, 18–21,
    25–6, 30–2, 34–7, 38, 45, 48–9, 66,
    67, 78, 80–1, 102–3, 108–10, 245,
    248
  as self-explanatory 163–4
  as self-knowledge of mind, *see* self-
    knowledge, history as
  senses of xviii, xx, xliii n. 73, xliv,
    lxix, lxxiv, lxxxii, 126–7, 171, 178,
    190, 245
  unlikeness to natural science xiv,
    xix, xlii, 4, 20, 56–7, 80, 137–8,
    162, 238, 245
  see also archaeology, resemblance
    to history; crypto-history; devel-
    opment in history; emotion as sub-
    ject-matter of history; fact,
    historical; human nature and his-
    tory; ideality of history; indeter-
    minism of history; individuality of
    history; knowledge, historical; lit-
    erature, historical; literature and
    history; logic and history; logic as
    history; memory and history;
    method, historical; methodology
    of history; moral judgements in
    history; morality, history and;
    morality, historical; natural history
    and human history; natural science
    and history; naturalism, historical;
    nature and history; object, histori-
    cal; objectivity, historical; the past,
    historical; patterns in history;
    philosophy and history; philo-
    sophy as history; philosophy of
    history; pigeon-holing in history;
    point of view in history; practical
    life and history; practice, histori-
    cal; principles, historical; prob-
    ability in history; problems,
    historical; process, historical;
    pseudo-history; question and
    answer in history; questions, his-
    torical; reality, historical; re-enact-
    ment, history as; relics, historical;
    res gestae, history of; research,
    historical; responsibility of histo-

rian; re-thinking, history as;
rewriting of history; scepticism,
historical; scholarship, historical;
scissors and paste, history as;
second-order history; selection, historical; sequence, historical; situations, historical; sources, historical;
spirit, historical; subject-matter of
history; theory of history; thought,
historical; thought, history being
the history of; thought in history;
time, historical; truth, historical;
understanding, historical; value
judgement in history
Hitler, Adoph 73 n. 41
Hobbes, Thomas 57 n. 24, 238
holism lxxxiv
Holmes, Oliver Wendell 111 n. 60
Holmes, Sherlock 37
human:
  anatomy 82
  nature xxxv, lxxiii, 82, 92, 124, 175,
    193–7, 201, 219–20, 225, 246,
    250 n., 252–3; and history 79–80,
    124, 190, 195, 197, 204, 220; as
    mind 220; rationality of, *see*
    rationality of human nature;
    science of, *see* science of human
    nature; theory of 219
  physiology 82
  rationality, *see* rationality, human
  reason, *see* reason, human
Hume, David 119 n. 2, 122, 150, 187,
    196, 207, 219, 225
Hundred Years War 4–5, 249
Huxley, T. H. 146

idealism xvi, 189, 206–7
  subjective lxix, 104, 128–9
ideality li, lxx, 136, 206–7, 222–3
  of history xxiii n. 28, lxv n. 110
  of the past, *see* the past, ideality of
imagination xiv, xxxi, xxxiii, liv, lxiv,
    49, 151–4, 162–6
immortality 129, 269
importance:
  analysis of lxxvi–lxxvii, lxxviii,
    144–6, 226–31, 240
  judgements of lxiii, lxxiv, 75, 86,
    129, 149, 150, 213, 214
Inca state 124
indeterminism of history lxxi, 163,
    194–5

Indians 243
individuality:
  abstract lxix, 137
  of biography 70–2
  of history xiv, xxv n. 30, xliii, 4–5,
    128, 134, 168–9, 178, 180–2, 221
  in literature 161–2
  of moral judgement xxv n. 30
Industrial Revolution lxxxiii
inference lii, 7–8, 11, 18, 32, 53, 147,
    169
  abductive xxxiii n.
  asserted 6, 32, 265
  constructive 150, 165
  deductive xxix, xxxiii, lxxii, 9–10,
    114
  denied xxxii, lxx, 140–1
  inductive xxix, xxxiii, lxxii, 9–10,
    16, 79, 81, 82, 187, 242
instincts 47, 82, 176–7, 195–6, 220,
    225
  natural lxxiv, 194
institutions 46, 64, 194, 195, 209
intention lxvii–lxviii, 67, 96, 147–8,
    247
interpolation xxxiii, 151–3, 158, 162
intolerance 41–3, 80, 88, 179
intuition 185
Iron Age 233
Italian idealists 170
Italy 85 n. 50, 167

James II lxxxvi, 264
James, Henry 214
Japan 183
Java lviii, lxiii, 97
Javanese agriculture 97
Jevons, W. S. 242
Jewish:
  people 236–7
  thought, see thought, Jewish
John, king 141
Joseph, H. W. B. 124
Jullian, C. 234 n.
Junius letters 50
Jupiter Capitolinus 239

Kant, Immanuel 19, 60 n., 119 n. 2,
    122, 152, 166–8, 203, 205, 207,
    219, 241
Keynes, J. M. 243
Klibansky, Raymond xxi n. 25, xli n.
    68, 171 n., 251 n. 1

knowledge 7, 131, 139, 159, 168–9,
    174–5, 177, 188–9, 207, 216, 220,
    239, 246, 248
  by causes 78
  historical 7–8, 12, 50–1, 65–7, 139,
    145, 147, 152, 156–7, 158, 165, 170
    n., 171, 177, 188, 210, 216, 220–1,
    234, 239, 265; advancement of
    164, 167, 218
  object of 172, 221
  problem of 178
  of situations, see situations, histori-
    cal
  theory of 174
  see also self-knowledge, history as
Knox, Sir Malcolm xiii, xv–xviii, xxii,
    xxiii, xxv–xxviii, liii–lx, lxiii, lxiv,
    lxxviii, lxxx n. 140, lxxxiii n., 37
    n., 103 n. 57, 219 n., 223 n., 251 n.
Kulturvölker 125

language 102
  as expression of thought, see thought
    as expressed in language
  and history xxxi–xxxiv, xlii, liv, 51,
    54, 67, 76, 111
  science of 52
  theory of 101
  understanding of, see understanding
    of language
  see also aesthetic as science of lan-
    guage; evidence readable as lan-
    guage; logic and language
Latin 3, 52–3, 74, 174
latitude and longitude of events
    216–17
law courts and history lxxviii, 23–4,
    231–2
law of wages 244
laws 177–80, 182–3
  of nature 61, 83, 97, 173, 187
  statistical, see statistical laws
  subsumption under general 182–3,
    185–6
League of Nations 203
Lee, Sir Sidney 73, 250 n.
Leibniz, G. W. lxxxv n. 149, 123, 132,
    205
Liberal party 239
liberalism 210
libertarianism lxxiii, 190, 204, 230
life 199–200, 208, 254, 256–8, 260–1,
    265

GENERAL INDEX 285

the present 192–3, 204
emotional idea of li, 112
historical liv, lxxxi, 136–7, 168, 222;
  as objective, see objectivity of the
  historian's past
ideality of li, 136, 222
as an innate idea 165–6
of life, see life, the past of
as living in the present xix, lxvii,
  lxxiv, lxxv, lxxix, 130, 132, 193,
  205–6, 222
of matter 202–3
of nature lxvi n., lxvii, lxxiv–lxxv,
  130, 205
as object of historical inquiry xx,
  55
picture of, see picture of the past
relation with the present xiv, lxx n.
  122, lxxi, 111–12, 126, 128, 130,
  132, 135, 138, 140–2, 191–2, 195,
  200, 204–5, 220, 222–4, 240,
  244–5, 255
pathfinding, art of 94, 97
patient, agent as 120
Paton, H. J. xxi n. 25, xli n. 68, 171 n.,
  251 n. 1
patterns 131, 133, 257
  in history lxxvii, 19–20, 105–6,
  214
Paul, St 237
pedigree 74, 197, 237
Peirce, Charles xxxiii n.
Peloponnesian War 16, 168, 210, 229
Peninsular War, history of the 69
pensiero pensante and pensiero pensato,
  Gentile on 122 n., 129
perception 172–4
  and history xxix, xxxvii–xxxviii n. 58,
  52–3, 76, 111, 132, 135, 151, 162,
  164–6, 168, 189, 265
  see also evidence, presently observable
Pericles 49
periods, historical xlv n. 77, 37
perspective:
  in history xxii, lxx
  of past time 128–9
Peters, Rik lxxxv n. 149, 122 n., 124
  n. 9
Petrie, Flinders 19
Peyrol 161–2
philology 52, 231
  comparative 180

philosophers:
  Christian and Mohammedan 213
  consulting lii, lxxx, 41–3
  eighteenth-century 219
  German 179, 252
  and historians 56–7, 158
  as inquisitors 41–3, 76 n.
philosophy xxxix, xl, lxv n. 110, lxxviii
  n. 133, 173
  Greek lxxxiv n.149, 172–4, 177–9,
  201
  and history xix–xx, lii, lviii–lix, 114,
  158, 167–8, 169 n., 241, 246
  as history lviii, lxxviii–lxxix, lxxxiii
  n., 238
  history of 106–7, 110, 167, 189, 211,
  218, 220, 224
  of history xvii, xxiv n., xxxviii n. 60,
  lxiv, lxxii, lxxx, 128; in narrow
  sense xv
  of man 198
  of mind xiii n. 1, xxxviii n. 60
  moral, see moral philosophy
  of nature 198, 253
  problems of 166–7
  and science, see science and philosophy
  subject-matter of, see subject-matter
  of philosophy
  the universal in, see the universal in
  philosophy
  see also method, philosophical;
  pseudo-philosophy; science,
  philosophical; understanding,
  philosophical
Phoenicians 160 n. 7
physician 147
  consulting 39 n.
physics 42, 56, 58, 60–1, 176, 200–1,
  204, 208, 219, 225, 253, 265
picture:
  historical xxiii, lxxii, 156, 162–5
  of the novelist 161–3
  of the past lxxii, 166
pigeon-holing in history 20–1, 216
Pithecanthropus Erectus 196
Plato 29, 58, 59 n., 198 n., 203, 214
Platonic forms 104
poem 184
poet 163
poetry 218
point of view in history 165, 213
Poirot, Hercule 37

thought (*cont.*):
  history of political, and political history 69
  Jewish 236–7
  modern 174, 177, 213
  nature of lxxvii, 188, 223–4
  about nature, *see* nature, thought about
  necessary 266
  object of 223–4, 266
  ordinary 143
  as being public 134
  rational and irrational xxxv–xxxvii
  in relation to nature in Hegel 104, 109
  science of human, *see* science of human thought; naturalistic science of human reason and thought
  scientific 30, 36, 123 n. 8, 162, 169, 175, 178–9, 181–2, 185, 215, 242; in relation to mathematical thought 180
  theory of 101
  types of 134
  validity in 242
Three Blind Mice 90
Thucydides 16, 25, 119, 145, 245
Tiger and Lady xli n. 69, 57
Timaeus 59 n.
time 132, 200, 203
  accumulation in 131
  clock- 199
  and existence 129
  geological 125
  and history xli, 55, 125, 199–200, 222, 244
  in nature 58–61
  in nature and history lxx, lxxiv, 56, 125
  velocity of 125
  see also events as temporally located; mind as being in time; order, temporal; process, temporal; pseudo-time; sequence, temporal
timefulness xli, lxxiv, 56, 58–60, 244
The Times Literary Supplement xiii n. 1
Tower of London 154
Toynbee, Arnold lxvii, 19
traces 111, 140
tradition 131, 143, 149, 222, 236
  cultural 193
  historical 222
Trafalgar, battle of 228

travelling 93
truth 209–10, 213, 242, 244
  historical 158, 160, 163–4, 166

understanding 54, 172–4, 178, 182–7, 246
  aesthetic 53
  of emotions lxvii–lxviii
  historical xviii–xix, lxvi–lxvii, lxxiii, 141–2, 184–7, 189, 212, 228; as critical lxviii
  of language xx, xxxii
  philosophical 224
  science of the human 225
  scientific 181, 184–7, 189
  in terms of generalities lxxiii
unique, the, in history 162
universal, the 186, 221
  in philosophy 114
  in relation to the individual in Hegel 128
  in science 162, 169, 186
universal history 20
universities 57

value:
  amusement 21, 37, 73
  gossip xxxix, 70, 73, 75, 77
  historical 73
  magical 21, 37, 73
  scales of 218
  snobbery 73 n. 41, 75
  see also fact as value-constituted
value judgement 209
  in history xlvii, lxxv–lxxvi, 214–18
  see also importance, judgements of; moral judgements in history
van der Dussen, W. J. xvii n. 13, xviii n. 15, xxi n. 24, xxv n. 31, xxviii n. 36, xxxiii n. 48, xxxviii n. 60, lv n., lvii n. 96, lviii n. 97, lix n. 99, lxxxiv n. 148
verification 234
vérité de raison and *vérité de fait* 220–1
Vespasian 140
Vico, Giambattista lxxix n. 135, 15, 19
Villeneuve, Pierre Charles de 228
Völkerpsychologie 180

Wales, kings of 216
war lxxiv, 4–5, 73, 96, 176, 194, 211, 249
  in 1914: 210

REFERENCES TO COLLINGWOOD'S WRITINGS

Published Writings

xx, xxi, xxxi, xxxii, xxxiii, xxxviii,
xxxix n. 62, xlvi n. 80, lv, lxv, lxvi,
lxviii, 21 n., 54 n. 20, 70 n.
Religion and Philosophy xiii n. 1,
xxxviii n. 60
Roman Britain xiv n. 4, lxxvi
*Roman Britain and the English
Settlements* xiv n. 4, liii, lxviii,
lxxvii, lxxix

'The Roman Frontier in Britain' xxx
n. 40
The Roman Inscriptions of Britain xiv
n. 4
Speculum Mentis xiii, xv
'The Three Laws of Politics' lxii n.
102

Manuscripts

'Can Historians be Impartial?' xxvi,
xlvii n. 82, li, liv n., lxxv–lxxvi,
209–18
'Conclusions to Lectures on Nature
and Mind' xviii, xxiv, xxvi, xxxii
n. 46, xli n. 68, xliii–xliv, xlv n. 77,
lii n. 90, lxvi n., lxix n. 118, n. 119,
lxx n. 120, lxxvii, lxxix n. 136,
lxxx–lxxxvii, 119 n., 170 n.,
251–70
Folklore manuscripts xxv, xxxvi, lxx
n. 121, lxxviii n. 134, lxxxiv
'History as the Understanding of the
Present' xxvi, lxx–lxxi, lxxix n.
136, 140–2
'Inaugural. Rough Notes' xix n. 20,
xxiv n., xxvi, xxx n. 41, lxxi–lxxii,
lxxiv n., 143–69
'Introduction to Metaphysics' 84–5 n.
48
Lecture Notes on Philosophy of
History for 1929, 1931, 1932:
lxxvi n. 130
Lecture Notes on Moral Philosophy
1921–40 xvii
'Lectures on Moral Philosophy' 1933:
xxxvi
'Lectures on Philosophy of History of
1936' xxii, xxiv n. 30, xxxiv n. 50,
lvi, lxiii, lxviii, lxxvi, lxxxii n. 144,
104
'Libellus de Generatione' 122 n.

'Metaphysical Epilegomena' 1936:
xxii, xxvi n. 33, lxiii, 223 n.
'Notes on Historiography' xvii, xviii,
xix n. 19, xxvi, xliv, li–lii, liv n.,
lvii n. 95, lxiii, lxvii, lxviii, lxix n.
119, lxxi, lxxvii n., lxxviii–lxxx,
lxxxiii n., lxxxvi, 3 n. 1, 73 n. 40,
235–50
'Notes on the History of
Historiography and Philosophy of
History' xxvi, xxx n. 41, xlvii n.
83, liii n. 91, lxxvi–lxxviii, lxxxii n.
144, lxxxv n. 150, lxxxvi,
219–34
'Notes towards a Metaphysic' xv n. 5,
xxvi, xliii n. 72, lxix–lxx, lxxiv n.,
lxxx–lxxxi, lxxxiv, lxxxv n. 149,
lxxxvi, 119–39, 138 n. 22, 170 n.,
251 n.
'The Principles of History' xv–lxvii,
lxix–lxx, lxxii n.123, lxxv n. 129,
lxxvii–lxxx, lxxxii, lxxxiv, lxxxvi,
lxxxvii, 3 n. 1, 85 n. 48, 111 n. 59,
114 n., 120 n., 235 n., 248 n. 21,
250 n., 251 n.
'Reality as History' xxvi, xli n. 68,
xliii, xlvi n. 80, li, lii n. 90, lxx n.
122, lxxi, lxxii–lxxv, lxxxi, lxxxii
n. 144, lxxxvi, 170–208
'Scheme for a Book' xviii–xx, xxxiii,
xxxv, xliii, xlv, li–lii, lx, lxiii, lxiv,
lxvii, lxxviii, 111 n. 59, 114, 245–6